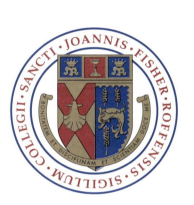

Teaching History
in the
Digital Classroom

History, Humanities, and New Technology

Series Editors: David J. Staley, Heidelberg College,
Dennis A. Trinkle, DePauw University,
Jeffrey G. Barlow, Pacific University

Sponsored by
The American Association for History and Computing

Teaching History
in the
Digital Classroom

D. Antonio Cantu and
Wilson J. Warren

with contributions by
John R. Barber
Joseph A. Braun, Jr.
Sandy Cantu
Alex Zukas

M.E. Sharpe
Armonk, New York
London, England

Library of Congress Cataloging-in-Publication Data

Cantu, D. Antonio.
    Teaching history in the digital classroom / D. Antonio Cantu and Wilson J. Warren;
with contributions by John R. Barber ... [et al.].
        p. cm.
    Includes bibliographical references and index.
    ISBN 0-7656-0992-4 (hardcover : alk. paper)
        1. History—Computer network resources. 2. Internet. 3. History—Computer-
assisted instruction. 4. History—Study and teaching. 5. History—Methodology. I.
Warren, Wilson J. II. Title

    D16.177.C36 2003
    907'8'5—dc21

                                                                    2002075861

Printed in the United States of America

The paper used in this publication meets the minimum requirements of
American National Standard for Information Sciences
Permanence of Paper for Printed Library Materials,
ANSI Z 39.48-1984.

∞

BM (c)   10   9   8   7   6   5   4   3   2   1

Contents

List of Tables and Worksheets

Tables

Worksheets

Preface

*Real teaching is never quite as straightforward as textbooks
and research papers would have it. It is always more
complex, more confused, and more idiosyncratic
than anticipated.*
—William H. Schubert and William C. Ayers

Schubert and Ayers' observation is perhaps more valid at the dawn
of the twenty-first century than it was at the close of the previous one.
In particular, history and social studies teachers are confronted with
the complex challenge of preparing the next generation's computer-
literate and technology-savvy students, with perhaps little or no training in the use of technology. In addition, they are about to spend the
next two to three decades teaching in a digital classroom, which many
find confusing because they were never taught in one themselves as
students and perhaps have yet to see the pedagogical use of technology
effectively modeled.

With the growing number of technology and Internet proficient students in middle schools and high schools, referred to by some educational demographers as the I-Generation, the need for digital
pedagogues in history classrooms is growing exponentially. In a recent

interview, Janet M. Healy, author of *Failure to Connect: How Computers Affect Our Children's Minds for Better or Worse*, outlined the potential benefits and shortfalls associated with the integration of computer technology in the classroom:

> I am intrigued by the possibilities of technology not only for teaching and learning but also for learning about the learning process. How can we plug in more effectively to kids who are at different stages of development and who experience learning in different ways? I am interested in applications that reach for that goal and don't simply recapitulate the old educational models. We haven't found a way yet—and I doubt whether we ever will—to let machine technology replace human technology in the education process. But through research, we may eventually combine human and machine technologies to discover why children are or are not learning certain things and to present information in a wide variety of modalities.[1]

Yet, the following statement by Thomas Edison in 1922 on the invention of film serves a reminder of the folly often associated with predicting how technology will impact education: "[This technology] is destined to revolutionize our educational system and . . . in a few years it will supplant largely, if not entirely, the use of textbooks."[2] Today, however, the impact of computer technology and the Internet on society and schools can be ascertained through the examination of empirical data, rather than by engaging in conjecture and speculation. The most recent set of U.S. Department of Education statistics concerning the integration of technology and the Internet, for example, show that nearly 90 percent of schools have the ability to support online initiatives.[3] Other data on the proliferation of computers in the classroom and on computer and Internet access in student homes, also serve to illustrate the increasingly important role such technology plays in society and schools.

The question, therefore, is not whether computer technology and the Internet will play a role in twenty-first century history education, but how extensive its impact is today on student learning. The critical question remains: What role will incoming history and social studies teachers play in preparing the next generation of students in today's digital and connected classrooms? This is a challenge and opportunity that D. Mark Meyers summarizes as follows:

Unless teachers are confident of their ability to use the computer, they tend to shy away from its use. Instead, they choose something they know they can handle; confronted by innovation, they may choose non-involvement. Exposing preservice teachers to technology increases their motivation to use technology and also increases the likelihood that they will use technology in their classroom. If preservice teachers develop confidence that they can control and use technology, they can then provide the same service to their students. There it will "trickle down" into the teaching practices of the schools. Teachers are not convinced by good ideas alone. Instead, it takes good ideas that have worked for someone else. Teachers will borrow successful ideas, not merely use ones they read about that might be good. These changes will involve the development of communities in which students and teachers investigate areas of interest and information is exchanged freely between school, university, and community.[4]

The salient questions, issues, and challenges confronting history and social studies teachers in this information age, as well as the curricular and instructional models, approaches, and strategies that are available to help better prepare individuals to teach in the digital classroom of the twenty-first century, serve as the focus for *Teaching History in the Digital Classroom*. We want to extend our heartfelt thanks to the following individuals who each contributed a chapter to this book as well: John R. Barber, Ball State University; Joseph A. Braun, Jr., Illinois State University; Sandy Cantu, Muncie Central High School; and Alex Zukas, National University.

Teaching History in the Digital Classroom is organized into four parts, each representative of a specific domain within the history and social studies curriculum. The first part, "Historical and Hidden Curriculum," traces the origins of history and social studies education in the United States and provides an overview of the standards and structure—the historical curriculum—of history, the social sciences, and social studies. In addition, it examines the role history teachers' beliefs—the hidden curriculum—play in the classroom, in particular how they impact teachers' perceptions of themselves, their students, what they teach (i.e., history and social studies), how they teach (i.e., pedagogical strategies and approaches), and where they teach (i.e., the classroom environment). The role technology plays in shaping how we define ourselves as teachers, and in our approach to teaching, is addressed throughout each of these chapters.

In the second part, "Intended Curriculum," curriculum design, those a priori desires and plans for what will take place in the classroom, is the primary focus. In the first of the five chapters in this section, the development of unit plans and lesson objectives is discussed. While in the next two chapters, the integration of online resources and design of Internet-based curricular and instructional strategies are examined. The final two chapters in this section delve into the myriad of lesson plan frameworks that are germane to history and social studies education at the middle school and high school level. As with each chapter in this book, the integration of technology and the Internet is addressed in every step of the curriculum planning process.

Part three, "Taught Curriculum," provides an extensive overview of instructional strategies that middle school and high school history and social studies teachers may employ in the digital classroom. Included in the four chapters that comprise this part are extensive examinations of the teaching of authentic history, the utilization of audiovisual and information technology in teaching historical thinking, the use of cooperative learning teaching strategies, and the integration of technology-specific teaching strategies and resources. Each of the chapters in this section introduce traditional, digital, and hybrid approaches to teaching middle and high school history and social studies in an engaging and powerful manner that take advantage of all of the resources that are now just a mouse-click away.

The final part in *Teaching History in the Digital Classroom* examines the "Learned Curriculum," those areas of teaching concerned with what the learners take with them when they leave the classroom. The four chapters in part four introduce a series of assessment and evaluation approaches and strategies that are ideally suited for the digital history and social studies classroom of the twenty-first century. The types of strategies that are addressed in these chapters are representative of the entire spectrum of assessment and evaluation approaches that are available to history and social studies teachers—to include both formal and informal strategies. In addition, the two assessment strategies that are perhaps most vital to the teaching of middle and high school history and social studies in the twenty-first century, performance-based assessment and document-based question (DBQ) analysis, are discussed at length in two of the chapters included in this part. Regardless of the particular focus, in each of these four chapters, traditional as well as digital approaches to assessment and evaluation are examined in detail.

The digital age that ushers in the twenty-first century offers history and social studies educators a unique opportunity to venture down roads never before taken by teachers in the history of education. Teachers, however, must be willing to take the first step in this process. Without their leadership, the use of computer technology and the Internet in history and social studies education will continue to lag far behind other core disciplines and sectors of American society. Therefore, teacher understanding of the role of technology in history and social studies education is absolutely critical. Chris Dede reminds teachers of the mistake made over the past decade that has hindered our ability to fully integrate such technology in history and social studies education:

> One of the mistakes we made in implementing educational technology was focusing first on students, rather than teachers, because when the computers on students' desks are mysterious devices to teachers, it's unreasonable to expect effective integration into the curriculum.[5]

That is the goal of *Teaching History in the Digital Classroom*, to provide middle and high school history and social studies teachers with the requisite knowledge and skills needed to not only teach in the classroom of the twenty-first century, but to thrive in that digital environment.

Part I

Historical and Hidden Curriculum

Chapter 1

Origins and Rationale for Teaching History and the Social Studies in the Middle and High School Curriculum

Never have ideas about children, and never have ideas for them.
—George Orwell

Origins

The teaching of history occupied a central place in the American secondary curriculum throughout the nineteenth century. However, history teaching in the nineteenth century was largely focused on myths about ancient Greece and Rome as well as national patriotic narratives that bordered on mythology. Because so few young people went through the secondary grades, it also tended to be a rather elitist subject, emphasizing ancient and classical studies often taught primarily to help students study for university entrance examinations.[1]

"Social studies," as defined simply as the secondary level subject that focuses on social issues by extracting from both history and the social sciences, emerged during the Progressive era. Several factors contributed to this emergence, particularly the role of historians, the special concerns of many Progressives who felt social problems could be solved if studied closely, and the firm belief of historians, social studies advocates, and a variety of reformers in the power of citizenship education.[2]

By the late nineteenth century, history as a discipline had become more scientific through hypothesis testing with more rigorous attention being paid to factual source material. Professional historians, especially those associated with the American Historical Association (AHA), founded in 1884, and who had often received Ph.D.s in Germany where "scientific" historical studies originated, wanted to infuse history teaching at all ranks with a more methodologically rigorous approach to the subject. The AHA wielded tremendous influence among not only historians and history teachers, but also among the fledgling social sciences. Historians were the accepted "spokespersons" for social scientists in general, with the AHA occupying a "preeminent position in shaping social science."[3]

The AHA's Committee on History, Civil Government and Political Economy, one of ten subcommittees of the so-called Committee of Ten formed by the National Education Association (NEA) in 1892, wrote one of the strongest statements of the "new" historians' perspectives at the turn of the twentieth century. The Committee of Ten was primarily interested in rectifying problems between secondary level and university programs and standardizing curriculum, but also ended up promoting work that led to deeper changes in American education. Led by Charles Kendall Adams, professor of history at the University of Michigan, the AHA committee's members, including Albert Bushnell Hart, a young Harvard history professor, and Woodrow Wilson, a young professor of political economy at Princeton University, wanted to make history a subject that would train students to critically think and avoid "mere lists of lifeless dates." The committee recommended that instead of haphazard study, history should be taught in all grades from five through twelve. To increase the amount of time devoted to history, the committee suggested that history, political geography, English, and/or civil government and political economy be combined as subjects. Instead of general history lessons, the committee wanted specific courses on Greek, Roman, English, American, and French history taught along with a general European history. Younger children should start by being exposed to biography and mythology along with other historical readings. The committee said that civil government should be allocated about half the time recommended for history. If possible, government should be integrated with history. The committee also stressed the importance of writing and critical examination of primary documents.[4]

Although few schools adopted the committee's recommendation for history at all grade levels, it seems that the report started the dominant twentieth century trend in social studies, though this term was not commonly used until after World War I, of making history the core social studies discipline. Subsequent AHA committee reports, particularly the one issued in 1899 by the so-called Committee of Seven, reinforced the importance of history in each grade level. The 1899 report urged that ancient history be taught in the first year of high school, medieval and modern history during the second year, English history in the third year, and American history and civil government during the fourth year. As many social studies educators would advocate later, both the 1892 and 1899 AHA committee reports emphasized how history courses would benefit from an interdisciplinary approach, or at least from drawing upon other disciplines.[5]

Social efficiency experts and their educational allies, who were typically followers of John Dewey's educational philosophies that advocated a more utilitarian approach to social education, laid the foundation for the citizenship education approach to social studies. Fundamentally, these reformers wanted education to produce social progress. They were skeptical of the professional historians' emphasis on intellectual development and reflection; they wanted a curriculum that addressed current social problems and needs. While arguably less central to social studies' origins than that sparked by professional historians, this approach has wielded a great deal of weight in the field since the early twentieth century. As the numbers of students attending and graduating from high schools increased rapidly during the first two decades of the twentieth century, social efficiency experts stressed that subjects offered should contribute to the social welfare of the nation. Many felt that young people needed to be better prepared for the travails of modern life. Subjects such as Latin, algebra, and even history, heralded during the nineteenth century as crucial for mental development, particularly for college-bound youngsters, were seen as impractical. Instead, the masses of new students attending high school needed subjects that would better prepare them for life and active participation as citizens. By the World War I era, many Progressives saw history as useful for examining problems of the present, but not particularly important as a subject in itself.[6]

This approach to social studies emerged most forcefully from the landmark NEA's 1913–16 Commission on the Reorganization of Secondary Education's Committee on Social Studies' report. Unlike the 1892 and 1899 committee reports composed by professional historians, professional secondary school educators comprised most of the twenty-one members of the Committee on Social Studies. Many of the members were sociologists, including the committee's chair, Thomas Jesse Jones, the originator of the term "social studies" and a student of sociologist Franklin H. Giddings of Columbia University. Interestingly, David Warren Saxe, the foremost scholar on the 1913–16 social studies committee's significance, notes that the first use of the term "social studies" in the United States was in the title of an 1887 book on the plight of urban workers. However, Saxe credits Jones with consistent use of the term for educational purposes after 1904. Two of the other four leading members of the committee, Arthur William Dunn and Clarence Kingsley, also were sociologists, and James Harvey Robinson was the only historian among the most influential committee members.[7]

The committee issued three reports, but its final report from 1916 defined citizenship education as the central focus of social studies education. This report stressed both social welfare and social efficiency for society's general improvement as the main rationale for social education. It also advocated the use of social education for making productive and contributing individuals. Jones's contributions to the report included an emphasis on teaching social problems and methods for dealing with them. Dunn's main contribution to the report was the notion of "community civics," a sort of precursor to contemporary ideas about service learning. Like many of the municipal reform advocates of the era, he wanted local governments to serve the health and welfare needs of communities. He also wanted students to see that civic education should be primarily concerned with responsibilities rather than rights. Arguably the most influential author of the 1916 report, Dunn felt that history, geography, and civics should be treated as integrated subjects with emphasis on giving young people training in how to live as citizens. James Harvey Robinson, the leading historian on the committee, wanted to dispense with traditional emphases on memorization of facts and dates and instead encourage students' understanding of historical methods of research and criticism.[8]

The core elements of the country's social studies curriculum emerged from the 1916 report. To date, most states still follow fairly well the subject matter scope and sequence advocated in the report: geography and history in grades seven and eight, civics in grade nine, followed by a repeat of this cycle in high school plus a new integrated course, Problems of Democracy, for grade twelve. The report stressed the teaching of modern history as more pertinent to students' needs. However, the new scope and sequence emphasis and the problems of democracy course irritated the AHA. The 1916 report did not include four years of required history courses. Instead, it advocated study of European, English, and American history for one-half to one year each depending on local curricular needs. More disconcerting to historians, the 1916 report focused on selectively using historical issues to study specific present-day problems. The problems of democracy course also downgraded history relative to government, economics, and sociology. The report was also precedent setting because it consistently used the term "social studies" to describe an integrated approach to social education related to the organization and development of human society.[9]

Although the problems of democracy course became widespread throughout grade twelve offerings in the country by the mid-1920s, the integrated approach to social studies education underlying its development has received only an episodic and half-hearted following among social studies practitioners. The contrast between the theoretical perspectives of social studies educators and actual classroom practice related to integration of disciplinary approaches is quite striking, yet two other trends clearly emerged from the World War I era. One was an instrumentalist approach to the teaching of history. Specifically, history should be used for the purpose of teaching citizenship. A second was an erosion of interest among historians in participating in social studies education for much of the rest of the twentieth century. It seems many historians saw little value in supporting this instrumentalist approach to the discipline. Instead, educators became more central to the profession, especially through participation in the newly founded National Council for the Social Studies (NCSS).[10]

Edgar Bruce Wesley, Alan Griffin, and, perhaps most important, the Rugg brothers, especially Harold, all leading members of the NCSS, were among the most prominent of the post–World War I generation of social studies advocates who downplayed history and stressed an integrated approach to social education. Wesley, a secondary social studies teacher in St. Louis before joining the faculty of the University of Minnesota in 1931, was famously misquoted as saying social studies are social sciences "simplified for pedagogical purposes." Nevertheless, he did stress that both history and the social sciences should not be taught per se but should be used in teaching social studies courses. Griffin, a successful secondary school teacher before becoming part of the faculty at Ohio State University in 1940, was the leading scholar in America in the development of reflective theories of teaching social studies. His reflective theories were grounded in his democratic ideals. Griffin felt history was primarily useful only if pursued in a "so what?" fashion. Otherwise, he believed it was only good for the acquisition of trivial knowledge.[11]

Harold and Earle Rugg were the most prominent conveyors of social studies as citizenship education during the 1920s and 1930s. Both brothers were important social studies educators, but Harold became the leading advocate of integration of the social science disciplines into social studies teaching during the post–World War I period. Rugg's ten principles of curriculum design, outlined in the NCSS publication *The Future of the Social Studies* in 1939, illustrate his approach to social studies education. Principle nine of his design stated that social studies "builds around problems and controversial issues, training in problem-solving and generalization." Principle ten focuses on the use of history for understanding contemporary problems. Rugg also stressed the value of using "dramatic episodes" in making a social studies curriculum more meaningful. According to Rugg, focusing on dramatic episodes that bear upon contemporary events and issues would make the past more relevant to young people.[12]

Ironically, Rugg's emphasis on controversial issues plunged not only him but arguably the entire critical-thinking movement in social studies education into trouble during the late 1930s and early 1940s. Rugg and his ideas about teaching social studies came under attack by conservatives during the 1930s. Many confused his emphasis on critical thinking with disloyalty and cynicism. Indeed, partly because of such attacks, the social issues discussed in Problems of Democracy texts throughout the country by the 1930s became formulaic and rigidly codified. United States entry into World War II and the subsequent cold war squelched the movement toward a critical-minded approach to controversial social issues as part of citizenship education.[13]

World War II and the cold war stifled critical thinking approaches to social studies education during the postwar years. The NCSS itself emphasized that more attention should be focused on American traditions and institutions with, by implication, less attention being devoted to the larger world. At the same time, despite a push for more emphasis on world history in reports issued in the 1930s, the AHA and the historical profession stressed consensus views of America and western civilization. McCarthyism obviously hurt the social studies profession; more than half of the states in the country required teachers to sign loyalty oaths during the 1950s.[14]

Although the larger malaise in the profession muted their impact, some social studies educators continued to push for a renewal of effort in conveying a more critical citizenship education focus. Maurice P. Hunt and Lawrence E. Metcalf's *Teaching High School Social Studies: Problems in Reflective Thinking and Social Understanding* (1968) is considered a crucial work in the Cold War era in attempting to return to critical thinking as the core of social studies education. Hunt and Metcalf's first chapter, "The Social Studies and American Society," explains the crux of their critical thinking and, perhaps more centrally, citizenship education perspective. The authors argue that effective social studies education must focus on "problematic areas of American culture," particularly in terms of beliefs and values in the "closed areas," or taboo topics of postwar America, such as racism, sexual relations, and religious beliefs. According to Hunt and Metcalf, a democratic society depends on understanding and shared points of view around common core beliefs and values, and that intelligent reflection and discussion is necessary for such understanding to begin to develop. Schools must play a role in helping students to understand the complex and divided nature of the society in which they live. Several chapters focused on reflective thinking, which, the authors point out, drew directly from John Dewey's *How We Think* (1933). These portions of the text regarding the core elements of effective citizenship preparation, including chapter 7, "Teaching History Reflectively," also caught the attention of many social studies educators.[15]

Shirley Engle, a longtime social studies educator at Indiana University, was another leader during the early cold war years in stressing critical thinking in citizenship education. Engle emphasized the importance of decision making in social studies instruction. He zealously upheld the value of social studies as preparing students for active citizenship. Teachers should stress decision making. Specifically, students should be confronted with issues and problems and work through alternatives before reaching conclusions. Such methods should replace what he termed "mere remembering" and "ground-covering techniques." In response to critics, many of whom were professional historians and social scientists, that his view of social studies as a "selection of distillation from the social sciences" watered down the curriculum, Engle emphasized that this approach did not neglect facts but actually required students to draw upon more information and do more reading. Like Hunt and Metcalf, Engle also emphasized how social studies education must help students deal with and make value decisions.[16]

Another effort to revitalize social studies education was the so-called new social studies movement of the 1960s and 1970s. Psychologist Jerome Bruner's emphasis on having students understand the "structure" of the disciplines prompted much of this work. Based on his principles, students would focus on the basic organizing principles underlying the structure of a particular discipline. As he explains in the introduction to his book, *The Process of Education*, Bruner felt that since students would be exposed only briefly to various disciplines in their elementary and secondary education the "teaching and learning of structure, rather than simply the mastery of facts and techniques, is at the center of the classic problem of transfer." In his chapter on "The Importance of Structure," Bruner goes on to explain how students should be taught to uncover basic structures and principles through methods of "discovery." Using more current educational jargon, Bruner advocated active and constructivist approaches because students could remember structure better than isolated facts and, by using these discovery methods, schools could narrow the gap between basic and more advanced approaches to various disciplines. In the social sciences, this led to efforts to involve students in inquiry and research activities, more emphasis on higher-level thinking skills, and activities that would help students understand how the scientific method worked in the social sciences.[17]

However, Engle's point of view and the work of "new" social studies proponents served to further alienate historians, most of whom had already withdrawn from social studies education circles after World War II. Engle's work tended to dismiss history as unimportant. For instance, as part of one of his summaries on the development of social studies, Engle recounted how despite the 1916 Committee on Social Studies' report that created a new social studies curriculum for the masses "only the most daring [schools and educators] departed from the safe haven of history." Although he commended historians such as Charles Beard who stressed the importance of social studies for citizenship education, Engle tended to dismiss the historical endeavor as the study of meaningless facts. Moreover, he felt history drove out the study of most other social sciences as well as social studies, which he defined as an integrated approach to social questions, issues, and problems. In his view, even the "new" social studies of the 1960s was still overly subject centered and paid too little attention to integration. Indeed, Engle said in 1971 that "the Social Studies do not, in fact, exist today." Edgar Bruce Wesley rankled historians in 1967 with an article titled "Let's Abolish History Courses." Repeating ideas he had stated throughout his career, Wesley said that history should be used but not taught as courses. Students could analyze historical documents and sources for the purpose of studying important historical issues, but history courses themselves were not necessary. Indeed, he claimed that the value of history would not be affected if all history courses were abolished. S. Samuel Shermis, another prominent post–World War II social studies educator, voiced similar ideas. He claimed that history teachers deluded themselves by thinking that students could not think about history without knowing many facts or studying it chronologically.[18]

Mark Krug was one of the most outspoken historians during the 1960s to pillory Bruner's ideas and the "new" social studies movement. When applied to history, Krug felt Bruner's ideas fell flat because the discipline has no underlying structure. Unlike the social sciences, which rely on theory and generalization, Krug said that historians basically endeavor to recount the uniqueness of events and ideas. Whereas Krug claimed that Bruner stressed the importance of the social sciences because understanding them would prepare young people to deal with changing patterns of human conditions, Krug said that history, like the real world, was "of the specific, of the unique, and of the separate." Other historians who commented on social studies education during the cold war years tended to agree that the field rested too much on generalities that disregarded evidence contrary to them. The activist citizenship education focus of Hunt, Metcalf, and Engle did not seem to sway many historians.[19]

It was not until the publication of Secretary of Education Terrel Bell's 1983 report, "A Nation at Risk," that professional historians once again became interested in the state of social studies teaching. Conservative ideologues' emphasis on cultural literacy as the answer to problems in K-12 education agitated and dismayed most historians and social studies educators alike. During the 1980s, the History Teaching Alliance, the National Council for History Education, the Bradley Commission on History in the Schools, National History Day, and the National Center for History in the Schools were all founded. Many of these groups played prominent roles in the history and social studies standards movements for the past two decades. Although the views of historians and social studies educators still often clashed on issues tied to standards and pedagogy, these groups provided fertile forums for historians and social studies educators to work together in a way not seen in the profession since before World War I.[20]

Despite the recent reinvigoration of the field, the two major streams of thought that emerged in the first two decades of the twentieth century still characterize and, sometimes, plague social studies education. The first is the place of history in social education. In a recent essay on the role of history education in America's democracy, historian Wilfred M. McClay voiced the still common lament of historians, especially those on the conservative end of the political spectrum, that educators "relentlessly sought over a period of decades to displace the study of history in our schools in favor of a 'social studies' curriculum that they believe is more conducive than the 'fact-grubbing' specificity of history to the creation of useful habits of problem solving, generalization, and harmonious living."[21]

The second thread, voiced by James Barth in an essay reflecting on the field of social studies in 1993, reasserted the vision of social studies providing all students with preparation for active citizenship. Barth outlined what he saw as social studies' four basic precepts: citizenship education; social science and humanistic concepts integrated for instructional purposes; a focus on "persistent and contemporary social and personal conflicts, issues, and problems expressed as concepts, topics, and themes"; and a practice of problem solving and decision making.[22] Where in these two contrasting visions of social education is a rationale for social studies' role in the secondary curriculum?

Rationale

Given the two major threads underpinning the origins and development of social studies, an examination of how they explain and uphold
the value of social education is necessary. From the 1890s to today,
professional historians have stressed how history education should
teach students to think critically about the impact of change over time.
Moreover, historians have stressed that history should be taught as
authentically as possible, allowing students on a small scale to engage
in historical exercises that reflect the way practitioners of the discipline actually work. Both the 1892 Committee on History, Civil Government, and Political Economy report as well as the American
Historical Association's Committee of Seven report in 1899 stressed
that history should be taught as an analytical, inquiry-based discipline.

The 1899 Committee of Seven report explicitly addressed the issue
of history's significance in the curriculum in their chapter on the
"Value of Historical Study." The committee's remarks centered on
four main values: ties to government, training in citizenship, training
in judgment, and training in character. They noted that knowledge of
history should inform a person's appreciation of how government
worked, both for good and ill. They boldly asserted that history prepared students to be "intelligent citizens" by exposing them to books
and other resources that would prepare them, as no other school subject could, to reflect on "good and useful citizenship." The committee
emphasized how history prepared students to exercise better judgments and "to see the relation between cause and effect." Finally, but
perhaps most importantly, the committee's report stressed that history
provided character training based on "a scientific habit of mind and
thought." They felt that all people need "to study and think and examine before [they] positively assert." In the Committee of Seven's
estimation, by reading "good books" and fostering a lively sense of
the "real past," historical training would enable people to do just
that.[23]

Charles McMurry's *Special Method in History: A Complete Outline
of a Course of Study in History for the Grades Below the High School*
(1909), drawing upon the principles of both the 1892 and 1899 AHA
reports, emphasized several related aims of historical instruction that
can be seen as authentic practices of the historical profession. Mc-
Murry stressed that history instruction should "bring the past into

manifest relation to the present." It should "interpret and value the present, to estimate properly the ideas and forces which are now at work around us." Instead of fostering uncritical patriotism, he suggested that students "should be made more intelligent about our country and more sensitive to its true honor and dignity." Moreover, historical instruction is primarily a "social and moral study" that should aid in making young people "less stubborn and isolated in [their] individuality." Not least of all, "historical studies, properly conducted, lead to a thoughtful weighing of arguments, pro and con, a survey of both sides of a question so as to reach a reasonable conclusion."[24]

The parallels between these two early statements of history's value in the elementary and secondary curriculum and the Bradley Commission on History in the Schools' more recent rationale are striking. Founded in 1987, in the wake of the history profession's reawakening about the importance of history in K-12 education, the Bradley Commission's academics and teachers, drawing on support from a variety of other newly constituted history groups as well as the AHA and Organization of American Historians (OAH), reviewed the current state of the history curriculum in the United States. It then proposed that students in all states in grades seven through twelve take at least four years of history. In the commission's statement on the value of studying history, two major aims of history education were identified: "the preparation of all our people for private lives of personal integrity and fulfillment, and their preparation for public life as democratic citizens." History not only constitutes a core humanistic discipline that gives meaning to people's private lives, it "convey[s] a sense of civic responsibility by graphic portrayals of virtue, courage, and wisdom." This statement virtually replicates the Committee of Seven's views on the same issue: by studying history, students "see tyranny, vulgarity, greed, benevolence, patriotism, self-sacrifice" in the lives of public officials. Moreover, according to the Bradley Commission, "history and geography provide the context of time and place for ideas and methods drawn from the social sciences—anthropology, economics, political science, psychology, and sociology." Furthermore, students prepared in history are needed in a variety of professions, such as "law, journalism, diplomacy, politics, and teaching. More broadly, historical study develops analytical skills, comparative perspectives, and modes of critical judgment that promote thoughtful work in any field or career."[25]

Citizenship education, the cornerstone of the 1916 report and most of the post–World War I social studies educators' arguments, obviously resonates throughout the historians' rationales. How have social studies educators' conceptions of citizenship education contrasted with historians'? Perhaps the central difference has been social studies educators' stronger emphasis on an activist approach to citizenship education. Arthur William Dunn, the central figure in the 1916 report on social studies, wanted students to identify and investigate social problems, ideally those found in their own communities, and work toward possible solutions. This Progressive faith in the ability of teachers and students to rationally examine and then tackle social ills underscores the rationales of most of the twentieth century's most prominent social studies educators.[26]

Shirley Engle, following in Dunn's footsteps, stresses repeatedly in his work that one cannot equate mastery of content with active, good citizenship. In Engle's view, it is not enough for students to have a critical understanding of persistent problems; they must have opportunities to engage in problem solving and decision making. Again, like Dunn and other Progressives, Engle wants students to use their abilities to make positive changes in society. Too often, Engle said, historians believe that students can become good citizens by studying past controversies. The key, though, is allowing students to not only reflect on past and present problems, but then to engage in exercises where they propose solutions to these problems. "Citizenship education needs to involve a continued conversation between students and their mentors while they search for better ways of doing things." Engle's views diverged again from historians in terms of the application of an informed understanding of the past's value for making changes in present society. He stressed that "the cutting edge of education must be at the emergence of new knowledge rather than at the persistence of old and frequently obsolete knowledge."[27]

This more explicitly activist conception of citizenship education in social studies has resulted in curricular proposals defined usually as either "issues-centered" or "social issues" education. Anna S. Ochoa-Becker, a colleague and collaborator of Engle's, explained the rationale for this type of social studies education as squarely centered on the question: "Can educators prepare young people for democratic citizenship?" Her conception of citizenship education rests on "the belief that democracy is preferred over other political systems, holds that democratic citizens must rise above pure self-interest and be sensitive to the needs of others and the common good."[28] Issues-centered education makes the public good the focus of students' problem solving and decision-making exercises. Designing an issues-centered curriculum requires educators to work not only with their students in defining relevant problems, but also with parents and the larger community.

As Ochoa-Becker and Engle further elaborated in *Education for Democratic Citizenship: Decision Making in the Social Studies* (1988) issues-centered citizenship education should create skeptical, proactive citizens, the cornerstone, in their view, of good citizenship. To do this, social studies teachers must emphasize both socialization and countersocialization. In the lower grades, socialization helps students to understand the basic elements of a democratic culture and practice the basic habits that can make a democracy effective. In the higher grades, countersocialization provides students with opportunities and support to develop their critical thinking skills and individual sense of responsibility. To create faith in the democratic ideal of the basic value of all individuals the schools themselves must provide opportunities for students to practice democracy and teachers must respect intellectual honesty in students. Crucially, teachers cannot solely rely on training students in the methods of social sciences because they do not help students make value judgments. Here, the humanities, including history, should play a role in a truly integrated social studies focus. When exposed to this process of social education, students would then be able to ask questions such as "How do we know that a particular statement is true? What must be done to improve specific social conditions such as crime, homelessness, foreign policy, inequalities, and so forth? How can I justify my decisions?" Both Engle and Ochoa-Becker downplay the importance of knowing the facts as isolated from a socially significant use of the facts.[29]

One of the essential points of difference between historians' and social studies educators' rationales for citizenship education is the contrast between reflections that inform and improve one's private life and the ability to use information to transform the larger society. Historians have emphasized the value of the former as much as the latter whereas educators such as Engle and Ochoa-Becker give much greater weight to the value of the latter. Yet there is little doubt that historians and social studies educators have consistently emphasized the central importance of citizenship education. No other subject in the schools addresses citizenship education, surely one of the most valuable elements of a child's education in the United States. The next chapter builds on the necessary foundation of history and social studies education by explaining the structure and standards of the disciplines.

Chapter 2

Overview of the Structure and Standards for History, the Social Sciences, and Social Studies

History is not Truth. Truth is in the Telling.
—Robert Penn Warren

Structure of History

Throughout the past century, historians and social studies educators stressed the value of citizenship preparation in emphasizing the role of social studies in the curriculum. Yet, clearly, historians stress elements of their discipline's value that differs from the social studies educators' perspectives and values. At this point, it is important to understand how historians, social scientists, and social studies educators have explained the structure of their disciplines and relate these understandings to current standards for teaching the disciplines.

Effective teaching of history rests in great part on a teacher's understanding of the discipline. Teachers need to understand the aims and purposes of historical inquiry, how historical inquiry compares and contrasts with other forms of social science inquiry, and how history can provide an integrative function in social studies teaching. This may be even more important today as the number and variety of electronic resources available to history teachers has proliferated. Those teachers who understand the nature of historical inquiry and have clear ideas about how to engage students most effectively in historical inquiry will be best able to take advantage of the resources now available.

Just what is the nature of history? R.G. Collingwood, one of the most notable philosophers of history, provided a deceptively simple definition when he said "History, like theology or natural science, is a special form of thought." More specifically, though, he went on to say that history is a kind of science since it involves inquiry focused on the actions of human beings in the past. It proceeds through the interpretation of evidence. Mark Krug, another important philosopher of history, emphasized history's grand purpose. It is concerned with the "totality of human experiences" and "attempts to provide society with an artificial collective memory." Yet, too, as one of the humanities, history also has characteristics of the arts. Where among these extremes of simplicity, grandeur, and artistic expression is history's structure and purpose as a discipline?[1]

History is, of course, the study of humanity's past. It is particularly, as Collingwood stressed, the study of people's actions in the past. Typically, though some social or cultural historians might disagree, history is concerned with actions that resulted in some larger social significance. But before one can investigate human activities with some larger significance, historians need to frame or limit their investigation. In other words, historians need to decide how they will approach a particular issue. Krug said that this basically revolves around the asking of three questions: What happened? How did it happen? Why did it happen? Answering the first question requires historians to gather appropriate evidence. Answering the second and third questions requires historians to interpret or make judgments based on their evidence.[2]

Historical evidence usually consists of written sources, but can also consist of oral records or artifacts. Since the evidence does not speak for itself, the historian's main task, as Oscar Handlin stresses, is to interpret the meaning of the evidence being examined. Indeed, Norman Cantor and Richard Schneider go so far as to say that historians *must* make such judgments. Credibility is one of the main issues a historian must consider. Who produced a particular source? What was the purpose in producing it? How does this evidence fit with other existing records? Understanding the answers to these questions requires historians to have contextual understanding of their sources.

When reading a word, Handlin stresses, one needs to understand that it might mean one thing at one time and something else at another. This may be even more important with numbers. The quality of the numerical data produced has generally improved over time. So one must know something about the process used in producing a numerical value, even when it looks very official in a published volume. Paintings and even photographs can conceal as much as they reveal. No matter what type of source is used, historians need to infer the intentions of those who produced them.[3]

Collecting and carefully scrutinizing evidence is the initial stage of historical investigation. Yet careful analysis, synthesis, and evaluation of historical evidence do not by themselves result in history. History is story telling. History is also concerned with explaining change over time. Therefore history combines a narrative framework with a focus on causation. Of course, narration and causation are linked to chronology. But historians cannot simply line up the appropriate evidence in a chronological order and call it history. On one hand, historians never have access to all the available evidence and, on the other hand, the evidence that is available to them is often fragmentary. Historians must therefore rely on their imaginations to interpolate from their evidence what might be missing to construct their explanatory narratives.

Imagination is often confused with bias. Yet, because history can never be fully recreated, as Collingwood stressed, "the historian must re-enact the past in his own mind." The historian must select the evidence that most accurately and fairly accounts for the changes perceived. This requires historians to not only use their imaginations to distinguish the important from the unimportant, but they also invariably stress factors or concerns that reflect their own standards of value. In this respect, history is always a product of the times in which it is written. This is also one of the reasons why history is always rewritten. Indeed, Lester Stephens contends that "revision of interpretations is inevitable." Of course, even though history is a product of the present, historians are still obligated to be fair in how they examine the relevant evidence. Fairness in this sense usually means that historians' accounts must be aware, as William H. Dray summarizes, of "alternative possibilities, to be willing to take criticism seriously into account, to be scrupulous and painstaking in presenting arguments, and to draw conclusions only where evidence for them can be adduced."[4]

More so than is true for other social scientists, historians focus on, as Mark Krug says, "the singular, the concrete, and the unique." But in addressing the how and why questions, historians are also concerned with generalization, at least limited or, to use Lester Stephens' qualifier, "tentative" generalizations. Historians' generalizations are almost always limited in space and time. Because historians must immerse themselves in understanding the milieu of a particular set of people in a particular place and time, they typically hesitate to generalize beyond that context. As noted later in the chapter, however, historians do often draw upon much broader theoretical frameworks, often devised by social scientists, for support in posing their own more constrained and limited generalizations. In addition to the limited, contextualized sort of explanations, historians also explain and generalize based on "how possibly" something might have happened. Such explanations are especially prevalent where evidence is fragmentary.[5]

Although historians' biases and perspectives invariably impact how they examine evidence and construct their analytical narratives, historians also are concerned with balance and perspective. Beyond the issues of fairness already noted, historians must take other historians' views into account in addition to weighing the relevant evidence that impacts a particular issue or event. Yet historians' writings about the past only can be impartial or objective to a degree much more limited than those of natural or physical scientists. Historical investigation unlike "hard" science cannot be undertaken under laboratory conditions and replicated precisely by successive investigators. This is especially true when historical work focuses on issues tied to values, attitudes, and beliefs. This affective focus is particularly slippery and very often reflects the historians' own values, attitudes, and beliefs. Historical accounts are products of the historians' imagination. Both Krug and Collingwood emphasize how history is a product of a particular historian's mind, which of course makes it a much different enterprise than that undertaken by other sorts of scientific investigation.[6]

Thus in many respects, history shares as much in common with those who engage in literary and humanistic endeavors as it does with social scientists' endeavors. Because great historical writing is an art, historians' efforts that have been discredited in terms of research or perspective are often still read and respected when they are well crafted.

Standards for History

One of the strengths of the standards movement has been the wide-spread adoption of authentic instructional language. This clearly is evident in the two major sources of standards for history teaching that many states' standards for preservice and inservice teachers have drawn upon: the *National Standards for History*, published by the National Center for History in the Schools (NCHS), and the National Council for the Social Studies' (NCSS) social studies standards. It is clear in the language of both organizations' standards that historians' methodological practices are advocated. The NCHS standards stress this in their five standards of historical thinking while the NCSS standards, though in a less systematic fashion, emphasize similar ideas in both the preservice and inservice history standards.

The NCHS's five standards for historical thinking are: chronological thinking, historical comprehension, historical analysis and interpretation, historical research capabilities, and historical issue analysis and decision making. In terms of historical comprehension, this standard emphasizes how students should be able to reconstruct literal meanings of historical passages, read historical passages imaginatively, describe the past on its own terms without judging it from their own present-day perspectives, and draw upon a wide variety of source materials. The standard on historical analysis and interpretation stresses how students should differentiate between fact and interpretation, consider multiple perspectives, analyze cause and effect, compare competing narratives, and remember that historical interpretations are tentative and subject to change. For historical research skills, the standard outlines how students need to formulate historical questions, obtain historical data, question their data by uncovering the context in which they were created, and identify missing data and imaginatively interpolate possible perspectives from those gaps in the record. The fifth standard dealing with historical issues analysis and decision making helps students to understand the value-laden nature of historical inquiry. It explains how students should be able to identify relevant issues and problems, gather evidence about contemporary factors and circumstances, identify relevant historical factors, evaluate alternative courses of action, formulate a position or course of action on an issue, and evaluate the implementation of a decision. As suggested by both the research and issues-analysis and decision-making standards' focuses, examples of students' achievements include primary source research activities for both the middle and high school grades.[7]

The NCSS's *Standards for Social Studies Teachers* focuses on history expectations for learners, teachers, and school applications. Students are expected to "develop historical understanding and competence in ways of historical thinking," including the ability to interpret sources and construct their own arguments. Teachers are expected to assist learners in understanding chronological thinking, developing historical comprehension, practicing analytical and interpretive skills, and undertaking historical research. Beginning during the middle grades, the NCSS history standards suggest that schools provide students with a more formal approach to their historical studies, including constructing timelines, studying and interpreting historical documents, thinking about historical context, formulating historical questions, and identifying the values and moral convictions of individuals. The high school applications builds on these ideas with expectations for "sophisticated analysis and reconstruction of the past" that includes such ideas as constructing bibliographies and considering multiple perspectives when formulating their historical arguments.[8]

Structure of the Social Sciences

While historical investigations rely on the use of a scientific method of research, the nature of historical evidence and writing requires historians to pursue understanding and insight in ways that are less scientific and more literary or creative perhaps than researchers involved in the other social sciences. Arguably the two most significant ways that the social sciences differ from history in terms of disciplinary structure are in the scope of their generalizations and in their focus on present concerns. As previously noted, historians are concerned primarily with limited generalizations. Such generalizations are grounded in particular contexts of place and time and even the peculiarities of specific individuals. Social scientists hope to generalize more universally. They do so especially with the intention of explaining human behavior present today. Certainly social scientists draw upon historical materials and references, but their focus is contemporary.

The more explicit emphasis on generalization for the purpose of understanding contemporary human behavior is evident when some of the key concerns of the various social science disciplines are outlined. Geographers view their field as a spatial science. The National Geographic Society's five themes of movement, location, region, place, and human-environment interaction encompass the major ways geographers examine human beings' ties to and impact on the environment. Geographers increasingly rely on a variety of technical applications, such as geographic positioning systems, geographic information systems, geographic information science, and remote sensing that have refined the analytical rigor of much of their work dealing with concepts of space.

Economists are especially concerned with issues related to the needs of humans to satisfy their material needs through production and consumption. The concepts of scarcity, allocation, and choice underlie their analyses of humans' material needs. Economists examine these concepts in terms of how different government structures influence and impact them. Perhaps more than the other social sciences, economists are particularly attuned to sophisticated quantitative analyses in formulating their examinations of people's material needs.

Political science focuses on issues of power among groups and individuals. Normally, power is tied to forms of government. Much of political scientists' work is therefore concentrated on government institutions and how groups and individuals relate to one another within and outside such institutions. In addition, political scientists examine how groups shape government policies through a variety of mechanisms such as pressure groups. They also focus a great deal of attention on how governments relate to one another. Political scientists deal with theoretical concepts such as democracy and citizenship.

Sociologists examine group behavior in many different contexts. They often examine small groups in order to generalize about human behavior in terms of norms, status, and roles. While sociologists tend to study modern, industrialized societies, anthropologists focus on many of the same concepts and concerns in terms of premodern or preindustrial societies. Both sociologists and anthropologists are broadly concerned with defining elements of human cultures and traditions. More so than sociologists, anthropologists often consider a broader sweep of cultural traditions.

Although normally considered part of the social science disciplines, psychologists also share concerns and techniques of biologists and medical scientists. Psychologists focus especially on understanding the nature of individual mental behaviors and processes. Their theoretical constructs, such as behaviorism and cognition, attempt to understand how human thought processes are translated into actions.

With each of these disciplines, social scientists' emphases on generalizations are striking when one considers the complexity of the conceptualization involved. Vast amounts of detail and variation are implicitly imbedded in concepts like norms, democracy, and culture. In contrast, historians find it necessary to explicate such details and variation in their descriptions and analyses. Reliance on generalization in the social sciences also allowed Jerome Bruner to stress the importance of structure in education. As contrasted with history, the social sciences emphasize fundamental concepts, principles, and theories that enable them to consider vast amalgams of ideas. Historical knowledge is very often the specific elements from which social scientists derive their generalizations. At the same time, especially over the past two generations, historians have drawn increasingly upon the conceptual and analytical tools of the social sciences in formulating a lot of the more global and comparative histories that have been written.[9]

Standards for the Social Sciences

The NCSS disciplinary standards for geography, civics and government, economics, and psychology underscore the importance of key concepts and generalizations within each of these fields. This is particularly emphasized in the teacher expectation components of each of these standards. To a large degree, the focus in the social science standards is on students' practice and facility in examining information to illustrate crucial conceptualizations and generalizations.

In geography, the NCSS disciplinary standard emphasizes that students should learn "the use of maps and other geographic representations, tools, and technologies to acquire, process, and report information from a spatial perspective." More specifically, teachers should help students understand the concepts of regions as an organizing tool for making sense of the Earth's complexity. Teachers should help students understand how culture, cultural mosaics, and experience influence perceptions of places and regions. Teachers should guide students' understanding of the Earth's ecosystems. Students need to understand how physical systems affect human systems. In terms of school applications, the geography standard, as contrasted with the history standard, focuses again more on activities that develop conceptual understanding than on analysis of actual data. Hence, high school students, for instance, need to understand "how multiple criteria are used to define a region and to analyze geographic issues." They should also "understand the spatial characteristics of cultural convergence and divergence."[10]

The NCSS civics and government disciplinary standard is directed primarily to issues and learning tasks that support the development of "competent citizens." Teachers are asked to focus primarily on issues tied to American government and civics. Students need to explore the meaning of democracy and develop an understanding of citizenship. They need to be made aware of "the full range of opportunities to participate as citizens in the American democracy." One strand of the teacher expectations notes that learners need to "understand the relationship of the United States to other nations and to world affairs," but clearly the standard emphasizes school applications as well that are squarely aimed at American government. As contrasted with geography and more akin to history, the government and civics standard emphasizes that high school students should explore the origins of the American political system through an examination of key foundational documents. Doing so will provide students with a "contextualized sense" of American political culture and values.[11]

The NCSS economics disciplinary standard includes a particularly strong focus on concepts and generalizations, primarily from a free enterprise economic point of view. Teachers are expected to emphasize tenets such as scarcity and cost-benefit decision making. Students should learn that people "respond predictably to positive and negative incentives." Competition is stressed as the mechanism that drives market performance. Students need to understand the concept of money. Teachers need to explain how government impacts the market economy, and how "costs of government policies sometimes exceed benefits." At the middle school level, schools should provide students with exercises that teach them the concept of scarcity. At the high school level, students should understand the concepts of marginal costs and marginal benefits as each relates to decisions concerning production and consumption.[12]

In a similar fashion as the economics standard, the NCSS psychology disciplinary standard is primarily oriented toward conceptualizations and generalizations. Students should understand major theories and be able to comprehend and apply "concepts, theories and principles associated with human cognition; emotional, social, and personal development; and growth and change." Nevertheless, as compared to the economics standard, the psychology standard does stress the application of these concepts and theories to the students' own experiences. They should "examine factors that may have influenced the development of personality and individual differences as well as psychological disorders." Some attention in the standard is devoted to having students "engage in preliminary behavioral science research."[13]

Structure of Social Studies

As explained in chapter 1, social studies, the new discipline that emerged out of the curriculum discussions and revisions during World War I, is not meant to involve students in full-fledged historical or social science investigations. Instead, social studies draws upon elements of history and social science primarily for the purpose of reflective inquiry into contemporary concerns. This focus has constituted what most social studies educators mean by citizenship education. Although troubling to some historians and social scientists, the use of historical and social science material in this way makes more sense today than it did when first proposed. Today, many fields of history draw upon social science concepts and theories for their thematic emphases. For instance, labor historians since the 1960s have drawn heavily upon sociological concepts like social class, economic theories such as socialism, and political concepts like ideology to both guide and bolster their historical investigations and arguments. In addition, like social scientists, historians generate their hypotheses about the past based on contemporary concerns. Although always trying to avoid imposing these present-day concerns on their interpretations of the past, historians' work inevitably reflects contemporary perspectives.[14]

As exemplified in the work of Hunt, Metcalf, Cox, Massialas, Oliver, Shaver, Engle, Ochoa-Becker, and many others since the 1950s, social studies is meant to involve middle and high school students in examining social issues using analytical and inquiry-based approaches, multidisciplinary sources of data, and opportunities to form judgments and evaluations. Hunt and Metcalf stressed that social studies should use elements of John Dewey's emphasis on controversy, values, and reflection to engage students in projects emphasizing meaning over facts and memorization. In particular, they emphasized that the primary objective of high school social studies should be to "help students reflectively examine issues in the problematic areas of American culture." Crucially, students' concerns should guide choices of issues. They felt that students' individual concerns would often intersect with larger societal problems. In this way, too, social studies would have more relevance because it would meet both individual and social needs. Moreover, they argued, students would only truly want to reflect on issues if they perceived them to be connected to their own problems. In terms of suggested "problematic areas of culture," Hunt and Metcalf outlined several ideas with the categories of power and the law; economics (particularly in terms of questioning the basic tenets of laissez-faire theories); nationalism, patriotism, and foreign affairs; social class; religion and morality; race and minority group relations; and sex, courtship, and marriage.[15]

C. Benjamin Cox and Byron Massialas examined texts in the mid-1960s, during the height of the "new" social studies movement, with an eye to the emphasis on inquiry. They believed, as it seems logical for social studies advocates to maintain in the early twenty-first century, that the subject focus nature of the curriculum is unlikely to change, but that social studies instructors could tailor the individual disciplines in a more issues-focused, interdisciplinary, analytical, inquiry-based, and reflective direction. In fact, their conclusions about textbooks in the mid-1960s would probably still hold true today. They found that practically any textbook could be used in an inquiry-oriented class. Yet, at the same time, no textbook alone would provide a sufficient research base for such a class. A wide variety of materials would be necessary. Moreover, very few texts in the mid-1960s, as would still hold true today, were structured to teach inquiry techniques in the various history or social science disciplines; that is left up to the knowledgeable and creative instructor. Cox and Massialas concluded that they hoped that future social studies instructors would make inquiry the emphasis of their courses and use it to have students examine contemporary controversial themes. Instead of subject-specific courses, the curriculum should be truly interdisciplinary. It should be built around key controversies, such as income distribution, minority relations, and ideological conflict. It must stress analytical concepts and generalizations, and must also push students to test hypotheses, gather data, and arrive at conclusions. Cox and Massialas stressed how the social studies really should be structured more around social science concepts than history. In fact, they recommended that much of the traditional chronological and political emphases of history could be done away with.[16]

During the same period of the mid-1960s, Donald W. Oliver and James P. Shaver recognized a similar problem as that identified by Cox and Massialas—How can greater attention be given to social science principles in the social studies? They felt that the two key problems that needed correction in the high school curriculum were transforming students from passive to active participants in the learning process and restructuring the social studies curriculum away from fragmented university disciplines into a focus on the "role of the citizen in the community." For Oliver and Shaver, the purpose of social studies is "to promote the dignity and worth of each individual who lives in the society." Ultimately, two criteria should guide content selection in the social studies: exposure of students to public problems and instruction of students of means to analyze these problems within political and social frameworks. They admit, however, that to emphasize these elements in the curriculum, students must already have a basic understanding of their own and other cultures and should be "committed to the basic ideals of American society emerging from the democratic traditions of Western civilization."[17]

Shirley Engle and Anna Ochoa clearly explained the delineation between social studies and the study of history and social sciences. For them, most broadly, the social studies should be defined as "the *critical* study of the social sciences and history," meaning "engaging directly in the intellectual process by which social scientists and historians verify truth." As opposed to the way the disciplines of history and the social sciences are taught in the middle and high schools, as facts and generalizations that students memorize for quizzes and tests, social studies should require students to "question the factual claims made or to argue with the authority." Engle and Ochoa also rejected the use of social studies as propaganda or indoctrination, the way, unfortunately too often, that citizenship education has been carried out in the schools. In the same way, Engle and Ochoa rejected the notion of equating social studies with the teaching of topics. For them, students should see all social issues as problems open to debate rather than topics for which all the answers are known and simply need to be passed on to students. Engle and Ochoa felt that the social studies best fulfilled its potential if students were able to pursue their own social science investigations, ideally focused on deeply rooted and enduring social problems. It seems fair to say, as Engle and Ochoa do, that the leading figures in the post–World War II social studies movement saw the structure of their discipline as a "hands-on, open, questioning, active enterprise, consistent with human intelligence and consistent with a democracy that presumably prizes the rational and the intellectual." Too often, however, this form of social studies classroom emphasis has been ignored or misunderstood.[18]

Historians, social scientists, and social studies educators would all agree about the vital importance of inquiry and reflection in understanding the structure of their disciplines. Nevertheless, many historians would likely object to the uses of history proposed by the social studies educators just surveyed. In particular, historians likely would feel uncomfortable with the contemporary socializing—citizenship education—purpose of social studies educators' views of the discipline. Hunt, Metcalf, Cox, Massialas, Oliver, Shaver, Engle, and Ochoa all emphasize how social studies inquiry should examine contemporary issues or problems. History is used as a means to understand current events, but not studied on its own terms. History educators such as Matthew Downey believed it is essential that history not be broken up into fragments and scattered through a social problem–centered curriculum. Kieran Egan has made one of the strongest cases for the weakness of this element of social studies' structure. As he explained, "the aim of history as a discipline is to come to understand the past in its own terms, in its uniqueness, for its own sake and the sake of the pleasure of such understanding." More fundamentally, history does not necessarily provide support for the basic ideals of American society, including a commitment to democracy, that social studies educators emphasize as crucial for the structure of the discipline. Egan scorned the aim of educators who saw social studies' structure as centered on critical thinking but neglected a focus on history because it is "austere, hard, and sterile." Furthermore, Egan contended that history used only to further an understanding of democratic Western ideals leaves out the very stuff of history that might serve to sharpen students' critical understanding of conflicting or competing points of view. Some took Egan to task for neglecting how much historians' concerns are connected to contemporary concerns, but Egan's central concern about the gulf in perspectives between historians and social studies educators, a divide noted in the history of social studies' development as a discipline, remains a persistent dilemma for the field.[19]

Standards for Social Studies

The standards that support current social studies practices, including the Interstate New Teachers Assessment and Support Consortium (INTASC), National Council for the Social Studies (NCSS), and various state discipline specific standards, represent a balance between discipline-specific elements and the citizenship education concerns, that is interdisciplinary, reflective emphases on contemporary social problems, advocated by social studies educators. On one hand, an emphasis on specific disciplines, as opposed to truly interdisciplinary social studies, is retained in the various social studies standards. Yet many elements underscoring citizenship education advocated by social studies educators also are emphasized. Five main elements of best teaching practice in the social studies field are evident in the INTASC and NCSS standards: multiple representations or perspectives, inquiry-based methodologies, critical use of appropriate source materials, interdisciplinary methods, and ability to construct new knowledge or sound interpretations.[20]

INTASC standard 1, focusing on content expertise and the ability of the teacher to create meaningful learning experiences, notes the importance of multiple perspectives in both its dispositions and performances sections. Teachers should "use differing viewpoints, theories, and 'ways of knowing.' " The NCSS's thematic standard for culture and cultural diversity, stresses that students "need to comprehend multiple perspectives that emerge from within their own culture and from the vantage points of the diverse cultural groups within that society and with whom the society may interact." The need for multiple perspectives is also cited in the NCSS history disciplinary standard. Multiple perspectives or representations are also evident in the

NCSS geography disciplinary standard in how teachers explain human interactions.[21]

INTASC and the NCSS standards are thoroughly infused with emphases on using inquiry-based methodologies. INTASC standard 1 starts by stating that the teacher "understands . . . processes of inquiry . . . that are central to the discipline(s) s/he teaches." In terms of dispositions, teachers should "convey to learners how knowledge is developed." In their performances, teachers need to "use . . . methods of inquiry" and "test hypotheses according to the methods of inquiry and standards of evidence used in the discipline." The NCSS disciplinary standards, especially in the sections on high school applications, emphasize how students should be allowed to analyze, explain, interpret, and solve problems.[22]

As might be expected if teachers introduce students to the use of inquiry-based methodologies in the various disciplines, the standards also emphasize that students should be taught to critically examine appropriate source materials. INTASC standard 1's emphasis on this is more implicit than the NCSS standards. The NCSS thematic standard on time, continuity, and change specifically notes that teachers should "guide learners as they systematically employ processes of critical historical inquiry." The NCSS geography standard says that teachers should "guide learners in the use of maps and other geographic representations, tools, and technologies." Psychology teachers are urged to have students "study personality and individual differences and commonalities."[23]

Great emphasis in INTASC standard 1 is placed on the importance of interdisciplinary perspectives. In the knowledge section of the standard, teachers are supposed to be able to "relate his/her disciplinary knowledge to other subject areas." In the performance section, the standard says that teachers should "create interdisciplinary learning experiences that allow students to integrate knowledge, skills, and methods of inquiry from several subject areas." A similar interdisciplinary focus is at the heart of the NCSS thematic standards. Indeed, this interdisciplinary focus underscores the use of the very term "social studies."[24]

Finally, and perhaps most important, the various standards stress an active, hands-on, "constructivist" perspective about the teaching of social studies. One can read the performances section of INTASC standard 1 and conclude that students should be engaged in authentic experimental or research type exercises as a core part of their instruction. The NCSS thematic and disciplinary standards refer repeatedly to enabling learners to predict, construct, explain, investigate, interpret, develop, explore, apply, and analyze new information to advance their own ideas about a particular subject.

Some social studies educators are likely to be disappointed that none of these standards suggest specific contemporary problems or issues that students need to specifically investigate. There is no explicit mention of either specific problems that should be focused on, nor is there emphasis on investigation of contemporary problems as part of citizenship education per se. Yet the standards are certainly malleable and open-ended enough for creative teachers of any of the history or social science disciplines to adopt a more explicitly citizenship education orientation to the problems or issues explored in their own courses. The same could be said of history teachers who see the value of reflective, inquiry-based social education. Michael Whelan offered one option for social studies educators who wanted to blend the social problems approach with history: "social problems are best studied in historical context and with the habits of mind of history study brought to bear."[25]

Chapter 3

Technology Integration in Preservice History Teacher Education

Be not the first by whom the new are tried, nor yet the last
to lay the old aside.
—Alexander Pope

At the dawn of the twenty-first century, it is rather inconceivable to think we would still be engaged in a discussion of how to integrate technology and the Internet into the history teacher education curriculum. However, this is the reality of the situation. Although American schools have witnessed the proliferation of computers and computer use in classrooms, going from 630,000 in 1985 to more than 8 million by the close of the twentieth century, this same pedagogical phenomenon has not been mirrored by teacher education programs.[1]

Researchers still find technology and Internet use in teacher education to be the exception rather than the norm.[2] Numerous research studies in both the United States and United Kingdom have found preservice teachers are "not well prepared for classroom use of computer technologies."[3] A recent report by the U.S. Office of Technology Assessment confirmed this dismal appraisal of computer use: "Despite the importance of technology in teacher education, it is not central to the preparation experience in most U.S. colleges of education today. Most new teachers graduate from teacher preparation institutions with limited knowledge of the ways technology can be used in their professional practice."[4]

Even in the midst of these turbulent waves of alarming reports on the status of computer use in teacher education, those who continue to champion the cause of technology education have weathered the storm and stayed the course. In the past five years, in fact, their voices have become stronger and their audience has grown dramatically.[5] A recent survey of preservice teachers found that 90 percent of them not only recognized the need for computer training, but lobbied strongly for such integration in their teacher education program.[6]

This plea for making technology an integral part of teacher education has been echoed by politicians as well. During his first term in office, President Bill Clinton made such a plea, positing that, "In our schools, every classroom in America must be connected to the information superhighway with computers and good software and well-trained teachers."[7] An even stronger statement was issued in a 1995 U.S. Office of Technology Assessment Report that placed teacher training as a top priority. The report proclaimed that preparing teachers to "effectively incorporate technology into the teaching and learning process is one of the most important steps the nation can take to make the most of past and continuing investment in educational technology."[8]

Three centuries later, perhaps neoclassical poet Alexander Pope's appraisal of societal acceptance of innovation is still valid. While computers have become nearly commonplace in elementary and secondary school landscapes, and the allocation for this technology has gone from millions to billions of dollars in annual spending, many of their classroom gatekeepers remain locked in an archaic pedagogical paradigm.[9] The result of this has been described by some researchers as an all too common, simplistic, classroom technology integration strategy of, "Do something. Do anything. Just use it!"[10]

While this may appear to be a rather extreme characterization of the current situation, it does raise a number of important questions for preservice history teacher education programs. In particular, there are two vital questions of greatest importance to the history education community: What is the current state of computer and Internet integration in teacher education? What theoretical and pedagogical frameworks and practices appear to be the most promising for history teacher education?

Although some researchers warn that any response to these questions is "hazardous in view of the fact that technological change has increased at such an accelerated rate that proposals for preservice and inservice teacher preparation in technology have a brief shelf life," this should not deter teachers and researchers from attempting to answer these queries.[11] The antithetical argument does not reconcile itself with the reality of the classroom. Many history education graduates will find themselves teaching in school districts where technology is already an integral, and evolving, component of the curriculum.[12] In addition, while education is more susceptible than any other profession to the swing of the innovation pendulum, nearly everyone agrees technology is one innovation that is here to stay.[13]

Status of Technology Use in Teacher Education

> Tens of millions of parents all across our nation have watched their children play every kind of video game from *Mortal Kombat* and *Primal Rage* to *Killer Instinct* and *Super Street Fighter*. But the really important new computer game in America is learning. And we are going to put it at the disposal of every child in this country by the end of the century.[14]

Although President Clinton's vision of universal computer access in America's classrooms has not yet been realized, it is much closer to reality today than it was just a few short years ago. The computer-student ratio has gone from 1:125 in 1984 to 1:5 today.[15] The question, however, is not whether the number of computers in American classrooms will continue to increase—this we have established. What remains to be seen is whether teacher education programs will be able to prepare new teachers to effectively incorporate computers and the Internet into their history curricula and instructional repertoires. While the statistical data concerning the proliferation of computers in American schools are indeed encouraging, the same statistical data regarding teacher preparation are quite depressing. For example, a 1995 report by the U.S. Office of Technology Assessment estimated that only 3 percent of teacher education program graduates felt, "very well prepared" to utilize technology in their classroom.[16]

Although the integration of instructional technology into teacher education curricula varies greatly from one institution to another, what remains constant is the disparity between the increase in access to such technology in K-12 classrooms and the caliber of technology training afforded to preservice teachers.[17] The current situation is perhaps best summarized by Howard Mehlinger and Jerry Willis in the introduction to their chapter, "Information Technology and Teacher Education," included in the most recent edition of the *Handbook of Research on Teacher Education*. They preface their review with the following statement:

> Much of the literature on information technology and teacher education could be summarized in one sentence: Most preservice teachers know very little about effective use of technology in education and leaders believe there is a pressing need to increase substantially the effective quality of instruction teachers receive about technology. The idea may be expressed aggressively, assertively, or in more subtle forms, but the virtually universal conclusion is that teacher education, particularly preservice, is not preparing educators to work in a technology-enriched classroom.[18]

Mehlinger and Willis are not alone in their assessment. Consider, as well, the following quotes by other educational researchers:

> Sadly, the need to train teachers in the effective use and integration of technology is not new information to teacher education training programs. Researchers have been reporting for at least a decade that schools and colleges of education are woefully behind schedule in areas related to technological uses in today's K-12 classrooms. Individually, most professors recognize technology training as a growing need in their preservice teacher education programs. Programmatically, though, they still think it should be taught as a stand-alone course, not necessarily integrated into their specific content area.[19]

> Teachers are emerging from their preservice training to become part of the problem of integrating technology into the classroom rather than part of the solution.[20]

> There is little argument among leaders in the field of educational technology that teacher training institutions are not adequately preparing undergraduate teacher education students to effectively integrate technology into their teaching. Thus, our education students are graduating

with little knowledge as to the instructional applications of one of the most revolutionary sets of instructional tools of the past two decades.[21]

While this picture of teacher education appears rather bleak, for many colleges and universities it is still an accurate portrayal. The only thing that has changed in the past few years is the increase in demand by school administrators for teacher education programs to graduate teacher candidates with the requisite skills necessary to integrate technology into their curricula. Economics is certainly a primary motivating factor in this scenario. As one teacher educator has pointed out, "more and more superintendents are reluctant to hire new teacher candidates that are not already trained in the use of technology. Their contention is that precious staff development funds are being eaten away by initial training that should, and could, be provided by preservice teacher education programs."[22] How then should history teacher education programs respond to this demand? What should guide history teacher educators in their attempt to design programs that meet the needs of the twenty-first century?

History Teacher Education Technology Framework: Standards

> If technology is to be widely used, teachers and administrators need training. Training to use technology must be a part of every entry-level teacher's preparation and should continue throughout a teacher's career so that he or she can keep abreast of developing technologies. The most effective training is accomplished within the curricular area in which the technology is to be used.[23]

Numerous events have played a role in determining the course of American education in the twentieth century. In the last quarter of the century, however, no event has played as critical a role as that of the standards movement. The power of standards to "catalyze change in fundamental components of the educational system" is without question.[24] Given this, an excellent starting point for history teacher education programs attempting to integrate technology into their teacher preparation curricula are the guidelines and policies imbedded in these standards. Although much is to be learned from the analysis of standards, it still represents only the first step in the development process.[25]

Numerous professional organizations lay claim to history or social studies teacher education; however most do not make mention of the role of technology in their standards, including those of the National Council for the Social Studies (NCSS). Other professional standards address technology education, though not in any degree of depth. In the Interstate New Teacher Assessment and Support Consortium (INTASC) Core Standards, for example, only one standard/principle mentions the utilization of technology. INTASC principle 6 states the following: "The teacher uses knowledge of effective verbal, non-verbal, and media communication techniques to foster active inquiry, collaboration, and supportive interaction in the classroom."[26] INTASC goes on to define media communication tools as audiovisual aids and computers.

The National Board for Professional Teaching Standards (NBPTS) Social Studies-History Standards also addresses the integration of technology in history teacher and education curricula. NBPTS social studies-history standard 6, *Instructional Resources*, states the following: "Highly accomplished teachers select, adapt and create rich and varied resources for social studies and history and use them productively."[27] The NBPTS document goes on to discuss how history teachers might apply this knowledge to the classroom:

> Teachers develop a deep and rich base of resources, choosing from written materials, electronic media, artifacts and other visual aids. They are aware that technological resources are important sources of information as well. Technology also promotes active learning and can facilitate student discussions in peer groups. They seek to expose their students to the broad assortment of resources, including primary and secondary sources, artifacts, video presentations, on-line services, CD-ROM, and community resources, among others. Such resources serve to make their students more capable and independent learners.[28]

These sets of standards are certainly of some assistance in helping teacher educators to integrate technology and the Internet into their history teacher education programs; however, their utility pales in comparison with the only nationally adopted standards for technology education, the International Society for Technology in Education (ISTE) Foundation Standards.[29] This set of fundamental concepts and skills for technology integration and classroom utilization is the most comprehensive and inclusive guideline available to history teacher educators. Not only do the ISTE standards serve as a valuable curricular planning resource, but they are also an integral part of the National Council for Accreditation of Teacher Education (NCATE) accreditation process.[30] The ISTE standards address the following eighteen technology concepts and skills:

Basic Computer/Technology Operations and Concepts

- Operate a multimedia computer system with related peripheral devices to successfully install and use a variety of software packages.
- Use terminology related to computers and technology appropriately in written and oral communications.
- Describe and implement basic troubleshooting techniques for multimedia computer systems with related peripheral devices.
- Use imaging devices such as scanners, digital cameras, and/or video cameras with computer systems and software.
- Demonstrate knowledge of uses of computers and technology in business, industry, and society.

Personal and Professional Use of Technology

- Use productivity tools for word processing, database management, and spreadsheet applications.
- Apply productivity tools for creating multimedia presentations.
- Use computer-based technologies including telecommunications to access information and enhance personal and professional productivity.
- Use computers to support problem solving, data collection, information management, communications, presentations, and decision making.
- Demonstrate awareness of resources for adaptive assistance devices for students with special needs.
- Demonstrate knowledge of equity, ethics, legal and human issues concerning use of computers and technology.
- Identify computer related technology resources for facilitating lifelong learning and emerging roles of the learner and the educator.
- Observe demonstrations or uses of broadcast instruction, audio/video conferencing, and other distance learning applications.

Application of Technology in Instruction

- Explore, evaluate, and use computer/technology resources including applications, tools, educational software, and associated documents.

- Describe current instructional principles, research, and appropriate assessment practices as related to the use of computers and technology resources in the curriculum.
- Design, deliver, and assess student learning activities that integrate computers/technology for a variety of student group strategies and for diverse student populations.
- Design student learning activities that foster equitable, ethical, and legal use of technology by students.
- Practice responsible, ethical, and legal use of technology, information, and software resources.[31]

Integration Versus Stand Alone Framework

In addition to reviewing national standards to identify the most efficacious application, another decision history teacher educators must make is how to best infuse technology education into their programs. One factor that certainly complicates this process is that *computer literacy* is still, very much, an ill-defined concept, as illustrated by the following quote by one educational researcher, "While computer literacy is still a popular concept, computer literacy is like motherhood in that most people are in favor of it. But unlike motherhood, it does not have a clear and precise definition."[32]

This definitional ambiguity is reflected in the status of technology infusion in teacher preparation curricula. Currently, teacher education programs are split in their allegiance to one of two prevailing technology literacy paradigms. Approximately half of the teacher education programs have adopted a "stand alone" approach that calls for a specific course to be designated for technology education purposes.[33] The other 50 percent of teacher education programs have instead adopted a more integrative approach, in a belief that "technology should be integrated seamlessly into all coursework making the need for a separate instructional technology course obsolete."[34]

Numerous professional organizations and governmental agencies have joined in this pedagogical crusade to make the latter of these two implementation paradigms the prevailing one. Perhaps the most influential recommendation was one issued by NCATE nearly a decade ago. In 1995, NCATE directed that all teacher education faculty should be "knowledgeable about current practices related to the use of computers and technology and integrate them into their teaching and scholarship."[35] Other agencies, such as the U.S. Office of Technology Assessment, have added that efforts must be made to not only implement technology education in preservice teacher preparation, but that such training must also include exposure to "more sophisticated tools (e.g., the Internet, integrated media, problem-solving applications) that support the development of students' higher-order thinking and problem-solving skills, leading to classroom integration."[36]

A major criticism of "stand alone" technology courses in teacher preparation is that they do not teach preservice teachers how to integrate technology in the manner described earlier.[37] Many teacher education researchers have investigated these two approaches and believe the integration approach to be more effective in preparing preservice teachers to teach in technology enriched K-12 classrooms.[38] On the other hand, a number of teacher educators still believe an introductory or foundational technology education course should remain in the teacher preparation curriculum. Both of these groups of integration proponents, however, agree that "unless students see the use of technology modeled in their other courses, unless they have an opportunity to make the connection between technology and instruction in the subject or level they will teach they are likely to graduate with limited professional skills in this area and harbor a questionable attitude toward the use of technology in education."[39]

Research data appear to support this type of integrative approach. In particular, a recent survey by ISTE of more than 400 teacher education programs in the United States identified a critical variable they term the *integration factor*. The ISTE found the integration factor, which they defined as the teaching of technology skills and classroom application, served as the best predictor of performance in the other technology education components on the thirty-two item survey.[40] The survey also found that "stand alone" technology course completion did not correlate well with preservice teacher technology literacy and classroom teaching integration.[41] The ISTE report concluded with a series of recommendations, many of which directly relate to integration, including a directive that teacher education programs continue to infuse technology education into other courses in the preservice teacher education curriculum and encourage individual faculty members to model such integration in their instruction.[42] The latter recommendation is echoed by NCATE in their 1997 report calling for universities to provide professional development incentives and academic rewards to faculty, to encourage this type of undertaking.[43]

Traditional Versus Constructivist Paradigm

Most history teacher educators today agree that the "mere presentation or demonstration of technology-related instruction by a Techie" is no longer a plausible option.[44] However, there still is great debate over which theoretical or pedagogical framework will best accomplish these ambitious technology goals for preservice history teachers. The current debate appears to center around two prevailing teaching and learning paradigms often referred to in the research literature as a traditional or rationalistic, transmission-oriented didactic approach versus a constructivist, learner-centered approach.[45] Another way of illustrating the distinction between these two teaching and learning paradigms is found in the comparison between Aristotle and Plato's epistemological positions. Aristotle's reality, founded in concrete knowledge gathering and experience, is analogous with the traditional or rationalistic pedagogical paradigm,[46] while Plato's concept of truth, which is similar to Piaget's concept of schemata, is more aligned with the constructivist pedagogical paradigm.[47]

Over the course of the past decade, a number of teacher education researchers and professional organizations have issued a call for a conceptual swing of the teacher preparation pendulum to the constructivist approach.[48] The constructivist teaching and learning paradigm appears to be an ideal framework for history teacher education programs. In particular, the emphasis on active and engaged student learning and the involvement of learners in the construction of representations of knowledge are germane to integrative history teacher education programs. In addition, the priority given to the connection of new knowledge and previously learned concepts and skills is another hallmark of history and technology education.[49] Cameron White perhaps most eloquently posited a rationale for adopting a constructivist teaching and learning approach in teacher education:

> The merging of technology and constructivism offers much hope for the future of social studies education. A constructivist orientation to teacher education is important if we are to encourage students in

schools to develop problem solving and critical thinking skills, and to apply, analyze, synthesize, and evaluate knowledge, skills, and attitudes.[50]

The final step in integrating constructivist teaching and learning strategies into the history teacher education curriculum is to make the students aware of the underlying theoretical basis for such activities.[51] Such conceptual elucidation is critical for students to understand the epistemological assumptions associated with the constructivist paradigm. If students are unsuccessful in making these connections, the concern by some teacher educators and researchers is that preservice teachers will simply convert these constructivist practices into traditional, rationalistic pedagogical strategies; perhaps the only ones with which they have any familiarity.[52]

Electronic Portfolio History Education Approach

Once preservice history teachers have gained an understanding of the theoretical foundation of the constructivist teaching and learning approach, the final step is for teacher educators to implement an integrative program that models and applies the constructivist praxis.[53] ISTE recommends that all education researcher and teacher educators attempt to "identify, study and disseminate" models of "effective technology integration."[54] One of the most promising of these models makes preservice teacher portfolios the cornerstone of its approach.[55]

Although research on preservice teacher portfolios has yielded limited information, many studies have suggested that students are more engaged and demonstrate more responsibility for their learning with this approach.[56] Since one of the "essential components of constructivist programs is active student involvement," teacher portfolios appear to be an ideal means for achieving this end.[57] Other benefits of this approach include the ability to document preservice teacher performance and professional growth; integrate technology into the teaching and learning process; introduce authentic learning activities in the teacher education curriculum; and produce an ideal marketing tool for future employment—an electronic portfolio.[58] The electronic portfolio approach is also an ideal pedagogical framework, not only for integrating technology in a constructivist manner, but also for addressing many national standards recommendations. The professional organizations that support utilization of portfolios in teacher education include the following:

- American Association of Colleges for Teacher Education
- National Board for Professional Teaching Standards
- National Council for Accreditation of Teacher Education
- National Project on the Quality of Teaching and Learning[59]

The teaching components included in preservice history teacher education portfolios may vary greatly, but they should always reflect the goals of the individual teacher education program. There are, though, certain elements that appear to be germane to most models. Utilizing Web authoring programs, such as *Netscape Composer*, preservice history teachers are able to create HTML documents containing their multimedia, electronic products. These items may then be published on student Web pages and/or burned on CD-ROM disks.[60] Some of the authentic, constructivist, and technology integrated activities that preservice history teachers may design for their electronic portfolios include the following:

- unit outlines
- lesson plans
- unit evaluation modules
- unit assessment devices
- *PowerPoint* presentations
- *Hyper Studio* learning programs
- Internet links pages
- performance assessment activities
- Web-based learning activities
- interactive and/or multimedia learning displays

Electronic portfolios allow preservice history teachers to demonstrate their computer and Internet skills, as well as their knowledge of history. Content knowledge plays an integral role in the development of teacher portfolios.[61] Such knowledge does not have to be sacrificed at the altar of pedagogical innovation. In fact, if implemented in a reflective and systematic manner, the electronic portfolio model is one of the most effective means for integrating technology and content currently available to history teacher educators.

Although a technology integrated, constructivist approach is a promising framework for preservice history teacher education, there are still a number of questions that remain unanswered.[62] For example, what is the relationship between integrative, constructivist teacher program graduates' classroom practice and student achievement? While optimism surrounds current reports that indicate students of teachers who had professional training in computers outperformed those who did not on the 1996 National Assessment of Education Progress (NAEP) exam, more studies, specifically focusing on history assessment performance, are clearly needed.[63]

Another question that remains unanswered is, what research paradigm and data collection and analysis methods will best guide practice? Because research and practice inform each other, "with research insights leading to program improvement as well as to contributions to the field's general knowledge," this is a critical question for both history teacher educators and preservice teachers.[64] Although most researchers will employ naturalistic or qualitative methods to investigate this phenomenon, which likely will be of greatest benefit to classroom history teachers and teacher educators, many educational and governmental leaders still will require quantitative evidence for them to continue their support of integrative, constructivist teaching and learning initiatives.

Conclusion

Fortunately, we find ourselves far removed from the time when many education and government leaders thought the mere presence of computers in K-12 classrooms was the final step in the technology integration process.[65] Today, there is a recognition by nearly everyone involved in education that this is but the first step in the process. The preparation of K-12 teachers to integrate technology in their history curricula, in a powerful and meaningful manner, is the next logical step in this journey. This is the challenge history teacher educators and preservice teachers face at the dawn of the twenty-first century. The goal, quite simply, is that this journey will eventually result in the same type of technology integration we have witnessed in other fields. Many history educators hope that at the close of the twenty-first century we don't find ourselves in the position we are in today, where many classrooms "resemble their ancestors of 50 and 100 years ago much more closely than do today's hospital operating rooms, business offices, manufacturing plants, or scientific labs."[66]

Chapter 4

History Teachers' Beliefs

I dream my painting, and then I paint my dream.
—Vincent van Gogh

During the past century, history teaching underwent a tremendous transformation. Perhaps the greatest change came about in response to the introduction of computers and the Internet in the classroom. As a result, a growing number of students are no longer content to have history fed to them through means of didactic lecture. Instead, they are beginning to demand that history teachers integrate the wealth of digital historical resources available on the Internet into their curriculum. In addition, these same students now expect history teachers to not only deliver their lessons using technology, but also to employ popular software applications, such as *PowerPoint*, and Internet-based teaching strategies, such as WebQuests, in the process. Teachers, however, remain the gatekeepers to the history classroom. The technological and information-processing advances of the twenty-first century will not see the light of day in the classroom unless the teachers allow them access. The role teachers play in this information age was recently highlighted in the *Second Annual Report* of the CEO Forum on Education and Technology:

> To thrive in today's world and tomorrow's workplace, America's students must learn how to learn, learn how to think, and have a solid

understanding of how technology works and what it can do. Teachers
hold the key. In fact, teachers are perhaps the single most important
factor determining the quality of education.[1]

Teachers, however, are forced to make decisions regarding technology, in addition to hundreds of other classroom decisions, with
little or no training. National data reflect, for example, that teachers
have fewer than nine clock hours of preparation in the use of computers in the classroom, and only rarely use the Internet for anything
other than as a source of personal information.[2]

What then determines whether teachers will allow technology or
the Internet to be integrated in the history curriculum and in their
instructional repertoire? To understand this issue and others concerning classroom practice, history education researchers have taken a deductive approach that has led them back to teacher thought. With
methodological and theoretical roots dating back to the 1960s, research on teacher thinking has flourished over the past three decades.
Examples of this include the establishment, by the American Educational Research Association, of the Special Interest Group on Teacher
and Student Cognitions, and the founding of the International Study
Association on Teacher Thinking.[3]

During the past decade, however, a number of researchers have
become highly critical of the findings these studies have produced.
These same researchers are advocating instead a focus on teacher beliefs, in an attempt to better understand teacher classroom practice.[4]
Numerous others have called for the investigation of beliefs as a
method of elucidating human behavior. John Dewey, for example,
wrote that beliefs, which he termed the third meaning of thought, play
a crucial role in human understanding because they "cover all the
matters of which we have no sure knowledge and yet which we are
sufficiently confident of to act upon and also the matters that we now
accept as certainly true, as knowledge, but which nevertheless may be
questioned in the future."[5] Arthur Combs is yet another example of
an early advocate of the primacy of beliefs. Combs's fervently claimed
that the "most important single cause of a person's success or failure
educationally has to do with the question of what he believes about
himself."[6] After a quarter of a century of research it appears that the
educational community has finally come back around to Combs' and
Dewey's emphasis on beliefs.

Origins of Teacher Thinking Research

Christopher Clark and Penelope Peterson in their chapter, "Teachers' Thought Processes," of the *Handbook of Research on Teaching*, credit Philip Jackson for publishing one of the first studies on teacher thought processes that underlie teacher practice.[7] In his 1968 book, *Life in Classrooms*, Jackson broke from the dominant experimental or rationalistic research paradigm and instead provided a descriptive portrayal of life in the classroom.[8] Jackson summarized the purpose of such studies two years earlier, a "glimpse at this 'hidden' side of teaching may increase our understanding of some of the more visible and well-known features of the process."[9]

The other event that marks the emergence of teacher thought as a legitimate topic of educational research was the 1974 National Institute of Education National Conference on the Studies in Teaching.[10] Ten panels of educators were organized at the conference to develop a research agenda for the educational community. One panel was entitled "Teaching as Clinical Informational Processing." The panel, chaired by Lee S. Shulman, issued a report the following year calling for much needed research on teacher thought processes:

> It is obvious that what teachers do is directed in no small measure by what they think. Moreover, it will be necessary for any innovations in the context, practices, and technology of teaching to be mediated through the minds and motives of teachers. To the extent that observed or intended teacher behavior is "thoughtless," it makes no use of the human teacher's most unique attributes. In so doing, it becomes mechanical and might well be done by a machine. If, however teaching is done and, in all likelihood, will continue to be done by human teachers, the question of the relationships between thought and action becomes crucial.[11]

A Paradigm Shift

The call for research on teacher thinking did not fall on deaf ears. The educational research community embraced the topic and within a relatively short period of time an overwhelming number of studies were produced.[12] Although the focus of teacher beliefs research was on teachers' interactive decision making and planning, little attention had been paid to the structure and function of teachers' beliefs.[13] This apparent lack of attention regarding participant beliefs and repertoires of understandings seriously weakens the educational value of many studies.[14]

Not all researchers overlooked teacher beliefs as a viable focus of teacher thinking investigations. Nearly thirty years ago, one of the earliest proponents of teacher beliefs, Gary Fenstermacher, prophetically posited that such studies would dominate teacher effectiveness research.[15] More than a decade later, Christopher Clark and Penelope Peterson presented their case in defense of shifting the focus of teacher thinking research to teacher beliefs, arguing that teachers' beliefs are a vital component to our understanding of teachers' thought processes:

> While we may learn much from a technical point of view from research on planning, interactive thinking, and teachers' attributions, we can make sense of these findings only in relation to the psychological context in which the teachers plan and decide.[16]

Optimistic predictions concerning the role of teacher beliefs studies are still being made by researchers, very similar to those made by Fenstermacher.[17] In his chapter of the *Handbook of Research on Teacher Education*, Pintrich, for example, even went so far as to declare that beliefs would become one of the most valuable psychological constructs in the field.[18]

Despite these strongly convicted arguments, teacher beliefs research often remains either poorly constructed or altogether ignored by history education researchers.[19] Although beliefs, including attitudes and values, have become a topic of legitimate research in fields such as political science, sociology, anthropology, and psychology, history education has, for the most part, avoided such types of investigations. Pajares, in a recent review of teacher beliefs research, attempted to explain why educational researchers have such an aversion to this topic:

> It is not surprising that researchers have avoided so formidable a concept as teacher beliefs, which does not lend itself easily to empirical investigation. Many see it so steeped in mystery that it can never be clearly defined or made a useful subject of research. For these reasons, it is often seen as the more proper concern of philosophy, or, in its more spiritual aspects, religion.[20]

It would appear that if teacher beliefs research is going to make significant inroads in education, the field that would be most inviting would appear to be history education, given how the various other disciplines of social studies have embraced such inquiry.

Nature of the Problem

The year 1994 represents a major turning point in the history of social studies education. For the first time, professional social studies organizations published national standards that either directly or indirectly addressed the K-12 teaching of history. Examples include the National Council for the Social Studies' *Curriculum Standards for Social Studies* and the National Center for History in Schools' *National Standards for U.S. History* and *National Standards for World History*. Although standards are not inherently problematic, their publication still represents a certain naiveté on the part of the authors, given that there still is not enough known about the players (teachers) to begin drafting the game plan (standards).

Walter Parker defines this problem as a linear conception of curriculum development and implementation.[21] Parker is critical of this approach which discounts or ignores teachers' mediation in social studies. He cites examples, such as the new social studies programs of the 1960s, of curricular programs that failed because they never viewed teachers as anything other than curriculum conduits.[22]

The crux of the problem, according to Jan Nespor is that not enough is known about teacher beliefs or how these beliefs relate to practice.[23] What is known, however, is that no matter how well packaged or documented standards and research findings are, their intent will not be translated into practice unless they pass what Sanders and McCutcheon refer to as a teacher's personal test for effectiveness, in which beliefs play the major role.[24]

The power of teacher belief studies has not been fully realized yet in history education. Mathematics researchers, however, have been making significant inroads into investigating the role of teacher beliefs in classroom practice. In the most recent *Handbook of Research on Mathematics Teaching and Learning*, Thompson refers to teachers' beliefs about the nature of mathematics as a "powerful driving force that has a major impact on their instructional practices; the more integrated their beliefs are with their practices, the more powerful the force becomes."[25]

The problem is therefore two-fold. Although the history/social studies community appears to be concerned with the current state of classroom practice, as evident in the proliferation of national standards, it remains reluctant to investigate one of the key variables, teacher beliefs, which has been identified by researchers as perhaps having the greatest influence on teacher instructional decisions and actions.[26] The other part of the problem is that many of those in history/social studies education who have initiated such research are producing studies that are seriously flawed and thus of little value to both practitioners and researchers alike.

To better understand the current status of history/social studies teachers' beliefs inquiry, it is important to first trace its roots to teacher thinking research. From this genesis, the study of teachers' beliefs evolved. Eventually, over time, history/social studies researchers began to initiate their own classroom investigations into this phenomenon.

Teacher Thinking Research

The past three decades has witnessed a proliferation of research on teaching and the teacher. Much of the focus has been on psychological aspects of teachers, particularly teachers' thought processes.[27] Some researchers, such as Raths and Katz, have criticized such research for being too expansive a topic for investigation, referring to this as the "Goldilocks Principle" in which the topic is just "too big."[28] Others, though, claim that teacher thinking research is "a respectable and rewarding way for researchers to spend time and energy."[29] A review of the research, however, should serve to illustrate the importance and potential teacher thinking studies hold for the educational community. Two pioneering works in the study of teachers' thought processes were Philip Jackson's *Life in Classrooms* and Dan Lortie's *Schoolteacher*.[30] Jackson's book helped bring legitimacy to the investigation of teacher mental constructs that underlie behavior.[31] He uncovered the complexity of the teaching task through examination of teachers' frames of reference in their reality, the classroom. Jackson's work, like none before, "called the attention of the educational research community to the importance of describing the thinking and planning of teachers as a means to fuller understanding of classroom processes."[32]

Dan Lortie's work also served to illuminate the ethos of teaching.[33] Among other topics, Lortie examined the preoccupations, beliefs, and preferences of teachers. Lortie's study relied heavily on qualitative methodology such as observations, interviews, and document analysis. Lortie noted that, "understanding the subjective world of people within a given field of work calls for long, detailed, and open-ended interviews."[34] Lortie provides, perhaps, the best rationale for classroom teacher thinking inquiry of any researcher before or since:

> Despite their pivotal role, public schools have received relatively little sociological study. Schooling is long on prescription, short on description. That is nowhere more evident than in the case of the two million persons who teach in the public schools. But although books and articles instructing teachers on how they should behave are legion, empirical studies of teaching work—and the outlook of those who staff the schools—remain rare. Changes are proposed and initiated without sure knowledge of the settings they are presumed to improve. Without a clear picture of school reality, efforts at rationalization can dissolve into faddism and panacean thinking.[35]

Clark and Peterson categorized teacher thought processes into three domains: teacher planning, teacher interactive thoughts and decision making, and teacher theories and beliefs.[36] To facilitate understanding, the same categories will be used to discuss teacher thinking research. The first category of teacher thinking research involves teacher planning. Instructional planning refers to "that component of teaching where teachers formulate a course of action for carrying out instruction. . . ."[37] Shavelson and Stern have defined the basic, structural unit of planning as instructional tasks.[38] The instructional task contains six elements: (1) content of subject matter, (2) materials or manipulatives; (3) instructional activity; (4) teacher goals or aims; (5) student abilities, needs, and interests; and, (6) social context of instruction.[39] Each of these elements has served as the focus of numerous research studies.

Findings that have resulted from teacher planning studies have been, for the most part, very consistent.[40] One of the earliest studies to investigate teacher planning was conducted by Peterson, Marx, and

Clark.[41] Through "think aloud" methods of investigation, these researchers found that the largest portion of planning time dealt with subject matter or content followed by instructional strategies. These same researchers confirmed their findings in a subsequent investigation of twelve junior high history/social studies teachers, who were asked to teach a new lesson to students they had no previous contact with, in a laboratory setting.[42] Although other researchers would arrive at similar conclusions to those of Peterson, Marx, and Clark's, all of the studies suffered from serious design flaws, including the use of experimenter-prescribed lessons and artificial, laboratory settings.[43]

As teacher planning research evolved, however, studies moved back to the natural environment of teachers—their own classrooms. A landmark study, in this regard, was conducted by Clark and Elmore.[44] After five weeks of observations and interviews of five teachers, in their respective classrooms, Clark and Elmore found that teachers were primarily concerned with social and structural features of the classroom.[45] These concerns served as a conceptual guide for their planning throughout the year.

Another factor found to have a direct impact on teacher planning is the area of student activities. Zahorik found, in his study of 194 teachers, that pupil activities were the greatest concern of teachers (81 percent).[46] He noted that learning objectives were, surprisingly, not viewed as a particularly important planning focus. Perhaps this observation is not as alarming as it first appears. In an earlier study, Zahorik found that adherence to a linear planning model, of objectives—activities—evaluation, resulted in instruction that was less sensitive to student needs.[47]

Although teacher planning research helps us understand teacher thought processes, it only begins to fully uncover the relationship between teacher interactive thoughts and decision making processes. To fully understand teacher thought processes, "researchers must look beyond the empty classroom and study the ways in which plans shape teacher and student behavior . . . in the interactive teaching environment."[48]

In a review of six interactive thought studies, Clark and Peterson found amazing similarity in findings.[49] The topic that encompassed the largest portion of teachers' thought processes was the learner (e.g., attentiveness, interest level). This was followed closely by concerns with instructional style (e.g., clarity, effectiveness). The two areas of concern which occupied the smallest portion of teachers' thought processes were instructional objectives and subject matter. Although objectives remained a minor focus during both planning and instruction, subject matter seemed to have dropped in importance, with respect to the role it played earlier during the planning phase. Meanwhile, students and instructional strategies remained as prominent elements in a teacher's thought processes during both phases.

Two models have been developed in an attempt to further define the interactive decision-making thought processes that go on in the classroom. Peterson and Clark developed the first such model. Set up as a task analysis schematic, a teacher has four possible routes to take in order to navigate through this conceptual maze.[50] The first involves a teacher recognizing cues that students are behaving correctly and understanding instruction, whereby instruction continues. The second route involves a teacher's recognition that students are behaving inappropriately and/or do not understand instruction. The teacher, however, has no alternative instructional or behavior management strategies available for use. A third path, again, involves teacher recognition of student misbehavior or confusion. The teacher, though, decides to bring behavior back on line through tolerance and continued instruction. The final route is similar to that described in the previous two scenarios. The teacher's reaction, however, is quite different. The teacher has a repertoire of alternative teaching strategies available and decides to implement one of those in an attempt to regain attention and control.

The other model, designed by Shavelson and Stern, posits that teaching is characterized by well-established routines.[51] The task analysis format is quite similar to that of Peterson and Clark. It begins with teaching routines that are monitored and/or modified through observation of student cues. The difference is that Shavelson and Stern add the dimensions of delayed action and storage of mental information for future use.[52] They also view teaching as more routinized or mechanistic than Peterson and Clark; stating that routines, "once begun . . . typically are played out, much as a computer subroutine is . . . [They] minimize conscious decision making during interactive teaching."[53]

Regardless of their differences, both of these models have served as conceptual frameworks for numerous researchers. They have found that teachers' plans are transformed into "mental scripts" or "images," which guide practice in a routinized manner.[54] Researchers have also found that many of their teacher participants were extremely reluctant to change these routines, which were broken only when classroom monitoring indicated a problem. McNair referred to this as teachers finally becoming "aware of reality."[55]

The final category of teacher thinking research is teachers' theories and beliefs. Clark defined teachers' implicit theories as "eclectic aggregations of cause-effect propositions from many sources, rules of thumb, generalizations drawn from personal experiences, beliefs, values, biases, and prejudices."[56] The problem with this definition and many of the implicit theory studies is that they are too expansive and poorly conceived.

This is the problem Kagan and Pajares, in their reviews of teacher thinking research, warn researchers about. Kagan found that numerous studies were too vague or ambiguous to promote their use or solve classroom problems.[57] Pajares noted that for teacher thinking research to play any role in educational inquiry it requires "clear conceptualizations, careful examination of key assumptions, consistent understandings and adherence to precise meanings, and proper assessment and investigation of specific belief constructs."[58] Perhaps, even implicit theory researchers are beginning to recognize this very fact. Clark and Yinger, in a review of teacher thinking research, concluded:

> The literature on teachers' implicit theories is more eclectic than the other material reviewed in the chapter. There appears to be little consensus. The common thread in these studies is the belief that teacher thinking and teacher behavior are guided by a set of organized beliefs, often operating unconsciously.[59]

Teachers' Beliefs Research

The theoretical roots of teachers' beliefs research can be traced to the work of social psychologists, in the 1920s, investigating the nature of beliefs and the role they play in individuals' actions.[60] Beginning in the 1930s, however, the study of beliefs fell into disfavor with the emergence of associationism and, later, behaviorism. In the 1960s, the roller-coaster history of the study of beliefs began another incline due in large part to the efforts of psychologists such as Milton Rokeach.

By the 1970s, educational researchers began to take note of this line of inquiry and initiate their own studies of teachers' beliefs. This represented a major shift in educational research, which had previously been entrenched in the process–product paradigm.[61] For history/social studies education, however, this evolutionary change in research focus was not realized until the 1980s.

Despite the fact that teachers' beliefs is now a popular topic of inquiry, there is still, according to Thompson and many others, a "scarcity of reasoned discourses on beliefs in educational literature."[62] This is due in large part to what Pajares refers to as "definitional problems, poor conceptualizations, and differing understandings of beliefs and belief structures."[63] An example of the definitional problem is illustrated by the number of terms used by researchers to describe teachers' beliefs. These terms include practical theories, practical knowledge, perspective, conception, images, implicit theories, and principles. These conflicting and sometimes confusing definitions not only distract from the intended research focus but also inhibit the potential impact of teachers' beliefs studies on informing classroom practice.

The conceptual structure of teachers' beliefs also is subject to debate among researchers. Freema Elbaz's case study investigation of one teacher's beliefs was conceptualized as teachers' "practical knowledge."[64] Elbaz defined "practical knowledge" as "a complex, practically oriented set of understandings which [teachers] use actively to shape and direct the work of teaching."[65] The components of "practical knowledge" included "rules of practice," "practical principles," and "images." Rules of practice were statements of "what to do or how to do it in a particular situation frequently encountered in practice."[66] Practical principles were "more inclusive and less explicit formulation[s] in which the teacher's purposes, implied in the statement of a rule, are more clearly evident."[67] These practical principles were more representative of the personal dimension of practical knowledge. The final component of practical knowledge was images. At this level, as Elbaz referred to it, teachers' "feelings, values, needs and beliefs combine as she [or he] forms images of how teaching should be. . . ."[68]

A correlation can be made between Elbaz's concept of practical knowledge and Rokeach's definition of "beliefs."[69] Elbaz's three components of practical knowledge are consistent with the three components of Rokeach's definition of beliefs. Rokeach's cognitive component of knowledge is reflected in Elbaz's rules of practice. His affective component of attitudes is found in both Elbaz's practical principles and images. Finally, Rokeach's behavioral component of values plays a major role in Elbaz's images level.

Other conceptual structures of beliefs are also consistent with Rokeach's definition.[70] Another example is Marland's four components of what he termed, "knowledge."[71] These components included reference to maxims on fundamental laws, attitudes, and rules that guide action. Once again Marland's concept of knowledge is consistent with Rokeach's definition of beliefs. Although it cannot be said that all teacher beliefs researchers' conceptual structures are perfectly consistent with Rokeach's definition, there is enough of a correlation to warrant adopting Rokeach's definition as a standard for defining history teachers' beliefs.

The findings of teachers' beliefs studies over the past two decades have produced a number of fundamental assumptions. Pajares attempted to synthesize these findings in a review of teachers' beliefs research. Some of these fundamental assumptions are that

1. beliefs are formed early and tend to self-perpetuate, persevering even against contradictions caused by reason, time, schooling, or experience;
2. individuals develop a belief system that houses all the beliefs acquired through the process of cultural transmission;
3. the belief system has an adaptive function in helping individuals define and understand the world and themselves;
4. thought processes may well be precursors to and creators of belief, but the filtering effect of belief structures ultimately screens, redefines, distorts, or reshapes subsequent thinking and information processing;
5. beliefs are prioritized according to their connections or relationships to other beliefs or other cognitive and affective structures;
6. belief substructures . . . must be understood in terms of their connections not only to each other but also to other, perhaps more central, beliefs in the system;
7. beliefs are instrumental in defining tasks and selecting the cognitive tools with which to interpret, plan, and make decisions regarding such tasks; hence, they play a critical role in defining behavior and organizing knowledge and information;
8. individuals' beliefs strongly affect their behavior; and,

9. beliefs must be inferred, and this inference must take into account the
   congruence among individuals' beliefs statements, the intentionality to
   behave in a predisposed manner, and the behavior related to the belief
   in question.[72]

It should be noted that while Pajares cited numerous authors for every
finding, Rokeach's research was credited as being a contributing
source for each.[73] Pajares's review serves as an excellent backdrop for
a detailed analysis of history/social studies teachers' beliefs studies.

History/Social Studies Teachers' Beliefs

Although history is not a new field of study, the construct referred to
as social studies is of a relatively new design. Perhaps this helps to
explain why social studies is usually ten years behind the various other
core subjects, such as mathematics and science, in recognizing the
value of educational reforms, innovations, and topics of inquiry. While
there are numerous examples to support this statement, the study of
teachers' beliefs is certainly an excellent case in point. At the same
time that other fields are conducting well-conceptualized and defined
studies of teacher beliefs, history/social studies was still wrestling with
definitional problems or embarking on scholarly quests for the "perfect
typology."

   Throughout this period, however, some history/social studies education researchers have attempted to demonstrate the powerful role
teachers' beliefs play in the classroom. One of the first, was historian
Charles Beard, who posited that every teacher had a "frame of reference" in his or her mind:

> Since all things known cannot be placed before children in the school
> room, there must and will be, inevitably, a selection, and the selection
> will be made with reference to some frame of knowledge and values,
> more or less consciously established in the mind of the selector.[74]

Shaver and Berlak suggested that beliefs were based on what Beard
referred to as "frames of reference."[75] While this may merely be an
exercise in semantics, what is important to note is that more than thirty
years ago history/social studies researchers were beginning to realize
the possible relationship between beliefs and practice.

   This same argument was echoed a decade later by two other social studies researchers, Brophy and Good, who suggested that a teacher's belief system played an important role in shaping curricular decision making.[76] Despite these observations, it was not until the 1960s that social studies researchers began to "dabble" in teachers' beliefs inquiry. Perhaps the impetus for this was the barrage of criticism directed at public education following the publication of various unflattering national reports during that period. Historian Hazel Hertzberg observed that most of the social studies reform movements failed to penetrate the classroom because reformers ignored the realities of that teaching environment.[77]

The stage was now set for history/social studies researchers to investigate teachers' beliefs as manifested in their natural environment, the classroom. While a number of teacher beliefs studies have been conducted over the past three decades, the following investigations best illustrate the current state of our knowledge regarding history/social studies teachers' beliefs.

One of the first studies to focus on the role of teacher thinking in history/social studies was conducted by Susan Adler.[78] Adler investigated the perspective of student teachers toward social studies. Her intent was to use such research to help bridge the gap between theory and practice:

> We know little about how practitioners, rather than scholars, give meaning and purpose to social studies and how these meanings, rather than scholarly definitions, give direction to classroom practice. We know little about the intentions and beliefs which underlie practice.[79]

Adler's work is important for the role it played in helping bring this type of research back to the forefront of discussion in history/social studies research journals. Adler's focus, however, was very narrow, only addressing preservice teacher perspectives toward social studies subject matter.

The next major study to follow Adler's was conducted by E. Wayne Ross.[80] Ross attempted to investigate those factors that affect preservice social studies teachers' perspective. He defined teacher perspective as a theory of action that takes into account "a broad range of factors, including the teacher's background, beliefs, and assumptions, the contexts of the classroom and the school, how these elements are interpreted, and the interpretation's influence on the teacher's actions."[81] Ross' investigation of twenty-one preservice teachers uncovered three interactive factors that combined to form teachers' perspectives. These included personal biographical factors (e.g., values, life experiences, content specialty), social structural variables (e.g., observations as a student, field experience), and interaction processes (e.g., role playing, selective rolemodeling). Ross concluded that the data supported his hypothesis that "teacher's perspectives are the product of a dialectical process of professional socialization."[82]

Another history/social studies education researcher who embarked on the same educational journey as Adler and Ross before him, was Ronald Evans. In his 1989 study of seventy-one secondary level history teachers, Evans investigated the factors that help determine a teacher's conception of history and the relationship between these conceptions and classroom teaching styles.[83] Evans used data gained from teacher surveys and interviews to formulate five distinct typologies of history instruction: storyteller, scientific historian, relativist/reformer, cosmic philosopher, and eclectic.[84] Evans noted distinct differences in teachers' conceptions of history that were directly linked to the teachers' background, knowledge, and beliefs. These conceptions of history were found to have a direct influence on classroom teaching styles.

Another study that set out to define history/social studies teachers' perspective was that conducted by Christine Bennet and Elizabeth Spalding.[85] In an attempt to define the multiple perspectives of social studies teachers, Bennet and Spalding conducted autobiographical and stimulated recall interviews, in addition to classroom observations of seven secondary social studies education students. Bennett and Spalding's defined "teacher perspectives" as "personal attitudes, values, beliefs, principles, and ideals that help a teacher justify and unify classroom decisions and actions."[86]

Bennett and Spalding identified seven teacher perspectives in an earlier study of sixty-eight student teachers representing such diverse fields as English, science, foreign language, math, and social studies. In this study, they try to fit the personal narratives of these seven social studies teachers into the a priori categories they had developed earlier: scholar psychologist; friendly scholar; inculcator; facilitator of thinking and lifelong learning; friendly pedagogue; empowerer; and nurturer.[87] Bennett and Spalding found that these teachers' conception of social studies was a major factor in shaping their teaching perspective.[88] They also found that these teaching perspectives, in turn, directly influenced teaching techniques.

Another study, by D.S.G. Carter, also attempted to examine teacher perspectives of social studies through use of three a priori categories defined years earlier by Barr, Barth, and Shermis.[89] These categories included knowledge transmitter, social scientist, and reflective thinker. After conducting observations of forty Australian high school social studies teachers, and placing them in one of these three categories, Carter chose one participant from each category for further in-depth analysis. Carter found that the teaching style used by social studies teachers was indeed purposeful. Each of the teachers in his study could "account for it in terms of an epistemological position regarding their personal construction of social studies knowledge and the aspirations they held for their students."[90]

Two other researchers, Susan Stodolsky and Pamela Grossman broke new ground in their 1995 study of the importance of subject matter on curricular activity.[91] Stodolsky and Grossman concluded that there are distinct features of subject matter that affect teachers' perceptions, thereby influencing practice. In particular, they found that teachers' perception of social studies is affected by four critical factors: (1) it is a poorly defined subject, with many disciplinary roots; (2) the broad scope of social studies results in less course rotation; (3) it is less sequential than other subjects; and (4) it is a more dynamic subject.[92] This study not only points out the importance of subject matter on teacher thought processes, but also the necessity of discipline-specific teachers' beliefs studies.

Samuel Wineburg and Suzanne Wilson's study of eleven experienced high school history teachers was also hailed by many as a groundbreaking work that did much to advance our knowledge of teacher beliefs or understanding.[93] The study, according to Wineburg and Wilson, was "guided by the belief that much knowledge about good teaching never finds its way into the professional literature, remaining instead in the minds of good teachers . . . [so] we attempted to cull, capture and describe what these . . . expert practitioners know, think and do."[94] Following a detailed analysis of classroom teaching activities, Wineburg and Wilson conclude that two factors greatly determine the instructional style of history teachers. First, teachers "turn inward" to their comprehension of subject matter content. Second, these same teachers also "turn outward," by considering student needs, motivations, and abilities.[95] For history teachers, the resolution of this conflict between these two competing forces will determine the instructional approach they will employ in the classroom.

A similar conclusion to that of Wineburg and Wilson is also reached by Stephen Thornton in the current edition of the *Handbook of Research on Social Studies Teaching and Learning*.[96] In his review of teachers' beliefs studies, Thornton posits that history/social studies teachers act as curricular and instructional gatekeepers in the classroom. One of the three components of Thornton's concept of gatekeeping involves teacher beliefs. He breaks this component down into two factions: (1) teacher beliefs about social studies subject matter, and (2) teacher beliefs about student thinking in social studies.[97] Based on his review, Thornton notes that while teachers' beliefs about subject matter and student thinking appear to influence the intended curriculum, "much less is known about their underlying beliefs about social studies."[98] Thornton's observation is indeed quite accurate. Although a tremendous amount has been learned about history teachers' beliefs, there remains much to be learned.

Two decades ago, history education researchers awoke from their catatonic state and entered the arena of teacher thought. As a result of this collective educational epiphany, we have been able to unlock the door to the once mysterious world of teacher beliefs, which provides us with a greater understanding of history classroom teaching and learning. In a recent investigation of American history teachers, Michael Romanowski, perhaps better than anyone else, summarizes the guiding conviction that has and continues to serve as the impetus for past, present, and, most likely, future history teacher belief research investigations:

> Few would argue that teaching is not a complicated task that is saturated with both explicit and implicit personal values and beliefs. Since teaching requires evaluation, interpretation, and choice, the process is never value-free or neutral. Located beneath the classroom practice of every teacher is an elaborate set of beliefs that are interwoven into the fabric of one's personal and professional life. This belief system serves as an organizing framework that establishes patterns of meaning, determines right and wrong, aids in historical interpretation, informs evaluations, and ... guide[s] teachers' decisions regarding curriculum and instruction.[99]

Part II

Intended Curriculum

Chapter 5

Developing Objectives and Plans for History and Social Studies Instruction

The mediocre teacher tells. The good teacher explains. The superior teacher demonstrates. The great teacher inspires.
—William A. Ward

Because of standards-based education, teachers are more aware than ever of the importance of clarifying their goals and plans in curriculum and instruction. Effective instruction, like any other important task, requires specific goals, organization, and planning. This is especially true for history, social science, and social studies educators who aspire to teach elements of their disciplines that stress inquiry, reflection, and, particularly, citizenship education. Although some studies suggest that most teachers start their planning by thinking about specific activities first, this is not effective for teachers who want to stress authentic instruction. Indeed, lack of specific goals and planning probably account in large part for why most teachers overemphasize factual recall in their classrooms.[1] Authentic instructional goals are just too complex to simply introduce to students without thinking carefully about how these instructional activities need to be developed and organized for students' benefit.

Instructional Objectives

Translating ambitious ideas about content into teachable ideas is one of the main challenges that teachers face. This is especially true for those teachers who attempt to use authentic, hands-on, or constructivist instructional methods. It is one thing for historians and social scientists to do research, but how does a teacher transfer elements of historical or social scientific methodology to the secondary school classroom in a way that students can actually use? David Kobrin has described the implementation of authentic instructional practices in secondary classrooms as a process of reduction and simplification. If, for instance, an instructor wants to engage students in an exercise analyzing the meaning of an important speech, such as Lincoln's Gettysburg Address, he or she must think about reducing and simplifying the tasks into steps that the students can follow. Moreover, the notions of reduction and simplification are at the heart of thinking about how one organizes not only discrete instructional activities, but also larger unit and course plans.[2]

The beginning point of this reduction and simplification process is the creation of instructional objectives. An instructional objective defines as specifically as possible what teachers want students to learn. Teachers should start by considering how the facts, concepts, higher-level thinking skills, and attitudes and values that students hopefully demonstrate will fit across the three learning domains: *cognitive, process*, and *affective*. Cognitive objectives focus on lower-level thinking skills while the process domain includes higher-level thinking skills. Bloom's work defined the cognitive domain as "those objectives which deal with the recall or recognition of knowledge and the development of intellectual abilities and skills," that included both basic and critical thinking skills. Here, however, the terms cognitive and process are used to distinguish between the two parts of this domain.[3] The affective domain allows students to examine and develop their beliefs, attitudes, and values.

Bloom's *Taxonomy of Educational Objectives* is especially useful as a guide to writing objectives for the cognitive, process, and affective domains. Bloom's taxonomy for the cognitive and process domains is a hierarchical sequencing of thinking values. The lowest level is *knowledge*. The knowledge level refers to factual recall of information. It is important that students have basic recall abilities since no intellectual activity at a higher level can otherwise take place. Next is *comprehension*. At this level one is able to define or explain the meaning of ideas or concepts. Remembering the name of a term is not the same as being able to explain what it means. Knowledge and comprehension together comprise the cognitive domain. This domain encourages *convergent* thinking, where students' answers or results are the same or very similar.[4]

The process domain moves from *application* to *analysis* to *synthesis* to *evaluation*. Application refers to the ability to transfer understanding from a previously learned situation to a new situation. The ability to place events in proper chronological context in a history class might be an example of application. Another example is the use of a term or concept learned in one unit then used in a new situation. Analysis is the ability to break down ideas or issues into their component parts. Very often in a history or social science context, analysis is equivalent to explaining *how* something happened or developed. Synthesis is the opposite of analysis. It refers to a process of seeing and integrating component parts into a whole or composite arrangement. Finally, evaluation, the highest level of Bloom's taxonomy, is the ability to assess, appraise, or make judgments. Evaluation is often equivalent to explaining *why* something happened or developed. When teaching in the process domain, teachers encourage *divergent* thinking. Students' work should result in multiple perspectives that may differ considerably. As such, the process domain allows students to develop their creative thinking skills as well as higher-level thinking skills. Of course, in a history or social science context, creative thinking still needs to be grounded in the use of relevant evidence.[5]

Teachers should also consider the affective domain when developing their instructional objectives. As defined by Krathwohl, Bloom, and Masia, the affective domain includes "objectives which emphasize a feeling tone, an emotion, or a degree of acceptance or rejection." Such objectives target "interests, attitudes, appreciations, values, and emotional sets or biases." For history, social science, and social studies teachers, the affective domain's focus on developing students' values and beliefs is vital to the process of inquiry. Historians' perspectives reflect their beliefs and values. Social studies' emphases on contemporary and controversial social problems demand that teachers make affective instructional objectives central to their instruction. Indeed, it is difficult to develop the process domain without spilling over into issues involving the affective domain. Bloom and his colleagues recognized the especially strong connections between the higher-level thinking skills and the affective domain. The affective domain's hierarchy, as developed by Bloom and his colleagues, moves from receiving to responding to valuing to organizing to characterizing by a value or value complex.[6]

The hierarchy in the affective domain parallels the levels of the cognitive domain. *Receiving* refers to an awareness of information. Consequently, a learner could receive information necessary for factual recall. *Responding* means a learner could demonstrate new behaviors as a result of learning experience. Thus, a learner could answer questions about a series of terms or concepts learned from reading or a lecture. *Valuing* suggests a sense of involvement or commitment so that after learning basic facts and demonstrating conceptual understanding a learner could apply this understanding in a new situation. *Organization* implies the integration of a new value into one's own value system. Critical or higher order thinking requires that learners prioritize their values and decision-making skills. Finally, *characterization by a value* refers to the ability to act upon one's values so that, as necessary for evaluation, learners could make judgments or appraisals about issues.[7]

The connection between the higher-level thinking skills and the affective domain is particularly evident in the interdisciplinary goals embedded in citizenship education. Inquiry and research centered on contemporary and controversial social issues require students to develop not only their abilities to apply, analyze, synthesize, and evaluate, but also reflect and clarify their own beliefs, values, and attitudes. Making a judgment about the worthiness of a particular form of government, for instance, demands that learners weigh a variety of evidence before deciding on a meaningful conclusion. In a social issue unit focusing on why a community should consider implementing a recycling plan, for example, the interchange between the process and affective domains is particularly strong. Analyzing, synthesizing, and evaluating the necessary information required in developing a plan of action also demands that learners clarify their values and take an ethical position about how recycling may or may not contribute to the betterment of one's community.

Table 5.1 provides a list of verbs that are useful in developing instructional objectives for the cognitive and process domains, for all six levels of Bloom's taxonomy. It also provides illustrations of each level of the affective domain. When stating instructional objectives using appropriate verbs that target specific levels of Bloom's taxonomy, it also is important to use behavioral or performance language. Such language is specific and precise in terms of what the intended student behavior or performance is supposed to be. Typically, good instructional objectives using behavioral language start by saying, "The student will . . ." or "The student should . . ." and then use appropriate verbs that indicate an outcome that a teacher can observe in terms of some sort of student activity. Instructional objectives that are general or imprecise, such as "Students will gain greater insight into the causes of the Great Depression," do not allow a teacher to determine whether students can actually accomplish this goal. "Gain insight" does not suggest observable behavior. Among the teaching materials in the appendix is a worksheet called "Developing Instructional Objectives" that provides a list of hypothetical instructional objectives covering the cognitive, process, and affective domains, some using behavioral language and others not, that can be used to check for understanding of these ideas.[8]

Planning Social Studies Units

Although clear statements of behavioral instructional objectives help teachers to define their specific instructional goals, such objectives also need to be organized into larger blocks of lessons called units. Teachers normally have considerable discretion in defining their units of instruction even though schools, districts, states, and national organizations, such as the National Council for the Social Studies, now provide considerable direction about organizational sequences for all subjects. Yet while a state history standard might note the importance of a particular event, such as the Great Depression, in U.S. history, these state standards do not suggest whether or not the Great Depression should be taught in a chronological unit focusing on the interwar period, for instance, or a thematic unit discussing the economic development of the United States. This is where a teacher's creativity and understanding of the content and its implications for students must be exercised in developing an appropriate unit.

So what is a unit? At base, a unit is a series of related lessons centered on a coherent set of instructional objectives. All units should

Table 5.1

Taxonomies of Educational Objectives

Cognitive domain	Process verbs	Possible activities/ Outcomes	Affective domain
Knowledge	define, list, identify, label, locate, memorize, name, recall, recite, state, match, name, order, place	List facts Worksheet Chart Oral recitation	Receiving (Attending)
Comprehension	describe, discuss, explain, restate, paraphrase, summarize, translate into your own words	Report Review Summary Discussion	Responding
Application	apply, construct, demonstrate, illustrate, employ, organize, predict, restructure, transfer	Map Model Interview Diagram Illustration	Valuing
Analysis	analyze, differentiate, categorize, separate, compare and contrast, classify, diagnose, dissect, induce, infer, subdivide	Graph Survey/Questionnaire Research Plan	Organization

| Synthesis | create, compose, design, invent, modify, revise, combine, assimilate, reorganize, generalize | Role play Mural Video production Newspaper Story Advertisement | Organization |
| Evaluation | assess, appraise, critique, debate, decide, judge, rank, rate, select, argue, validate | Panel discussion Editorial Debate Mock trial Book review | Characterization by a value or value complex |

Sources: Bloom et al., ed. (1956); Krathwohl, Bloom, and Masia, ed. (1964).

include the three learning domains: cognitive, process, and affective. That is, students should acquire knowledge and comprehend basic concepts and principles, develop critical thinking skills, and form and reflect on beliefs, attitudes, and values. The types of units a teacher develops obviously depend on the subject being taught. History teachers typically organize units chronologically, social science teachers stress thematic units, and social studies instruction focusing on social issues emphasizes interdisciplinary approaches.

Most units developed for history classes emphasize chronological organization. At base, history explores change over time. Generally, students in middle and high school levels need to develop their ability to think chronologically and they do so best by moving from the past to the present. Some teachers make good use of "telescoping" past to present, where contemporary issues and developments are connected to similar elements in the past to enhance its meaning and relevance. But it is much more difficult to develop units that move backward in time from the present. Within the chronological organizational scheme, history units typically stress generalizations dealing with causes, effects, and large-scale developments. Here, history units very often incorporate concepts and terms that draw upon social science concepts. If a history unit is focusing on American imperialism at the turn of the twentieth century, a teacher may very well ask students to examine the impact of economic expansionism, Christianity, racism, militarism, and social Darwinism. It also may be appropriate to ask students to compare American imperialism in Cuba and the Philippines at the beginning of the twentieth century with America's economic, cultural, and military impact on the rest of the world at the beginning of the twenty-first century.

In social science classes, a typical unit plan is more conceptually oriented than a history unit. In geography classes, units often center on particular regions of the world; however, depending on the relative emphasis on physical or human geography, units might stress elements focusing on place as well as issues related to the human interaction with their environment. Comparative emphases are crucial in geography units as they are in most social science units. Political science units typically stress theoretical topics such as political philosophy, institutions, behavior, and comparative themes. Very often they focus on case studies, sometimes historical and sometimes contemporary in nature. Because citizenship education is often seen as particularly central in political science courses, the affective domain is more centrally incorporated into units dealing with topics such as voting and political participation. Economics, arguably the most theoretical and abstract of the social sciences, emphasizes themes and concepts that require elements that bridge the gap between theory and practice. Teaching the concept of supply and demand requires teachers to incorporate concrete illustrations of this concept's application and use in the real world. Psychology and sociology typically focus on case studies as a means of teaching principles and other generalizations.

In history and social science classes, it often is useful to adopt an interdisciplinary social issues focus for developing unit plans. Whereas traditional unit plans in history and social science classes start with general topics, either chronological or thematic in focus, a social issue (or issue-centered) unit plan starts by raising a central unit question—basically a hypothesis. When considering a good central unit question, a teacher should ask four main questions: Is it controversial? Is the issue important? Is the issue interesting? Can the issue effectively be researched? Of course, answers to these questions depend on the grade level and types of students one has. But social issue plans, as emphasized in social studies scholarship over much of the twentieth century, must reflect students' interests and concerns that help to mold effective citizenship. They should also stress research and help to develop students' critical thinking skills. Worksheet 5.1 provides lists of questions that can be asked when developing social issue units.

After choosing an effective central unit question, the format for a social issue plan starts with an introductory "grabber" that piques students' interests. The teacher then develops one or two days' worth of lessons that provide students with the basic information they need to start their investigations of the central unit question. Most of the remaining days of the unit are then spent pursuing research. Crucially, however, students are not left to their own resourcefulness to find appropriate information. The teacher provides detailed lists of books, articles, films, Web sites, and community resources for students to examine. Ideally, these resources should be provided for students in the classroom as much as possible. Of course, before doing their research, students need to know what their culminating projects will be. In the social issue unit plan, such projects can take the form of a paper, but might also include a speech, debate, panel discussion, news broadcast, poster display, video, role play, or same other sort of dramatic performance. Worksheet 5.2 highlights some general objectives of social issue plans. Worksheet 5.3 provides a list of possible social issue units, based on the curriculum ideas of several leading figures in social studies education.[9]

Developing Lesson Plans

Regardless of the specific history, social science, or social studies class being taught, there are several elements that normally should be included in an effective lesson plan. Teachers need to know how their lesson's objectives reflect their instructional objectives. They need to introduce the lesson to their students, have clear goals about the activities and materials to be used, and explain those to the students. They then need to assess students' understanding of what they have done. With all this, teachers need to be mindful of how they allocate their time.[10]

Because it may take more than one day's lesson to teach a specific instructional objective, it is a good idea to start a lesson plan by writing a daily instructional objective. Each daily objective should reflect the instructional objectives that teachers developed for their units, but

---

Worksheet 5.1

Reflective Teaching Process

In identifying a problem, how well does the teacher:
- Ask divergent questions to identify a problem?
- Use materials to introduce conflicting ideas?
- Ask probing questions that identify inconsistencies or contradictions in the beliefs, opinions, or ideas of students?
- Ask students to state the problem/question in their own words?
- Ask students to define ambiguous or new terms to help make the problem or question clear and precise?

In developing hypotheses for social issue problems, how well does the teacher:
- Present students with a hypothesis to test?
- Ask divergent questions to solicit hypotheses?
- Present data and then ask questions to solicit hypotheses?
- Ask probing questions to help students identify and locate sources that could be used to generate hypotheses?
- Provide time for students to gather sources and formulate hypotheses?

In facilitating open discussion, how well does the teacher:
- Arrange chairs in seminar or small-group style?
- Direct student-to-student interaction?
- Direct the discussion to many students, not just a few?
- Talk briefly and then stop so that he or she does not monopolize the discussion?
- Allow time for students to reflect on the topic being discussed?
- Point out what is relevant and not relevant to the discussion?

Source: Adapted from Engle and Ochoa (1988), Appendix A.

---

should also indicate more specific language about the activities and/ or materials that will be used to develop a part of the larger instructional objective. For instance, if the Vietnam War unit's instructional objective is "Students will interview a Vietnam War veteran to gain an understanding of how the war affected soldiers," it will probably take at least two days of class time to help students think through and design their questions for such a project. On the first day, the daily objective might be, "Students will examine a list of suggested topics about soldiers' experiences and, in a small group, discuss which would be most appropriate to ask a veteran," assuming that such a list could be distributed. The list might also explain how a good interviewer asks open-ended questions and focuses on eliciting personal perspectives rather than information that might be better culled from second-

---

Worksheet 5.2

Suggested General Objectives for Issue-Based Units

1. How can social justice be achieved in a democratic society?
2. What social activities can citizens undertake to remedy society's ills?
3. How can citizens use their critical judgment to see through propaganda?
4. How can citizens demonstrate tolerance for differences in a democratic society?
5. How can citizens pursue conservation in their community?
6. What scientific advancements or applications will promote the general welfare?
7. What are specific civic duties that demonstrate political citizenship?
8. What are ways to support democratic institutions in one's community?
9. How can citizens contribute to the improvement of the public's health?
10. How can citizens demonstrate respect for the social value of a particular occupation?
11. What safeguards should be established to protect consumer's interests?

Source: Adapted from Table 1: "Representative Curriculum Goals Pertaining to Issue-Focused Curriculum and Instruction," Wraga (1996).

---

ary sources. The second class day's objective might then be "Students will write their interview questions and have them approved by the instructor."

Each daily lesson plan starts with some sort of initial or introductory activity. As in the case of the social issue plans previously discussed, these activities are sometimes meant to "grab" students' attention. Such "grabbers" help to arouse students' curiosity and involve them in activities that set the stage for further investigations. But more often the initial activities are explanatory in nature and are meant to allow the teacher to provide directions or facilitate students' continued development or attention to the tasks at hand.

The activities and materials for the daily unit constitute the core of the lesson. There are two types of instructional activities, *direct* (expository) and *indirect* (constructivist, hands-on). Direct instructional activities are teacher led while indirect activities are student centered. Among the most commonly used direct instructional activities of history, social science, and social studies teachers are lectures, class discussions centered on assigned readings, and films or videos. Some of the more commonly used indirect activities are individual or group research, various types of reading assignments, simulations or role

Worksheet 5.3

Suggested Social Issue Unit Plans

Hunt and Metcalf's Problematic Areas of Culture[a]	Oliver and Shaver's General Problem Areas[b]	Engle and Ochoa's Guidelines for Social Studies Curriculum Development[c]

• Power and the Law
  Sovereign Citizen v. Powers Centers
  Law as Protection of the Weak v. Law as a Weapon of Power
  Courts as Dispensers of Justice v. Courts as Dispensers of Injustice
• Economics
  Government Frugality v. Government Financing of Needed Projects
  Taxes and Government Spending
  Monopoly and Free Competition
  Free Enterprise and Socialism
  Prosperity and Population Growth
• Nationalism, Patriotism, and Foreign Affairs
  War and Peace
  National Honor and Foreign Commitments
  Self-Determination of Nations and Puppet Governments
  Patriotism as Obedience and Patriotism as Critical Inquiry
	• Racial and Ethnic Conflict
	  School Desegregation
	  Civil Rights, Education, Housing, and Job Opportunities for Minorities
	  Immigration Policy
	• Religious and Ideological Conflict
	  Rights of Dissident Political Parties, Religion and Public Education, Control of Subversive Literature
	  Religion and National Security: Oaths, Conscientious Objectors
	  Taxation of Religious Property
	• Security of the Individual
	  Crime and Delinquency
	• Conflict among Economic Groups
	  Organized Labor and Monopoly Capital, Agribusiness and the Family Farmer, Economic Growth and Environmental Protection
		1. The curriculum should be highly selective of a relatively small number of topics or episodes, each of which will be studied in great depth.
		2. The topics of episodes to be selected should be those with the greatest potential for encouraging thinking, or even controversy, about matters or fact, or about matters of historical interpretation of events in the past, or about alternative resolutions to social problems in the present.
		3. Students should continually be asked to make judgments about such matters as what really are the facts, how facts should be interpreted, what should be done about a problem or, if the problem is historical, what should have been done differently. Students should continually be asked to make value judgments as to whether the decisions made or about to be made, past or present, are good or bad.
		4. Geography, history, and the other social science disciplines will be treated not as an end product or summary of supposed knowledge to be accepted as true and then memorized but rather as alternative sources of information to be utilized in resolving questions such as those suggested above.

- Social Class
  Rank in a Classless Society
  Earned Success and Fortuitous Success
  Success and Happiness
  Liberal v. Vocational Education
- Religion and Morality
  Religious Belief and Practice
  Science and Religion
  High Pleasures and Low Pleasures
  Democracy and Religion
- Race and Minority-Group Relations
  Racial Differences and Human Similarity
- Sex, Courtship, and Marriage
  Purity v. Experience
  Chastity and Peer-Group Status
  Modesty and Sex Appeal
  Career v. Housewifery

- Health, Education, and Welfare
  Medical Protection for the Poor and Elderly, Social Security
  Protection for Displaced Workers
- Security of the Nation
  Balancing National Security Interests with Individuals' Civil Liberties

5. Since questions of what is good and what is bad are involved in most or all of these kinds of questions and since models for thinking about questions of good and bad are more likely to be found in the humanities than in the social sciences, selections from literature, art, music, religion, philosophy, and journalism would be utilized alongside and on a par with selections from the social sciences and history in the thoughtful study of any topic, episode, or problem.

6. The curriculum should utilize relatively large quantities of data from a variety of sources to study a relatively small number of topics.

7. The firsthand experience of students and teachers would be respected as one of the important sources of information bearing on any question or problem.

Sources: [a]Adapted from Hunt and Metcalf (1968).
[b]Adapted from Oliver and Shaver (1966).
[c]Adapted from Engle and Ochoa (1988). Reprinted with permission of Teachers College Press via Copyright Clearance Center.

playing, and field trips. Of course, many daily plans blend elements of both direct and indirect instruction. Indeed, to effectively set the stage for any indirect instruction, teachers normally engage in direct instruction to explain what students will need to do. Later chapters provide specific ideas about developing lesson plans centered on a variety of themes and incorporating both direct and indirect instructional activities. See Worksheet 5.4 for issues to consider when using various direct and indirect instructional activities in history, social science, and social studies classes.

Although not necessarily the concluding part of the lesson, assessment of student learning also should be incorporated into each lesson. As discussed earlier in regard to instructional objectives, the teacher needs to know if students are actually learning. Assessment can be done both formally and informally. Formal assessment means testing where the student writes down answers or ideas that you collect and check. Informal assessment is typically an oral surveying of what students think. Here teachers often query the class on the reading that they did to gauge whether or not students seemed to understand the material. Or teachers might engage students in a discussion following a lecture to see if they comprehended the key points. Assessment is discussed at greater length in the book in later chapters.

When constructing lesson plans, teachers need to be particularly mindful about how they allocate their time. Indeed, time management is one of the most difficult parts of effective instruction. New teachers very often prepare too little or far too much for a typical class period, which is normally around forty-five to fifty minutes in length. Although the typical class period may seem like a very long period to accomplish one main activity, very often teachers need to think in terms of using that length of time to accomplish at least two related instructional tasks. Particularly with middle school students, it is important to consider their limited attention spans and consider ways to retain their focus through related yet different instructional activities. Block scheduling, where schools have reoriented their class lengths to longer periods, often seventy-five minutes to as much as two hours in length, requires teachers to be even more creative in the use of their time. Such longer periods of time are ideal for indirect instructional activities, such as research efforts, simulations, role playing, and debates, but are not very good for some types of direct instructional

Worksheet 5.4

Direct and Indirect Instructional Activities: Considerations for Social Studies Teachers

Direct instruction

- Lecture
  1. Use "interactive" methods: Encourage student participation
  2. Lecturing should not be a passive exercise; require students to take notes and ask questions
  3. The younger the students, the shorter the lectures
  4. Lecturing is not the same as "giving notes" on the overhead.

- Class discussions
  1. Need to have a central focus
  2. Teacher needs to prompt, redirect, and moderate; no "free for all"
  3. Students need to learn to understand the difference between informed and uninformed opinions
  4. Discussion should combine elements of direct and indirect instruction

- Videos
  1. Best to use portions that specifically portray or highlight ideas made in other lessons
  2. Always use study guides
  3. Keep in mind that students are used to watching videos for recreation not learning

Indirect instruction

- Individual/Group Research
  1. Needs to be well structured
     —teacher gathers materials
     —teacher models how to use
     —teacher requires hypothesis testing
     —teacher requires interpretations and drawing of inferences
     —teacher should encourage divergent thinking
  2. Projects should encourage divergent thinking
  3. Group work should require a "contract" so that the teacher can assess who did what

- Reading assignments
  1. Use "directed reading lessons" as much as possible
     —provide prereading strategies
     —provide specific reading instructions and outcomes
     —require some sort of postreading activity
  2. For higher-level thinking, require students to review or critique the meaning of a text

- Role play
  1. Requires considerable background preparation
  2. Emphasizes creativity and involvement, not rigid memorization

Worksheet 5.5

Lesson Plan Template

Sample Lesson Plan

Name: School:

Subject: Grade Level:

Number of Students: Date/Time:

Unit Instructional Objectives:

Lesson Activities, Procedures, and Time Allocations:

Teaching Resources Needed:

Informal/Formal Assessments:

Teacher's Bibliography:

activities, such as lectures and films. Unfortunately, some teachers see block scheduling as an opportunity to simply talk longer on topics or show entire Hollywood films at the expense too often of students' interest in the issues or topics at hand. Worksheet 5.5 provides a basic template for lesson planning that can be modified depending on the specific focus, activities, and materials that will be used.

Chapter 6

Teaching Early American History: A Curricular Model for Integrating Online Resources

It is not important that we go beyond
where we have been before.
Neither should we assume that we can't.
The question should never be how far, how
high, how fast, or how much—
but simply how?

—Anonymous

Most teachers recognize the critical need to establish a strong conceptual stage or foundation for students to build upon throughout the learning process. Those students that fail to acquire the requisite knowledge and conceptual foundation often struggle to understand new material, because they lack the cognitive framework or schemata necessary for deeper understanding and comprehension. The *National Standards for History* refers to this framework constructed in the minds of students as "mental scaffolding."[1] The study of American history is greatly enhanced by careful and comprehensive construction of mental scaffolding. As such, the critical period for American history is the point at which the middle school and high school history curricula often begin—the pre-Columbian through colonial and revolutionary eras to the founding period. For most students, the foundation of their understanding of, and interest in, American history is formed in the first few weeks of school, when these critical periods in American history are being addressed in the classroom. Therefore, it is vital that middle school and high school history teachers provide students with a clear understanding of the significance of these early periods in our nation's history. For many classroom teachers, the *National Standards for History* provides perhaps the most eloquent and concise rationale for why students should study these periods of early American history; some of which are examined further.

The key architects of the *National Standards for History* assess the importance of the pre-Columbian era in American history as follows:

> The study of American history properly begins with the first peopling of this continent some 30,000 years ago, and then proceeds to the epic events of the late 15th century when three worlds met: when Europeans, the inhabitants of North and South America, and the peoples of Africa entered upon a historic convergence that was to shape much of modern history in over half the world.[2]

These same authors of the *National Standards for History* also note the important role the study of the colonial period plays in providing the foundation for understanding major political, economic, and social developments in subsequent periods of America's national history:

> The study of the colonial era in United States history is essential for all students. . . . Without an understanding of the seedtime of the American nation, it is almost impossible for students to understand such critical developments as the formation of our political institutions and values; our economic system; our multi-ethnic and culturally diverse composition; our troublesome history of slavery and the enduring problems of race that were its legacy; and the special sense of destiny or mission in the American culture.[3]

One of the most popular topics in early American history for middle and high school students and teachers is the American Revolution. The importance of this period is perhaps best reflected in the following statement by some of the former authors of the *National Standards for History:*

> Thus, the American Revolution . . . was the first great collective step in the journey of democracy that we in the United States are still embarked

upon at home. Together with the French Revolution a few years later, it proclaimed to the world's peoples that three great human aspirations were not only right but reachable: national unity and independence, democratic self-government and civil equality; economic and social justice.[4]

The study of the American Revolution, however, should also include an examination not only of the "causes for the outbreak of the war" and "main stages of the Revolutionary War," but also the resulting "economic, regional, social, ideological, religious, and political . . . debate over the Constitution."[5]

Just as the study of United States history is enhanced through careful and comprehensive examination of these early periods, so too can the Internet enhance the learning opportunities accorded to students. In particular, students can greatly benefit from the availability of historical resources on the World Wide Web. These resources serve to build or refine each of the five elements of historical thinking outlined in the *National Standards for History* and address a number of "history's habits of the mind."[6] This chapter outlines one approach to integrating specific Web resources into the history curriculum to facilitate the development of student historical thinking, utilizing the *National Standards for History* as the overarching curricular framework.

Curricular and Instructional Framework

Classroom history teachers must march to the beat of numerous "curricular drummers." Therefore, this chapter references each of the three nationally recognized curriculum documents for the teaching of American history in middle school and high school: the National Center for History in the Schools' (NCHS) *National Standards for History;* National Council for the Social Studies' (NCSS) *Curriculum Standards for Social Studies;* and the Bradley Commission on History in Schools' "habits of the mind." The primary curricular structure used in the design of this chapter, however, is a direct reflection of the *National Standards for History*, in particular the eras and themes outlined in Table 6.1.[7]

Although the NCHS's *National Standards for History* focuses solely on the teaching of United States and world history, the stan-

Table 6.1

National Standards for History

Era Standard	Description
Era 1—Standard 1	Comparative characteristics of societies in the Americas, Western Europe, and Western Africa that increasingly interacted after 1450.
Era 1—Standard 2	How early European exploration and colonization resulted in cultural and ecological interactions among previously unconnected peoples.
Era 2—Standard 1	Why the Americas attracted Europeans, why they brought enslaved Africans to their colonies, and how Europeans struggled for control of North America and the Caribbean.
Era 2—Standard 2	How political, religious, and social institutions emerged in the English colonies.
Era 2—Standard 3	How the values and institutions of European economic life took root in the colonies, and how slavery reshaped European and African life in the Americas.
Era 3—Standard 1	The causes of the American Revolution, the ideas and interests involved in forging the revolutionary movement, and the reasons for the American victory.
Era 3—Standard 2	The impact of the American Revolution on politics, economy, and society.
Era 3—Standard 3	The institutions and practices of government created during the Revolution and how they were revised between 1787 and 1815 to create the foundation of the American political system based on the U.S. Constitution and the Bill of Rights.

Source: National Center for History in the Schools (1996).

Era 1—three worlds meet (beginnings to 1620); Era 2—colonization and settlement (1585–1763); Era 3—revolution and the new nation (1754–1820s).

dards document drafted by the NCSS does not. The NCSS's *Curriculum Standards for Social Studies* attempts to encompass all of the disciplines that comprise the social studies, including history. The theme and performance expectation in the NCSS standards that are addressed in this chapter, are shown in Worksheet 6.1.

The Bradley Commission on History in Schools developed the final historical framework used to guide the design of the themes and se-

Worksheet 6.1	
NCSS Standards	
Theme II—*Time, Continuity, and Change*	
Performance expectation	Description
d	Systematically employ processes of critical historical inquiry to reconstruct and reinterpret the past, such as using a variety of sources and checking their credibility, validating and weighting evidence for claims, and searching for causality.
Source: National Council for the Social Studies (1994).	

lection of Internet-based resources. In their book, *Historical Literacy: The Case for History in American Education* the commission identified a set of "perspectives and modes of thoughtful judgments" the study of history should encompass.[8] Two of these "habits of the mind" addressed in this chapter are as follow:

1. Distinguish between the important and the inconsequential, to develop the "discriminating memory" needed for a discerning judgment in public and personal life.
2. Read widely and critically in order to recognize the difference between fact and conjecture, between evidence and assertion, and thereby to frame useful questions.

These standards serve as a nationally recognized foundation upon which to develop the curricular scaffolding for middle school and high school classroom history teachers to structure their utilization of Internet-based resources in an organized and comprehensive manner. It must be made clear, however, that any value obtained from this curricular framework or these Internet-based resources rests, as it should, solely on the shoulders of classroom teachers. The value of technology and the Internet in the teaching of early American history, and their impact on the classroom, were all but predicted a few years ago by Howard Mehlinger, former NCSS president, who observed the following:

> It is no longer necessary to learn about the American War of Independence by sitting in Mrs. Smith's classroom and hearing her version of

it. There are more powerful and efficient ways to learn about the Revolutionary War, and they are all potentially under the control of the learner.[9]

That is the purpose of this chapter, to examine these more powerful and potentially efficient methods for teaching early American history—from pre-Columbian through colonial and revolutionary eras to the founding period.

Pre-Columbian American Societies

Prior to discussing the "great convergence," all history teachers recognize the need to provide students with opportunities to examine pre-Columbian American history. Certainly, the debate surrounding the 500th anniversary of Columbus' landing in this hemisphere serves to remind us all that American history did not begin in 1492, and it was incredulous to promulgate that premise in K-12 history curricula. Although that position is all but universally recognized today, there are still questions to be answered concerning the salient individuals, events, themes, and issues to address in the teaching of this period of history. While there are numerous responses to this pedagogical query, the focus of this chapter will remain with the curricular approach outlined in the *National Standards for History*. The chief architects of the standards remind us of how important this period is for future student understanding:

> Although the Europeans were the active forces for change at this time, students will not grasp the import of the "great convergence" without understanding the extensiveness and complexity of the societies of pre-Columbian America and West Africa—regions that were to be centrally involved in the events following 1492 and, like Europe, were to undergo profound changes as a consequence. Developing accurate perspectives on these pre-1492 societies will dispel stereotyped images of American Indians and Africans and prepare students for the complexity of the often violent meeting of these three worlds.[10]

Although there are numerous resources available on the World Wide Web to utilize in teaching this, as well as any, period of American history, their credibility and utility varies greatly. The Internet resources examined below represent the type of Web sites history teachers and students benefit from the most. Their individual content and design are reviewed, as well as their application to teaching historical thinking skills and content outlined in the *National Standards for History*. These particular Web sites focus on events, individuals, issues, and themes identified in *National Standards for History* Era 1, "Three Worlds Meet," Standard 1, "Comparative characteristics of societies in the Americas, Western Europe, and Western Africa that increasingly interacted after 1450."[11]

First Nations Histories
http://www.dickshovel.com/Compacts.html

This site, maintained by Lee Sultzman, provides history teachers and students with short histories of nearly fifty Native tribes. In addition, a bibliography of print resources is available to assist students in their research projects. Perhaps the most valuable resource for young researchers is the listing of current contact information (e.g., addresses, phone and fax numbers) on those Native tribes that still reside in the United States and Canada.

WWW Virtual Library-American Indians
http://www.hanksville.org/NAresources/indices/NAhistory.html

Another valuable resource for classroom teachers is available at this portal, maintained by Karen M. Strom. Hundreds of Internet sites are indexed according to the region in which the Native tribes were indigenous. In addition to these regional history sites, there are also links to Internet resources containing Native American history timelines, oral and written accounts, and photographic archives.

On This Date in North American Indian History
http://members.tripod.com/~PHILKON/

The name of this site developed by Phil Konstantin, a member of the Cherokee nation, is somewhat misleading. While there is a daily listing of events in Native American history, that is not the most valuable pedagogical asset available on this Web site. Teachers will find the links page, listing over 7,000 Web sites dedicated to Native American tribes and history, an invaluable tool for developing lesson plans, home page links, or student research projects.

Native Americans-Internet Resources
http://falcon.jmu.edu/~ramseyil/native.htm

James Madison University's *Internet School Library Media Center* sponsors this portal for educators. Although it includes numerous links to sites containing primary and secondary resources on Native American history, there are some differences between this site and other portals reviewed earlier. In addition to links to historical documents and e-texts, this Web site also provides middle school and high school classroom history teachers with links to specific teaching resources, such as a link to an Internet site that cross references Native American history topics with Virginia's K-12 standards—Standards of Learning (SOL).

Age of Exploration

While the characterization of Christopher Columbus is the subject of heated debate among historians and the public at large, what is certain is that he embodies the dichotomy that the age of exploration and discovery represents. The following passage in Columbus' diary illustrates this point in a hauntingly prophetic manner:

> They ... brought us parrots and balls of cotton and spears and many other things, which they exchanged for the glass beads and hawks' bells. They willingly traded everything they owned. . . . They do not bear arms, and do not know them, for I showed them a sword, they took it by the edge and cut themselves out of ignorance. . . . They would make fine servants. . . . With fifty men we could subjugate them all and make them do whatever we want.[12]

Although the period or age of exploration is quite expansive, the following Internet resources focus on many of the individuals and events that epitomize the importance of this period as it relates to American history. The issues and themes addressed in these Web sites represent the same knowledge and conceptual foundations the *National Standards for History* call for in Era 1, "Three Worlds Meet," Standard 2: "How early European exploration and colonization re-

sulted in cultural and ecological interactions among previously un-
connected peoples."[13]

The European Voyages of Exploration
http://www.acs.ucalgary.ca/HIST/tutor/eurvoya/index.html

The University of Calgary's history department has designed one
of the most comprehensive multimedia accounts of European explorers. The site contains a number of features teachers and students will
find of great interest. In addition to a short written narrative, the site
contains a number of primary source materials, maps, paintings, photographs of historical artifacts, and illustrations. All of these resources
are linked together to form a tutorial framework that provides for
independent learning opportunities as well.

Christopher Columbus and the Age of Discovery
http://marauder.millersv.edu/~columbus/

As mentioned previously, the quincentennial of Columbus' voyage
sparked heated debate. This site, developed and maintained by Mill-
ersville University of Pennsylvania, provides teachers and students
with an electronic database of over 1,000 articles from magazines,
newspapers, and journals that address the role of Columbus in history
and the legacy of the "great convergence." While all of the information available at this site is textual, it still represents a valuable resource for classroom discussion, debates, and research projects.

Age of Exploration Time Line
http://www.mariner.org/age/histexp.html

The Mariners' Museum of Newport News, Virginia maintains this site.
Although the design is rather simplistic, it includes a useful hypertext
time line that connects users to a comprehensive collection of biographical data on a number of explorers. The time line framework is
not only easy for students to navigate, but it also reinforces one of
the *National History Standard*'s thinking skills, that of "chronological
thinking."

1492: An Ongoing Voyage
http://metalab.unc.edu/expo/1492.exhibit/Intro.html

In 1992 the Library of Congress unveiled its *1492: An Ongoing Voyage* exhibit. This site makes many elements of that exhibit available online. Students may choose to navigate one of six sections of the exhibit. As they navigate through each section, they have the option to "continue the voyage" or "abandon ship" at any point in their tutorial voyage. Students who don't particularly care for this type of simulated navigation design may opt to utilize the hyperlinked index, which takes them directly to the section and information they are researching.

Immigration and Colonization

In the decades that followed this initial contact or "convergence of three worlds," countless Europeans migrated to the "New World, motivated by a myriad of catalytic factors, ranging from the noble to the indefensible." Although their intent varied as much as their treatment of the indigenous population, the motivation of one group—the Puritans who migrated to Plymouth—is perhaps summed up in the following passage by William Bradford, taken from *Of Plymouth Plantation*:

> Thus out of small beginnings greater things have been produced by His hand that made all things of nothing, and gives being to all things that are; and, as one small candle may light a thousand, so the light here kindled hath shone unto many, yea in some sort to our whole nation.[14]

The following Web sites address many of the salient themes germane to this period in American history, identified in the *National Standards for History* Era 2, "Colonization and Settlement." In particular, these online historical resources focus on individuals, events, and themes outlined in Standard 1: "Why the Americas attracted Europeans, why they brought enslaved Africans to their colonies, and how Europeans struggled for control of North America and the Caribbean."[15]

Virtual Jamestown
http://jefferson.village.virginia.edu/vcdh/jamestown/

Although there are a number of teaching resources available at this site, developed by Virginia Tech and the University of Virginia, students will undoubtedly find the Quick Time Virtual Reality (QTVR) panoramas the most interesting feature. Those students engaged in research projects on Jamestown or colonial Virginia, however, will find the plethora of resources (e.g., census data, letters, maps) available at this site invaluable.

Colonial North America: 1492–1763
http://www.ucalgary.ca/HIST/tutor/colony/home.html

Once again, the University of Calgary's history department has designed an attractive, multimedia site for history educators. In this case, the focus is on the convergence of European, African, and Native American societies. As was the case with the University of Calgary site reviewed earlier, this Internet resource also contains multiple types of media, utilized to enhance a hypertext narrative. Teachers will find the images, personal accounts, and Internet links valuable resources for designing lesson plans, *PowerPoint* presentations, or assigning research projects.

AMDOCS: Documents for the Study of American History
http://www.cc.ukans.edu/carrie/docs/amdocs_index.html

Teachers in search of primary documents for lesson plans or student research projects on this era in American history will want to include a link to this site in their home page. The site, part of the University of Kansas' *Carrie* (electronic library) system, contains links to a variety of primary source materials germane to fifteenth-, sixteenth-, and seventeenth-century American history. Students have access to the full text of select historical documents, such as treaties, proclamations, acts, ordinances, letters, journals, and diaries.

Plymouth Colony Archive Project
http://etext.virginia.edu/users/deetz/home2.html

History teachers and students will find the design of this site as interesting and engaging as the Jamestown site discussed earlier. The designers use the blueprint or floor plan from a seventeenth century house as the index for their Web site, with each room containing a link to specific historical data on the Plymouth colony from 1620 to 1691. Teachers and students will find a number of valuable resources available at this site, including historical documents, seminar papers, legal records, and brief biographies of select Plymouth historical figures.

Colonial Society

While it is difficult, if not impossible, to accurately portray colonial society in one broad stroke of the historian's pen, there are certain characteristics that came to define what we commonly refer to as colonial America. While Jean de Crevecoeur made the following observation during America's revolutionary period, it illustrates the same qualities that characterized colonial American society when compared with European society and the "Old World" paradigm:

> The American is a new man, who acts upon new principles; he must therefore entertain new ideas, and form new opinions. From involuntary idleness, servile dependence, and useless labor, he has passed to toils of a very different nature, rewarded by ample subsistence. This is an American.[16]

Although the theme of colonial society is an extremely inclusive curricular focus, the following Internet resources address many of the key individuals, events, and issues that capture the essence and importance of this period in American history. In particular, they address many of the topics and issues outlined in the National Standards for History Era 2, "Colonization and Settlement," Standard 2: "How political, religious, and social institutions emerged in the English colonies."[17]

Colonial American History and the Early Republic to 1812
http://web.uccs.edu/~history/index/colonial.html

Teachers will find a number of useful links for teaching colonial American history at this portal, sponsored by the Department of History at the University of Colorado, Colorado Springs. The site contains more than a hundred links to Internet resources that are organized in both a chronological and thematic manner, making the site especially easy for students to navigate. Teachers will also find the links to online journals on colonial American history and the student "research toolbox" of great pedagogical benefit.

Thirteen Originals: Founding the American Colonies
http://www.seanet.com/users/pamur/13colony.html

An ideal curricular framework for teaching colonial American history, at the K-12 level, is the use of the thirteen British colonies as a conceptual outline. This site allows classroom teachers to combine this teaching framework with World Wide Web resources, providing for much needed depth. Teachers and students can access a brief history of each colony and links to a variety of resources, such as online databases and historic sites' Web pages. The databases for each colony are rich with primary and secondary source materials, including government documents, photographs, maps, and links to state professional and historical societies.

Rare Map Collection—Colonial America
http://scarlett.libs.uga.edu/darchive/hargrett/maps/colamer.html

The *National Standards for History* emphasizes the need for students to draw upon data in historical maps. This site, maintained by the University of Georgia, provides classroom teachers with online access to more than sixty rare maps from this period in American history, making it an ideal resource for teaching this historical thinking skill.

The American Colonist's Library
http://www.universitylake.org/primarysources.html

One of the most expansive online collections of primary documents from this period is available on this site maintained by Richard Gardiner, a history instructor at University Lake School in Wisconsin. Teachers and students will find links to a variety of historical documents, such as journals, colonial charters, treaties, and personal writings, arranged in a user friendly chronological format. Gardiner's claim that "if it isn't here, it probably is not available online anywhere" is not far from the truth.

Colonial Economy and Slavery

Slavery was the most controversial, divisive, and debated feature of colonial society. The following metaphoric statement by Thomas Jefferson, perhaps better than any other, illustrates the economic and moral dilemma that confronted the colonists, and later founders of the republic: "We have the wolf by the ears; and we can neither hold him, nor safely let him go. Justice is in one scale, and self-preservation in the other."[18]

There are two major foci for this particular period or theme: the colonial economic structure, and the institution of slavery. The following Web sites address many of the critical individuals, events, concepts, and issues of this period in American history. This theme reflects the same knowledge and conceptual foundations outlined in the *National Standards for History* Era 2, "Colonization and Settlement," Standard 3: "How the values and institutions of European economic life took root in the colonies, and how slavery reshaped European and African life in the Americas."[19]

Quantitative Data—The Colonial Era
http://www.imsa.edu/edu/socsci/jvictory/q_summary_pg.html

For those teachers and students attempting to locate quantitative data on the colonial period in American history, this site will prove invaluable. Maintained by the Illinois Mathematics and Science Academy, the site is designed specifically for students attempting to get a quantitative snapshot of the colonies. Even though the data available on the site illustrates tremendous breadth, ranging from economic and census data to information concerning colonists' diet, it does, however, lack depth. It is still an ideal teaching tool for introducing students to the type of statistical data they will encounter on other Web sites and how to analyze them.

North American Slave Narratives
http://metalab.unc.edu/docsouth/neh/nehmain.html

The University of North Carolina at Chapel Hill received a National Endowment for the Humanities (NEH) grant to digitize nearly 200 narratives of fugitive and former slaves. The result of their efforts is this invaluable site for history educators to use in their classroom teaching. These primary source materials provide students with a tremendous resource for learning about this topic from the perspective of those who lived through it. This collection of electronic materials is arranged in an alphabetical hypertext format that makes it easy for students to access and utilize in their research and/or individual study.

Excerpts for Slave Narratives
http://vi.uh.edu/pages/mintz/primary.htm

Steve Mintz of the University of Houston provides history teachers and students with another online collection of slave narratives. The difference between this site and the former one, however, is that Mintz has selected fewer, yet more recognized accounts typically found in print sources. In addition, he organizes his site thematically, which may make it easier for teachers to integrate many of the selections in their teaching. Teachers, for example, could easily include hyperlinks in their *PowerPoint* presentations or Web pages to specific accounts of the middle passage or slave family life and religious beliefs.

Africans in America
http://www.pbs.org/wgbh/aia/part1/title.html

PBS has designed one of the most interesting, engaging, and informative sites on the Internet for the teaching of African American history. Designed to accompany the four-part PBS series of the same name, this site provides students and teachers with a myriad of textual and multimedia resources. In addition to the primary and secondary documents available at this site, teachers may also access a narrative, which is enhanced with a number of images of the period, and a teacher's guide, making it the most teacher- and student-friendly site of all those reviewed.

Causes of the American Revolution

Although there are myriad resources available on the Internet and World Wide Web to use in the teaching of those events that led to the American Revolution, their credibility and utility varies greatly. The sites included in this section represent the type of Internet-based resources history teachers and students benefit from the most. Each of these Web sites focuses on events, individuals, issues, and themes identified in *National Standards for History* Era 3, "Revolution and the New Nation," Standard 1: "The causes of the American Revolution, the ideas and interests involved in forging the revolutionary movements, and the reasons for the American victory."[20]

The American Revolution Home Page
http://webpages.homestead.com/revwar/files/index2.htm

This site provides an overview of the major events leading up to the American Revolution—from the French and Indian War to the Declaration of Independence. A rather comprehensive description of the causes and consequences of each event, as well as the identification of key players, is provided for each item. The chronological structure and inclusion of numerous paintings, prints, and illustrations, make this an easily navigated and engaging site for students.

PBS' Liberty: The American Revolution
http://www.pbs.org/ktca/liberty/index.html

This companion Web site for the 1997 PBS series *Liberty* contains a number of stand-alone resources and activities for classroom teachers. In particular, the time line and newspaper headline sections present students with a chronological overview of the key events leading up to as well as those that took place during the American Revolution. Both of these sections include a brief analysis of the events, enhanced by images (e.g., paintings, illustrations, broadsides) germane to the period. In addition, an interactive review game, "The Road to Revolution," is also made available for students.

Colonial Hall: A Look at America's Founders
http://www.colonialhall.com/index.asp

The primary pedagogical utility of this site is quite simple, yet invaluable to classroom teachers. The premise—to provide a brief biography of the key players in the American Revolution—is certainly not a novel online phenomenon. What is unique, however, about the Colonial Hall site is that it includes the biographies of more than a hundred of the signers of the major documents of this period: Declaration of Independence, Articles of Confederation, and Constitution of the United States. Such a site serves as an ideal companion for teacher-created online activities.

Founder's Library: Founding Era Documents
http://www.founding.com/library/lbody.cfm

The name of this site is not an overstatement. The full-text collection of founding era documents included at the Founder's Library truly comprises a virtual library for students and teachers alike. The collection includes both American documents, such as the Declaration of Rights and Grievances (1765), Olive Branch Petition (1775), and Declaration of Independence, and British government documents, such as the Sugar Act (1764), Stamp Act (1765), and Tea Act (1773).

Library of Congress Exhibit: Thomas Jefferson
http://www.loc.gov/exhibits/jefferson/

The Library of Congress' Jefferson exhibit includes a number of resources teachers should find of tremendous value. Arranged thematically, the resources are representative of every phase of Thomas Jefferson's life. The collection includes a number of documents germane to the American Revolution (e.g., a draft copy of the Declaration of Independence), the founding period (e.g., letters between Jefferson and James Madison), and from his presidency (e.g., Jefferson's First and Second Inaugural Addresses).

American Revolution

Regardless of whether teachers and students trace the origins of the American Revolution to the conclusion of the French-Indian War in 1763 or founding of Jamestown in 1607, the event itself still represents the culmination of a "long human struggle for liberty, equality, justice, and dignity, and the ideas, people, and conditions that carried the struggle forward."[21] The individuals, events, issues, and themes addressed in the following Web sites represent the same knowledge and conceptual foundation called for in the *National Standards for History* Era 3, "Revolution and the New Nation," Standard 2: "The impact of the American Revolution on politics, economy, and society."[22]

The History Place: American Revolution
http://www.historyplace.com/unitedstates/revolution/index.html

Those history educators who use a chronological approach to teach the American Revolution will appreciate the overview of the American Revolution provided at the History Place Web site. The site contains a time line that includes an almost daily overview of events from 1775 to 1783. Brief summaries of events are accompanied by thumbnail images that are linked to larger versions. Although there are no primary source materials available at this site, it is still a great companion to classroom lectures or online activities.

PBS' **Africans in America:** *Revolution*
http://www.pbs.org/wgbh/aia/part2/index.html

While it is not dedicated to study of the American Revolution, the PBS series *Africans in America*'s companion Web site contains a number of primary and secondary source documents that might be integrated into the curriculum of middle school and high school history teachers. In particular, teachers will find the accounts and personal narratives of African Americans during the revolution of great interest and utility, and the many salient documents included at the site, such as the 1775 Proclamation of Earl of Dunmore. The organization of the site—a hypertext thematic outline—makes it quite easy for students to navigate.

Library of Congress's Collection of Maps and Charts: American Revolution and Its Era
http://memory.loc.gov/ammem/gmdhtml/armhtml/armhome.html

Teachers will find the collection of maps at the Library of Congress site a valuable addition to their American Revolution curriculum. The Library of Congress has compressed each image so that downloading time is kept to a minimum. In addition, the site is arranged so that teachers and students can choose between a zoom view and navigator view of each map. The collection includes not only military battle maps, but also city and state maps of the period, as well as cultural landscape maps.

A Revolutionary WebQuest
http://library.thinkquest.org/11683/HomeMain.html

For those teachers desiring to either introduce or review key individuals, events, and issues of the American Revolution with their students, the Revolutionary WebQuest represents an engaging and comprehensive option. Teachers familiar with the WebQuest teaching format will appreciate the sophistication of the activities offered at the site. Included among the seven different WebQuest activities are: descriptions of key events; an overview of heroes of the revolution; a lifestyle and culture activity, which includes links to the music of the period; an overview of the major battles of the war; and a "Road to the Revolution" interactive simulation emphasizing economic issues germane to the American Revolution.

University of Virginia's Papers of George Washington
www.virginia.edu/gwpapers/index.html

The name of this site is somewhat misleading. Although the University of Virginia site contains a number of George Washington's papers, including correspondence between Washington and his generals and his farewell address to the Army (1783), it also contains a number of other format type resources. In particular, teachers will appreciate the numerous maps, illustrations, portraits, and sketches also available at the UVA site.

Founding of the American Republic

According to the chief architects of the *National Standards for History*, the study of the founding period "demonstrates why the Constitution was the culmination of the most creative era of constitutionalism in American history and perhaps of all modern Western history."[23] The following Internet-based resources address many of the individuals, documents, events, and issues germane to this period in American history; identified in the *National Standards for History* Era 3, Revolution and the New Nation, Standard 3: "The institutions and practices of government created during the Revolution and how they were revised between 1787 and 1815 to create the foundation of the American political system based on the United States Constitution and the Bill of Rights."[24]

Library of Congress's Documents from the Continental Congress and the Constitutional Convention
http://memory.loc.gov/ammem/bdsds/bdsdhome.html

More than 200 documents relating to the work of the Continental Congress and drafting of the Constitution are available at this Library of Congress site. The documents, which range in size from one to twenty-eight pages, include laws, treaties, land grants, public addresses, and proclamations. As with all Library of Congress' sites, users can search the database by either keyword or subject.

Library of Congress Exhibit: Religion and the Founding of the American Republic
http://lcweb.loc.gov/exhibits/religion/rel06.html

The Library of Congress's Religion and the Founding of the American Republic exhibit includes more than 200 objects from the library's collection that examine the role religion played in the founding of the American Republic. The collection includes covers and excerpts from books and manuscripts, as well as letters, prints, illustrations, paintings, and other artifacts. Examples include a 1787 request by Benjamin Franklin for a prayer at the beginning of each session of the Constitutional Convention, a 1788 Baptist preacher's objections to the Constitution, and an 1800 cartoon attacking Jefferson as an infidel.

National Archives and Records Administration Exhibit: The Bill of Rights
http://www.nara.gov/exhall/charters/billrights/billmain.html

The National Archives has made available to teachers an ideal site for the teaching of the Bill of Rights. Not only can teachers access a transcription of the preamble and first ten amendments, but they also can download all constitutional amendments that have been passed since then. In addition, the NARA has also made available a high-resolution image (339K JPEG) of the Bill of Rights. The other component in the exhibit that teachers will find of interest is an excerpt from "A More Perfect Union" that provides a detailed look at the proceedings of the Continental Congress.

Yale University Avalon Project: Eighteenth Century Documents
http://www.yale.edu/lawweb/avalon/18th.htm

Teachers will want to include a link to the Avalon Project at the Yale University Law School on their home page for every unit they teach in American history. Of particular interest for the teaching of the founding of the American Republic are full-text transcriptions of late eighteenth-century state constitutions, the Constitution of the United States, state ratification proceedings, and Kentucky and Virginia resolutions, to name just a few.

James Madison Center's James Madison: His Legacy
www.jmu.edu/madison/

James Madison University's Madison Center has developed a Web site that provides teachers with a well-organized, easily accessible database that includes hundreds of pages of documents penned by the "Father of the Constitution" and fourth president of the United States. Included in the collection of full-text transcriptions are Madison's notes on the Constitution, inaugural addresses, and state of the union speeches.

Conclusion

The teaching of early American history is indeed a challenge. It is not typically the historical period that attracts most students to the study of history—that "honor" being reserved for the Civil War. Unfortunately, far too many students view the pre-Columbian through founding period in American history with as much enthusiasm as they typically do the Gilded Age. Although this certainly is not a fair assessment on the part of students, it does present an academic hurdle or challenge history teachers must overcome if they are to successfully engage students in the salient issues, events, and themes germane to these periods. The online resources discussed in this chapter represent but a fraction of the plethora of Web sites dedicated to the study of these early periods in American history. Although the quality of online resources addressing these and other periods in United States history varies greatly, just as with history tomes, it does not diminish the tremendous potential of the Internet and World Wide Web. These Internet resources have the potential to provide a conceptual hook that combines pedagogical features most students find quite appealing and engaging, such as computer technology, multimedia components, and student autonomy.

It is perhaps this final element—student autonomy—that will prove to be most beneficial in the development of student historical thinking skills. For too long, many teachers have been unwilling to relinquish their role of informational gatekeeper. The Internet, however, is perhaps much more democratic, granting access to more historical resources than ever could have been imagined even five years ago, all a mere mouse click away. Therefore, teachers must concentrate even more intently on providing students with opportunities for developing historical thinking skills and habits of the mind, such as the ability to "read widely and critically in order to recognize the difference between fact and conjecture, between evidence and assertion, and thereby to frame useful questions."[25]

The challenge for teachers, however, is not only to provide the knowledge and conceptual foundation for students to build upon throughout their study of American history, hopefully dispelling many of the myths and historical inaccuracies along the way, but also to engage students in the type of historical inquiry and investigative activities that serve to further their interest and understanding of this critical period. Students are leaving the safety of the academic nest much earlier than before, attempting to fly in the cyber sky and encountering countless historical resources along the way, from the invaluable to the dubious. Our goal, therefore, should be to teach them how to fly better in this uncharted electronic environment.

Chapter 7

Active Learning, World History, and the Internet: Creating Knowledge in the Classroom

Alex Zukas

We can't solve problems by using the same kind of thinking we used when we created them.
—Albert Einstein

In our so-called "Information Age," teachers in elementary, middle, and high schools are being increasingly exhorted to use computer applications and Internet resources to teach history. The amount of information on the World Wide Web (WWW), however, is overwhelming and its quality is often inconsistent.[1] Teachers could easily spend the whole summer prepping for the fall semester and still not find the best or most appropriate sites for their courses. From a pedagogical perspective, even worse, as one recent article pointed out, information is not knowledge.[2] Such an insight should not be shocking to history teachers since a good part of what happens in any social studies class is demonstrating and encouraging critical-thinking skills to create knowledge. However, it is important to remember that the Internet can store and convey huge volumes of information, which are only of limited use until they are converted into knowledge by the mental work of real human beings—students. In fact, this process by which students create knowledge makes the role of the teacher indispensable because students need some guidance and feedback as they practice specific critical-thinking skills in creating their own knowledge. This chapter focuses on how using the World Wide Web can help students master the skills and subject matter necessary to succeed in one area of social studies—world history. After examining some curricular goals and issues germane to middle and high school world history education, this chapter presents some of the best practices found in the literature and draws on classroom world history and global studies experiences using the Internet. The chapter concludes with some thoughts on the future prospects, both positive and negative, of using the Internet to teach students about the world and its history. In the end, the Internet can assist teachers in reaching their curricular goals for world history education but only if the strengths and weaknesses of this unique medium are fully understood.

Curricular Goals

What are some important curricular goals in world history? The *National Standards for History* is a good place to begin the discussion, despite or maybe because of the controversy generated in the past decade. Granted, these standards were written with a United States curriculum in mind but they were developed to convey a non-Eurocentric and non-Western perspective on global history. They also took years to develop and were written by a task force of teachers "drawn equally from elementary, middle, and high schools" who "worked with a battery of historians of world . . . history and the resulting collaborative work was reviewed, draft by draft, by thirty-three national organizations" including the American Historical Association and the National Council for the Social Studies.[3] These standards, then, provide a collaborative and collegial entry point for a discussion of shared curricular goals and issues in teaching a world history perspective and content in grades five through twelve. They do not need to be accepted as the final word on curricular goals, especially by teachers in other parts of the world who did not contribute to their development, but should be seen as raising important issues for discussion by teachers of world history. In addition, they provide excellent teaching suggestions and guidance on how to integrate historical understanding with historical thinking skills in a large number of exercises that can be used immediately in the classroom.

The authors of the standards write that knowledge of history is the precondition for informed citizen participation not only in one's nation but in the world: "Without history, we cannot undertake any sensible inquiry into the political, social, or moral issues of society."[4] Therefore, one curricular goal is to educate students for civic responsibility on a global scale. A related goal is the use of inquiry and critical thinking to examine the problems of past cultures and societies, how those problems were resolved (or not), and the consequences of these decisions. The objective is to foster in students a deeper awareness of the alternatives they face when they confront today's problems and the likely consequences of each alternative. The idea is to bring "sound historical analysis to the service of informed decision making."

Beyond civic education, the study of world history can help students develop a fuller sense of self: "Historical memory is the key to self-identity, to seeing one's place in the stream of time, and one's connectedness with all of humankind." Another curricular goal, therefore, is to help students understand their place in world history, to realize that who they are and what they believe are the result of a long historical process, which will not end even when they are gone. In other words, they are part of a larger (historical) community that may not yet be apparent to them. Studying world history may help them find their "place," but it is a place that is not static. They will in turn create the conditions for the self-identity of future generations. The intent is to enable students to see themselves in relation to their societies and to the larger world.

Another related goal is to create for students the opportunity to develop a "comprehensive understanding of the world and of the many societies whose traditions and values may in many ways be different from their own." The idea is for students to "acquire the habit of seeing matters through others' eyes and come to realize that they can better understand themselves as they study others" so that they can see the relationship between themselves and the wider world and develop a critical perspective on their own views, values, and beliefs. These are important elements in critical thinking.

Further curricular goals fall into two main areas: developing historical thinking skills (critical thinking) and historical understanding (learning content). The first area emphasizes process while the second stresses knowledge. Historical thinking skills are essentially critical thinking skills and involve such activities as evaluating evidence, developing comparative and causal analyses, interpreting the historical record, and constructing sound arguments and perspectives. Historical understanding refers to the knowledge students create by applying their critical thinking skills to six major spheres of human activity: social, scientific/technological, economic, political, and cultural, and ecological. Historical understanding also involves issues of chronology, causation, outcomes, and diversity.[5]

In the area of diversity, "schools must teach a comprehensive history in which all students may share. That means a history that encompasses humanity" and a "forceful commitment to world-scale history." In terms of chronology, the *National Standards for History* suggests grouping world history into eight broad eras to make its broad sweep and massive scope intelligible and more coherent for teacher and student.[6] The eras make no claim to being definitive and represent broad shifts rather than rigid delineations. They are heuristic devices that teachers may or may not adopt for their own classrooms. The authors of the *National Standards* recognize that the standards they have set forth need to be converted into achievement expectations that are appropriate for students in grades five and six, seven and eight, and nine through twelve. The authors have endeavored to create examples of appropriate student achievement or outcomes at these different grade levels. For example, in the area of historical research capabilities, the authors recommend that students in grades five and six study historical documents to formulate significant questions such as: Who produced the document? When, how, and why was the document produced? What does the document tell us about the person(s) who created it? What do students need to find out to "tell a story" about the document and the people and events connected with it? For grades seven and eight, the assignment involves a higher level of critical thinking and entails examining historical documents to *determine* what voices are missing from mainstream narratives, *explain* the reasons for the omissions, and *challenge* generalizations and interpretations in text accounts. Finally, for grades nine through twelve the authors suggest that students use book reviews and critiques to make choices about which historical sources to consult, examine references to determine the context in which the documents were produced, and develop the habit of cross-referencing sources and asking probing questions to determine the authenticity and credibility of the references.[7]

While not nearly as encyclopedic in its detail, the National Council for History Education (NCHE) made comparable recommendations in 1996 to improve history education in the United States. Its recommendations include a suggestion that "historical inquiry should involve the use of visual materials, artifacts, [and] community resources" and that effective teaching practices for the K-12 classroom would involve more "lab-based" activities, critical and creative thinking, and multiple materials and venues that went beyond the textbook.[8] The NCHE also recommended that

> Teachers should be seen as trail guides rather than dispensers of information; Classroom practices should include assessments that are authentic and appropriate . . . ; Classroom methodology should center on active processes of research and interpretation . . . and pursue connections among historical ideas . . . ; Successful classroom practices should be shared through an electronic clearinghouse . . . [and] include resources, sample lesson plans, and model units.[9]

We will return to some specific suggestions in a later section of this chapter to show how the Internet not only facilitates communication among teachers of successful pedagogical approaches to the teaching of world history but also promotes students' critical- and historical-thinking skills and their creation of historical understanding, all key curricular goals for world history in the twenty-first century.

Pedagogy

Another curricular issue that is really pedagogical in nature concerns how students learn best. Some important current theories stress active questioning and learning rather than rote memorization or passive absorption of information (e.g., names, facts, dates), the older style of learning history in grades five through twelve that most of us grew up with that bored even the most dedicated and motivated of students. The two most relevant theories about teaching and student learning are constructivism and learning styles.

Constructivism asserts that individuals actively construct their knowledge of the world.[10] Knowledge is not something that is passively received but which is the result of active analysis and synthesis. Constructivists also assert that

> knowledge resides in individuals and that knowledge cannot be transferred from the brain of a teacher to the brains of students. The student

tries to make sense of new knowledge by trying to fit it with his or her experience. Consequently, words are not containers whose meanings are encapsulated in each word itself; words gain meaning through an individual's construction of knowledge. We can communicate with another person because the meaning of our words is compatible with the meaning others give the same words. Communication is an important act to constructivist teachers.[11]

Lorsbach and Basolo claim that constructivism is associated with many current reform efforts in education in the United States.[12] It has a great deal in common with the critical pedagogy of Brazilian educator Paolo Freire, with its emphasis on making sense of the world (rather than on abstract mental exercises or thought problems) and its insistence that teaching and learning are active, social processes that make sense of experience. Some of the educators closely associated with constructivism, like Ira Shor, come from the critical pedagogy tradition.[13] One application of constructivism is "problem-based learning," an approach to student learning ideally suited to the Internet. We will return to problem-based learning in the next section as one solution to many of the curricular issues raised so far.

Harvard psychologist Howard Gardner developed the theory of multiple ways of knowing twenty years ago. In a series of books, he popularized the notion that students have preferred and optimal ways of knowing that are not the same for all students in a class. He identified seven major pathways by which students learn. All students possessed and used all seven modalities for learning because they often reinforced each other, and the use of more than one modality made learning more enduring. Gardner encouraged teachers to develop teaching and learning strategies that did not favor or privilege one learning style over another and to present material in ways that appealed to multiple ways of knowing. Not only would learning in one style be reinforced by the others but, in keeping with our concerns as teachers of world history and the *National Standards'* emphasis on teaching a comprehensive history all students may share, the classroom becomes more inclusive. No student needs to feel left out or left behind because of the way world history is taught. In other words, the medium should be part of the message. In most traditional classrooms where teachers lectured and students read a textbook, certain learners were privileged and went on to perform better on written tests of their knowledge and understanding. Other students, however, whose preferred learning style was not the same were then regarded or regarded themselves as somehow deficient in ability and knowledge, when in fact the source of the problem was not their intelligence but how they were taught. Gardner defines this idea as his theory of "multiple intelligences."[14] Others have since developed different versions of multiple intelligences and different typologies based on different psychological theories.[15] However, all could agree with the statement that we should "provide a learning environment in which all learners feel embedded or connected."[16] Given the curricular goals of the *National Standards* toward inclusiveness, multiple perspectives, and critical reflection, creating such a rich learning environment would be a worthy project for middle and high school world history classrooms. Would use of the Internet really advance such curricular goals?

Uses of the Internet in World History Classrooms

There are some uses of the Internet with which this chapter does not deal, especially technical issues such as conducting effective Internet searches, creating classroom Web pages and Web boards, and using the class Web site to communicate with parents and post student assignments.[17] This chapter does, however, examine possible uses of Internet content to achieve certain curricular goals in teaching world history. It is based on the assumption that students and teachers see each other in actual classrooms and use the Internet as an additional resource for teaching and learning. This chapter does not deal with the cyber classroom.[18] The assumption that students and teachers have access to the Internet through a local server or service provider may not be reasonable for all schools, a problem that will be discussed in the concluding section of this chapter. An understanding of the many resources available on the Internet for student learning might, however, encourage school districts to request funding for a school district server.

As one recent contributor to the discussion on using the Internet in social studies classes wrote:

> The Internet makes available an unparalleled, and seemingly unlimited, repository of resources and ideas for social studies teachers. It offers access to library catalogs and historical archives; viewings of exhibits

in art and historical museums; material from the latest editions of popular magazines and newspapers; . . . [and] communication with like-
minded individuals about a topic of mutual interest. With the Internet,
teachers now have the ability to reach far beyond the traditional sources
of social studies curriculum material . . . [but] the Internet is only a tool,
and like any tool, its use can be very enriching, or frustrating and even
dangerous.[19]

This ability to reach beyond traditional materials brings a new set of
problems for teachers because too much information can be as much
of a problem as too little. Selection becomes even more difficult for
teachers as Web sites constantly are updated, disappear, and reappear,
which can be as frustrating as outdated textbooks. There is no guar-
antee that the information on a Web site is accurate or reliable since
anyone can post a Web site with no editing or peer review. These are
only some of the problems teachers will face when they begin to use
the Internet in their classrooms, but like many problems, they have
an effective solution that can become part of the curriculum, depending upon grade level.[20]

For instance, to help students develop their critical-thinking and
research skills, teachers could ask tenth graders to review a number
of Web sites that deal with the same problem or topic and determine
which ones seem more reliable and trustworthy as sources of information and ideas, and then use the most reliable information in their
reports or essays. Since students will undoubtedly use the Internet as
a source of information and analysis in their future studies and oc-
cupations, and given the fact that thousands of new Internet sites are
posted daily, learning how to vet these sites is an important real-world
skill that students should master as early as possible. Kathy Schrock
has developed K-12 Web site evaluation forms that students could use
to decide if the site is suitable and/or useful for their project. These
forms are available at http://school.discovery.com/schrockguide/
eval.html. More adventurous teachers who have the necessary technical support could have their students create virtual tours of historic
sites, events, or areas and share them with their classmates.[21] One
innovative high school teacher assigns "virtual treasure hunts" and has
students go to Russia, Africa, or China on quests for artifacts and
information that create a rich and challenging learning environment
for the students.[22]

For younger students in fifth and sixth grades, WebQuests may be a more appropriate assignment. A WebQuest is a structured exercise created by the teacher that asks students to solve problems or find answers to questions on the Web. Developed by Bernie Dodge at San Diego State University, "a WebQuest provides a framework in which active learning and knowledge construction can take place" and so fits in quite well with recent theories about how students learn best.[23] A WebQuest requires some rudimentary ability to search the Web using a number of search engines, but simple strategies are easily taught to young students who love to play on a computer keyboard anyway. As they get older, the searches can become more advanced. Older students can construct WebQuests with the assistance of their teachers and further the construction of their own knowledge. The WebQuest page at http://edweb.sdsu.edu/webquest/webquest.html outlines the components of a WebQuest for teachers and provides links to sample WebQuests.

Teachers also can create classroom Web sites where they post links to relevant online resources and ask students to follow the links and answer a series of questions. This can be a more guided exercise than a typical WebQuest and is very suitable for lower grades and novice users as it does not require the use of search engines. It also gives the teacher more control over the content to avoid inappropriate or misinformed sites.[24]

The issue of juvenile access to the Internet is, of course, an important factor for teachers to consider when they design their Web assignments.[25] Included at the end of this chapter is a "Webliography" of sites that may be helpful in using the Internet to craft interactive, problem-solving activities in world history classes. A few outstanding sites, and how they relate to the curricular goals discussed earlier, will be discussed in detail. Teachers looking for suitable Web sites may want to keep in mind that starting with recognized authorities such as government agencies, educational institutions, news media, reputable nonprofit organizations, and established business firms will increase the likelihood of finding reliable information. This does not mean, however, that the sites can be taken at face value or that there are no biases in the selection and organization of information or opinion. A visitor is not relieved of the responsibility of evaluating the worth of the site, but the chances of finding good solid data and research are greater at these sites than ones run by organizations which put ideology over information. Remember that the Web sites of the World Bank, the U.S. government, CNN, the Environmental Defense Fund, and so forth, also have ideological purposes, but the information placed on these sites has been checked against other references and is open to criticism and revision. Sites run by groups for whom information is subordinate to ideology are less likely to be useful as sources of dispassionate information, but students can, of course, access those sites if the assignment is to understand the worldview and tactics of such groups. A teacher would need to frame such an assignment very carefully to prevent students from accepting the information on these sites as having great scientific or methodological accuracy and would need to use the assignment as a critical-thinking exercise for students, although all sites require the use of skills of analysis to detect bias and reliability.

A classroom Web site also can be a place to publish student work in history and allow them to present themselves to the world.[26] Such publications can give students a new sense of self and help them understand their place in the world, especially when a number of students from a learning community post their work on an issue and create links to each other's work and to local and global resources. In cyberspace, the sense of community can be extended to include students in other parts of the world who collaborate on a common world-history project and who are in frequent e-mail contact.[27] One Internet project that facilitates such communication is ePALS Classroom Exchange. Teachers register their class through an online form at http://www.epals.com and use tools at the site to find a class with which to create a liaison and common learning activities. Other Web sites that create dialogue between students in distant locations include The Global Schoolhouse at http://www.gsh.org, KidLINK at http://www.kidlink.org, and Learning Circles at http://www.att.com/education/lcguide/p.intro/a.intro.html. Through this process of collaboration, students can acquire a global perspective that facilitates a study of world history, cultural diversity, global connections, an appreciation of the views of others and others' views of oneself, and a kind of global political and cultural education.[28]

In terms of world history content, students and teachers may access the Internet to read letters from American soldiers in the Philippines in 1901 or the testimony of female factory workers in England in the nineteenth century, view photographs of archaeological sites in Mesopotamia or Greece, or examine satellite photos of the growth of the Sahara Desert or the deforestation in Brazil in the past twenty years. So much good material exists on the Web that the limits to what historical resources may be brought into the classroom really are set by the teacher's imagination, the hardware and software available at the school, any legal stipulations regarding appropriate subject matter for minors, and the time it takes to surf the Internet. The latter issue is very important because a teacher, whose day is already very full, can spend hours a day for weeks sifting through the thousands of Web sites which have historical content to find the two or three dozen that really fit the assignments or purpose of the class. One book that can help teachers get started searching for Web sites is *The History Highway*.[29] This book, designed for the novice, explains how to send and receive email, post messages to newsgroups and discussion lists, and many other technical operations. The bulk of the book, however, is a wonderful annotated listing of Web sites, resources, and discussion lists for historians and history teachers. The discussion lists allow teachers to communicate with each other electronically about peda-gogical issues and share advice concerning lesson plans, appropriate material, and strategies for student learning.

There are Web sites that contain lesson plans and teaching strate-gies. Some of these are commercial sites while others are maintained by universities, museums, and institutes. Additional sites contain pri-mary sources, maps, pictures, paintings, and historians' interpretation of the past, which teachers can integrate into their own lesson plans. Among other places to find lesson plans, are the History Channel Web site at http://www.historychannel.com or R. Jerry Adams' site at http://www.awesomelibrary.com/history.html, which has links to lesson plans in history at all grade levels and links to history Web sites.[30] Another excellent place to start is an article by Gregory Levitt in which he outlines ten instructional approaches to using the Internet: projects, problem-based inquiry, issue-centered instruction, discussion, simulations and role plays, panel discussion, resource person/guest speaker, case studies, debates, and mock trials. Levitt also annotates more than sixty other Web sites that confront a number of crucial global issues: the environment, gender and class, globalization, inter-national conflict, and regional relations.[31] These sites are most suitable in a lesson on contemporary historical problems. To enhance history lessons, the use of art resources on the Internet invariably piques student interest. As David Williams writes, "The arts . . . carry the critical affective and aesthetic messages that are so important to truly experiencing an enriched telling of the stories of people, society, and history."[32] In his article, Williams provides wonderful examples of the use of art-based resources in creating an imaginative, stimulating, and enticing curriculum for students in which the teacher brings in materials from art, photography, painting, music, and theater to build a story for students to explore. His extended examples include discussion of technical issues as well as curricular ones.

Teachers need to be aware of how much work is involved in creating a classroom Web site. It easily can consume a tremendous amount of time. Joe Cain makes a number of important points that any teacher who wants to put up a classroom Web site should be aware of: Consider the target audience and make explicit assumptions about their skills; consider the physical learning environment in which the students will access the material; consider the alternative means of information or lesson delivery; be clear about the purpose of the Web site; and, consider the available (that is, limited) resources at your disposal and the technical problems that will invariably arise.[33] Paying attention to these issues will save teachers and students hours of frustration and wasted effort. As Cain writes, "Thinking deeply about pedagogy and design is crucial if resources, money, and time matter while you create your Web pages."[34] Beyond providing these caveats, he also stresses that the Internet is an excellent medium for active learning.

Sample Solutions

Using the Internet can give teachers access to real-world problems that can cause students to question their understanding of the world and prompt them to test their own assumptions about what they know.[35] Lesson plans built around such problems are very consistent with the pedagogical goals of constructivism and multiple intelligences mentioned earlier and with the curricular goals of world history that have been outlined. These lessons involve political education and informed decision making, historical understanding, problem-solving skills, consideration of multiple perspectives, and locating where one stands in relation to a problem. One example of such a lesson is a virtual field trip or WebQuest to China.

Tom March of San Diego State University created this WebQuest, available at http://www.kn.pacbell.com/wired/China/, to involve students in independent and collaborative work to solve a problem: "What actions should the United States take in its policy toward China?" The purpose of the quest is for students to understand Chinese history, culture, practices, and recent policies. The outcomes of the quest meet many of the curricular and pedagogical goals outlined in the paragraph above, to include the opportunity for students to develop an interest in the study of China and learn information about six key aspects of Chinese culture, realize that complex topics can be looked at from various perspectives, formulate and support an argument from one of the six perspectives, work with teammates to problem-solve a combined action plan, and question the nature of international relations in our more interdependent world. The design of this WebQuest is excellent and could serve as a model for other historical WebQuests because it clearly outlines the steps and requirements for students. The only drawback to this particular WebQuest is that the perspectives from which the students are working are almost completely Western. Some of the links provide Chinese perspectives on the issues raised (economics, religion, culture, environment, human rights, international relations), but the students see themselves as representatives of the United States and one is even a U.S. senator (the others are a business person, a human rights advocate, an environmental activist, a religious leader, and a museum curator). To teach a truly global perspective, it might have been better to have had the group represent the United Nations, with representatives from six different continents or cultural traditions.

Even with that reservation, the site outlines the elements of a successfully designed WebQuest and demonstrates the importance of individual and collective work using problem-based learning, which, according to Lorsbach and Basolo, reinforces crucial critical-thinking and process skills such as observing, classifying, measuring, predicting, inferring, identifying and controlling variables, formulating and testing hypotheses, interpreting data, experimenting, constructing models, and communicating.[36] Consistent with this, the WebQuest asks students to publish their findings on an electronic bulletin board or in a chat room using the link provided to "China on the Net" to get real-world feedback on their ideas and proposals, thus closing the link with the community and involving themselves as citizens in global issues.

The China WebQuest is the last and most complex of six possible strategies for using the Internet for learning available at the Pacific Bell Web site, at http://www.kn.pacbell.com/wired/China/index.html. The other strategies include a gateway called "China on the Web" which has links to useful and stimulating Web sites on China; a multimedia scrapbook idea called "Exploring China" which asks students to surf the Net and download images, text, video, and music to use in their own multimedia scrapbook (suitable for middle school students); a treasure hunt called, of course, "The Treasures of China" which has students find "hard knowledge" (facts, information, news, history) about China (suitable for high school students); a subjective sampler called "My China" which invites students to record their personal ideas, feelings, and experiences on some specific aspects of China (suitable for elementary school students); and, an introductory WebQuest called "Does the Tiger Eat its Cubs?" which requires students to investigate the reported mistreatment of orphans in China (appropriate for high school students). This last inquiry-based activity, which requires higher-order thinking and collaboration, can lead students to successfully complete the larger WebQuest outlined above.

World history teachers who would like to develop their own WebQuests can look at the sites that explain how to construct a WebQuest in the Webliography at the end of this chapter. For those who want to create a less structured Internet field trip, there are still some tips to follow. Planning is essential for success. Teachers need to preview Internet sites to make sure they fit the purpose of the exercise and are relevant to the curricular goals of the lesson. Some authors suggest teachers develop an Internet travel guide for each Web site students visit.[37] It should provide the Internet address of the site at the top of the page, directions for touring the Web site, especially where to begin, questions to be answered after students go through the site, directions for keeping a travel journal of the Web sites they visit, and other activities for learners who are less print and visually oriented. All of these activities encourage active learning.

There are certainly other activities that encourage greater historical understanding and skills by allowing students to examine world history issues such as chronology, causation, and outcomes or consequences, as well as diversity and inclusivity. One large question would be to have students examine why civilizations collapsed. Another would be to compare civilizations and their essential features. A final exercise might be to combine these first two exercises into another: What happens when one civilization conquers another? Is the latter totally extinguished?

A good place to begin looking at the issue of civilizational collapse is the Annenberg Web site "Collapse: Why Do Civilizations Fall?" available at http://www.learner.org/exhibits/collapse/. Based on a PBS video series, the site examines the Maya of Central America, Sumer in western Asia, the Anasazi in New Mexico, and the Mali and Songhai in West Africa. The site thus covers four continents and a variety of time periods. It teaches students how archaeologists find and interpret evidence and asks them to become detectives themselves. The site is well constructed with good visuals, and invites student involvement. The resources available at the site are not exhaustive, therefore high school teachers should integrate other Web sites into the lesson so that students may compare the information and perspective provided at the Annenberg site. Teachers could ask students to explain what it means for a civilization to collapse. What does "collapse" imply? Total loss? Extinction? What were the causes? Were they the same in each case? What were the consequences? Did the people disappear or simply assume a new cultural form? Teachers could also expect students to examine the role of theory in history. The Annenberg site contends that "The history of humankind has been marked by patterns of growth and decline." Students could be asked to test this theory on other civilizations to see if it serves as a plausible explanation.

Two other sites with which the Annenberg site could be compared are the Lords of the Earth site at http://www.historyserver.org/lords/ and the Ancient Civilizations Web site, available at http://www.awesomelibrary.org/Classroom/Social_Studies/Ancient_Civilizations/Ancient_Civilizations.html. The Lords of the Earth site has extensive information on the art, culture, beliefs, cosmology, practices, and descendents of the classic Maya, Aztec, Mixtec, and Inca peoples as well as North American native peoples. This site celebrates the accomplishments of these peoples and defines these civilizations as having "collapsed" in the sense that they disappeared. The Ancient Civilizations site includes an examination of the ancient Aztecs, Celts, Chinese, Egyptians, Greeks, Incas, Indians, Japanese, Maya, Mesopotamians,

Native Americans, Nubians, Romans, and Vikings. Some of these ancient civilizations and their languages are dead and there has been a nearly complete rupture with the present, even if some of the values and perspectives live on in the successor cultures in one form or another. But for other cultures, most notably the Chinese and Egyptian, there has been a fairly unbroken history for four thousand years. It would be hard to talk about civilizational collapse in their cases even if the civilizations are much different today than they were two thousand years ago. This site would allow teachers to ask students to compare the structure, values, practices, and beliefs of various ancient civilizations and so promote an understanding of the diversity of the human experience. Such an assignment would also encourage active learning and could be crafted to appeal to different learning styles and grade levels where some of the outcomes could be a written report, an oral report, a craft or drawing, a map, an architectural sketch, or a story.

Another aspect of the civilization theme that involves collapse and comparison is the arrival of Europeans in the Americas and the ensuing massive dislocation and destruction of the native peoples. There are numerous Web sites that examine Columbus and his impact and legacy with the Spanish, Portuguese, French, and English who followed him. Students could investigate the similarities and differences between indigenous and nonindigenous cultures, economic systems, ecological practices, flora and fauna, and social structures. They could revisit the question of civilizational collapse and find causes not enumerated on the Annenberg Web site and also question whether Mayan civilization has really disappeared in Chiapas, in Guatemala, or the Yucatan just because Mayan cities were abandoned. This issue provides a rich field for students' historical inquiry, and it is an issue whose relevance has reemerged in the last decade with the quincentennial of Columbus and the indigenous rebellion in Chiapas.

A more critical examination of the history of the modern world that includes great links to a plethora of resources, is available at the Global Problems and the Culture of Capitalism Web site at http://www.plattsburgh.edu/richard.robbins/legacy/. This site invites high school students to question assumptions about the role of capitalism in the world since 1500 by considering the role of the consumer, laborer, capitalist, and nation-state in a system of global capitalism. It has an historical emphasis and stresses issues of current concern such as population growth, hunger, poverty, economic development, environment, consumption, disease, indigenous peoples, protest, rebellion, and resistance. The Web site has links to hundreds of content sites on all of these issues and would allow teachers to construct a myriad of assignments that would heighten students' critical-thinking skills and historical understanding. It also would give them a new awareness of the complexity of the global problems, both current and future.

Conclusion: Benefits and Problems

Where does all of this leave us? To summarize, the Internet can help teachers create a stimulating and enhanced world history curriculum that will reach the objectives of the *National Standards for History* and ideas proposed by the National Council for History Education. Online projects demand higher order thinking skills and require students to create solutions to complex problems. Teachers can modify and adapt resources very quickly to incorporate new material and new perspectives, keeping the curriculum current and engaging, both for teachers and students. The data that students access will be relevant and current. Online learning can serve both linear and nonlinear thinkers, and assignments can be more learner-centered. Teachers can create links to community and global resources and have students publish their findings on the Internet, electronic bulletin boards, list servers, or in discussion groups. The richness of the material posted on the Internet, in terms of audio, visuals, and textual data, provides teachers with a wonderful opportunity to enhance the curriculum without sacrificing the quality of instruction and learning. The "bells and whistles" of the Web create a new substance as well as a new form. Finally, Web-based assignments allow students to explore "real world" problems using the latest information. In addition, students also cultivate a greater sense of civic responsibility, acquire new knowledge and the skills to acquire more, and build connections. Assignments can cease to be simulations, and instead deal with actual real world problems for which students can propose and post real solutions for others to read and consider.

The problems of using the Internet to teach world history are only in part curricular and pedagogical; most are technical as well, and fall out of the scope of this chapter. They need, however, to be kept in mind if they are not to undermine the pedagogical function of the Internet. The major technical hurdle concerns teacher access to adequate computing resources, Internet connections, and projectors. Without these resources, all of their great plans will come to nothing. Teachers must ensure that students have adequate Internet skills and access to equipment in order to complete the assignments, otherwise their frustration will cancel any pedagogical advantage of using the Internet. At least one expert warns that teaching using the Internet will take a significant commitment of time, more than teachers will expect, and that many school budgets will never be adequate to sustain such online endeavors.[38]

Other curricular and pedagogical obstacles concern issues of plagiarism and inappropriate Web sites. The Internet makes it easier for students to plagiarize. Well-crafted assignments, however, can reduce the tendency of students to copy information verbatim from the Internet especially if they are required to draw conclusions, make comparisons, and engage in high-order thinking skills. With respect to inappropriate Web sites, teachers will have to guide students in the selection of material or select such resources a priori. The student's desire to explore and evaluate new sources of information, however, must never be thwarted. If teachers notice a persistent problem regarding student use or viewing of inappropriate sites, the school can purchase software which blocks certain kinds of Internet sites.

The final curricular issues concern Web site instability and gender and class technology bias. Web sites come and go, and one of Joe Cain's major lessons was that he spent enormous amounts of time checking links and updating his Web sites.[39] When a Web site is gone, the teacher must either locate its new URL, find a substitute, or modify the lesson plan.

Experts have noticed that technology, including the Internet, is not a neutral medium. It has historically privileged some individuals over others. Some prepackaged software has shown gender and class bias, while much of the language of the Internet reveals a masculine bias.[40] As Cameron White and Trenia Walker note, "access is still primarily available to middle and upper class individuals, so the issue of the Internet becoming the great equalizer or democratizer has yet to come to fruition."[41] As with many problems associated with using the Internet to teach world history, this one can be addressed directly in the classroom by asking the students to employ the critical thinking skills they have acquired in their WebQuests and other assignments in order to analyze the language of the Internet and put it in historical perspective. The Internet presents a challenge to middle and high school world history teachers, but it also represents an opportunity to promote active learning and student created knowledge.

Webliography

Gateway Sites

The following three sites are excellent and provide wonderful ideas on designing school Web sites and/or how to contact other schools in the United States and around the world:

American School Directory (Internet Gateway to108,000 K-12 Schools' websites): http://www.asd.com
Connected Teacher K–12 School Sites: http://www.classroom.com/community/connection/states.jhtml
International School Registry: http://web66.umn.edu/schools.html

The following sites have links to Web sites that contain world history content and great lesson plans:

History/social studies for K-12 teachers: http://my.execpc.com/~dboals/boals.html
K-12 sources—curriculum—lesson plans: http://my.execpc.com/~dboals/k-12.html
EduNET world history sites: http://www.edunetconnect.com/index_n.html
Global problems and the culture of capitalism: http://www.plattsburgh.edu/richard.robbins/legacy/
The History Channel: http://www.historychannel.com
Awesome Library world history resources: http://www.awesomelibrary.org/Classroom/Social_Studies/History/History.html
Exploring, teaching, and learning world history with new media: http://www.accd.edu/sac/history/keller/WHAsess.htm
National Council for the Social Sciences history links: http://databank.ncss.org/links.php
History online: http://www.jacksonesd.k12.or.us/k12projects/jimperry/history.html

Maps on the Internet: http://www.lib.utexas.edu/Libs/PCL/Map_collection/
map_sites/hist_sites.html; http://www-sul.stanford.edu/depts/ssrg/medieval/
atlas.html

History gateway: http://www.arts.gla.ac.uk/www/ctich/histlink.html

Art history gateway: http://www.arts.gla.ac.uk/www/ctich/arthistlinks.htm

Web Pedagogy Sites

Kathy Schrock's guide: http://school.discovery.com/schrockguide

WebQuest sites: http://edweb.sdsu.edu/webquest; http://school.discovery.com/
schrockguide/webquest/webquest.html

Research and critical thinking: http://my.execpc.com/~dboals/think.html
(This is part of the history/social studies Web site for K-12 teachers. It
discusses concept mapping, Web site evaluation, research skills and
tools, search tools and how to use them, critical thinking and the Web.)

ePALS: http://www.epals.com

The Global Schoolhouse: http://www.gsh.org

KidLINK: http://www.kidlink.org

Learning Circles: http://www.att.com/education/lcguide/p.intro/a.intro.html

Selected World History Content Sites

World history timeline: http://www.hyperhistory.com

History of costume through the ages: http://www.siue.edu/COSTUMES/
history.html

Images of ancient Egypt: http://homepages.tcp.co.uk/~nicholson/egypt.html

Assyrian-Babylonian myths: http://members.bellatlantic.net/~vze33gpz/
assyrbabyl-faq.html

Greek myths: http://www.desy.delgna/interpedial/greek_myth//greek_myth
.html

The agricultural revolution: http://www.wsu.edu/gened/learn-modules/
top_agrev/agrev-index.html

Harappa: http://www.harappa.com/

Nippur, sacred city of Enlil: http://asmar.uchicago.edu/OI/PROJ/NIP/PUB93/
NSC/NSC.html

Ancient Egypt virtual walking tour: http://www.sonic.net/~exactsci/ancient/
egypt/egypt.html

Life in Ancient Egypt: http://www.carnegiemuseums.org/cmnh/exhibits/
egypt/

Virtual tour of ancient Athens: http://www.sonic.net/~exactsci/ancient/greek/
greek.html

Virtual tour of ancient Rome: http://www.sonic.net/~exactsci/ancient/rome/
rome.html

Archaeological excavation at Isthmia in Greece: http://isthmia. ohio-
state.edu/

The Roman forum: http://www.crystalintes.com/romeforum.html

Roman emperors online encyclopedia: http://www.roman-emperors.org/

Diocletian's palace in Split: http://sunsite.unc.edu/expo/palace.exhibit/
intro.html

Roman art and architecture: http://harpy.uccs.edu/roman/html/roman.html

History of India: http://www.historyofindia.com/home.html

Eyewitness: History through the eyes of those who lived it: http://
www.ibiscom.com/ (mostly primary sources for U.S. history except for
material from the ancient and medieval worlds)

Indigenous Peoples: http://www.indigenouspeople.org/natlit/natimage.htm
(Maya, Aztec, Mixtec, Native North Americans, Inca, links to other sites—
culture, customs, poetry, lifestyles, beliefs, religion, practices, etc.)

Ancient civilization resources: http://www.awesomelibrary.org/Classroom/
Social_Studies/Ancient_Civilizations/Ancient_Civilizations.html

Internet global history sourcebook (documents from around the world from
2000 BCE to the present): http://www.fordham.edu/halsall/global/
globalsbook.html

Exploring ancient world cultures: http://eawc.evansville.edu/index.htm

Collapse: Why do civilizations fail?: http://www.learner.org/exhibits/
collapse/

Forbidden City—virtual tour: http://www.chinavista.com/beijing/gugong/
!start.html

Chinese culture: http://www.chinavista.com/experience/index.html

Searching for China WebQuest: http://www.kn.pacbell.com/wired/China/
ChinaQuest.html

Six paths to China: http://www.kn.pacbell.com/wired/China/index.html

Japanese history timeline: http://www.askasia.org/frclasrm/readings/
t000013.html

Japanese history: http://www.japan-guide.com/e/e641.html

Views of Kaaba (Islam): http://www.al-islam.org/gallery/photos/
images_1.htm

Sufism: http://www.archives.uga.edu/~godlas/sufism.html

Life in medieval England (complete with feasting and Vikings): http://
www.regia.org/village.htm

Shagrat al-Durr (a female Muslim commander who fought Crusaders): http:/
/www.womeninworldhistory.com/heroine1.html

Lady Murasaki (Heian Japan): http://www.womeninworldhistory.com/
heroine9.html

Virtual tour of Isfahan (architecture inspired by Sufism): http://
isfahan.anglia.ac.uk:8200/

The Book of Hours (medieval illumination): http://humanities.uchicago.edu/
images/heures/heures.html

Aztecs: http://www.indians.org/welker/aztec.htm

Maya: http://www.indians.org/welker/maya.htm

The Inca trail and Machu Picchu: http://www.raingod.com/angus/Gallery/
Photos/SouthAmerica/Peru/IncaTrail/index.html

Ancient Mesoamerican Civilization: http://www.angelfire.com/ca/
humanorigins/index.html

Maya civilization: http://www.mexconnect.com/mex_/travel/ldumois/maya/
mayanindex.html

Jainism: http://www.jainworld.com

Buddhism: http://www.sukhi.com

Taoism: http://www.clas.ufl.edu/users/gthursby/taoism/

Hinduism: http://www.famnest.com/hinduism/index.htm

Chinese philosophy: http://www.chinesephilosophy.net

Confucianism: http://www.ciolek.com/WWWVL_Buddhism.html

Tour of Renaissance-era gardens: http://www.boglewood.com/palladio/
home.html

European medieval and Renaissance architecture: http://www.netserf.org/
Architecture/

Trans-Atlantic slave trade: http://library.thinkquest.org/13406/ta/index.html

History of the East India Company: http://www.theeastindiacompany.com/
history.html

Russian history: http://www.ucr.edu/history/seaman/

Modern Asia: http://coombs.anu.edu.au/WWWVL-AsianStudies.html

Child labor in the nineteenth century: http://www.earlham.edu/~pols/
globalprobs/children/Laila.html

U.S. imperialism in the late nineteenth and early twentieth centuries: http://
www.smplanet.com/imperialism/toc.html

"The White Man's Burden" and its critics: http://www.boondocksnet.com/
kipling/

Images of war and empire (United States): http://www.boondocksnet.com/
centennial/image.html

Images of U.S.-Philippine War and soldiers' letters home: http://
www.boondocksnet.com/stereo/parlor_index.html

Dutch colonialism in Indonesia: http://www.aseanfocus.com/gateway/
indonesia/colonialismP2.asp

Early western explorers in Kenya: http://www.kenyalogy.com/eng/info/
histo8.html

The partition of Africa and the "Lunatic Express": http://www.kenyalogy
.com/eng/info/histo10.html
Great Depression in Vancouver, British Columbia: http://
www2.excite.sfu.ca/pgm/depress/greatdepress.html
Historic forest resources and problems: http://www.lib.duke.edu/forest
Tropical forests: http://www.rainforest-alliance.org/
The Sahel from satellites: http://www.eden-foundation.org/project/
desertif.html

Chapter 8

Sequential Lesson Plan Frameworks

The aim of education should be to teach the child how to think, not what to think.
—John Dewey

The first formal educational approach, sophistic dialogue, dates back to the fifth century. In an attempt to impart knowledge, the elder Sophists employed a group discussion or what became known as the sophistic dialogue technique, that would remain the dominating pedagogical approach for centuries thereafter.[1] By the late seventeenth century, however, John Locke's *tabula rasa* or blank slate theory became the guiding philosophical force in academia.[2] Following the efficiency movement of the early twentieth century, championed by the psychologist Edward Thorndike, American education entered the modern era. Ralph Tyler's "rationale" served to usher in this new age of teaching, with its emphasis on curriculum design and educational objectives.[3] Soon, other educators would develop similar curriculum and instruction models that provided teachers with a series of sequential frameworks for designing lesson plans, each with their own unique curricular syntax.

In the digital classroom of the twenty-first century, it is crucial for history teachers to be armed with a variety of curricular and instructional arrows in their teaching quiver to take advantage of all of the resources at their fingertips and to address the needs and concerns of a diverse student population. The critical role of the intended curriculum on classroom instruction is perhaps best reflected in the following observation by Bruce Joyce, Marsha Weil, and Beverly Showers:

> Models of teaching are really models of learning. As we help students acquire information, ideas, skills, values, ways of thinking, and means of expressing themselves, we are also teaching them to learn. In fact, the most important long-term outcome of instruction may be the students' increased capabilities to learn more easily and effectively in the future, both because of the knowledge and skill they have acquired and because they have mastered learning processes.[4]

This chapter provides an overview of seven of the most popular sequential curricular and instructional models for teaching middle school and high school history: Tyler's "Teaching by Objectives" Method; Gagne's "Behavioral Method"; Bloom's "Mastery Learning"; Hunter's "Mastery Learning"; Karplus and Thier's "5-E Learning Cycle"; Oliver and Shaver's "Jurisprudential Inquiry"; and Cantu's "Educate Model." These models are meant only to broaden a history teacher's instructional repertoire, not to serve as prescriptive pedagogical dogma. Perhaps a better analogy is that first posited by Lawrence Stenhouse a quarter of a century ago, who suggested that lesson plan frameworks and the greater classroom curriculum are like a cooking recipe:

> It can be criticized on nutritional or gastronomic grounds—does it nourish the students and does it taste good?—and it can be criticized on the grounds of practicality—we can't get hold of six dozen larks' tongues and the grocer can't find any ground unicorn horn! A curriculum, like the recipe for a dish, is first imagined as a possibility, then the subject of experiment. The recipe offered publicly is in a sense a report on the experiment. Similarly, a curriculum should be grounded in practice. It is an attempt to describe the work observed in classrooms that it is adequately communicated to teachers and others. Finally, within limits, a recipe can be varied according to taste. So can a curriculum.[5]

Table 8.1

Tyler's Teaching by Objectives Method Syntax

Teaching step	Central components
Lesson title	Identify title and focus of lesson.
Educational goals	List educational purpose and goals of each learning activity.
Instructional objectives	List the behavioral objectives for each learning activity.
Curricular resources	Identify materials needed to conduct each learning activity, and the estimated time required for each.
Instruction	List and describe each teaching activity, in the order in which they will be introduced.
Evaluation	Identify the specific assessment strategies that will be used to evaluate student performance.
Post-reflection	Discuss how the lesson and teacher performance will be reviewed and/or assessed.

Tyler's "Teaching by Objectives" Method

Noted educational researchers Decker F. Walker and Jonas F. Soltis once remarked that "the most influential set of ideas about how to make a curriculum is embodied in the 'Tyler rationale.'"[6] They were making reference to the course syllabus for Education 260 Basic Principles of Curriculum and Instruction, by Ralph Tyler at the University of Chicago, which was published as a monograph in 1950. The Tyler rationale quickly became the guiding paradigm for curriculum development in the United States.[7]

Over time, Tyler's rationale was translated into a curricular framework that became commonplace in classrooms as a template for designing lesson plans.[8] The lesson plan development model, which is known as the "teaching by objectives" method, contains seven distinct components. The lesson should begin with the listing of the *lesson title,* which includes a brief one paragraph description of the lesson content focus. Closely associated with this step is the next one in which the teacher should clearly identify the *educational goals* for the lesson to include the purpose and meaning of the learning activities contained within. Teachers should then identify the *instructional objectives,* using any or all of the three domains—cognitive, affective, and psychomotor—as the guiding hierarchical framework for organizing them. Next, teachers should identify all of the *curricular resources* they will need to conduct each of the learning activities that comprise the lesson. The heart of this lesson framework is the listing and description of each of the teaching activities that constitute the formal *instruction* phase or step in the lesson (e.g., *PowerPoint* presentation, online module, lecture). The final two steps in the teaching by objectives framework are closely mirrored. First, teachers should identify the assessment strategies that will be included in the lesson to *evaluate* student understanding and performance. Finally, an activity should be integrated at the end of the lesson to allow for *post reflection,* which includes evaluation of the lesson and individual performance through a variety of means (e.g., discussion boards, e-mail messages, chat rooms, online interactive critique forms).

Gagne's "Behavioral Method"

Robert Gagne, father of the 1960s curriculum strategy Instructional Systems Design (ISD), was one of the first in the education community to advocate the use of sequential lesson plans—an approach that calls for breaking down each lesson into individual teaching components.[9] A behaviorist, Gagne felt that such a series of stimuli—teaching components or events—when taught sequentially, would result in respective student responses or learning moments. To this end, Gagne identified five distinct types of learning that go on in the classroom: verbal information, intellectual skills, cognitive strategies, attitudes, and motor skills.[10]

To achieve these various types of student learning, Gagne developed a framework that included nine instructional steps or events that he felt were requisite for any lesson plan.[11] Teachers should begin the lesson by introducing the focus or topic in an engaging manner that captures *student attention* (i.e., through use of powerful video or audio clips or *Flash* presentations). This is followed by an overview or discussion of the goals and *teaching objectives* of the lesson with the students. The third preinstructional step of the behavioral method is a review of *prior learning* knowledge and student experiences that are related to the focus of the lesson. Next is the formal *presentation* step,

Table 8.2

Gagne's Behavioral Method Syntax

Teaching step	Central components
Student attention	Introduce the topic in a manner that gains the students attention.
Teaching objectives	Inform students of the goals and objectives for the lesson.
Prior learning	Review prior student knowledge and experiences that are germane to the lesson.
Presentation	Present the lesson by introducing a series of learning prompts or stimuli.
Coaching	Guide students through the learning process through use of questions and reinforcement.
Student performance	Provide an opportunity for classroom student performance to demonstrate understanding.
Provide feedback	Develop and implement a means for assessing student performance to offer formative feedback and reinforcement.
Testing	Develop an assessment device that will be used in the summative evaluation process.
Enhance retention and transfer	Provide a final review and introduce an example of an authentic application of learning concepts discussed in the lesson.

which calls for more formal, teacher-centered instruction (e.g., *PowerPoint* presentation, online module, lecture). The next component or step in the lesson planning process is to incorporate a *coaching* activity or session that helps to check for student understanding (e.g., *Hot Potatoes* quiz, question and answer session, timed *PowerPoint* or *Flash* Question and Answer session). In addition to the coaching activity, Gagne also calls for teachers to include a means for assessing students and *providing formative feedback* to help shape their classroom performance. This step is followed by yet another assessment activity, however this time the *testing* is more formal and serves a summative evaluation purpose. The lesson concludes with a final review and authentic application activity that allows for *enhanced retention and transfer* of student knowledge and understanding.

Table 8.3

Bloom's Mastery Learning Syntax

Teaching step	Central components
Knowledge	Engage students in a learning activity that allows them to recognize or recall information.
Comprehension	Engage students in a learning activity that allows them to demonstrate an ability to translate, interpret, or manipulate material.
Application	Engage students in a learning activity that allows them to apply previously learned material to other contexts or situations.
Analysis	Engage students in a learning activity that allows them to think critically, breaking down material into component parts.
Synthesis	Engage students in a learning activity that allows them to think creatively, reassembling knowledge to form a new whole.
Evaluation	Engage students in a learning activity that allows them to offer an informed opinion on or judge the value of material for a given purpose.

Bloom's "Mastery Learning"

In 1948, Benjamin Bloom and his colleagues embarked upon a project that would change the face of American education. Shortly after the annual American Psychological Association convention that year, Bloom began work on identifying and classifying "the goals of the educational process."[12] The result of their efforts was the development of three hierarchical domains that were to be used for the formulation of educational objectives—the cognitive, affective, and psychomotor domains. Although all of these domains are germane to history education, classroom teachers found the cognitive domain to have the greatest utility in their curriculum planning. The cognitive domain hierarchy, which became known as Bloom's taxonomy, includes six levels in its classification of intellectual abilities and skills: knowledge, comprehension, application, analysis, synthesis, and evaluation.[13]

Today, Bloom's taxonomy serves not only as a guide for teachers in the development of learning objectives, but also as a curriculum design framework. One of the most popular sequential lesson plan frameworks in middle school and high school is what is often referred to as Bloom's mastery learning model. Teachers have translated each level of Bloom's taxonomy into a six-step lesson plan model that begins with the lowest end of the cognitive hierarchy, knowledge, and works its way up to the higher order thinking levels. Teachers should begin their lesson with a basic *knowledge* level activity that may include more traditional components—such as lecture, concept mapping, or outlining—that help to build the conceptual foundation for subsequent learning steps. Next, teachers should engage students in a learning activity that provides an opportunity for individual interpretation or translation (e.g., document or event summary, restatement of historical accounts) to help check for *comprehension*. Once these basic levels of understanding have been established, students should be engaged in a learning activity that calls for them to *apply* their newfound knowledge to another situation or context (e.g., Cognitive WebQuest, online scavenger hunt). Next, students are encouraged to engage in an *analysis* or critical thinking activity that demands they break down material into component parts (e.g., document-based questions, primary and/or secondary document analysis). Teachers should then design a *synthesis* activity that allows students to reassemble knowledge to form a new whole (e.g., student developed Web page, *PowerPoint*, or *HyperStudio* presentation). Bloom's mastery learning lesson concludes with an *evaluation* activity that calls for students to offer an informed opinion or judgment on a historical individual, event, or movement (online decision-making scenario, affective WebQuest).

Hunter's "Mastery Learning"

Madeline Hunter received national attention in the 1960s as the principal of University Elementary School (UES) in Los Angeles. With the assistance of Professor John Goodlad of UCLA, Hunter led a crusade to renew her lab school's curriculum.[14] Within a few years, Hunter's new educational approach, which became known as direct instruction, was reaping tremendous rewards, in the form of increased student achievement. It wasn't long before Hunter began touring the country touting the merits of her direct instruction, or what later became known as mastery learning approach.[15] Hunter's original curricular framework contained four essential elements: teaching to the objectives, teaching at the appropriate level of difficulty, monitoring and adjusting instruction as needed, and using recognized principles

Table 8.4

Hunter's Mastery Learning Syntax

Teaching step	Central components
Anticipatory set	Introduce the lesson through student engagement in a brief activity or prompt.
Purpose	Inform students of the lesson objectives and purpose.
Input	Provide instruction that addresses key knowledge, concepts, processes, and skills.
Modeling	Model ideal behavior to demonstrate learning exemplars.
Check for comprehension	Check for student understanding through use of a variety of questioning strategies.
Guided practice	Provide an opportunity for guided student practice of new learning.
Independent practice	Provide an opportunity for independent student practice to verify understanding.
Closure	Review or wrap-up current lesson and provide a segue or tie-in to the next.

of learning.[16] Over time, however, Madeline Hunter's research and curriculum theories would take on a life of their own.

By the late 1980s, Hunter's original direct instruction approach was transformed into an eight step—the last step, however, is often omitted in the seven step design—lesson-planning framework. Although Hunter, as well as some others, found a certain degree of fault in the way her original approach had been resurrected, teachers and administers quickly took the new mastery learning framework to heart; making it the most popularly used lesson plan design framework of the late twentieth century.[17] Despite certain abuses of Hunter's mastery learning approach, it remains an extremely popular framework in the twenty-first century. The first step in the model, *establish set*, calls for teachers to introduce the lesson in an engaging manner to help provide a conceptual hook that captures students' attention (i.e., through use of powerful video or audio clips or *Flash* presentations). Teachers should then inform the students of the lesson *purpose and objectives*, in an attempt to provide learners with a conceptual roadmap for the lesson (i.e., discussion, *PowerPoint* slide, whiteboard listing). These two pre-instructional activities help to set the stage for the next step, *input*, in which the teacher provides instruction over the key knowledge, concepts, processes, and skills germane to the lesson (e.g., *PowerPoint* presentation, online module, lecture). In addition to providing teacher-centered instruction, Hunter's mastery learning model also calls for teachers to *model ideal behavior* (e.g., photograph or cartoon analysis, document interpretation) for students. Teachers should also allow time for an activity that helps to *check for student comprehension* (e.g., question and answer session, timed *PowerPoint* or *Flash* Question and Answer session). The next two steps, *guided practice* and *independent practice* involve the engagement of students in learning activities (e.g., online decision making scenario, virtual field trip, cognitive and affective WebQuests, document analysis, reading critiques) that are first supervised or facilitated by the classroom teacher and then completed by students on their own (i.e., homework). The lesson concludes with a review or wrap-up activity or session that serves as *closure* for that day's lesson as well as a conceptual springboard for the next.

Karplus and Thier's "5-E Learning Cycle"

In 1967, Robert Karplus and Herbert Thier introduced their 5-E learning cycle model to the science education community.[18] Later modified by Rodger Bybee for the Biological Science Curriculum Study (BSCS) program, this new constructivist model for curriculum planning, which became known simply as 5-E, spread from science to other core curriculum disciplines to include history.[19] Although numerous variations of the 5-E approach have surfaced over the past few decades, to include a 3-E, 4-E, and 7-E version, the basic philosophical and curricular premise has remained true—that students experience phenomena in a similar manner when attempting to learn a concept.[20]

The most popular learning cycle model today remains the original 5-E approach first designed by Karplus and Thier nearly forty years ago. In keeping with the constructivist paradigm, teachers who implement the 5-E lesson plan approach in the classroom foster the development of student understanding of new concepts through a series of activities that allow students to learn in an engaging and experiential

Table 8.5

Karplus and Thier's 5-E Learning Cycle Syntax

Teaching step	Central components
Engagement	Introduce the focus of the lesson by engaging students in a learning task that also connects previous learning.
Exploration	Provide students with an opportunity for guided exploration of relevant data and materials.
Explanation	Provide instruction that explains key information, concepts, processes, and skills.
Elaboration	Accord students an opportunity to apply their knowledge and abstract experience to authentic situations.
Evaluation	Implement formal and/or informal assessment strategies to evaluate student understanding of lesson concepts and knowledge.

manner.[21] Every 5-E lesson begins with an *engagement* activity that provides both a focus for the lesson and a connection with previous student learning, all in as engaging a manner as possible to pique students' interest (i.e., through use of powerful video or audio clips or *Flash* presentations). Once teachers have captured their students' attention and have instructed them on the lesson focus, they should accord them an opportunity to *explore* historical documents and data in a lab-like, hands-on environment (e.g., document analysis, multimedia scrapbook analysis, cognitive WebQuest, virtual field trip). Following the guided exploration session, the 5-E model calls for a more traditional *explanation* activity that introduces key historical individuals, events, issues, movements, and developments germane to the lesson focus (e.g., *PowerPoint* presentation, online module, lecture). The next step, the *elaboration* stage, requires teachers to design an activity that calls for students to apply their newfound knowledge to another situation or context (e.g., affective WebQuest, online scavenger hunt, decision-making scenario). The 5-E lesson concludes with a formal or informal assessment activity designed to *evaluate* student understanding and/or proficiency (e.g., *Hot Potatoes* quiz, question and answer session, timed *PowerPoint* or *Flash* Question and Answer session, document-based question).

Table 8.6

Oliver and Shaver's Jurisprudential Inquiry Syntax

Teaching step	Central components
Orientation phase	
Orientation to the case	Provide instruction that orients students to the controversy/case and introduces relevant concepts, facts, and materials.
Identify the issues	Accord students an opportunity to synthesize facts into public issues and identify values and questions.
Position formulation	
Take a position	Allow students to take a position on the case/controversy and outline their rationale.
Explore underlying beliefs	Provide a means for students to examine their position by identifying the embedded values and establishing priorities.
Refine and qualify position	Provide a forum for students to restate/clarify their position and apply it to similar situations.
Authentic application	
Test the assumptions	Allow students to determine predicted consequences of their position through an authentic application activity.

Oliver and Shaver's "Jurisprudential Inquiry"

More than thirty years ago, social studies education researchers Donald Oliver and James Shaver developed an approach to teaching that allows students to think systematically about contemporary issues.[22] A replica of the judicial process, the jurisprudential inquiry approach, as it was named, lets students explore controversial issues in much the same way as participants in a trial are introduced to and must evaluate or weigh evidence that is admitted. While Oliver and Shaver's teaching approach predates the performance assessment movement in American education, it serves today as a model for performance-based instruction, with its emphasis on both process and product. In addition, many also consider the jurisprudential inquiry approach to be a model for citizenship education today.

Although originally designed for use in middle school and high school social studies classrooms, the jurisprudential inquiry model has found an educational niche in almost every core discipline classroom. For the history classroom, the jurisprudential inquiry approach is perhaps best suited for engaging students in discussions and investigations regarding historic court cases and presidential decisions.[23] The jurisprudential inquiry lesson contains three distinct phases: orientation phase, position formulation, and authentic application. The first phase of the lesson, the orientation phase, contains two steps. First, teachers should provide instruction that *orients student to the case*, presidential decision, or controversial issue (e.g., *PowerPoint* presentation, online module, lecture). The second step in the orientation phase involves the *identification of the issues*, in which students are engaged in an activity that calls for them to synthesize facts into public issues, as well as identify relevant values and questions. The next stage of jurisprudential inquiry is position formulation. This phase includes three steps: *take a position*, *explore underlying beliefs*, and *refine and qualify position*. In these three steps, teachers should design multiple learning activities that guide students through this process, which includes not only taking a position, but also developing a rationale, evaluating the embedded values of the position, and engaging in an activity that demands the restatement or clarification of their original position in face of new information or contexts. The final phase of the jurisprudential inquiry model, authentic application, includes one final step—*test the assumption*. For this step, teachers should develop a divergent thinking activity that allows students to determine the predicted outcome or consequences of their position, within the context of an authentic situation.

Cantu's "Educate Method"

In 2001, social studies education researcher D. Antonio Cantu developed a new curricular and instructional approach for teaching middle school history, using technology and the Internet. The approach, which became known as the Educate method, serves as an ideal introductory lesson plan framework for teaching history, while at the same time introducing students to historical online research and basic computer and Web design skills. In keeping with the constructivist tradition, the Educate method first orients students to the requisite

Table 8.7

Cantu's Educate Model Syntax

Teaching step	Central components
Stimulate	Introduce the online learning module and scenario in an engaging and stimulating manner that serves as a conceptual hook.
Navigate	Orient students to the learning environment that will be used to navigate the Internet for research purposes.
Locate	Integrate multiple opportunities for students to utilize search and metasearch engines to conduct their research.
Evaluate	Define for students the assessment criteria that will be used to evaluate online resources and require its use throughout.
Collate	Introduce and model for students the protocol for collecting, storing, and indexing data obtained during their research.
Demonstrate	Identify the format that students will use to display their research data and findings.
Communicate	Systematically allow students to reflect upon and evaluate their learning experience.

knowledge and skills needed to conduct historical research and design digital display formats, followed by an extended opportunity for hands-on student experiences, which allow learners to apply these new or refined skills in the course of completing authentic learning activities. Although originally developed for the middle school classroom, the model has been successfully modified for use at the high school level as well.

While designed specifically for a digital environment, the Educate model also contains a number of traditional learning components indigenous to other history and social studies curricular approaches, making it ideally suited for integration in other lesson plan frameworks as well. Although it can be modified to fit teacher needs, the ideal Educate model lesson includes seven steps. First, teachers need to *stimulate* student interest in the lesson scenario or focus (i.e., through use of powerful video or audio clips or *Flash* presentations). Next, it is necessary to orient students to the physical and virtual learning environments in which the research will take place, in order to equip students with the skills necessary to *navigate* online. Once students feel comfortable navigating in that environment, they need to be instructed in the use of search and metasearch engines needed to identify and *locate* online resources. The fourth step of the Educate model requires students to utilize specific criteria, such as the CARS method, discussed further in chapter 16, to *evaluate* online resources they encounter in the research process. While the first four steps of the Educate model address process, the final three stages involve the design and development of the student product. In the *collate* phase of the lesson, students are introduced to the protocol for collecting, storing, and indexing historical data they encounter during the earlier research steps. Next, students must display their research data and findings in one of a variety of digital formats (e.g., *PowerPoint, HyperStudio,* or *Flash* presentation, Web page, hypertext or PDF report) to *demonstrate* proficiency. Finally, the Educate model concludes with an activity designed to provide students with a means to *communicate* or reflect upon their learning experience (e.g., discussion boards, e-mail messages, chat rooms, online interactive critique forms).

Conclusion

Nearly a century ago, John Dewey observed that the "core of the process of teaching is the arrangement of environments within which the students can interact."[24] This is perhaps even truer today in this information age—where an environment can now be real or virtual—than it was a century ago. Technology and the Internet are indeed dual-edged swords for history educators. Although these innovations and advances can positively impact classroom teaching efficacy, they also present teachers with myriad problems and dilemmas never even imagined a generation ago. The need, therefore, for middle school and high school history teachers to enter the profession armed with a plethora of a priori curricular and instructional frameworks in their pedagogical repertoire is greater now than ever. Such frameworks are, according to Lawrence Stenhouse, mere proposals for experimentation:

> The idea is that an educational science in which each classroom is a laboratory, each teacher a member of the scientific community. . . . The crucial point is that the proposal is not to be regarded as an unqualified recommendation but rather as a provisional specification claiming no

more than to be worth putting to the test of practice. Such proposals claim to be intelligent rather than correct.[25]

These seven frameworks should therefore be viewed not as educational panaceas, but as intelligent approaches to teaching history in classrooms that foster both student and teacher experimentation.

Chapter 9

Brain-Based Lesson Plan Frameworks

Minds are like parachutes.
They only function when open.
—Author Unknown

For many experienced middle school and high school history teachers their original conception of teaching and learning has undergone a tremendous evolution. One of the most common observations teachers make after their first year in the classroom is that they never truly realized how complex students were and just how many different ways teachers can achieve the same learning goals or objectives. Brain-based lesson plan frameworks attempt to address these concerns by providing teachers with models for integrating both resources and learning activities in a way that addresses the multiple dimensions of student cognition and learning, in an attempt to truly engage all learners in a productive and meaningful manner. Two brain-based lesson plan frameworks in particular appear to hold the most promise for history teachers who seek to fully integrate primary sources and technology in their classroom teaching—Multiple Intelligences and Left- and Right-Brain 4MAT. An overview of these two brain-based approaches serves as the focus for this chapter.

Multiple Intelligences Lesson Plan Framework

In 1983 Howard Gardner, a Harvard University professor, introduced his theory of "multiple intelligences." Nearly two decades later, his original book, *Frames of Mind: The Theory of Multiple Intelligences*, has been translated into twenty languages and countless "Multiple Intelligences (MI) schools" have been established throughout the United States.[1] Since that time, Gardner's original list of seven distinct forms of intelligence has grown to eight.

Today, Gardner's theory serves as one of the most effective curricular and instructional frameworks for classroom teachers to use in designing their lesson plans. While even the most ardent supporters of MI would never claim this framework is a curricular or instructional panacea, Gardner's theory certainly provides one approach that at least attempts to address the multiple ways of learning and understanding that our students bring with them to the history classroom.[2]

Perhaps what is most surprising is that Gardner's initial intent was, in his words, "[to attack] the standard notion of intelligence as a single capacity with which an individual is born, and which proves difficult, if not impossible, to alter. In the place of this construct, I offered a more pluralistic cognitive universe."[3] The result, however, was "a revolution of sorts in classrooms around the world."[4] Gardner expected to "stir controversy among my fellow psychologists," which did occur, yet he was taken aback by the "largely and mostly positive reaction" to his theory by educators.[5]

As we enter this new millennium, high school history teachers struggle to keep pace with all of the demands placed upon them. The educational pendulum continues to swing back and forth, with educators patiently waiting to see what course they are expected to take. One of the appealing elements of the MI framework is that it allows teachers to teach in a manner that does not ask them to sacrifice verbal and analytical skills for, what some might term, more affective or nontraditional forms of intelligence.[6] Instead, it provides a model for educators to provide students with a deeper understanding, which Gardner defines as "a sufficient grasp of concepts, principles, or skills so that you can bring them to bear on new problems and situations."[7]

The multiple intelligences framework seems ideal for history teachers who already provide students learning opportunities that involve maps, documents, political cartoons, broadsides, video and audio clips, and other forms of primary and secondary resources. In addition, computer technology and the Internet seem only to enhance the opportunity to combine these resources into comprehensive multiple intelligences lesson plans that can potentially address each of the eight student capacities for learning.[8] Gardner even refers to this marriage between technology and his MI theory as a "comfortable fit."[9]

History of Multiple Intelligences

Howard Gardner's theory of multiple intelligences resulted from his work with brain-damaged patients in a Boston area hospital.[10] Over the years, he discovered that the brain appeared to possess several distinct abilities or intelligences. Eventually, he created a list of criteria in which to judge what constituted each of the types of intelligences he was attempting to identify. Gardner's eight criteria for determining what constitutes intelligence are:

- potential isolation by brain damage
- existence of idiot savant, prodigies, and other exceptional individuals
- an identifiable core set of operations, basic kinds of information-processing operations, or mechanisms that deal with one specific kind of input
- a distinctive developmental history, along with a definite set of "end-state" performances
- an evolutionary history and evolutionary plausibility
- support from experimental and psychological tasks
- support from psychometric findings
- susceptibility to encoding from a symbol system[11]

By the early 1980s, Gardner had identified seven intelligences that met his criteria. He unveiled his seven intelligences to the academic community in his 1983 book *Frames of Mind: The Theory of Multiple Intelligences*. While he was prepared for the criticism his fellow psychologists would launch at him, he was quite surprised at the interest and warm reception it received from educators throughout the world.[12] By 1984, following his presentation at a New York education conference aptly named "The Coming Education Explosion," nearly all education practitioners and researchers throughout the United States were familiar with the MI theory and each of the seven intelligences outlined by its author.[13]

The 1980s witnessed the proliferation MI programs (e.g., Indianapolis's Key School, Saint Louis's New City School), and the publication of countless articles and books on the topic.[14] The director of the New City School best describes the impact Gardner's theory had on education:

> Sure, Copernicus and Columbus caused paradigm shifts; so, too, did Charles Darwin, Harriet Beecher Stowe, and Rachel Carson. Our thinking remains altered by their insights. But, much of what we termed paradigm shifts really were not shifts in paradigms at all. At best they were new treatments of familiar theories and practices. That is no less true in education. Rarely does an insight have the potential to change how we view students, teach, assess, and communicate with their parents. The theory of multiple intelligences (MI), however, does just that. . . . MI theory is a paradigm shift because it changes the way we look at students and their potentials. As a result, we view our roles and responsibilities quite differently.[15]

The impact of the revolution launched in 1983 by Gardner, intentionally or not, is still felt today. Every year more schools are added to the growing list of MI schools and hundreds of studies, articles, and books continue to mark the educational landscape. Case in point of the continued popularity of Gardner's MI theory include the tenth anniversary publication of his *Frames of Mind* and the addition of an eighth intelligence or way of knowing—*naturalist intelligence*.[16] Through it all, Gardner has remained loyal to his original premise that MI is "not for the faint-hearted, nor for those in search of a quick fix."[17] Instead, it represents a model that places student understanding at the forefront of educational reform. Even Gardner will admit this sounds simplistic; he goes on to explain however, that "nearly every teacher I know—myself included—would claim to teach for understanding. In practice, it's really quite difficult, though. . . . Curiously, this failure is not so much deliberate as unwitting. Knowing how kids learn is key."[18] That is what the MI model provides middle and high school history teachers, a model that provides for deeper student understanding.

Table 9.1

Summary of Gardner's Eight Intelligences

Form of intelligence	Central components
Logical/Mathematical	Discern logical or numerical patterns; deductive reasoning
Verbal/Linguistic	Use written and spoken language to express complex meaning
Visual/Spatial	Perceive the visual world accurately; create mental images
Musical/Rhythmic	Produce and appreciate forms of musical expressiveness
Body/Kinesthetic	Control body movements and handle items skillfully
Naturalist	Recognize patterns and distinctions in the natural world
Interpersonal	Understand others; discern verbal and nonverbal cues
Intrapersonal	Understand oneself; engage in self-reflection and meta-cognition

Sources: Campbell et al. (1996); Mjagkij and Cantu (1999).

Gardner's Multiple Intelligences Theory

Gardner defines *intelligence* as the "capacity to solve problems or to fashion products that are valued in one or more cultural settings."[19] As mentioned previously, Gardner's MI theory includes eight distinct intelligences or ways of learning (defined in Table 9.1). His theory of intelligence went well beyond the traditional focus on logical-mathematical and linguistic intelligence, which all too often is the sole focus of standardized tests and classroom instruction.[20] Perhaps the goal of the multiple intelligences model is best summed up by Sue Teele of the University of California, Riverside:

> The theory of multiple intelligences provides different windows into the same room. We need to unleash the creative potential in all our schools to open as many windows as possible for every student to succeed. We must move forward together in a way that builds on our mutual strengths and respects our unique differences.[21]

Just as there are certain characteristics germane to each of the eight intelligences identified by Gardner, so too are there specific teaching

Table 9.2

Multiple Intelligences Instructional Strategies

Form of intelligence	Teaching activities
Logical/Mathematical	Problem solving, investigation, experimentation, questioning
Verbal/Linguistic	Discussion, narration, advanced organizers, writing activities
Visual/Spatial	Imagery, map analysis, observation activities, construction of dioramas or posters
Musical/Rhythmic	Simulations, song analysis, creative song writing, performances
Body/Kinesthetic	Simulations, modeling, role playing, analyzing manipulatives
Naturalist	Recognize and classify cultural and natural artifacts, data gathering in natural setting
Interpersonal	Cooperative learning, peer teaching, brainstorming, shared inquiry
Intrapersonal	Decision making, journal writing, self-discovery, independent learning projects

Sources: Chapman (1993); Meyer (1997); Weber (1996).

strategies that address each of these student ways of learning (see Table 9.2). The introduction of MI activities into the classrooms of history teachers, however, must be accompanied with a change in how educators view student thinking. The following quote by a former high school English teacher, reflecting on his classroom experience, illustrates this point:

> If a teacher who lectures incessantly suddenly starts assigning journals, the introduction of journals into students' meaning-making repertoire will likely change very little else about the class unless the teacher makes an effort to make wholesale changes in the overriding conceptions of classroom process that govern life for teacher and students.[22]

Internet-Based Multiple Intelligences Model

The Internet and World Wide Web provide both an ideal resource and platform for MI lesson plans. Middle and high school history teachers may now design lesson plans that incorporate Internet based materials into their MI lessons. In addition, many of the classroom activities they produce may be placed on the Internet for student use. Both of these innovations enhance multiple intelligences lesson plans in a manner never imagined. Even Gardner believed the potential impact of computer technology would not be felt until 2013.[23] The pedagogical impact of the Internet and World Wide Web is being experienced now, however, and the role they play in providing for deeper student understanding through MI teaching can also be realized today.

How do middle and high school teachers combine the potential of the Internet with the promise of the MI model? What rationale is there for implementing such a model? One necessary prerequisite for implementing this model is an understanding of both the MI model and the potential the Internet and World Wide Web hold for such a curricular design. Many of the activities which teachers might incorporate into Internet-based MI lessons are outlined in Table 9.3. While the key to implementation of this model is providing teachers with the necessary information and resources, it is just as important to recognize the incredible amount of time and sacrifice necessary to implement this model. Perhaps the key to the success of the MI model lies in the fact that it is not a prescriptive model, but instead an approach to teaching and learning that allows for individual interpretation, design, and implementation.

The Internet and World Wide Web present teachers with an entirely different dimension for implementing the MI model in their classroom. As mentioned previously, the Internet provides not only an invaluable resource for MI classroom activities, it also serves as an excellent pedagogical platform for launching such lessons.[24] Many of the resources on the World Wide Web, which can be introduced into MI history lessons, are outlined in Table 9.4. In addition to these resources, teachers may also use the following Internet instructional tools to address each of the eight student ways of learning:

- *E-mail.* Students and teachers can use e-mail to share multimedia and textual data relevant to MI activities they are working on. Not only can this enhance interpersonal activities, providing another dimension, but it also can be used for teacher-student communication concerning intrapersonal and verbal/linguistic products such as essays or journal entries.
- *Chat rooms.* Class chat rooms can be ideal means for sharing information or checking on the progress of classroom MI projects. While this

Table 9.3

Internet-Based Multiple Intelligences Activities

Form of intelligence	Teaching activities
Logical/Mathematical	Analyze statistical historical data, create graphic representations of historical data, create hyperlinked timeline
Verbal/Linguistic	Compose essays, poetry, etc. for publishing on Web page, critique written resources through an annotated bibliography (hypertext)
Visual/Spatial	Construct thematic Web pages that include various visual images (e.g., posters, political cartoons, broadsides, photos, illustrations), construct hyperlinked timelines and maps
Musical/Rhythmic	Analysis of song lyrics, composition of song lyrics, design and publish *PowerPoint* presentations which incorporate music and visual elements
Body/Kinesthetic	Internet based simulations, cooperative Web searches or WebQuests, role playing activities that incorporate Web resources, classroom presentations
Naturalist	Design virtual landscapes, analyze computer simulated topographic battlefields, cities, maps, etc.
Interpersonal	All of the above activities that might be designed to incorporate cooperative learning groups
Intrapersonal	All of the above activities that might be completed through reflective individual projects

Sources: Bergman (1995); Melton and Pickett (1997); Lazear (1991); Soares (1998).

is an especially useful tool for addressing interpersonal learning needs, it can be used to assist with activities representative of each of the seven other intelligences.

- *Individual Web sites.* Designing and publishing individual Web sites to showcase student projects from activities representing each of the eight intelligences is another ideal pedagogical tool for implementing the MI model. In addition to textual data, graphics, images, and audio and video clips, students can include hypermedia and hypertext links to other resources on the World Wide Web on their individual Web pages.
- *Class Web sites.* Teachers may choose to synthesize student products into a course or class Web page. In addition to providing a means for comparison, these Web sites also serve as excellent examples for future classes attempting to complete MI activities.[25]

Table 9.4

World Wide Web Multiple Intelligences Resources

Form of intelligence	Teaching resources
Logical/Mathematical	Charts, diagrams, government reports, statistical demographic and population data
Verbal/Linguistic	Diary entries, government documents, personal narratives, historical documents, letters
Visual/Spatial	Maps, diagrams, illustrations, battlefield representations, historical timelines
Musical/Rhythmic	Lyrics or audio files of patriotic, protest, period and other historical music
Body/Kinesthetic	Illustrations and descriptions of historical costumes, cooking, dance, etc. for role playing or simulation
Naturalist	Illustrations, paintings, maps, personal narratives and photographs of historical and contemporary environments
Interpersonal	All of the above resources that might be used in cooperative multiple intelligences activities
Intrapersonal	All of the above resources that might be used in reflective, individual multiple intelligences activities

Sources: Lazear (1991, 1992); Gutloff (1996).

Implications for History Education

Howard Gardner has often used history to illustrate the potential of his model, remarking that there "is no reason why everyone has to learn history. . . . in the same way."[26] Gardner frequently uses the study of the American Revolution to illustrate the MI approach to history education:

> All of us have studied the American Revolution, for example. And some of us have studied it several times. But we almost always study it from the point of view of U.S. history: The Tories are bad, the colonists are good, and in the end goodness triumphs. Read about the American Revolution from the British perspective, though, and things appear quite different: The American Revolution isn't a revolution, it's a rebellion—a revolt of those dastardly colonists. . . . In other words, if

you approach a topic from different perspectives, you get a much richer view about what the American Revolution, or Yankee Uprising, was really like.[27]

Three benefits result from this type of MI teaching strategy.[28] First, because not all students learn in the same way, teachers are able to meet the needs of more students in their class. Second, the students realize that historians, teachers, and students view history from a variety of perspectives and they learn more about how to evaluate and analyze historical evidence. Finally, the MI model allows for students to demonstrate understanding in a variety of ways, to include individual Web pages, Internet annotated bibliographies, hyperlinked maps or timelines, and student generated *PowerPoint* presentations and Internet links pages.[29]

Already, there are thematic and constructivist adaptations of this model available for middle and high school history teachers to use as further examples for their classroom use.[30] While there are no guarantees provided with any curricular or instructional model, the Internet-based MI model represents an approach that seems ideally designed for those teachers desiring to provide content driven, thematic, powerful, and meaningful history education for their students.[31] Certainly, no other model attempts to address all eight intelligences. Nor does any model take as comprehensive an approach to utilizing the Internet and World Wide Web. Still, many questions regarding the impact of the MI model on standardized test scores remain unanswered, with far too few longitudinal studies having been conducted on this topic to inform classroom teachers.[32]

Although much research remains to be done, the promise of marrying technology with the MI model is still one that can be realized today, nearly a decade before MI founder Howard Gardner's original 2013 forecast.[33] The Internet-based MI model, however, is just that, a model. It is designed to give middle and high school educators the flexibility to adapt it for use in their classroom to meet individual needs. Such a model serves as a "bare-bones framework for interaction, a skeleton to be fleshed out by individual school communities at their own pace, in their own time, using their own resources."[34] Teachers hold the key to unlocking student understanding. This model simply provides history teachers and students with one of two powerful brain-based means for achieving that goal, with the left- and right-brain 4MAT approach serving as the other.

Left- and Right-Brain 4MAT Lesson Plan Framework

> For almost a century, students of education have suffered under the yoke of the behavioral psychologists, who see learning as synonymous with a *change of behavior*. We reject this view, and observe instead that learning by humans leads to a *change in the meaning of experience*. . . . How can we help individuals to reflect upon their experience and to construct new, more powerful meanings?[35]

Although Joseph D. Novak and D. Bob Gowin first posited their distinction in how educators should perceive of learning two decades ago, it is even more valid at the dawn of this new century than it was at the close of the previous one. With the increasing number of technology literate and Internet savvy students in schools, referred to by some educational demographers as the I-Generation, the need for digital curricular and instructional frameworks is greater today than ever. In a recent interview, Jane M. Healy, author of *Failure to Connect: How Computers Affect Our Children's Minds—for Better or Worse*, outlined the potential benefits and shortfalls associated with the integration of computer technology in the classroom:

> I am intrigued by the possibilities of technology not only for teaching and learning but also for learning about the learning process. How can we plug in more effectively to kids who are at different stages of development and who experience learning in different ways? I am interested in applications that reach for that goal and don't simply recapitulate the old educational models. We haven't found a way yet— and I doubt whether we ever will—to let machine technology replace human technology in the education process. But through research, we may eventually combine human and machine technologies to discover why children are or are not learning certain things and to present information in a wide variety of modalities.[36]

The impact of computer technology and the Internet on education is no longer a topic of conjecture and speculation. The most recent set of U.S. Department of Education data on the integration of technology and the Internet, for example, shows that nearly 90 percent of schools have the ability to support online initiatives.[37] Other data on the proliferation of computers in the classroom, as well as computer and Internet access in student homes, serve to illustrate the increas-

Table 9.5

Left-and Right-Brain Characteristics

Left brain	Right brain
Verbal	Visual
Sequential/linear	Holistic/simultaneous
Logical/mathematical	Artistic/musical
Reasoning/cognitive	Emotional/affective
Analytical	Creative

ingly important role such technology plays in society and schools. The question, therefore, is not whether computer technology and the Internet will play a role in twenty-first century education, but how extensive its impact is today on student learning. A critical factor in the integration of technology and the Internet into middle and high school history classrooms is the curricular and instructional approach teachers use to achieve such integration. One framework that seems ideal for such integration is the left- and right-brain 4MAT teaching model.

Left- and Right-Brain Learning Modalities

In 1980, Bernice McCarthy, a former classroom teacher, developed an open-ended, holistic teaching model that took into consideration individual learning styles, in particular those characteristics associated with right- and left-hemisphere dominance. This pedagogical framework became known as the left- and right-brain 4MAT teaching model. The purpose of the model, according to McCarthy, was simply to "raise teacher awareness as to why some things work with some learners and other things do not."[38] One way for teachers to attend to the needs of left- and right-brain learners is to develop lessons that sequentially incorporate multiple activities that call on students to utilize both left- and right-brain learning modalities. Characteristics associated with left- and right-brain learners are listed in Table 9.5.

Table 9.6

Left- and Right-Brain 4MAT Instructional Sequence

Left brain	Right brain
Experiencing	
Examine	Connect
Reflect, analyze experience	Engage in experience
Conceptualizing	
Define	Image
Learn concepts and skills	Imagine or "picture" the concept
Applying	
Try	Extend
Practice with content	Apply to more complex experience
Creating	
Refine	Integrate
Analyze application for relevance, usefulness	Share and celebrate learning

4MAT Curricular Framework

Even though the issue of left- and right-hemisphere dominance still remains the subject of debate in the psychology community, the left- and right-brain 4MAT approach has been well received by educators. It seems especially well suited for the teaching of middle and high school history, given its sequential and multidimensional approach to learning. In particular, it provides students with opportunities to build upon previous learning, engage in critical analysis and decision making, develop historical empathy, and gain a deeper understanding of those events and issues that have shaped our nation's history. The instructional sequence/learning cycle associated with the 4MAT model is outlined in Table 9.6.

Left- and Right-Brain Teaching Approach

A number of topics and themes addressed in middle and high school history courses provide teachers with a plethora of ideal primary and

---

Table 9.7

Primary and Secondary Resources for Left- and Right-Brain 4MAT Curricula

Left brain	Right brain
Speeches	Posters and broadsides
Memos and letters	Songs
Newspaper headlines and articles	Historical artifacts
Political party platforms	Political cartoons
Supreme Court decisions	Photographs
Statistical data	Historical vignette
Literary works	Newsreel/video clips
Historical timeline	Maps
Government documents	Radio/audio recordings

---

secondary resources for classroom use. The left- and right-brain 4MAT curricular and instructional model also allows teachers to categorize these materials in accordance with the specific learning needs they address. Examples of some of the primary and secondary resources teachers might integrate into their curricula are listed in Table 9.7.

Just as there are multiple resources for teaching middle and high school history, so, too, are there myriad products that can result from student interaction with these materials. Once again, the left- and right-brain 4MAT curricular model provides history teachers with an excellent framework for classifying these students' activities and products. Some of the student activities and products that can be included in a middle or high school history teacher's instructional repertoire include those listed in Table 9.8.

Technology and Internet Integration

The Internet and World Wide Web provide both an ideal resource and platform for left- and right-brain 4MAT lesson plans. Middle and high

Table 9.8

Student Activities and Products

Left brain	Right brain
Research paper	Readers theater project
Essay	Political cartoon
Speech	Poster or broadside
Annotated bibliography	Web page
Book review	Film critique
Newspaper account/story	Fictional newscast
Crossword puzzle/quiz	Graphic organizer
Fictional diary entry/letter	Song
Timeline	Poem

school history teachers may now design lesson plans that incorporate Web-based materials into their 4MAT lessons. In addition, many of the classroom activities they produce may be placed on the Internet for student use. All of these innovations enhance 4MAT lesson plans in a manner never imagined. Table 9.9 outlines some of the Web-based activities and student products that teachers can integrate into their 4MAT lessons.

Conclusion

The digital age that ushers in the twenty-first century provides social studies educators with a unique opportunity to venture down roads never traveled before by teachers in the history of education. Teachers, however, must be willing to take the first step in this process; without their leadership, the use of computer technology and the Internet in education will continue to lag far behind other sectors of society, such as government, business, military, and the legal and medical professions. Therefore, teacher understanding of the role of technology in social studies education is absolutely critical. Chris Dede reminds teachers of the mistakes we have made over the past decade, which

Table 9.9

Web-Based Activities and Products

Left brain	Right brain
Analyze statistical historical data; create graphic representations of historical data	Construct thematic Web pages that include various visual images (e.g., posters, political cartoons, broadsides, photos, illustrations)
Create hyperlinked timelines and maps	Design virtual landscapes, analyze computer simulated topographic battlefields, cities, maps, etc.
Write and publish hypertext essays and papers on the Web; critique written resources through an annotated bibliography	Analysis of song lyrics, composition of song lyrics, design and publish online presentations that incorporate music and visual elements
Develop content-focused *PowerPoint* classroom presentations	Develop multimedia *Hyper Studio* classroom presentations
Design Web-based, interactive games, puzzles and quizzes; develop or complete cognitive WebQuests	Internet based simulations, cooperative Web searches, and role playing activities that incorporate Web resources, classroom presentations

has hindered our ability to fully integrate such technology in education:

> One of the mistakes we made in implementing educational technology was focusing first on students, rather than teachers, because when the computers on the students' desks are mysterious devices to teachers, it's unreasonable to expect effective integration into the curriculum.[39]

The potential and use of technology and the Internet in history education, from the middle school to the high school level, is dependent upon the curricular scaffolding with which learning will be constructed. The MI and left- and right-brain 4MAT brain-based approaches are two such models that teachers may employ to build a digital learning environment in their classroom. In addition, they provide much-needed curricular frameworks for organizing primary and secondary resources for student classroom use. The result is a primary document-based, multidimensional approach to teaching middle and high school history in a digital age.

Part III

Taught Curriculum

Chapter 10

Teaching Authentic History

A teacher is one who makes himself progressively
unnecessary.
—Thomas Carruthers

One of the most common complaints about secondary school history instruction is that it lacks a critical research focus. It seems that few junior high or high school history teachers do much besides teach the textbook. Whereas high school science classes typically require students to dissect frogs, mix chemicals, and test hypotheses, high school history classes seldom require students to analyze historical documents. Instead, too many history classes focus on memorization of factual material as their dominant activity.

Although problematic for a variety of reasons, memorization exercises do not lend themselves to authentic instruction or assessment. That is, when an emphasis on recall of facts is the predominant classroom activity, students are often not required to engage in tasks that are either meaningful or professionally valid. Authentic achievement requires students to pursue learning exercises that reflect the type of inquiry used in the discipline, show evidence of understanding relationships among the various fields that comprise their learning (such as English and history), and develop competencies and culminating exercises that have value beyond the classroom.[1] Over the past decade, authentic instruction and assessment has resulted in greater emphasis on tasks that are not only more meaningful and professionally valid but more challenging for students. History lends itself quite well to authentic assessment since scholars in the discipline use research materials to produce written interpretations.[2]

The traditional history classroom emphasis on memorization also contributes to another common complaint about secondary history instruction—its dullness. As sociologist James W. Loewen says in the opening sentence of his widely acclaimed *Lies My Teacher Told Me: Everything Your American History Textbook Got Wrong*, "[h]igh school students hate history." Students typically think of history as not only the most boring but also the most irrelevant subject they take in school. This perception is again directly related to the pedagogical emphasis of most secondary-level history instructors on textbook readings combined with rehearsal and regurgitation of factual material. Students are not exposed to the interpretive dimensions of the discipline when this type of pedagogy dominates. They also miss out on the potential for interest created by examining the "mysteries" posed by actual historical documents. Indeed, as Howard Gardner has said, introducing students to the "intellectual heart" or "experiential soul" of the disciplines should be at the center of a truly worthwhile educational experience for all children.[3]

Of course, until recently nearly all secondary history teachers could have honestly protested about limited access to primary sources. For instance, school libraries typically do not collect letters, correspondence, diaries, newspapers, journals, maps, paintings, photos, broadsides, and other items from various historical periods. All these items are more typically associated with university or research libraries' archival collections. Before the emergence of widespread Internet and World Wide Web access, providing students with primary source materials would have entailed photocopying items from a nearby research library or considerable logistical creativity and use of class time in transporting students to larger public libraries, local history museums, or county courthouses. Other options for identifying and using primary sources are also problematic. Some history textbooks include primary source vignettes, but these are often more decorative than anything else. Ready-made primary source packets, such as those produced by Jackdaws Publications, are relatively expensive and, of course, cannot cover all possible issues that teachers might like. But with the explosion of materials available on the World Wide Web and increasingly widespread Internet access in schools, teachers can no longer legitimately complain about lack of availability of primary source materials.[4]

Historians see the advantages of primary source research without need for explanation, but middle and high school history teachers need to identify the benefits for their students. Several can be stated succinctly. Students need to develop the historian's critical thinking perspectives, or "habits of mind," that can be acquired only through the systematic analysis of historical materials. As David Kobrin has outlined in his valuable text, *Beyond the Textbook: Teaching History Using Documents and Primary Sources*, students involved in historical research can learn how to "pose pertinent questions, define problems, analyze relevant information, support their conclusions, and understand their own values." While developing these skills and a more critical perspective, primary research exercises also help students learn to question authority, particularly the typical reliance created by the repetitious use of textbooks and direct instruction by teachers. By helping students pursue primary source analysis and their own construction of history, teachers also can motivate students to become more active learners. In the process of engaging in primary source research, many students become enthusiastic about history rather than being bored by it.[5]

Some secondary history teachers may still question whether students can adopt historians' "habits of mind." Do adolescents have the intellectual ability to engage in serious historical inquiry? Educational researchers have found that the typical adolescent believes that he or she can understand history without using a process of inquiry and that authorities should not be questioned. Certainly during the middle school grades, many students are only starting to develop formal operational thinking skills and many are still immersed in what Lawrence Kohlberg identifies as a "conventional" stage of moral development, specifically stages three and four where the individual focuses on abiding by the society's rules.[6]

Instead of simply accepting students' natural limitations, however, teachers need to direct students' intellectual development. Studies suggest that students can follow teachers who model good historical practices. Ronald Evans, for instance, has argued that teachers who have clear conceptions of the nature of the discipline not only can make appropriate curriculum decisions, but also can successfully shape their students' understanding of history. Other researchers have found that secondary-level students need active, hands-on instructional activities in order to develop their abilities to think more abstractly and ideologically across the entire spectrum of the social sciences.[7]

The most effective (and attention-grabbing) way to engage students in hands-on primary source exercises is by provoking interest, particularly in the affective learning domain. That is, adolescents will be most interested in exercises that challenge their values and beliefs. Kieran Egan has noted that teachers who use historical materials that involve "abstract binary opposites" create dramatic tension that is compelling to students. Egan argues that this can be done without reducing historical issues to simplistic black and white explanations. Interesting details that emerge from strange, awe-inspiring, or unexpected historical episodes are the most effective fodder for historical inquiry activities. Peter Frederick also explains how students learn history best when they are confronted with "a compelling human historical problem, decision, or personal question." With either Egan's or Frederick's example, these strategies are quite similar to those posed by social studies educators who have called for focused examination of controversial social issues or problems.[8]

Many teachers are likely to protest about the time required for such inquiry-type research exercises. How can teachers have students investigate historical issues and still "cover" all the essential topics in their curriculum? While it is obviously true that having students engage in primary source research takes time away from other activities, the time required does not need to be excessive. Brief exercises, requiring two or three fifty-minute periods, are probably much more effective for secondary students than longer exercises. The exercises described below are designed to take no more than a couple of days of instructional time.

The first type might be called a "prepackaged" primary source exercise. There are now many teaching sites on the Web consisting of structured instructional activities that focus on analysis and evaluation of primary documents. For instance, the Library of Congress's American Memory Learning Page (memory.loc.gov/ammem/ndlpedu/), History Matters (historymatters.gmu.edu), PBS (www.pbs.org/neighborhoods/history/), and the Primary Source Network (primarysources.

msu.edu/) all provide teachers with examples of historical materials structured for student examination. Some of the most carefully structured activities can be found on the National Archives and Records Administration teaching materials site (www.nara.gov/education/ teaching/teaching.html). The site contains nearly twenty sets of documents on topics ranging from the Constitution, the *Amistad* case, black soldiers in the Civil War, the development of barbed wire, women's suffrage, the Zimmermann telegram, World War II poster art, Jackie Robinson, to Watergate. Each document site contains reproducible copies of primary documents from the National Archives' holdings. The introductory material for each theme is also linked to the National History Standards and National Standards for Civics and Government. Other related curricular connections are suggested as well. The main national archives teaching Web site also has reproducible document worksheets that can be adapted for use with other primary source documents a teacher might want to use.[9]

The site on the development of barbed wire lends itself nicely to an integrated thematic approach to industrialization and frontier settlement in the late nineteenth century United States. Students are likely to be curious about how barbed wire, a material most of them would consider mundane, is worthy of serious historical investigation. One would also hope that they would be intrigued: Just *how* did the development of barbed wire link the frontier's development to industrialization? An investigation of this site might be ideal in an eleventh-grade U.S. history class after students have finished units on the westward movement and the growth of urban-industrial America. Although complete in virtually all other respects, the National Archives sites typically do not provide teachers with suggestions about context. Students should be asked to examine the site with this question in mind: How did the introduction of barbed wire shape the settlement of the West *and* necessitate an urban-industrial society?

The following procedural steps are all provided in the teaching activities on the site. After a nicely focused, yet concise historical background reading, the site provides links to a precise reproduction of Joseph Glidden's 1874 patent application and the accompanying drawing of the barbed wire itself. If computers with Web access are available for the entire class, students working in pairs (as suggested in the teaching activities) could then examine the documents and answer the document analysis questions provided at the site. The teacher should replicate these questions on a study guide for each student. Or, as the site's instructions also suggest, the instructor might make transparencies or *PowerPoint* slides of both artifacts and project them for the entire class.

For document analysis, the site suggests three related steps. (See Worksheet 10.1) The first is free association and brainstorming about images associated with barbed wire. Students then examine the drawing and text of the patent application to answer the following questions: For whom was the drawing intended? Why was it created? What is the inventor actually seeking to patent? What are the strengths of the invention? How well does the written description depict the physical design and intended use? What aspects of the description need enhancement? After these questions have been answered, students are asked to ponder more complex historical connections to previously learned material: What skills were necessary for the inventor to design these improvements? What skills were required to manufacture, market, and sell the product? What are some connections to professions and technical skills of the era?

Although an instructor might reasonably choose to end the activity at this point, the site provides several ideas for related activities (though pursuing any of them would add to the amount of instructional time needed). In "Writing and Defining a Position," instructors are asked to divide students into four groups, which then write about how the development of barbed wire affected various groups (cowboys or herders, farmers, Native Americans, and wire manufacturers). In "Comparing Written and Visual Descriptions," students are asked to write a description of how they might improve an object they commonly use in class (like a pencil sharpener). Once students have redesigned this object and compared it to their description, they could discuss why the patent office requires both visual and written descriptions of inventions.

In "Relating Personal Experiences," students could discuss their personal encounters with barbed wire and speculate about why people today are interested enough in the material to collect it. "Creative Interpretations" suggests that students listen to Cole Porter's "Don't Fence Me In" and read the lyrics. They would then translate the images suggested by the song to some other written medium. The "Further Research Activity" offers the possibility of structuring a similar

---

Worksheet 10.1

National Archive Teaching Unit Worksheet: Barbed Wire, the West, and Industrialization

Research Question: How did the introduction of barbed wire shape the settlement of the West and necessitate an industrial society?

Procedure: Use the documents included in the National Archives Teaching Unit (www.nara.gov/education/teaching/glidden/wire.html) and follow the steps outlined in "Document Analysis" under the heading "Teaching Activities." You may work in pairs to complete the questions below.

Step One: Free Association and Brainstorming
What words or images do you associate with barbed wire?

Step Two: Document Analysis
After viewing the patent drawing and reading the written description, answer the following questions concisely.

1. For whom was the drawing intended?
2. Why was the drawing created?
3. What is Glidden actually seeking to patent?
4. What are the strengths of the invention?
5. How well does the written description depict the physical design and intended use?
6. What aspects of the description need enhancement?

Step Three: Linking Previous Knowledge and Making Connections

1. What skills were necessary for the inventor to design these improvements?
2. What skills were required to manufacture, market, and sell the product?
3. List some connections to professions and technical skills of the era.

Step Four: Essay
Based on the answers provided to the questions in Steps One, Two, and Three, compose a concise response to the research question: How did the introduction of barbed wire shape the settlement of the West and necessitate an industrial society?

---

exercise around another invention that shaped the West, such as the plow or firearms.

Once the students complete the document analysis and discuss their findings, it is crucial to then return to the original historical question: How did the introduction of barbed wire shape the settlement of the West and necessitate an urban-industrial society? Students should be asked to write a coherent essay response to this question that draws upon their document analysis. A culminating discussion based on their responses also may prove worthwhile.

Although the number of sites offering "prepackaged" exercises using primary documents is steadily increasing, history instructors interested in constructing their own exercises also have a wide array of sites to choose from. Primary source exercises constructed from material on sites not specifically designated for instructional use are the second type of lessons that will be highlighted here. Perhaps the two greatest challenges to teachers interested in constructing their own primary source exercises are identifying contextually relevant and accurate materials and leaving enough time to locate materials and structure them in exercises that students can actually use.[10]

As Dennis Trinkle and Scott Merriman's *The History Highway 2000* (published by M.E. Sharpe) makes quite explicit, there are dozens of such sites that one might develop lessons around. Perhaps the safest way to begin to identify accurate primary source materials is to use their suggestions and rely on collections maintained by universities and other reputable historical organizations. The University of Kansas maintains one of the richest of such collections called AMDOCS—Documents for the Study of American History (history.cc.ukans.edu/carrie/docs/amdocs_index.html). Many of these sites include sources of quantitative data. Because students need more exposure to the manipulation of numerical data outside mathematics classes, the United States Historical Census Data Browser lends itself nicely to quantitative research exercises. Created by the Inter-University Consortium for Political and Social Research (ICPSR), the site provides access to state and county level data for each of the censuses from 1790 to 1960 (http://fisher.lib.Virginia.edu/census/).

The "virtual" census is not as complete as the published census. Nevertheless, it provides a wealth of data and is certainly more user friendly, especially for younger students, than the bound census volumes. Instead of having to handle heavy, dusty, and intimidating tomes, students can learn very quickly how to click on various categories to compile the data they need. While many secondary-level students will initially be intimidated by an exercise focusing on the use of numbers, the potential attraction is not unlike that raised by the national archives' teaching unit on the introduction of barbed wire. Students are likely to be mystified by how numbers convey important historical insights. It is incumbent upon the creative and adventuresome secondary history teacher to "sell" the use of census data to clear up this mystery.

Envision teaching a unit for an eighth- or eleventh-grade United

States history class on Gilded Age industrialization. After discussing this era for the nation as a whole, the class might turn to how industrialization impacted their own region. Following is an example of one such project I have my students engage in regarding Vigo County, Indiana. To understand Vigo County's economic development from the late nineteenth through the mid-twentieth century, students must examine changes over that period. The research question that frames students' investigation might be: How did Vigo County change as a result of industrialization from the late nineteenth through the mid-twentieth century? This is a particularly relevant question, too, since the region has a long industrial heritage.

To begin, provide each student with a blank chart on which to record census data. (See Worksheet 10.2) Students use the virtual census to look up county-level data on a variety of variables for four sets of "snapshot" years: 1870, 1900, 1930, and 1950. The variables used in this example, but which could certainly be modified depending on the interests of teachers and students, are: total population, total number of foreign-born, total number of whites, total number of blacks, total number of manufacturing plants, total number of semiskilled who worked in manufacturing, and total number of illiterates (as defined by inability to read). Although it might be better for the purpose of more closely tracking historical developments to have students collect data on each decennial year for the period, for the purposes of consolidating use of class time these snapshot years provide a view at the beginning, middle, and end of the industrialization era.

As is true of the published census volumes for these years, the census categories that record these variables change somewhat over the period, particularly those involving manufacturing employment. Students need direction to help them combine categories to come up with the most meaningful and consistent answers over time. For instance, while the 1870 and 1930 census categories provide straightforward calculations for the number of people who worked in manufacturing, the 1950 census includes a much more detailed (and convoluted) breakdown by occupation. Students would need to think about the types of jobs involved in manufacturing before realizing that male and female operatives were the most relevant census categories in 1950. Similarly with the issue of illiteracy, students would need help in understanding why the inability to read is an issue impacted by industrialization. Teachers could talk about how a manufacturing

Worksheet 10.2

Virtual Census Data Worksheet: How Did Industrialization Affect Vigo County?

Research Question: How did Vigo County change as a result of industrialization from the late 19th through the mid-20th centuries?

Procedure: Using the data collected in the United States Historical Census Data Browser (fisher.lib.Virginia.edu/census/) answer each of the following questions by writing the appropriate number in the blanks provided.

Step One: Collecting the Data

Categories	Vigo County 1870	Vigo County 1900	Vigo County 1930	Vigo County 1950
Total Population?				
Total No. of Foreign Born?				
Total White Population?				
Total Black Population?				
Total No. of Manuf. Plants				
Total No. of Semi-skilled Workers in Manufacturing				
Total No. of Illiterates? (i.e., can't read)				

Step Two: Convert Absolute Numbers to Relative Numbers
In order to effectively analyze the data you've collected, you should convert the total numbers to percentages. In some cases, a ratio may be more meaningful (e.g., the ratio of manufacturing plants to blue-collar workers). Write the percentages below the total number in each box where this is relevant.

Step Three: Analysis
Using the data you have collected, write a concise answer to the research question: How did Vigo County change as a result of industrialization from the late 19th through the mid-20th centuries? Be sure to cite relevant numbers or percentages in your analysis.

economy required basic literacy, especially reading, among its work force. Teachers would again need to prompt and direct discussions about such interpretive dimensions of the data.

After students have gathered the raw data on their census chart, the next step in analyzing the data involves converting, where relevant, the absolute numbers to relative numbers (percentages) for the purpose of comparing the data over time. This type of statistical calculation draws upon skills already learned by middle school students. Still, teachers would need to explain why percentages are the most useful way of comparing, for example, the number of foreign-born to the total population or changes in the number of manufacturing workers to total employment over time. In the manufacturing category, students might also calculate the ratio of workers to individual manufacturing plants for each of the four years.

Once the percentages are added to the census chart, students could then focuses on the research questions: How did Vigo County change from the late nineteenth century through the mid-twentieth century? Encourage students to start by listing visible trends before composing a more structured essay. As noted, teachers should point out that the categories indicated here are not the only relevant measures of industrialization's impact over time. One should therefore expect variations among students in how they analyze the information, including, of course, how carefully or diligently the data are scrutinized. For instance, while nearly all students will note that population increased over time, only some will point out that the rate of population increase slowed considerably. Many will point out that the total number of manufacturing plants declined drastically over time, but only a certain number will note that the relative number of manufacturing workers increased steadily over the period.

Students should be encouraged to explain county-level trends in reference to national trends they learned earlier in the industrialization unit. Students should be urged to postulate why their findings either affirm or diverge from what they might have expected. In this way, this type of primary source exercise would help students learn to construct meaningful historical hypotheses that could be "tested" as they learn more history.

A third, and perhaps easiest, type of primary source exercise is having students analyze a document using a "background worksheet" such as the one described by David Kobrin in *Beyond the Textbook*.

Worksheet 10.3

Background Worksheet for Documents

Name of Document: _____

1. What are the names of the important people mentioned? What are their positions? Why are they important?

2. What are the names of places mentioned in the document? Where are they? Why are they important?

3. What are difficult words in the document? What are appropriate definitions for them?

4. Who is the speaker or author's intended audience?

5. What is the larger picture for the document? What's going on at this time that you would need to know in order to understand this document?

In many cases, it may be more appropriate during a unit to have students examine a particular document rather than embark on a longer, structured exercise. Students receive practice in using critical thinking skills without needing to use too much class time. As can be seen in Worksheet 10.3, the activity engages students in a thorough, systematic examination of a document. Students need to name who the people are, noting what their positions are and why they are important. They would do the same thing in terms of the source's setting. What places are noted? Where are they? Why are they important? To focus attention on difficult, archaic, or contextually challenging terminology, students would then note any difficult words.

Instead of allowing students to read around or skip such terms, as they are prone to do, the background worksheet forces students to not only note such terms but define them as well. The next question requires students to think about the source's intended audience. When thinking historically (and critically) students need to be aware not only of who the speaker is but to whom that person is speaking. Students need to be able to not only know literally what a source says, but also understand the context in which its information is given. The last question is the necessary follow-up to the previous one. Given the intended audience, what is the "larger picture" or appropriate historical context surrounding the source? Without an awareness of this context, it is indeed quite easy to try to understand issues or ideas out of context. The national archives Web site has a similar type of worksheet, called a "Written Document Analysis Sheet," that includes most of the same elements. One nice feature of it is that it includes a heading where students can check the type of document as well as any "unique physical qualities" of the document.

The three examples of primary source analysis activities described all lend themselves to short classroom exercises. They each engage students in active, inquiry-based, and reflective examinations of historical documents, and are particularly well suited to the availability of World Wide Web sources now on the Internet. Students who engage in such instructional activities will not only learn a more authentic brand of history, but, hopefully, they will also become more enthusiastic about learning history in general.

Chapter 11

The Montage Class:
Teaching Historical Thinking
with Audiovisual and
Information Technology

John R. Barber

*A teacher who can arouse a feeling for one single good
action, for one single good poem, accomplishes more
than he who fills our memory with rows and rows of
natural objects classified with name and form.*
—Johann Wolfgang Von Goethe

On a cold gray morning, a college freshman rushed from a physical
education class to a history lecture. In the small room warmed by the
bodies of about thirty students, two radiators, and an open gas heater,
he soon forgot the cold. The professor sat behind her desk about ten
feet away, teaching in her usual fashion: with little movement and in
a very even voice she paraphrased the reading assignment of the day.
The student fought boredom and an urge to sleep as he struggled to
write a summary of the teacher's summary of the information in the
text. He persisted because he knew that he could prepare for the next
test more easily by numbly taking notes than by thoughtfully listening
and reading the assignment.

Less than five years after that gloomy day, the former student,
armed with a master's degree, began to teach the same course in the
same room using essentially the same method of instruction, except

that he stood, and spoke somewhat more forcefully. His techniques did not change at all for three years. Thereafter, for a decade he made a slow transition toward more varied methods. He still lectured a lot despite having lost his faith in the idea that a class session filled with teacher talk was the best way to encourage students to gain knowledge of the past and learn to think historically.

Should he have kept his faith in the old pedagogical religion of the spoken word? Lectures, well done and in moderation, have a certain role to play. Lectures are not used in moderation, however. A report published in 1987 indicated that

> the most recent extensive survey of U.S. university professors found lecturing to be the mode of instruction of 89 percent of the physical scientists and mathematicians, 81 percent of the social scientists, and 61 percent of the humanities faculty (although 81 percent of art historians and 90 percent of the philosophers lectured).[1]

Classroom teachers probably talk less than college instructors, but at all levels this technique is immoderately used and too often is not "done well." It seems fair to say that good lectures at least should hold an audience's attention. One might also reasonably expect well-done lectures to convey information effectively and encourage its retention. Lectures almost certainly fail when judged by these standards. The following quotation pertains to a special lecture rather than an ordinary class session, but it differs little from the way researchers describe what happens during and after course lectures:

> Ten percent of the audience displayed signs of inattention within 15 minutes. After 18 minutes one-third of the audience and 10 percent of the platform guests were fidgeting. At 35 minutes everyone was inattentive; at 45 minutes, trance was more noticeable than fidgeting; and at 47 minutes some were asleep and at least one was reading. A casual check 24 hours later revealed that the audience recalled only insignificant details [that] were generally wrong.[2]

Teachers can help students to learn by speaking to them, but they could achieve much more, especially in the effort to teach thinking, if they would end the primacy of this method in the classroom.

This criticism of the overdependence on lectures and the description of alternative methods in this chapter should not be construed as an argument that highly effective class presentations alone ensure success in teaching for improved thinking. Successful instruction for this or any other purpose certainly depends also on overall course design, reading and other resources selected for students, activities and assignments carried on outside of class, matching of methods to student abilities, testing and evaluation, and much more. Classroom teaching sessions, however, are an important part, and perhaps the critical mechanism, in the system that encourages and guides education. It is during these times together with students that the teacher can most directly spark enthusiasm for learning, convey information, spur thought, promote awareness and understanding, and, above all, promote the development of thinking and learning skills. These purposes of the classroom session cannot be served effectively when the students' minds are too frequently elsewhere, when the level of attention is low, and when students are not regularly engaged in the guided practice of thinking.[3]

A Primer on Teaching Thinking

The pedagogical literature on thinking exhibits a startling lack of consistency in definitions but reasonable agreement about the ways to teach for improved cognitive ability. The contradictory definitions perhaps result from the very complex and highly varied nature of thinking; and the somewhat paradoxical accompanying circumstance of agreement on methods for teaching thinking, might simply mean that thinking in all its forms, however described, improves when teaching is done in certain fairly apparent ways.

The muddle of definitions will pose no particular problem in teaching for cognitive growth if the teacher and her or his students have a clear idea about the meanings they attach to several important words. Teachers could use the following statements to guide their planning, or do enough reading in the literature to write their own:

- Thinking is the use of the brain and related nervous-system structures to process imaginary concepts or information gained from the external environment through the senses. Thinking may take the form of simple contemplation of whatever is perceived or recalled, in which case the mental activity is not directed toward a particular kind of processing or result. Much contemplation, however, is one of two types, either critical or creative thinking.

- Critical thinking is contemplation in the form of evaluative processing, the purpose of which is to judge the quality of an object, device, idea, theory, source of information, problem solution, or any other focus of attention. Creative thinking is contemplation, the intention of which is to produce a mental image that is new to the thinker and that will be viewed as innovative when communicated to other qualified observers.
- The two special forms of thinking are closely related. There might be much that is creative in the way critical thinking is done, and the conclusions drawn in the process of evaluation might be innovative. In critical thinking, however, the emphasis is on the process of discrimination rather than on the creative product. Similarly, in creative thinking much evaluative processing probably occurs, but the primary objective is the innovative result.

Teachers need general definitions of the kind offered above, but success in cognitive instruction will depend even more on having an understanding of thinking strategies and skills. Fortunately, experts on cognition usually agree in their descriptions of these aspects of thinking. Barry K. Beyer, for example, identifies three strategies—problem solving, decision making, and conceptualizing—with a list of steps involved in each. In problem solving, Beyer suggests that a person tends to proceed in this way: he or she becomes aware of the problem, expresses it, decides how to solve it, carries out the solution, and evaluates the results. Beyer describes a similar sequence of steps in thinking through goal oriented alternatives to arrive at a decision (decision making) and working through the attributes of a concept to imagine a new version of it (conceptualizing). Beyer groups recall, interpretation, analysis, synthesis, evaluation, and several other mental processes under the heading of "micro-thinking skills." He includes inductive, deductive, and analogical reasoning in the micro skills category as well. Following is a complete, verbatim list of his idea of critical thinking skills:

- Distinguishing between verifiable facts and value claims
- Distinguishing relevant from irrelevant information, claims, or reasons
- Determining the factual accuracy of a statement
- Determining the credibility of a source

- Identifying unstated assumptions
- Detecting bias
- Identifying logical fallacies
- Recognizing logical inconsistencies in a line of reasoning
- Determining the strength of an argument or claim[4]

As further steps in the process of definition, teachers need to learn more about the meanings of words such as analysis and induction, which are forms of thinking of special importance to history students. For purposes of lesson planning, one might begin with these definitions: analysis means a determination of main points in a printed or visual document or an explanation of documentary points using rewording or personal examples; induction is determining a pattern in or drawing a conclusion from points of historical information. Once teachers have a set of definitions of forms of thinking and of the related cognitive strategies and skills to guide their planning, one of their first steps should be to translate the definitions into statements that their students can readily understand. Then the teaching effort can begin.

Barry K. Beyer's review of a vast amount of research leads him to the conclusion that teachers who want to encourage cognitive growth above all must realize that they have to teach thinking directly. When students experience methods that encourage thought, hear admonitions to think, or confront tough problems to solve, they still will not make adequate progress in thinking ability. For real effectiveness, teachers must periodically and with some regularity overtly identify as a learning objective a specific thinking strategy, skill, or disposition. They also "must employ direct, systematic instruction in these skills prior to, during, and following student introduction to and use of these skills. . . ."[5] Beyer and others emphasize that the direct instruction has to include repeated practice on differing material under the teacher's guidance, with feedback, "until they can individually initiate and employ the skill and evaluate their use of it."[6] Wilbert J. McKeachie, one of the most widely respected cognitive psychologists, offers views on how to teach thinking that agree with Beyer's admonitions. McKeachie makes such additional points as these: research suggests that "explicitly focusing on the specific methods and strategies to be used in solving specific types of problems and noting different approaches helps novices." He further affirms "that at least three elements of teaching seem to make a difference in student gains in thinking skills: (1) student discussion, (2) explicit emphasis on problem-solving procedures and methods using varied examples, and (3) verbalization of methods and strategies to encourage development of metacognition." (Metacognition is thinking about the nature of or planning the thinking process.) Then he concludes that "because productive thinking involves knowledge, it seems likely that this kind of teaching is likely to be most effective in the context of subject-matter courses."[7] (The latter is good news for history teachers.)

Although thinking is best taught "in the context of subject-matter courses," the tendency of teachers in history and other fields to concentrate too much on "covering" the required subject hinders instruction for mind development. The requirement of standards-based instruction likely will strengthen the coverage obsession among teachers. Despite the critical importance of student absorption of knowledge, teaching thinking effectively requires the devotion of less time and effort to *giving* them the required information, and the commitment of more time to activities planned to ensure that they gain the knowledge in conjunction with a thinking process. Joanne Gainen Kurfiss offers this cogent observation on the problem caused by the urge to cover the subject and the way to resolve it:

> If we believe students cannot think until they "know" a lot, and if teaching for information crowds out learning to think, how and when will critical thinking abilities develop? To escape this impasse, let's explore an alternative proposition: *students' ability and willingness to think critically are most likely to develop when knowledge acquisition and thinking about content are intertwined rather than sequential.*[8]

A Starter Set of Strategies to Teach Thinking

Instruction to develop a particular cognitive ability ordinarily should begin with (1) an introduction that clearly and quickly explains or (2) leads to a discovery of the meaning of the skill. In the first of these introductory approaches, the teacher states the definition, describes and models the skill's use, provides an opportunity for students to practice the process, and then guides them though a review of the thinking method. The second method of skill introduction involves immediate movement from stated definition to student application followed by alternating activities to review and practice it. When the understanding of the meaning of a skill seems adequate, teachers can proceed to repeated "guided practice."[9]

Teachers can use text or visual documents presented on paper or projected in conjunction with strategies to direct students through the use, for example, of "the skill of distinguishing statements of fact from value judgments," one of the thinking abilities that Beyer contends should be among the first taught.[10] Historic documentaries offer countless segments of widely varied lengths that contain both hard data and opinions. (Consider, for example, any film that portrays the effects of the industrial revolution or the origins of World War I or II.) After viewing a brief presentation from such sources, students could individually write a list of facts/value judgments and then form pairs or triads for comparative discussion. Thereafter, the interaction could expand to involve the whole class and should include discussion of the process of using the skill. A very similar approach could encourage the development of a somewhat more advanced thinking activity—the identification of bias in sources.

Historical analysis in its simplest form—recognition of main points—might pose even less difficulty for students than deciding between facts and opinions. Teachers could teach this skill with the strategic steps described above or by using creative variations. Have the students watch a CBS *60 Minutes* segment, available commercially, that provides historical background on a topic, and then ask them to "shout out," or quietly speak out, a list of main points. Or, use this same technique with a portion of a movie based on historic events. *PowerPoint*, *HyperStudio*, or *Flash* presentations that include text, visual images, and video and audio clips also provide opportunities to guide students in learning more complex forms of analysis such as the explanation of historic events—listing main points and then using their own words and examples to clarify meaning.

Even middle school students could learn at least a rudimentary form of an extremely important thinking process for history students—inductive reasoning. Much more complex induction should fascinate advanced classes when taught in the right way. Audiovisual and information technology will facilitate this kind of teaching at all levels. For this thinking process in particular, a *PowerPoint*, *HyperStudio*, or *Flash* sequence probably is the best way to offer an introductory definition and display to illustrate the steps by which students can

draw conclusions from a list of historic points or a body of information about past events. Students need to practice all thinking skills,
but especially such complex operations as induction, in a variety of
ways; for example, by writing about and discussing different forms
of both visual and print documents, sound recordings, artifacts, or any
other source of information about the past. The directed and varied
repetition that follows the *PowerPoint, HyperStudio,* or *Flash* introduction of inductive thinking might follow this pattern in a class
studying the American Revolution:

- Show selected portions or all sixty minutes of "The Reluctant Revolu-
  tionaries" (Part 1 in a series titled "Liberty," a 1997 PBS Video production).
- Have students determine main points using the analysis strategy described above or imagine other ways—engage your creative teaching
  mind again (long walks help).
- Ask individuals, pairs, or triads to write statements of their conclusions
  about the causes of the revolt or, perhaps somewhat differently, the
  pattern of justifications offered for rebellion.
- Discuss and evaluate the mental steps involved in drawing conclusions.
- Repeat this pattern using printed excerpts from the writings of revolutionary figures.
- Have students write their own tracts, working individually outside of
  class or in groups in class, justifying or opposing the revolution. They
  could display their work, graphically enhanced or not, or incorporate it
  into a *PowerPoint, HyperStudio,* or *Flash* presentation on the coming
  of the revolution.

Each of these strategies, but especially activities that focus on the
search for bias or inductive thinking, involves critical thinking in the
sense defined in this chapter. If teachers intend to concentrate on
building this set of evaluative skills, they should periodically make
students aware that the cognitive technique under development is not
only the "determination of bias," for example, but also critical thinking—questioning in a search for better answers and a refined ability
to find them.

Technology in a Grand Scale Cognitive Teaching Process

In her discussion of an extended set of strategies for cognitive development aligned with the National Standards for History, Gina Hogue

recommends "Using Computer Technology to Record and Present Family History and to Enhance Historical Thinking Skills."[11] She contends that "most students are eager to engage in any project involving the use of a computer and can learn a great deal about the United States and the world just by interviewing an elderly relative."[12] The summary of the steps in this strategy includes suggestions about a thinking skills development exercise in which students, guided by a list of questions, analyze an LCD projection of an early twentieth century photograph of "a man and his horse" standing at the site of a saw mill in Arkansas. Hogue also briefly summarizes a possible second instructional stage in which students develop or refine the necessary computer skills for the activities and assignments that follow.

Thereafter, the teacher directs students through the process of selecting a person for an interview, developing a reasonably limited topical focus, and formulating questions for use in the interview. Hogue indicates that students should tape the dialogue with an older person, apparently implying audio only. The option of videotaping seems appropriate. The collection of photographs, visits to sites of importance in the interviewee's family history—possibly a cemetery, and the study of sources to provide historical context will enhance this learning effort. Additional steps in organizing material, digitizing visuals, writing, and typing are all requisite preparation for the development of a computer-assisted presentation. Hogue estimates that a project of this kind will require a month to five weeks, and she notes that it could be extended. (This description of the strategy closely follows Hogue's outline, but her article provides additional details.)

Before proceeding with this approach to the development of historical thinking, teachers will need to gather information about the ethical and legal implications of conducting oral and audiovisual history projects that involve interviewing and recording subjects. Studying family history also risks embarrassing students or causing other negative emotional consequences for them or their relatives. Teachers, therefore, should always offer alternatives from the outset, such as interviewing a World War II veteran who is *not* a relative. This approach enables students to select a nonthreatening assignment without revealing any hint of why they made their particular choice.

Audiovisual Primacy

To teach thinking by following the general principles and using the types of strategies indicated in the preceding sections of this chapter might ensure that the majority of the time most students remain actively engaged in classroom activities. Additional steps, however, might involve still more students and deepen the concentration of all. This and the following sections of the chapter will focus primarily on one methodological objective and one means of its achievement—student concentration in class and the audiovisual means of affecting attention.

With respect to the way classroom sessions are taught, teachers in the twenty-first century should have a new leading concern in planning. Lectures still have primacy in college history courses, almost to the exclusion of all other teaching techniques. Middle and high school teachers probably are not nearly so passionately devoted to the lecture creed, but very likely too many still practice the faith. This *long*-standing teaching tradition should end, and audiovisuals should supplant lectures as the mainstay in middle and high school history courses. The more complete realization of the potential of class sessions requires that teachers abandon the perception that visuals are "aids" to the real stuff of instruction.

This recognition of the primacy of audiovisual methods is the first and most important step in the effort to use class time most effectively in the promotion of thinking ability. An approach that makes visual teaching its primary concern means that history teachers should give audiovisuals first consideration as a means of conveying, promoting study of, and encouraging thought about the content of their courses. They also should devote special attention to the visual elements of content. Teachers often can depict the subject and make it more complete and real and thus more thought provoking.

Teachers, that is, should view the discovery and preparation of audiovisuals as the most important methodological task in class preparation. Thus, audiovisual primacy also means that teachers use any method in almost every session, techniques that involve depictions, usually with transparency projection, videotape, DVD, or computer technology (e.g., *PowerPoint, HyperStudio,* or *Flash* presentations), are the ones they virtually always should employ. Primacy does not mean, however, that the majority of class time should be devoted to such multimedia presentations. Instead, discussion and other active student involvement should take place during most of the typical classroom session.

But why should audiovisual primacy not also mean filling most of the class time with visual images? To be practical, time is a factor—it takes longer and demands a greater effort to teach visually. As one advocate of visual teaching has put it, "words are dominant over pictures in academic and serious circles because they're easier to produce."[13] The time and energy required explains why the indolent will lecture on, but it also indicates why the conscientious majority also cannot make *most* of their teaching visual—teachers generally are already loaded to the limit.

Practicality also suggests another reason for limiting the time devoted to visual teaching more than its "prime" importance might indicate is desirable. The young learners who fill our classrooms might have had their capacity for visual thinking significantly diminished by the way society operates and especially by the way teaching shifts toward a verbal emphasis as students advance through the grades.[14] A sudden plunge into mostly visual teaching *might* cause students, especially those who are inclined to aural learning, to have a sense of being overwhelmed by the images or lost for lack of guiding words.

Finally, among the reasons for continuing to spend much class time on verbal activities, it is very important to avoid the kind of either-or thinking that often arises in a challenge to the conventional wisdom and to realize that the need is for *both* visual and verbal teaching, as well as any other kinds that are appropriate to the education of students in the twenty-first-century world. Robert H. McKim, one of the strongest advocates of visual thinking, is exactly right on this point. He has been paraphrased by Doug Stewart as saying that

> he doesn't expect people to do all their thinking in images. Words, logic and numbers are indispensable, he says, especially in refining and testing an idea. Rather, images provide a rich, expressive medium for thought that complements analytical reasoning and offers quicker, more unexpected jumps and connections.[15]

So, lecture, discuss, turn the class into a workshop, and in other ways make use of students' verbal-logical-mathematical intelligences. But consider the argument for audiovisual primacy, in the sense defined above. And, if the contention about the special importance of depiction seems valid, prepare to engage the students visually.

The Rationale for Visual Primacy

Research in cognitive psychology provides important support for the idea of audiovisual primacy. It indicates that much of the brain, especially the right hemisphere, is dedicated to "visual thinking." Rudolf Arnheim, a leading figure among those who study the psychology of perception, describes his conclusions on sight and thought as follows:

> A review of what is known about perception, and especially about sight, made me realize that the remarkable mechanisms by which the senses understand the environment are all but identical with the operations described in the psychology of thinking. Inversely, there was much evidence that truly productive thinking in whatever area of cognition takes place in the realm of imagery.[16]

Thus to Arnheim, visual thinking is the most important and perhaps the only form that ideas take. Even if this view exaggerates the significance of visual thinking, Arnheim is right in his suggestion of visual primacy.

Other studies further confirm the special value of visuals in thoughtful communication. Jacob Bronowski in his essay on human nature includes a section on the brain. He reports the scientific evidence that the eyes, as well as other parts of the nervous system outside the brain, are not all passive receptors that flash neutral messages to the brain. A nerve fiber leading from the eye, he states, "often does not so much inform the brain as instruct it, by sorting its messages in advance; and it does this most effectively by simply withholding information— judging for itself what is irrelevant, and discarding it, without leave from the brain."[17] Similarly, a *Science News* article affirmed that "surprisingly, scientists now report, the [stimulus] screening process begins before the signals reach the brain's complex processing centers, perhaps even before they reach the brain."[18] Visuals, therefore, have the potential to engage much of the brain *and* other parts of the neurological thought system that otherwise would remain much more nearly quiescent. There is more to mind-brain function than lining up words or any other logical sequence at some point deep inside one portion of the brain.

Robert McKim, an expert on visual thinking mentioned above, is another of the specialists on thought who emphasize that the highest levels of cognition involve images and activate portions of the brain too often neglected in teaching. In his commentary on the importance of visual thinking, he mentions Einstein's observation "that he 'rarely thought in words at all' and that his thinking processes were represented to his consciousness by 'more or less clear images . . . of visual and some of muscular type.'" McKim also reports this widely known finding that warrants repeating: "Recent neurological research has provided objective evidence that the right hemisphere of the brain is involved in the holistic, spatial operations of visual thinking and the left hemisphere with the more analytical, linear operations of verbal and mathematical thinking."[19]

Richard L. Hopkins refers to this same discovery about brain structure and function, but his article also adds an important corrective point. He urges that "it is probably best not to reduce the left and right hemispheres of the brain to a simple dichotomy. . . ." We must recognize, he continues, that functions are not so sharply separated, that people vary in "hemispheric specialization," and that various structures connect the hemispheres. With these important cautions, Hopkins goes on to delineate the usual hemispheric specializations. The left brain generally handles most aspects of "sequential" tasks such as "speaking, reading, writing, and simple calculation—though the right hemisphere plays a role in these processes, it seems, when we become more involved in patterned thinking." Further, "the right hemisphere seems to be better at simultaneous patterned thinking and integrating parts into wholes. Often this has been associated with the visual world. . . ." But the right side has other duties. "The patterning of the right hemisphere is in the abstract, tactile, kinesthetic, and auditory worlds as well [as the visual]."[20] This typical summary of findings argues for the acceptance of visual primacy as a principle in instructional preparation.

Studies that focus more directly on the learning process also support the view that audiovisual techniques deserve first consideration in class planning. The Second World War provided a powerful incentive in the United States to the rapid discovery of ways to teach with the greatest speed and effectiveness. According to J.R. Kidd, educators decided on an approach in which films and simulations would be used more extensively than in the past.[21] In Second World War era instruction, motion picture films proved particularly valuable. Kidd's view of the traits of motion pictures indicates why they worked so well: "Films are concrete and real; often closer to the experience of men and women than are more abstract printed materials." And because films "combine all the arts," they have the power "not only to attract an audience, but to hold attention." Kidd concluded that in certain respects motion picture films had a unique potential in teaching. He contended that film audiences can see in ways that are

> in some respects better suited to learning than is nature or actual experience. Telescopic photography can bring distant objects close up for study; microscopic photography can allow direct observation of objects otherwise too small; time-lapse and slow-motion photography make possible the study of growth or motion which one otherwise could speculate about but never observe.[22]

Such portrayals, thus, have unique capacities to convey information and, it is clearly implied, assist comprehension.

David Berliner, a noted educational researcher, points to another important learning benefit of visual teaching. He reports that "the research [on brain hemispheric functions] implies that the more ways you can enhance imagery when teaching verbal material, the more likely it is that your students will remember what you taught." Berliner also uses an example to suggest the power of vision to assist memory, as he tells of a memory specialist who studied a complex, meaningless mathematical formula for seven minutes then, fifteen years later, without forewarning that he would be tested, recalled it precisely. The mnemonic's technique involved the use of multiple sense impressions, including visualization. Both Kidd and Berliner report the great value of visual methods as part of a "multiple sensory approach" to complete and long-term retention of information.[23]

The discussion thus far indicates that visual teaching offers benefits to learning not only in holding and intensifying attention but also in other ways, such as the enhancement of comprehension and memory. Most teachers probably would agree that these are worthy goals of classroom instruction. A similarly wide consensus very likely exists that class presentations should encourage active and creative thinking. These aims of instruction, especially the latter, provide an additional reason for the advocacy of visual primacy.

Professors, such as Jim Rymarcsuk of Stanford, who specialize in visual teaching, appear to do so mainly because this approach supports the development of creative thinking skills so well. The aim of these visual thinking courses "is to free the eyes and the mind from stereotypes and taboos and to see surroundings in new ways, make connections between unlikely elements, and sketch, tinker and imagine until ideas emerge." In a conversation with Doug Stewart, McKim expressed his commitment to the goal of the cultivation of imaginative minds, and, by a statement on the barrier to this learning, conveyed his idea of the visual route to creative thinking: "'Back in the early Sixties here, I was teaching students how to design new products,' he recalls. 'I noticed that many of our students had trouble generating new ideas. They'd say, literally, "I don't have any imagination." What they'd been rewarded for in school was to manipulate words and numbers and pick single answers on multiple choice quizzes.' They were, McKim decided visual illiterates."[24]

Business people also attest to the benefits of creative thinking through visualization. William Gordon, the man in charge of SES Associates and its program of seminars that teach creativity to the business world, affirms the conviction in this way: " 'The basis of creativity has always been a new connection,' he says. 'To make connections would take hours using words. Your subconscious has to use pictures.' " (Gordon and the SES group came up with the Pringles shape by *visualizing* leaf raking and piles of wet leaves. Teachers will not profit in the same way as they use visual approaches in their professional tasks, but visual teaching should prove quite valuable in the cultivation of creative minds.)[25]

The Montage Class

The following description of "the montage class" suggests one approach to the organization of presentations and activities during a class period. The primary aim of this overview of the montage class is to indicate an effective way to integrate audiovisual, other technological presentations, and nontechnical learning activities into a coherent lesson or class session. The use of the term "montage" emphasizes not only the special importance of visuals and computers in instruction for cognitive growth but also the vital need to divide most class periods into segments that yet remain closely unified. More specifically, the objective of the montage class is the creation of a dynamic learning environment through periodic changes in the nature of class presentations during most sessions and through the use of active learning methods (student writing, discussion, etc.) in every class period.

Teachers should aim to make individual presentations gripping. Even though not everything of importance is interesting, teachers should look for as many interesting elements as time and imagination allow. The proportion of presentations or activities in which one tries for dynamism would be smaller, but most periods need one or more lively occurrences. High interest levels and dynamism are especially easy to achieve with certain forms of audiovisual or computer based programs, simulations and demonstrations, group opinion expressions, and educational drama. Whether such devices have the desired effect often depends on the extent to which they involve action by the students or encourage intense observation. A typical class using the principles noted above would proceed as follows:

- A short video segment (five minutes or so) or simulation that suggests the theme of the session and, if possible, links the previous class to the present one
- A brief lecture, discussion, handout, or *PowerPoint, HyperStudio*, or *Flash* presentation that emphasizes the main elements of the topic and places it in the context of assigned reading
- A longer visual presentation, usually a videotaped segment, expanding on an aspect of the topic at hand
- A group expression activity such as a standing bar graph, hand vote indicating levels of agreement-disagreement with a values statement, anonymous opinion survey on paper, or a five-minute topical essay
- Position statements from a sample of the group, indicating, for example, more about why they responded to the expression action as they did
- Introduction and brief practice of a thinking skill as described in the sampler set of strategies
- Teacher comment to conclude, or a two-minute essay by students describing "Something important I learned today" or discussing some other concluding point of emphasis

The teacher could devote the following day to extended work on the thinking skill introduced in the class described above. In general, it helps to vary the pattern not only within a session but also over the course of several classes to avoid a sense of routine. Teachers also should pay much attention to elements or measures that clarify connections among the segments so that students will remain aware of subject-matter unity. The goal, thus, is an *integrated* series of presentations and activities—a "montage" session.

Points on Audiovisual Techniques

Class sessions of the kind described for the montage class incorporate a great many more audiovisual presentations than is typical of history instruction. The effectiveness of such visual teaching probably can be insured by a not overly rigid adherence to several principles for audiovisual use:

- Introduce presentations with a brief but carefully thought out oral or duplicated statement, usually given in conjunction with a session outline (handed out, on overhead, *PowerPoint* or *HyperStudio* presentations slides, etc.), that will increase student comprehension of the experience.
- Be brief, usually. Class sessions seem to work much better with presentations that are seldom more than five or ten minutes in length. Especially in large classes, segments of lecture and discussion also should be short, although the period overall might be devoted mostly to lecture, discussion, and writing. Once or twice in a term, a carefully selected film, about thirty-minutes long (much more rarely, fifty minutes or an hour) can have a very powerful effect.
- As the above point and previous commentary should make clear, the largest portion of most sessions should not be devoted to audiovisual presentations. That is, not only is it important to be brief, it is necessary also to devote most of a class to activities or presentations other than audiovisuals.
- Vary the forms of audiovisuals and distribute them within and among sessions so that the flow is almost never from audiovisual to audiovisual.
- How can presentations be kept brief, varied, and so forth? Use segments of videos. They are all made up of small pieces. Study them carefully and select parts that are meaningful and visually effective. Variety comes in part from using segments with significantly different contents—different pace, color, mood, intellectual depth, and so forth. Intersperse audiovisual presentations among other kinds of presentations and activities.

The discussion of the montage class reveals much about the integration of audiovisuals, if integration is taken to mean the incorporation of these presentations into sessions to make a class as effective as possible. In addition, it is important to realize that the task is not "integrating audiovisual aids into instruction." Instead, the objective should be the structuring of a series of presentations and activities into a meaningful whole shaped especially by attention to audiovisuals. Computer presentation software makes this "best practice" especially easy. More points on ensuring class session coherence are:

- Each session ordinarily should have a theme that runs clearly through all presentations, *especially* the visual ones. This principle is vital to success in an hour class, and it is still more important in a class comprised of segments, the most important of which are visual.
- Reinforce the awareness of a classroom session's theme by distributing or projecting an overview in outline or paragraph form and by periodically referring to the theme, with special reference to theme elements in the audiovisuals.
- Select or prepare audiovisuals so that their relationship to the whole is as evident as possible.
- Plan or conduct session closure so that students leave with a reminder of the logical ties among class presentations. This could be accomplished by a statement from the teacher or by a brief class discussion that focuses on student views of the session theme.

The Classroom of the Future

Classrooms that teach for our future must encourage the development of capacities for "patterned thinking." This more advanced kind of thinking, which requires visual as well as verbal approaches to its cultivation, holds special promise in helping us "explore the world of process and structure that we live in—of bodily processes, urban life, forces in a bridge, world trade patterns, multiple causation, and the historical flow of complex interaction."[26] In short, our classes soon must begin to do much more to develop the whole mind with its power to think in nonlinear as well as linear patterns, to imagine, and to envision solutions. Our future needs a turn toward more visual teaching if we want to cope with the world that is coming out of the past.

This redirection is important also in order to take advantage of the opportunities that lie ahead, especially those presented by the technology of the communication and information sciences. Many people still have a difficult time grasping the potentials of the least of the personal computers. And far too few probably have begun to see the way to the "global village" or to notice other bright prospects on the horizon that voice and video electronics might be opening. Our rapidly changing tools in the realms of communication and information science indicate a need to expand greatly our capacity for visual thinking. As implied in the Hopkins article on "Educating the Right Brian," teachers in "the emerging electronic culture" should see this challenge clearly as they enter their classrooms of the future today.[27]

Chapter 12

Cooperative Learning

Sandy Cantu

Cooperate with each other, compete only against yourself.
—Harry and Rosemary Wong

Compromising, sharing, assisting, caring: Are these the verbs that come to mind when describing the majority of high school history classrooms? Or, would "yawning" or even "sleeping" be more accurate? More than 700,000 students drop out of school each year.[1] Social studies classes are ranked as the least favorite of all core subjects. Scores on most national and state assessments are lowest in social studies. The greatest discrepancy between white and nonwhite students on formal testing occurs in social studies.[2] Why does this happen, and more important, what can be done to correct this phenomenon?

Maybe instead of sitting passively while the teacher plays the role of storyteller, a more interesting strategy such as cooperative learning could be integrated. Rethinking cooperative learning is an effective and engaging way to teach history. Imagine a middle school classroom where the teacher stands at a podium, lecture notes in hand. All twenty-five sixth graders get out a piece of paper and take notes for almost an hour. Now imagine this taking place three or four days a week. Add three or more years to this scenario and that is exactly what is taking place too often in many high school classrooms. If student achievement as measured by test scores, attendance, graduation rate, SAT scores, and so on, peaked with this type of pedagogical approach, there would be no need for an alternative to lecture. But, current research suggests otherwise.[3] Many classrooms today look strikingly similar to those at the beginning of the last century. Students are sitting in straight rows, the teacher is at the front of the room and chalk is still being ordered in bulk.

If history teachers are teaching the same way at the beginning of the twenty-first century as they did at the beginning of the twentieth century, a hundred years of pedagogical studies are being ignored. The bottom line is accountability. The old methods are not working. Students are not succeeding under the didactic lecture method. History is the most textbook reliant core subject.[4]

Too often enthusiastic history teachers try "TYNT" or "this year's new thing." The results can be like dynamite if the approaches are not based on solid principles—a big bang with someone left to clean up the mess. Cooperative learning is an essential component to a successful classroom not because it is this year's new thing but because it has been tried and tested, and is flexible enough to still evolve.[5]

Some teachers choose to structure lessons competitively, with students competing against each other to reach a goal.[6] Other teachers structure the lesson individualistically, where students have unrelated, individual goals.[7] Teachers also may choose to structure the lesson cooperatively where students are "cooperatively linked" to achieve their goal.[8]

The dominant lesson structure for the past half century has been competitive and individualistic.[9] Research, however, shows that cooperative learning strategies are "instructionally effective in elementary and secondary schools."[10] Certain cooperative learning strategies have been found to be even more "effective than traditional methods in increasing basic achievement outcomes, including performance on standardized test of mathematics, reading and language arts."[11]

Cooperative learning includes a number of strategies designed to "promote academic learning through peer cooperation and communication."[12] Cooperative learning is becoming a popular strategy on the east and west coast (especially California) and is becoming increasingly popular in the midwest.[13] Brandt observed that cooperative learning is found primarily in upper-middle class suburban school districts, where college enrollment is a major objective.[14] If the upper-middle class school districts have found success with cooperative learning in assisting the college bound student, what might happen if the same strategies are applied to all students?

Cooperative learning has been researched longer than any other aspect of education, including class size, departmentalizing, or even reading readiness.[15] The first study of cooperative learning was completed in 1897.[16] A number of researchers have developed cooperative learning curricula, including Spencer Kagan in Riverside, California, Schlomo Sharan in Israel, and Robert Slavin at Johns Hopkins University.[17] Johnson and Johnson's University of Minnesota cooperative learning model contains five basic elements:

1. Positive Interdependence. Students must feel that they are linked together in a "sink or swim" relationship.
2. Face-to-Face Interaction. Students explain, discuss, argue, encourage, assist, and support each other.
3. Individual Accountability. Each member of a group must understand that they must learn, there is no academic "hitchhiking."
4. Social Skills. Students must be taught leadership, conflict resolution, communication and trust-building skills.
5. Group Processing. Students must assess how well they are working together and achieving their goals.[18]

Every time a teacher creates a lesson plan, he or she must decide what teaching strategy to use. Teachers choose cooperative learning structures only 7 to 20 percent of the time.[19] Research, however, shows that cooperative learning strategies should be used when teachers want students to "learn more, like school better, like each other better, have higher self-esteem, and learn more effective social skills."[20]

The teacher in a classroom can set up activities to reinforce competition, individualism, and cooperation.[21] The cognitive outcomes in a competitive classroom are speed and quantity of work in simple drill activities, and competitive skills. The affective outcomes are negative, such as ranking students in a classroom from "worst" to "best," fear of failure, obstruction of individuals' goals accomplishments, belief that a person is valued only for winning, and the lack of intrinsic motivation for learning and thinking. Education has perpetuated "myths" for the positive use of outcomes of competition in the class-room for the last several years. One myth is that our society is highly competitive and students should be educated to survive in this kind of society. The truth is that most of our interactions in society are cooperative, not competitive. A second myth is that the qualities of achievement, success, outstanding performance, drive, ambition, and motivation are dependent upon competition with others. The truth is that cooperation facilitates these qualities to a greater extent than competition. A third myth is that competition will build character and toughen children for life in the real world. Instead, cooperative learning helps students develop a sense of interdependence.[22] If students enjoy the class, the activities, and their groups they are more likely to have better attendance and experience more success. Other recent research has shown that students prefer cooperative learning situations to competitive ones.[23] The last myth is that competition builds self-confidence and self-esteem. Students frequently experience failure under the competitive goal structure and if students are not winning, their self-confidence and self-esteem suffer.[24]

In an individualistic goal structure the cognitive outcomes are mastery of factual information and the development of individualistic and simple mechanical skills. The affective outcomes are minimal. Some students may feel satisfaction after material is mastered. Most students interviewed by Johnson and Johnson experienced loneliness, isolation, alienation, and feelings that the teacher did not give them enough time when working on individualized activities.[25]

In a cooperative goal structure the cognitive outcomes are retention, application, and transfer of information; mastery of concepts and principles; increased verbal abilities; development of problem-solving abilities, cooperative skills, and creative abilities; awareness of an individual's capabilities; and the ability to take on roles. The affective outcomes are the development of interpersonal skills, group skills, and democratic values; acceptance and appreciation of cultural, ethnic, and individual differences; valuing education; positive attitudes toward school and related areas; positive enjoyment and satisfaction of learning; positive self images; and increased emotional capacity.

Each goal structure can be used in the classroom, but in the correct proportion of time. Competition can be used in a productive manner when students are to review, drill, or achieve quantity of material, or when students are engaged in low anxiety producing and relatively unimportant activities. If there are no set criteria to evaluate skills and abilities, some students may measure themselves against others. Each student should be able to monitor the progress of competitors, believe they have a chance of winning, and have access to specific criteria of a right or wrong answers. These conditions need to be met to make good use of the competitive goal structure in a classroom.[26] This goal structure ideally should be used about 10 percent of the classroom time. Individualized instruction is desirable if the goal is for each student to master the objective, and the materials, time, space, and teacher assistance are adequate. An ideal amount of time for this goal structure is 20 percent.[27]

The cooperative goal structure should be used when problem solving is wanted, creativity is necessary, the task is difficult, learning goals are important, and social development is a major instructional goal. Cooperation should be used about 70 percent of the time in a classroom. Cooperation is the unconscious goal of interaction. More than 90 percent of all human interactions are cooperative.[28]

There is a crisis in education. The most recent woes attributed to education are lower student scores on the SAT test, the lack of capability seen in the work force by employers, lower achievement in math and science in comparison to other industrialized countries, and the rising rate of illiteracy among United States citizens. There are also crises cited in the socialization of children, teenagers, and young adults. Crime rates in most areas have indicated a decline in all but crimes committed by youth. Changes in the composition and characteristics of family add to the challenges.

The primary goals of our schools should be to master facts, theories, and information, and to develop critical thinking strategies and skills. Students also should develop positive attitudes toward subject areas; be able to use knowledge gained on the job, in the family, community, and society; and acquire the psychological well being needed to function in society. Cooperative learning at all levels can be used to further achieve all of these aims and reduce the crises in education in our society.

Cooperative learning also plays a role in classrooms that include students with learning disabilities, because cooperative experiences encourage interaction between individuals of different learning abilities and learning modalities. This interaction is characterized by involvement and friendship.[29]

Another purpose cooperative learning serves is to maximize achievement when using computer-assisted instruction.[30] Students of different educational levels can work cooperatively using each other's special areas of expertise. One student may be proficient in word processing while another finds the challenges of tables and charts rewarding. Yet another student may be a *PowerPoint, Hyper Studio,* or *Flash* whiz, and the last member of the group may find comfort in using the templates offered in *Inspiration.*

Some researchers feel that cooperative learning serves as a catalyst for empowering both students and teachers. They believe that cooperative learning can turn schools into "models of democracy."[31] By creating "communities of caring and support," cooperative learning my transform not only classrooms and schools but society itself.[32]

David Johnson and Roger Johnson are quick to point out that their cooperative learning model is not a new concept—"It is as old as humankind."[33] They trace the roots of modern cooperative learning to Colonel Francis W. Parker (1837–1902). As superintendent of public schools in Quincy, Massachusetts, Parker promoted cooperative learning procedures. Parker was a strong advocate of "freedom, democracy, and individuality" in schools.[34]

Parker's emphasis on placing the child "center stage in the educational process" and educating "the whole child" is an example of child-centered progressivism which was popular during the early part of the twentieth century.[35] Another progressive educator who favored similar strategies was William Heard Kilpatrick (1871–1965). Kilpatrick advocated the use of student projects with the teacher serving as a guide for "meaningful learning activities."[36]

John Dewey's (1859–1952) pragmatic use of cooperative learning groups in his "famous project method in instruction" is another case of a well-known educator understanding the value of cooperative learning.[37] The root word of pragmatism is a Greek word meaning "work." Pragmatism is a philosophy that encourages us to seek out the processes and to do the things that work best to help us achieve desirable ends. Pragmatism seeks to examine traditional ways of thinking and doing, and where possible and desirable, to reconstruct our approach to life more in line with the human needs of today.[38] Cooperative learning is an example of these perspectives. David Johnson, however, credits Morton Deutsch's theory for cooperation as the theoretical foundation of their model.[39] Deutsch, building on Kurt

Lewin's theory, formulated a "theory of cooperative and competitive situations."[40]

There is also a great movement toward humanistic education, of which cooperative learning is a branch. Because the compassionate use of reason in dealing with other humans is vital in the type of relationships created between students, teachers, principles, and other school personnel, education needs to focus on the attitudes, values, and beliefs that promote humane interaction and the skills and capacities needed for building and maintaining humanizing relationships.[41] Humanizing relationships cannot be built upon the competitive goal structure that takes place often in the classroom. They also cannot happen under a bureaucratic organizational structure that many schools and school districts have.

Aims

Johnson, Johnson, Holubec and Roy have outlined five school aims for students:

1. Achieve the mastery of facts, information, and theories that are taught in school.
2. Develop critical thinking competencies and the use of higher-level reasoning strategies.
3. Develop positive attitudes toward subject areas . . . so those students are motivated to study these subjects and to learn more about them.
4. Acquire the ability to use their knowledge and resources in collaborative activities with other people in their careers, families, communities, and the larger society.
5. Acquire . . . the psychological health and well being required to participate effectively in our society.[42]

Cooperative learning serves a "special function in reinforcing these general aims."[43] Five basic elements are necessary for cooperative learning to be successful: positive interdependence, face-to-face interaction, individual accountability, interpersonal and group skills, and group processing.[44]

Positive Interdependence

Students must feel that they are dependent on each other to complete the group's task. This can be achieved mutual goals or goal interdependence, or through divisions of labor for *task interdependence,* by dividing resources or information among group members, or through *resource interdependence.* Role interdependence can be achieved by assigning students different tasks, while giving joint rewards leads to reward interdependence. A helpful tip that will conserve paper but will more importantly lead to student responsibility, is for the teacher to limit the amount of copies made of an individual task sheet, written directions, or primary documents. Too often teachers are guilty of making excessive copies and then providing these copies whenever students misplace or fail to bring theirs to class. This leads to the student devaluing whatever was written on the copy. To correct this and to promote sharing, teachers could make only one copy of a document per group or post online.

Face-to-Face Interaction

Beneficial educational outcomes are due to the interaction patterns and verbal exchanges that take place among students in carefully structured cooperative learning groups. This can be achieved through appropriate room arrangement, oral summarizing and elaborating, or relating what is being learned to previous learning. The appearance of the room should not be taken lightly. One of the basic elements of behavior management is that the teacher cannot do anything to change the behavior of the students; instead he or she can only change their own behavior. One of the simplest ways to change a behavior is to change the environment. When a student walks into a classroom the room arrangement can predispose the student's mood, excitement level, and behavioral expectations. It is important to take a look at the amount of teacher space, student space, and shared space. If a classroom looks the same as every other classroom in the building then the same discriminating stimuli exist. To evaluate a particular classroom, follow these steps:

1. Determine where the fixed areas are. This can include phones, computer outlets, windows, doorways, affixed bookshelves.
2. Figure the percentage of space being used for the teacher's preparation, and assess whether this area is being used efficiently. Some teachers need more space for storage and development of lessons but most could

benefit from a self-assessment of how productive their space is being utilized. Visiting other teachers' workspaces also may prove beneficial in gaining organizational tips. Perhaps a "trading spaces" for teachers would be a fun and helpful activity.

3. Decide what percentage of space is being used for students and if groups can be spread farther apart.
4. Check traffic flow in the room and see if exits are easily accessible. Can the instructor walk from group to group? It is important that the room still be functional and safe when not using the traditional straight rows.
5. Determine whether or not supplies and resources are in a central location. Establishing an art cart or designating a shelf or file cabinet drawer to hold different types, sizes, and colors of paper products can assist with both storage and creativity. Requesting additional supplies from parents can lead to more parental involvement and an interesting inventory. A simple letter asking if the parents could send (or even better, bring) various excess craft items, paper products, or surplus items from their work can produce a plethora of resources.
6. Decide if the overall appearance of the room is attractive, clean, orderly, or sterile. The personality of the teacher can be reflected in room decorations. Some teachers interact better in an environment with more plants or different fabrics or flowers or collections. Color, organizational arrangement, and decorations and furnishings make a classroom stand out from the others, and are important in establishing a pleasant climate for both the teacher and the student. Color is important in that it can provide warmth, excitement, or even a sense of calmness depending upon what the school environment and the students need most.

Individual Accountability

The purpose of a cooperative learning group is to enhance the learning of each member. A learning group is not truly cooperative if individual members let others do all the work. To ensure that all members learn and that groups know which members to provide with encouragement and help, teachers will need to assess frequently the level of performance of each group member. This can be accomplished by giving individual tasks, randomly selecting members to explain answers (by using a die, a spinner, drawing out numbers), having members edit each other's work or by having members use different colors of ink, or on computer projects, different font colors.

Interpersonal and Group Skills

Students do not necessarily come to school with the social skills they need to collaborate effectively with others. Teachers need to use direct instruction to teach the appropriate communication, leadership, trust, decision-making, and conflict-management skills to students. Teachers also should provide the motivation to use these skills for groups to function effectively. As teachers monitor their students working in cooperative learning groups, they will notice in which areas students lack important skills. There are four levels of cooperative skills: forming, functioning, formulating, and fermenting.

Forming

The skills needed to establish a functioning cooperative learning group is the formation of the group. These skills are directed toward organizing the group and establishing minimum norms for appropriate behavior. Some of the more important behaviors in this category are:

1. Move into cooperative learning groups without undue noise or excessive time.
2. Stay with the group unless getting resources.
3. Use different levels of voices (i.e., discussion voice, secret voice, presentation voice).
4. Encourage positive vocabulary.
5. Establish size of group.

When forming groups, Johnson and Johnson believe in the magic number of four. Groups of four do work well with some activities. However, groups of two, three, five, and half of the class also can be highly effective. It is important to understand why groups are being formed and what the expected outcome of the group is before determining group size. Knowing the students and the particular class dynamics also will help a teacher decide if a successful outcome the previous year on a certain project with groups of four may be more successful this year with smaller or larger groups. Varying groups can be beneficial, but having a "home" group that stays constant throughout the semester has it benefits. Perhaps having study buddies who stay the same can be a source of comfort for some students and can be treated like a standing group for providing materials and instruction for absences. Setting cooperative teams of two groups of study buddies can be helpful in schools with frequent transfers or if attendance is a problem.

Functioning

These functioning levels of cooperative skills are involved in managing the groups' efforts to complete their tasks and maintain effective working relationships among members. On the first day of school most students are bored by seventh hour because each teacher has laid out his or her expectations for the entire school year with a primary emphasis on discipline. This can be as exciting as hearing how a certain accounting firm counted the votes at an awards show. Yet, establishing behavioral expectations before students break into groups, reviewing these expectations, and overtly teaching these behaviors is crucial to continued cooperative learning experiences.

Rules should be set up with the following in mind: Each teacher follows up to seven sets of rules. The hierarchy includes guidelines from the federal government, the state government, the school district or corporation, building guidelines, department rules or protocols, the teacher's own set of beliefs and practices concerning discipline, and the students input. A classroom is a small society existing within these larger frameworks, so some rules are nonnegotiable and some are more flexible.

Examples of federal rules, which are important in cooperative learning, are those ensuring that every student regardless of race, income, or ability level has the right to participate in the learning environment to the fullest extent. State guidelines determine standards, and district guidelines can influence a number of factors such as peer grading and Internet access. Building rules help the teacher identify procedures such as where activities are held, and access to areas and server space to display finished projects. Department rules or protocols vary according to the size of the district but can include pacing requirements and primary text use.

Of course, the area where the teacher has the most control is their own set of beliefs and practices. By asking what the desired outcomes of a particular project or lesson might be, examining personal tolerance levels, and by conducting surveys and listening to feedback, teachers can incorporate their own teaching style into their own set of behavior expectations. Student input is the most crucial part of emulating a social contract. Once students understand which roles are non-negotiable, contracts or compromises may be made. Students in each class could make up their own word for off-task behavior or they could help establish a "quiet signal." Quiet signals can be anything from a particular noisemaker to everyone raising their hand when the teacher raised his or hers. This allows those whose face is turned away from the teacher to know when to be silent. Quiet signals must be taught and practiced early and reinforced often. They are useful for transitions, when the teacher wants to give additional instructions or information, or when the class is too loud.

Formulating

This set of skills is requisite to provide the mental processes needed to build deeper understanding of the material being studied, stimulate the use of higher quality reasoning strategies, and ensure mastery and retention of the assigned material. The following skills are specifically aimed at providing formal methods for processing materials:

1. Summarize out loud. Every group member must summarize from memory often if learning is to be maximized.
2. Seek accuracy by correcting, adding information, or pointing out ideas or facts that were summarized incorrectly in a member's summary.
3. Seek elaboration by asking other members to relate the material being learned to earlier material and to other things they know.
4. Utilize a variety of graphic organizers such as t-charts, Venn diagrams, Vee heuristics, concept maps, time lines, and decision-making scenarios to help retain important ideas and facts.[45]

Fermenting

Some of the most important aspects of learning take place when group members skillfully challenge each other's conclusions and reasoning. Skills involved include the abilities to:

1. Differentiate when there is a disagreement with the learning group.
2. Integrate a number of different ideas into a single position.

3. Ask for justification of a member's conclusion or answer.
4. Extend another member's answer by adding further information or implications.
5. Probe by asking questions that lead to deeper understanding.
6. Keep "rough notes" to visually show the group's processes.

The fermenting skills are the most complex and the most difficult to master. They ensure that intellectual challenge and disagreement take place within learning groups.

Group Processing

Groups need specific time to discuss how well they are achieving their goals and maintaining effective working relationships among members. This may be achieved by having the groups describe what member actions were helpful or unhelpful, and by the groups making decisions about what member actions should continue and what actions need more work.

The Teacher's Role in Cooperative Learning

The teacher's role in cooperative learning situations includes five major sets of strategies. The first strategy is that the teacher clearly should state the essential question, the objectives, and the standards for the lesson. The academic objective needs to be specified, at the correct level for the students, and matched to the right level of instruction according to a conceptual or task analysis. The collaborative or social skills objective details what collaborative skills are going to be emphasized during the lesson. In regard to timing, the teacher may remain flexible but must keep in mind semester goals and overall pacing requirements.

Making decisions about assigning learning groups prior to the lesson being taught is the second major strategy a teacher must initiate. The size of the group as mentioned earlier may be changed based on the lesson objectives. The more group members, the more chance to have someone who has special knowledge helpful to the group, hence more minds and talents are available to do the task. Sometimes just breaking the class into two large groups further aids academic achievement. The larger the group, however, the more skilled they must be at providing an opportunity for everyone to participate and in reaching consensus. The availability of materials, including computers; the time allowed; and the nature of the task may determine group size. Allowing students to choose their own groups is not always a poor idea as long as students in the class have been familiar with cooperative learning rules; are sensitive to heterogeneous benefits; and do not group according to ability, gender, ethnic background, and task orientations. Yet, there are times when homogenous grouping, according to gender or some other factor, may enhance the learning of a particular topic. The assigning of student roles can be accomplished in a number of ways. Titles such as summarizer, checker, researcher, data processor, and so on, may be effective. Using models of government such as president, cabinet members, senators, pages, and staff members also may serve as additional role-playing activities. When studying America at war it may be helpful and stimulating to have roles with military titles. Students also can volunteer based on their specific strengths where they can help the group the best.

The third strategy is in explaining the instructional task through direct instruction. Cooperative learning is not just providing group work so the teacher can complete paper work. Direct instruction is still a vital role for the teacher who should be clear and specific about the assignment. The essential question should be posted and presented in a clear and enthusiastic manner. Essential questions for the unit should be broad enough to incorporate several questions. An example of an essential question for a unit on the Gilded Age could be "Why can't I as an immigrant work harder to improve my position in life?"

Positive goal interdependence can be structured by asking the group to produce a single product and by providing group rewards. Structured individual accountability can be obtained by giving individual tests, randomly selecting students to explain answers, randomly picking one paper from the group to grade, or by having group members use different font colors or pen colors. Rubrics assist with explaining criteria used in the evaluation. The teacher also could have each member of a group explain how they arrived at the answer.

The fourth strategy is in monitoring the effectiveness of cooperative groups and intervening only to provide task assistance or to increase students' group skills. A formal observation sheet, a student observer, or student feedback can assist with this. It is very important after the charge has been given to a group to step back and not intervene unless absolutely necessary. It is with this type of problem-solving situation that students will build valuable skills; therefore the teacher should not act as an enabler to solve all problems.

The final strategy for teachers to implement is in evaluating and processing. The quality and quantity of student's mastery of concepts should be as creative as the cooperative learning process. Unit tests can go beyond multiple choice and essay and include a variety of assessment devices such as document-based questions, t-charts, and persuasive writings and drawings, just to name a few. Tests should be challenging and not just knowledge based. Choice is important for the student as some aspects of the particular question are more relevant to individuals than others and application skills still are measured.

Cooperative learning also serves to create a democratic social system in which the students determine how to reach their mutual goal. Teachers serve as facilitators, not as "workers trying to sand, polish, and paint students into educated objects."[46] As a facilitator teachers must make the transition from being "in authority" to being "an authority."[47] Students, on the other hand, must learn to trust one another and learn to resolve conflicts constructively.[48]

Instructional Support System

W. Woolworth said, "I never got very far until I stopped imagining I had to do everything myself."[49] Harry Wong admonishes teachers to look at themselves at the end of the day and assess who is more tired, the teacher or the student. If the answer is the teacher then something is wrong since it is the student who was supposed to be engaged in the learning.[50] Teachers need more than books and workshops to become proficient in cooperative learning. They become proficient through practice and through support groups.[51] In *The Fifth Discipline*, Senge discusses the importance of professional learning groups and how student achievement can be a direct result of teachers using action-based research to implement new strategies or improve on existing ones in their classrooms.[52] When teachers are asked who their primary source of assistance is, the most common reply is, "other teachers."[53]

Teachers need emotional support from colleagues who will "cheer success" and encourage them through difficult times.[54] The role of the principal and superintendent in providing administrative support to cooperative learning is important because students are not seated in silent rows and the noise level in a cooperative classroom can escalate. An administrative collegial support group can be implemented, structured in a similar manner to the teacher's cooperative classroom structure to assist in providing support for best practices.[55]

The last variable in the instructional support system is that of parental support. In an interview with Ron Brandt, Roger Johnson noted that cooperative learning receives a great deal of support, especially from upper-middle class parents.[56] Parents view cooperative learning as a "bonus" because it provides their children with leadership, conflict resolution, and decision-making training; all of which are necessary skills for future success.[57] This type of parental support is a prerequisite to successful cooperative learning. In the age of project-based learning, parental support is further encouraged if most of the structure of the project can be worked on at school in the cooperative learning group. This is preferable to the more common method of assigning a project with little direction at school and parents scrambling to assist their child in completing the project. Communication is the key and with classroom Web pages, e-mail, online classroom newsletters, and so forth, parents can become actively involved. The use of a Web cam for presentations of final projects could allow many parents a chance to see their child perform at a time that may have been impossible in the past.

Cooperative learning is not a "quick-fix panacea" that teachers can master in one workshop.[58] It takes a great deal of patience, time, commitment, and support to refine the techniques. Spencer Kagan developed *Kagan's New Cooperative Learning* which includes a "Smart-Card" that illustrates fifty-six simple strategies for cooperative learning.[59] Strategies that have been successful in secondary history classrooms are those where the teacher takes the fundamentals of cooperative learning and then uses a little creativity. Using playing cards, especially those designed for young children, can be helpful and fun in assigning groups, developing lessons, and helping students meet objectives.

Cooperative learning never should be viewed as a reward that can be taken away if the students do not behave, instead it should be viewed as an effective teaching technique. Flexibility, established ground rules, and a little imagination can revitalize a classroom. Accountability can be increased by providing group incentives, such as extra points for the entire group if the group average exceeds the past test by a certain number of points. Publishing examples of excellence from different groups will lead to increased self-esteem and increased intrinsic motivation. Participatory education beats passive education every time.

Chapter 13

Teaching Strategies and Resources for History and Social Studies Education

Joseph A. Braun, Jr.

In the beginner's mind there are many possibilities.
—Shunryu Suzuki

William Kennard, chair of the Federal Communication Commission (FCC), has described the inevitable future of a wireless information superhighway that will democratize the Internet and make the availability and power of the new information technologies cheaper and more widespread. According to Kennard, the availability of more bandwidth for greater technological development will result in "making the Internet available to those who can't afford a $5,000 computer."[1] His words portend that soon teachers can download clips (even entire movies) or television programs with an amazing array of choices instead of the relatively few channels currently available. Cable seems to offer a wide variety of choices; however what is coming will make the current fifty channel package seem paltry in comparison. This means that in the not too distant future, it will be possible to cheaply and quickly deliver instructionally valuable video, linked with text and primary source resources, to students over desktop monitors (or handheld devices like PDAs). Essentially, for about the current cost of textbooks, students will have in their hands access to the Internet and multimedia. including full-motion video capabilities, all with access speeds faster than current T-1 lines deliver.

There is a catch, however, to optimizing the educational potential of this future: preparing social studies teachers who can take advantage of the information technologies that are currently available, not to mention the next generation that Kennard forecasts. As Jamie McKenzie has aptly argued, we have spent much too much time and effort on information technology and not near enough time on information literacy.[2] He takes the position that there is not enough emphasis on professional development and program development to take advantage of the networks and information technologies that are now available. While the FCC points out the proliferation of information technology, Mackenzie contends that schools don't make a strong commitment to student questioning and research.

In this chapter, the focus will be on what teachers can do to promote information literacy in the history and social studies education classroom. The ideas outlined in the chapter will be limited to a dozen notions that seem crucial in teaching history and social studies in the twenty-first century.

Searching and Researching: A Key to Information Literacy

As argued elsewhere, a fundamental element of realizing the educative power of the Internet is making students critical consumers of what they encounter as they search for information.[3] Essentially, they need to be what Beyer described as judges of the authenticity, relevancy, and worthiness of information.[4] Before evaluating whatever information they encounter, however, students need to know how to plan for finding information, and this starts with the basic step of posing the right questions. We will look at Beyer's concern in more depth in the next section, but first how do students go about systematically finding information?

In a short, but gem-packed book, Jamie Mackenzie claims that the most important technology ever invented is the human question.[5] He goes on to present a typology of seventeen questioning tools that are appropriate not only for the Internet but for any research quest. Also offered is a solid rationale for why this typology should become part of what a school district offers as a toolkit for students to use in their search for information. In addition to the role of questions in an information literacy school, Mackenzie describes the research cycle. Finally, in the latter portions he provides a thorough description of the various strategies (beginning with the organization into research teams) that students could use to plan, execute, and report on the research they conduct. Although much of what is presented is relevant to any student-initiated research, he does include many elements that focus on technology—such as presenting and analyzing data.

Although Mackenzie's book is a generalized treatment of conducting research on the Internet, a chapter in the recent National Council for the Social Studies (NCSS) bulletin is a more specific look at search engines. In addition, it also includes some good ideas that students and teachers can use in planning to conduct research.[6] Essentially, a five-step plan is outlined for searching the Internet: (1) choose a keyword; (2) choose the search engine to use; (3) enter advanced search techniques; (4) choose relevant returns; and, (5) refine or expand search. Of course, this is really only an Internet adaptation of the above-mentioned scientific method of inquiry. Brehm also offers some teaching guidance for helping students learn how to be more effective in searching the Internet, such as understanding that it is a gradual process that probably should not be taught until fourth or fifth grade when students are a bit more mature. Prior to that, teachers should preselect sites.

"Search Engine Watch" teaches more about the specifics of learning how to search online. It has a complete review of all the major search engines, strategies for using them, reviews and rankings of search engines, and tips for getting URLs identified by search engines. Teachers may also subscribe to a free monthly online newsletter that gives up-to-date information on search engines.[7]

Assessment: The Missing Link

Fred Risinger and others have argued that the evaluation and validation of information on the Internet is a central issue. Teachers and students must openly confront these issues, or run the risk of putting our students at great intellectual jeopardy.[8] Before the printing press, monks and imams of the church or mosque and scribes for the royal court served as the filters of information for the masses. With the printing press, it became the academics, the publishers, and eventually teachers who filtered information. In the age of the Internet, the responsibility for determining the worthiness, authenticity, and relevance of information is now left to the masses. Brehm's caution against providing much free searching for students before around fourth grade notwithstanding, it is imperative that we give later elementary-aged students some tools by which they can critically assess information they encounter online.[9]

Evaluating information found on the Internet is not as daunting as it might seem. In fact, the criteria are not unfamiliar; they are almost the same that would be applied to any other written information or primary source document. Some of the criteria Risinger identified for evaluating an Internet site include: (1) How congruent is the online information with what you already know? (2) Who is the author and what credentials do they possess? (3) What is the currency of the information? (4) What is the scope and depth of the information? (5) Is the information clearly presented and well organized? (6) Has anyone recommended this site to you? (7) How true do you think this information is and why do you think so? (8) If there are photos, what point of view is the photographer trying to take? (9) How important is the information and why do you think it is?[10] Of course, the particular ability of a given student to use these criteria will be contingent on the ability to use skills such as detecting bias and separating fact from opinion. Although these skills are not really "new," they are needed more often now and must be applied to new media.

A second dimension of assessment also is not new, but this dimension seems to be like the "missing link" whenever reviewing Web pages purporting to be for social studies education. In this context, assessment is applied not to the World Wide Web itself, but rather to how we know students learned anything from their experiences in using whatever technology might be employed as a learning tool. The importance of assessment cannot be understated, for it is the basis by which we determine the value of any educational endeavor.[11] Although some Web-based curriculum designs, such as WebQuests, which will be described shortly, do have a strong assessment component, many others do not.

Numerous state boards of education have developed booklets on authentic assessment that contain excellent rubrics, information about using authentic assessments in social studies, and examples of prompts and scored student-responses as illustrations of how the rubrics work.

Such booklets and packets are valuable resources for teachers, and often can be accessed online.[12]

Antidotes for Plagiarism in the Information Age

It is no secret to students that term papers are available over the Internet for almost any topic. But as Mackenzie points out, this isn't what we should be worrying about.[13] Rather, he argues that we ought to be developing some approaches that go beyond the typical "go find out about" assignments that students get as their research project. Instead, he advocates a more sophisticated approach to having students engage in research assignments given the available technologies. His antidotes for the urge to plagiarize in this digital age are sensible but require some of the following changes.

First, distinctions in the type of research we ask students to engage in should be established. One level of research is "just the facts"; while a more sophisticated level is "other peoples' ideas." The most significant level, however, is what Mackenzie calls "in my humble opinion," where students are asked questions or given problems that have never been adequately addressed. He offers, "How can we have peace in Northern Ireland?" as an example.[14] The emphasis should be on this level, but that will require breaking the dominance of "trivial pursuits" that pervade many students' experiences with doing research on the Internet. We should ask essential questions and questions that cause (and enable) students to construct their own answers. This will go far in reducing the tendency among students to look for an easy answer or good essay on the Internet and pass it off as their own.

Another antidote that Mackenzie identifies is "focus on systematic storage," which includes having students become systematic about their note taking and the storage of their notes in an electronic database.[15] In addition to the ease of storage and retrieval, electronic notes could be used as part of the assessment process. In developing note-taking skills, students learn how to construct a list of subject-level words and create a deeper level of categorization with keywords. Finally, students learn to write an abstract of the information they acquire. So the database entry has three fields (or categories): subject, keywords, and abstract.

Perhaps the best antidote among McKenzie's suggestions is the one he calls "green ink and stressing citations."[16] Most current versions of word processing programs allow the user to choose the color of the font, in addition to the font itself. Building on the above idea of electronic notes, McKenzie suggests that starting with the abstract, student can identify the ideas of others by using black, and can select a different color (such as green) their own comments. The teacher can then select yet a different font color (such as blue) and respond to the student's notes and ideas about the information. Thus, the note card is transformed into a tri-color record of the information found by the student, the student's responses, and the teacher's guidance on what to do next. This might be viewed as the technological application of the content area literacy strategy known as "reader response."[17] Of course the culminating step would be to compile this into a "final paper" that is published as part of the multimedia presentation.

Databases

Because databases appear to be the most logical way to store electronic notes, it seems logical to follow the idea of electronic note cards with a discussion about databases as a tool in social studies education. Hunter was the first to suggest three stages of student use with databases.[18] At the initial level, students are searching databases compiled by someone else, which is a good way to introduce them to the functions of the particular database being used—*Clarisworks* and *File-Maker Pro* are the most common in K-12 education.

Most research studies on database instruction support an initial whole-group model followed by small groups and individual practice with the various database construction and search strategies.[19] As an example of the first stage of databases use is to begin each semester by administering a brief survey of "favorites" (categories include fast food, toothpaste, designer label, pizza topping, holiday, etc). Also ask students how much television they watch and how many hours they spend reading about current events on a daily basis. This provides some numeric data in addition to the text data generated by the other categories. Next, enter the data and deliberately falsify some of the numeric data. As students begin to learn how to search a database, some become affected by the falsifications and are outraged, which is the first point to be made about any database—it is only as useful as the information in it is reliable.

Once students learn how to manipulate the database someone else provided in the first stage, higher order thinking skills are developed as they think about ways to sort and organize the information they add to predetermined records (or note cards), which is Hunter's second stage of database use.[20] Initially, the teacher (in consultation with the student) might define the subject and keyword descriptors that are developed. Thus, the student is adding information into a template and then searching it for trends and other relationships.

The final stage is when students design and construct the database independent of the teacher. It is in the creation and definition of the categories (or fields) of information and then the construction and use of the database to answer questions that students develop skills such as classifying, defining, categorizing, inferring, comparing, and contrasting.

As teachers we want to model problem solving with databases through a progression of the following tasks: determining information needs, formulating expectations, drawing a tentative conclusion, and presenting the results. Furthermore, we need to help our students comprehend some other general considerations for good social studies teaching such as using cooperative learning, providing adequate structure in the initial stages of working with databases and promoting higher order skills, and adjusting instruction for different grade levels.

Spreadsheets

Understanding the use of spreadsheets is an example of the kind of skill students need so they can become competent in what has become known as social mathematics. Social mathematics is the ability to understand basic statistical concepts (ratio, percent, mean, etc.) and apply these concepts in order to recognize trends and make predictions based on quantitative data.[21] There are a number of examples of how spreadsheets are used in history and social studies.

Using data collected from three graveyards in South Africa by twelve year olds, Paul and Kaiser point out several outcomes that students learned as they organized the data, developed their own hypotheses, and searched for answers employing the computational and representational properties inherent in spreadsheets.[22] Students cooperatively interacted with each other, engaged in lively discussions during hypotheses formation and testing as graphs of the data were prepared with the spreadsheet application, and furthered their cross-curricular understanding by applying mathematical principles, skills, and concepts to historical data.

An exploration of geography and climate served as the focus of one particular spreadsheet activity used with fourth graders.[23] The project focused on United States weather patterns for three cities at the same latitude but having very different climates: San Francisco, California, Dodge City, Kansas, and Richmond, Virginia. Students entered the mean temperatures for each month and then used the graphing function of their spreadsheet program to examine trends and anomalies (i.e., comparatively, San Francisco is much nicer to spend the winter in than the summer). The varieties of graphs give students ample opportunities to compare and discuss the differences in what the visual displays convey. Ideas for extending this project and processing the ideas encountered are provided.

The final strategy for using a spreadsheet fits in nicely with our role as teachers—recording and reporting student scores on projects, exams, and assignments. Instead of purchasing a grade program, however, most spreadsheets will serve the function just as well. Multiple uses such as this (i.e., as an instructional and classroom management tool) make spreadsheets and databases valuable tools in a history and social studies teachers' repertoire.

Word Processing and Other Forms of Electronic Writing

In addition to Mackenzie's "green ink" antidote for plagiarism outlined earlier, there are some other ways that features of word processing programs can be used to promote better history and social studies teaching. In addition to discussing how to use some of the features commonly found in current versions of word processing programs, some ideas used to prevent e-mail overload but still encourage online discourse will be described.

Social studies teachers need to provide for the conceptual development of their students. The use of computer-based webbing as a way of providing a conceptual map has been advocated and examined.[24] Just as there are specialized software programs for recording and calculating grades, there also are particular software applications designed for the specific purpose of developing concept maps.[25] And, just as spreadsheets can be easily used for recording grades, the more current and popular word processing programs feature drawing tools that can be enlisted for the development of concept maps. Drawing tools can appear as a pallet or part of a pull down menu depending on the application. Regardless of how the feature appears, virtually every drawing tools offering contains all that is needed for concept map production: ovals and other geometric shapes in which students can insert brief amounts of text (all that's needed for a concept map) and lines for connecting different parts of the web. Of course, drawing tools allow for other shapes besides ovals, thus permitting the user to design complex maps with different shapes representing various dimensions of the concept.

In addition to the function of drawing tools, the insertion of graphics is another feature that is becoming commonplace with word processing programs. Graphics can be obtained from clip art, downloaded from the Internet (in compliance with copyright laws), or scanned in by students. Graphics can be used to enhance a concept map (picture a middle school student developing a concept map on geographic forms who has incorporated pictures to illustrate a bay, peninsula, and isthmus on her concept map). Students can also incorporate graphics into reports. Additionally, word processing programs often contain features for placing text in columns, thus allowing students to create desktop-published newspapers that include graphics. All of these represent ways students can display and communicate what they are learning using tools that they will more than likely encounter as they begin working in a few years.

Undeniably, e-mail has become a common element in the world of work and at times it can feel overwhelming with the number of messages arriving on any given day. Therefore, in addition to the delete key, teachers are always looking for ways to reduce the volume of incoming mail. Rather than relying on e-mail or list servers, one way to reduce e-mail overload is to encourage students to use a discussion group or newsgroups, which can be Web-based, to communicate with others and with the teacher. To initiate their use of this Internet tool, ask students to post a response to "What concerns you about this class?" Then collect their concerns and synthesize them into a set of discussion threads and post them. Students are then assigned the task of finding a thread they want to respond to and posting a response to it. By the end of the semester or school year, a variety of topics should have been raised and discussed by different members of each class who offer their expertise and experience to the online conversation.

Similarly, students learn how to create discussion threads and post questions about assignments or other matters that concern them in relation to the class. Teachers then can direct student e-mail for personal matters that do not concern other class members.

From Atoms to Bits: Computer Hardware and Multimedia Experiences

As Nicholas Negroponte has explained, the world used to consist only of atoms but computers changed this: now our world is made of atoms and bits.[26] It is an intriguing concept to mull over and it is the computer's capacity to store and manipulate the bits of information that form into the amazing array of multimedia experiences that make current computers such a captivating experience for students. Bits, by the way, refers to an encoding system using only 0s and 1s, which the computer then processes to produce items such as documents, databases, spreadsheets, and images.

The computer peripherals designed to accomplish the process of transposing images into bits were initially somewhat expensive for most school budgets. As with other technological advances, the cost associated with purchasing the most current image processing products has rapidly become less expensive and is now within the budget of many schools, particularly those savvy enough to seek technology support through grant programs. The following describes the basic hardware and software applications associated with the power to create, manipulate, and produce multimedia for instructional purposes in history and social studies education.

Digital cameras are a prime example of the power, simplicity, and affordability of computer peripherals that can be used to develop multimedia. By running off a disk or by storing the image internally until it is transferred to a hard drive through a connecting cable, digital cameras can record images with almost the same fidelity as a 35mm camera. Photographs of geographic forms, famous landmarks, or dramatic productions related to social studies easily can be taken and stored.

Scanners are a second good example in the evolution of computer peripherals and their adaptability to meet history and social studies goals. As with the digital camera, a scanner performs its functions much the same way as a checker at the grocery store scans the prices of your groceries with bar codes. The computer chips inside these devices read and record all the colors (or just black and white bar codes) as "bits" of information that are then translated by the computer (or cash register) into images and text. Scanners can reproduce photographs of people and places, historical documents (including text), and artist renditions of social studies related content. As with a digital camera, once the information is recorded as bits, the files can be stored on a disk or hard drive. It should be noted that graphic images can be quite large; however they easily can be manipulated within a graphics program to make them manageable.

Creating digital versions of audio and video tape recordings is also relatively cheap and can be an excellent way for history and social studies teachers not only to provide curriculum material for students, but also to record examples of teaching vignettes for inclusion in a teaching portfolio. Depending on file size, which is the number of bits used, digitized versions of teaching episodes could be transferred to a CD or stored and made available over the Internet using a particular format for delivering all the bits in a "stream" instead of downloading them onto the user's computer through a File Transfer (FTP). Therefore, the file is never really transferred when it is streamed to users. When on the Internet, there are commonly agreed upon universal formats for the digital media: GIF and JPEG for graphics; AU, WAV, AIFF, and RA for audio; and AVI, MPEG, and QuickTime (MOV) for video.

From Atoms to Bits: Computer Software and the Multimedia Experiences

Graphics software is used to manipulate digitized images. Photoediting software makes it possible to manipulate an image by resizing it or by changing the coloration and contrast. Paint tools also are usually included in photoediting software, which allows images, such as a banner, to be generated for a homepage.

PowerPoint is a special form of multimedia software that is primarily used for making presentations. While certainly appropriate as part of the history and social studies curriculum, this particular technology, when used in a minimalist manner to assist a teacher's lecture, does not represent the more sophisticated levels of instructional uses of technology. Nonetheless, when used appropriately, such software applications can provide combinations of text, images, video, and audio to focus student attention and present the main points of a lecture. Additionally, *PowerPoint* programs easily can be uploaded to the Web for later recall and downloading.

Hypermedia software is used to link several pages of text and graphic material together allowing the user to navigate through links and buttons to related text, graphic, and audio files. The Internet is a hypermedia environment and the software used to create Web pages has become as easy to use as word processing applications. In fact, many of the latest word processors offer not only paint tools but also a feature that automatically generates an HTML file (which stands for hypertext markup language) that can be read by an Internet browser.

A popular hypermedia software program that students and teachers can learn easily is *HyperStudio*. Like Web pages, a *HyperStudio* stack has links to a variety of pages containing graphics, text, and possibly audio files. The organization and path through the stack is left up to the author's design. Teachers can construct stacks to guide student learning through a particular topic or concept, such as a tutorial on various landforms or variety in housing of Native Americans. Also, students can create multimedia reports of historical or geographic information, such as architectural changes in homes, and include maps, digitized photos taken of examples found locally, or scanned images of examples not locally available. Such multimedia reports offer students multiple ways of expressing their learning by demonstrating their understanding of concepts and ability to report factual content. *HyperStudio* stacks not only operate similarly to many home pages on the World Wide Web, but also can be linked to the Web, and many such social studies learning modules of student multimedia reports are currently available on the Internet. In addition, online rubrics are available that can be employed in evaluating multimedia productions of students.[27]

FTP: Transferring Files Over the Internet

Before teaching students how to create a Web page, it is important to first teach them a skill that they will need to publish their Web site on the Internet. It is the same skill that allows teachers to use the "green ink" strategy described earlier and to avoid massive amounts of e-mail from students when it comes time to turn in their assignments. This skill involves using an Internet software tool that allows the user to transfer files across the Internet. Most commonly, on the PC platform, this software is called FTP (which stands for file transfer protocol); on the Macintosh platform the most popular FTP software is called *Fetch*. Because it is a relatively simple tool to use, in a sense it provides "the keys to the kingdom," it is curious why so many schools still deny teachers access to it.

Students actually have used FTP before if they have ever downloaded a file from the Internet, such as the popular audio files known as MP3, which provides free musical entertainment. In this case, FTP is operational, but it works automatically in the background and the user is not really aware of its operation. An analogy might be how a clutch is incorporated into an automatic transmission on a car and its use is not apparent to the driver. When students learn to use FTP software, they are provided with accounts on the school's server. A server is a computer that is dedicated to a particular function, in this case a gateway to the Internet, and an account provides disk space for the storage and retrieval of computer files, such as word documents, Adobe Portable Document Format (PDF) files, spreadsheets, databases, or files formatted for viewing on the Internet.

To actually launch and operate the software involves typing in the address of the Internet server the user wants to connect with and account information (i.e., user ID and password that the "network administrator" provides when the account is registered). It takes about a minute or two to teach students this procedure and then they have access to a class folder that contains individual subfolders for storing digital files, such as reflection papers to an assignment, or Web pages (these folders are also called directories but serve the same purpose). In addition to their individual folders, students can have access (transmit files) to a "public" folder where they initially store their work for grading. Once the student's work is evaluated, it is returned to the individual's folder to which the network administrator has granted "permission" for both the student and teacher to access.

What seems puzzling about the current practices of most school systems is why they do not give teachers their own accounts so they (and their students) can publish on the Internet and transmit work electronically. The only plausible explanation (but few would say this publicly) is that teachers cannot be trusted to use the technology properly. This is certainly akin to the administrator who denies teachers the keys to the building precluding them from coming to work during the summer or on weekends. It is demeaning and no longer makes sense.

Students learn that they are capable of using the Internet for purposes beyond viewing Web pages and downloading MP3 music files. In the short time that it takes students to learn FTP, they acquire the skills of organizing and managing folders for storing digital files, publishing their own Web site, and transferring files from one computer to another over the Internet.

Publishing on the Web: WebQuests as an Internet Instructional Design Model

Less than five years ago, students had to create Web pages by learning the HTML tags (tags are the little codes in brackets that are translated by your Internet software-browser into text and images). However, software soon became available that would allow anyone familiar with word processing software to learn the basic functions of HTML text editing in an hour or two. Because students already know how to use FTP, they can be publishing their own Web pages in a relatively short period of time.

One path for publishing on the Web is a class home page. Examples of these abound on the Internet.[28] The value of such a home page could be to keep parents and students advised of course assignments or as a repository for students to display their work (i.e., links to multimedia reports described above). In this case, the home page serves as a "public" version of the curriculum that summarizes what students are learning. Obviously, school district approval must be attained before any such home page bearing the name of a school or individual students is posted to the Internet. And, as described above, individual teachers often are not given the right to post anything to the Web except through a network administrator, often called the Webmaster.

The second path for a teacher-produced Web page is by far the more interesting and is a specific example of Internet-based curriculum—the WebQuest.[29] An inquiry-oriented approach first described by Bernie Dodge, WebQuests can be either short term (lasting one to three class periods) or long term (from a week to a month duration). WebQuests transform students into what Mackenzie calls "infotectives" and creates the kind of technology supported environments where students become "engaged learners."[30]

WebQuest's critical attributes include: an introduction that sets the stage and provides information; a task that is doable; information sources embedded as Internet links pointing the user to relevant home pages or the e-mail addresses of experts; the process for completing the task; some guidance on how to organize the information (guiding questions or organizational instructions for completing a concept map or a cause and effect diagram); and, a conclusion that encourages students to extend the experience into other domains. The advantage of such an online structure for Web-based learning experiences is the guidance the teacher builds into the problem to be solved or project to be completed. Students are not left to aimlessly "free range" on the Internet—a practice that Jamie Mackenzie avers against.

A final guide to Internet curriculum design is called Module Makers, a program conceived by Mackenzie. He provides templates in both a Web-based format and a word document that can be downloaded from the Web site by FTP (which is operating in the background). Mackenzie maintains that the hard-pressed teacher does not always have time for constructing a Web page and he provides Internet-based lessons in a word processing format that teachers can easily modify to meet their particular instructional goals.[31]

Social Studies Software: Concerns and Development of New Forms

One of the most prevalent forms of social studies computer software is simulation, a teaching strategy which long predates computers.[32] Not all simulations, however, are what they appear at first glance. For example, from a critical theorist's perspective, Bigelow reviewed an acclaimed software simulation, *Oregon Trail*.[33] In addition to raising many valid criticisms about this particular software, Bigelow concluded his review with six important questions for social studies teachers to consider before using any simulation:

1. Which social groups are students invited not to identify with in the simulation?
2. How might these social groups be portrayed differently than framed in the simulation?

3. What decisions do simulation participants make that may have consequences for social groups not highlighted in the simulations? And what are these consequences?
4. What decisions do simulation participants make that may have consequences for the earth and nonhuman life?
5. If the simulation is time specific, as in the case of the Oregon Trail, what are the social and environmental consequences after the time period covered in the simulation?
6. Can we name the ideological orientation of a particular simulation?

What seems to separate simulations from other computer-assisted forms of learning such as arcade games are two characteristics: realism and relevance.[34] As important as these variables are to meaningful social studies learning, the critical factor in the effective use of technology as part of a social studies curriculum will always be the teacher. It is the teacher who helps students process the information and experiences encountered, so that they can construct meaningful learning from any experience with software. Chiodo and Flaim analyze several models for debriefing simulations and then apply a four-stage model of their own to *Oregon Trail*.[35] Essentially, their instructional model begins in the first stage with students experiencing the simulation, and then the teacher leads the students to make inferences, analyze, and compare the computer simulation to the real world.

Perhaps the newest form of social studies software to become available is the recent release of mapping software based on Geographic Information Systems (GIS).[36] An analogy that helps explain GIS as a concept was provided by Keiper who described it as similar to the process of laying overhead on top of overhead with each one representing a different layer of map information that is added to the base.[37] Unlike simulations and other forms of social studies software, GIS software is a tool that students or teachers can use to construct maps and topographical representations—a very powerful and expressive tool that makes such practices as coloring in maps obsolete.

Two Enduring Concepts for Coping with Future Shock

There are two concepts that students often are taught to consider as constants in life. These concepts are embodied in what Alvin Toffler was describing when he coined the term "future shock" almost thirty

years ago.[38] In a general sense these concepts are experienced throughout life, but particularly in relation to technology do we encounter the
concepts of *change* and *conflict* on an ongoing basis. As software
developers work to incorporate more features into their programs, they
often render earlier versions of the same software obsolete. Users ac-
customed to working with a particular software product find that the
new version often conflicts with their previously learned skills and
knowledge. The changes and conflict that technology inevitably brings
into our lives are not insurmountable, but they require new attitudes
and new strategies for accommodating the relentless pace of technological development. As Kuriloff pointed out recently, educators must
prepare students to control, rather than react to, the changes that new
technology will bring.[39]

Misery loves company, so the solution for dealing with the never-
ending changes and conflicts that technology brings into our lives is
simple—get a buddy with whom you can share your woes. In other
words, find a technology mentor—another teacher, media-center director, student, professor, or personal friend—who would be willing
to share their expertise and help you answer questions that arise as
you work with new software programs or Internet tools. What is important, beyond a mentor's expertise with technology, is his or her
ability to not overwhelm you with information that is beyond your
level of comprehension, thereby leaving you frustrated. Most teachers
with some expertise in technology often are more than willing to help
a newcomer figure out what is causing the glitch.

Mentorship might not always come from a single individual. There
are presentations at conferences, workshops, and institutes that focus
on instructional uses of technology. The National Council for the Social Studies (NCSS), the Association of Supervision and Curriculum
Development (ASCD), and the National Association of Middle-
Schools Education (NAME), all have strands that address technology
at their annual national conferences; the same is true for the majority
of affiliated regional and state association conferences. Presentations
and opportunities for hands-on exploration facilitate acquiring
technology-related skills and also provide ideas for incorporating these
skills. The NCSS provides a technology lab at their annual conferences that highlights current versions of a wide variety of social studies software. Other applications, such as *HyperStudio* or *PowerPoint*

also are available for preview and experimentation by conference participants.

Sometimes mentors come in the form of authors, both online and in print. Advice and information can be gained from the Internet itself by posing questions to newsgroups and list servers. A number of publications feature a section devoted to technology-related curricula and instruction. Two NCSS journals are must-reads for current trends in using technology in social studies: "The Media Corner" section in *Social Studies and the Young Learner* (elementary and middle school education); the "Instructional Technology" section of *Social Education* (high school and middle school education) includes not only reviews of software and articles on using technology, but a monthly feature on using the Internet as an instructional tool. The International Society for Technology in Education publishes *Learning and Leading with Technology*, which has a special section on social studies and features articles germane to middle school social studies. "Power Tools" in *Phi Delta Kappan* is a column that provides a brief but informative look at cutting edge applications of technology to education.

Where Do We Go From Here? The Next Step

The next step novice and experienced teachers should take to help students develop the information literacy skills they will need for this new millennium can be found in the standards set by the International Society for Technology Education.[40] Many of the ideas enumerated above are embedded in these standards. History and social studies teachers who can meet this set of standards are well equipped to use technology in powerful ways in their teaching. For others, the journey of learning how to integrate technology into their curriculum and instructional practices certainly can begin with these standards.

Anyone who embarks on the journey to become proficient in the above mentioned standards, however, should keep in mind the ancient Chinese proverb, "The journey of a thousand miles begins with a single step." Thus, it does take time to become masterful in using technology and incorporating it into teaching so that students are engaged and working in ways that allow them to use these powerful tools for obtaining information and constructing knowledge. But, when done in ways that are beginning to take shape in more and more classrooms, the possibilities are absolutely astounding in how they alter teaching and learning.[41]

In a recent article, the venerable social studies educator Howard Mehlinger speculated what the life of a teacher of social studies might be like given the predicted changes in technology and how it will be adopted to educational needs. He outlines exciting changes, which already are technologically feasible, such as visualization software and virtual environments for learning. He also alludes to the powerful communication link that can be built between parents and teachers.[42]

In contrast to the future that Mehlinger projects, educational historian and Stanford professor Larry Cuban avers that teachers and students do use computers, but more at home than at school. From his research findings he offers two reasons why there is such infrequent and limited use of computers even in schools where abundant technology resources are available.[43] First, there are institutional forces currently impeding the more imaginative and creative ways that computers can be used, such as the use of age to determine grade placement and the departmentalization in the secondary schools. A second reason is that the technology sometimes is flawed, and when it fails it leaves teachers scrambling to complete a lesson and substituting plans on the fly.

Given the transformational changes in the multimedia possibilities described in the beginning of this chapter, and the fact that teachers and students make significant use of computers at home, it seems the technological issues Cuban raises will dissipate over time. The forecasts of Negroponte, Mehlinger, and Kennard suggest that computers will become much more prevalent and easier to use over the next decade, which will lessen the technology flaw phenomenon. The school organization and management issue, however, is a human-thinking problem that can be changed, but it requires the development of instructional and curricular models.

Over the past twenty years, we have too often observed classrooms with banks of computers sitting idly by while the "teacher talk" that Goodlad documented prevailed.[44] On the other hand, we have all been in classrooms where computers are in constant use and students move back and forth in small groups conducting research or getting more individual instruction from their teacher than possible when whole class instruction is the predominate instructional model. Perhaps that could be our own step for the coming year: to encourage even more multiple group work time around computers in our own history and social studies classroom. What will yours be? Just remember: One step at a time will do it.

Part IV

Learned Curriculum

Chapter 14

Informal Assessment and Evaluation Strategies

To make someone smart, you can't make them know the
answers, but you have to teach them to ask the
right questions.
—Author Unknown

Without question, assessment is one of the most vexing and taxing issues associated with teaching. It is also one of the most important, both for students and teachers. Good assessment and evaluation strategies provide students and teachers with information about how well students are learning and about the effectiveness of teachers' instructional practices. Of course, any kind of assessment or evaluation can examine only a snapshot or small percentage of the total possible understandings or abilities that students have. That reality makes it crucial that teachers think carefully about the development of their instructional objectives and the relationship between those objectives and their choice of assessments. Students and teachers cannot benefit from assessments that focus on relatively unimportant aspects of the material presented or demonstrated by students.

With the advent of standards-based education, *performance assessment* has become more widespread. In general, performance assessment focuses on students' authentic or real-world demonstrations of competencies as opposed to more traditional paper and pencil tests. "Performance assessment requires examinees to construct/supply answers, perform, or produce something for evaluation."[1] Performance assessment is actually a much older type of testing than the relatively modern paper and pencil tests. The Chinese civil service examination system and medieval European craft guilds both required potential practitioners to demonstrate real-world "job" skills. It was only in the nineteenth century with Horace Mann's replacement of oral tests with written exams and, more directly, the development of standardized testing in the twentieth century that paper and pencil "traditional" tests eclipsed performance assessment.[2] As discussed in chapter fifteen on formal assessment and evaluation strategies, there are many performance assessments that work well in history, social science, and social studies classes.

But these types of performance-based assessments are generally *summative,* or end point, evaluations. This chapter focuses on *formative* assessment and evaluation strategies that allow teachers to gauge how well students are learning so that instruction is more effective and deficiencies or problems in students' understandings or abilities can be corrected. Thomas A. Angelo and K. Patricia Cross describe formative assessment as "almost never graded" and intended to "provide faculty with information on what, how much, and how well students are learning, in order to help them better prepare to succeed—both in subsequent graded evaluations and in the world beyond the classroom." Formative assessment, as opposed to summative types of assessment, is also very often anonymous; teachers attempt to gauge how well all students are doing as a whole. This chapter will highlight three major categories of informal or formative evaluations: assessments in the cognitive domain, assessments in the process and affective domains, and portfolios that document activities in all domains.[3]

Cognitive Domain

Teacher dialogues and discussions with students are the most basic and essential element of informal assessment. Generally, such conversations emphasize relatively quick checks for knowledge and comprehension. When lecturing, for instance, teachers should try to incorporate questioning techniques into their presentations. This style of lecturing might be seen as a modified Socratic style in which the teacher directs questions about the material to students, to check for both content understanding and higher-order thinking. When most effectively conducted, such lectures actually become more like discussions and opportunities for sharing of teacher and student points of view on the material. By listening to students' responses, a teacher can determine whether it may be necessary to reteach material or move expeditiously on to the next topic.

Very often what one discovers when asking students questions is that they have faulty understandings based on misconceptions or stereotypes about the issues. Angelo and Cross suggest a "Misconception/Preconception Check" as a useful assessment tool for helping teachers to uncover students' misunderstandings. With this formative assessment exercise, before starting a new unit the teacher asks students to list answers on key questions about the main themes in the unit. For instance, in a United States history class unit on the Great Depression, a teacher could list on the board: (1) What were the causes of the depression? (2) What did the Hoover administration do about the depression? (3) What did the Roosevelt administrations do about the depression? (4) What event was most important in lifting the country out of the depression? After the students write down their answers, the teacher could have the students work in small groups and pool their answers to provide to the rest of the class. Before providing the right or most plausible answers, the teacher would ask the students to reflect on how they formed their judgments about the questions.[4]

Discussion with students can also take the form of written checks for understanding. For instance, teachers can ask students to write for one minute to explain what they learned about a particular topic or issue. Normally, these one-minute writing exercises should be done near the end of class when a teacher will ask students to respond to variations of the following questions: What was the most important thing you learned during the class? What unanswered questions do you have about the lesson? Teachers can then collect students' answers, read through them, and gain an understanding of where they need to proceed or how they should adjust their instruction. This same idea can be applied to almost any type of direct instruction. For instance, following a video clip, a teacher might ask students to write down the main ideas or themes from the clip. These can be scanned quickly after class and used to help direct further discussion of the importance of the segment the students watched. Teachers might also ask students to take a very short quiz at some point during a lesson to see how well they understood key concepts or ideas.

The "K-W-L format" also provides useful formative assessment information: Using the KWL acronym as a guide, students indicate what they *know*, then note what they *want* to learn, followed by some indication of what they have *learned*. This process can be conducted orally or in written form. With each of these types of formative assessments, the emphasis is not on scoring the students' work as it usually is with a summative assessment. Instead, the information gathered helps the teacher focus on how students are either learning or not learning the material. This again helps teachers decide how they might proceed.[5]

Another type of written formative assessment is initialing students' work on projects that have been scaffolded. Any fairly involved research projects in which students test a hypothesis should be structured to help students understand the process involved in examining the document or documents, analyzing their meaning or meanings, and then composing their responses to the hypothesis. These scaffolded assignments require the individual or groups of students to receive a teacher's check or initials before moving to the next step. As teachers move from one student or group of students to the next, they can gauge the students' efforts, talk to them if needed about how they are doing, and then indicate, with their initials, if the students should proceed to the next part of the project. Worksheet 14.1 provides a template for a scaffolded project.[6]

Pretests can provide useful information for formative evaluation, particularly for judging students' basic knowledge and comprehension. Used in this way, pretests provide diagnostic information that allows teachers to determine what students know before they begin a unit. By identifying students' understanding or gaps in understanding, teachers can then modify their unit design accordingly. Normally, pretests, like most formative assessment tools, should not be graded.

Process and Affective Domains

Although usually more time consuming, there are several more intensive types of formative assessment. Here, instead of relatively quick checks for understanding or comprehension, the teacher engages in

---

Worksheet 14.1

Steps for Developing a Scaffolded Cooperative Project Centered on a Reading Assignment

Directions: Each student will work in a small group and read the selected passage(s).

Step One: Read the passage(s).

Step Two: Rewrite the passage(s) in your own words.

Check Point: Teacher must initial before the group is allowed to proceed. _____

Step Three: Summarize your passage(s) in your own words to the other people in your group.

Step Four: Select a facilitator for the group's discussion about the meaning of the various passages.

Check Point: Teacher must initial before the group is allowed to proceed. _____

Step Five: Each member of the group must write a three-paragraph essay explaining what the passages mean.

   Source: Adapted from Kobrin (1996).

---

more in-depth questioning or written assessments of students' abilities in the process and affective domains. By using "probing" questions during a classroom discussion, for instance, a teacher can gauge students' analytical or evaluative abilities in the process domain. In history and social studies classes, questions that require students to explain how or why target their higher-order thinking skills. These questions can be asked not only during a class discussion on a topic, but are also ideal for when students are working on research projects, either individually or as part of a group.

Angelo and Cross describe several variations on these sorts of higher-order questioning techniques. For instance, students can be asked to explain the "pros" and "cons" of a decision-making process. In a political science class, a teacher might ask students to list the pros and cons of eliminating the electoral college from the presidential election process. In this case, rather than simply checking students' comprehension of factual issues, the focus is on decisions, judgments, dilemmas, or issues that are central to the unit being taught. These answers can then be collected and assessed to see how balanced students' perspectives are and where they may have gaps in their analytical skills.[7]

Very often asking higher-order questions during such interviews requires teachers to follow up with questions that ask students to elaborate on their answers. Here are some possible follow-up statements or questions.

- I am interested in your thinking. Please tell me more.
- Please help me to understand. Suppose you are the teacher and I am the student.
- I don't think this issue is easy to understand. Sometimes I get confused, don't you?
- Sometimes when I have difficulty with an issue, I break it down into small steps. Let's do that here.
- Take your time and think about your answer.

Each of these prompts asks students to reflect further on their ideas. Indeed, formative assessment is especially useful for providing students with opportunities to develop their reflective abilities.[8]

Questioning and interviewing individuals or groups of students also allow the teacher to assess students' dispositions in the affective domain. Teachers frequently should ask students to elaborate on their beliefs, values, and attitudes. This type of discussion is useful not only in developing students' beliefs, but also in providing teachers with important information about their students' attitudes, particularly in terms of whether or not such attitudes have changed over time. In fact, the citizenship education function of so much of history and the social studies demands that teachers engage in informal assessment of students' developing belief structures.

Angelo and Cross outline several types of reflective formative assessments that focus on students' attitudes and values. One is the classroom opinion poll. Teachers can use such polls to help students prepare for a discussion of a controversial issue and as a pre- or post-assessment device "to determine whether and how students' opinions have changed in response to class discussions and assignments." Opinion polls are ideal in history, social science, and social studies classes. In a United States history class before discussing the debates surrounding the use of the atomic bomb, a teacher could ask students whether or not the United States should have used the bombs to end the war. This question is ideal to use both before and after discussing the use of the bombs.[9]

Although informal interview assessments suggest an oral approach, this type of formative evaluation also can be practiced through a variety of written exercises. Journals are particularly useful for asking students to reflect on their beliefs, values, and attitudes. When used informally, students may actually provide more honest remarks since they know that their attitudes are not being graded. Indeed, in these cases they may be more likely to express their reactions and beliefs in a journal rather than in open discussion. One type of written exercise focusing on students' values and analytical abilities is the double-entry journal. Many teachers require their students to keep their lecture and reading notes in a journal. The double-entry journal takes this one step further by having students write their reactions to their lessons in a separate column. On the left side of the page, students should take their lecture or reading notes, while on the right side, next to the appropriate issue, they should write their comments. Such responses help teachers to evaluate their students' reading, analytical, and reflective abilities. Requiring students to prepare longer profiles on individuals or issues is a variation on the same type of analytical and reflective journal entry. Here, however, the time required to read students' entries is greater.[10]

Another way to use students' written work for formative assessment is by evaluating drafts with qualitative assessments of their idea development. Instead of assigning a score based in part on mechanical and grammatical proficiency, teachers can develop rubrics that provide written feedback about their essay's audience awareness, development, organization, coherence, and unity. Worksheet 14.2 provides a sample rubric for this type of formative writing assessment.[11]

Since one of the main purposes of formative assessment is to provide teachers with feedback on how students are learning, teachers should also ask students for their reactions on what they have learned. This can be done orally at the end of the class by asking the question, "What did you learn today?" But it may be more reliable and systematic to ask students to jot down their answers on a piece of paper and turn them in anonymously at the end of class. With the advent of e-mail and its widespread use, this can also be accomplished electronically. Although not quite as anonymous, its use may save class time since the messages can be sent to the instructor following class. Students can even engage in electronic conversations among themselves through class list servers.[12]

Portfolios

Typically, portfolios, or collections of students' work, are used for summative evaluation. Teachers might ask students to save and or-

---

Worksheet 14.2

Writing Idea Development Instrument

Audience awareness

The writer has a purpose.	No	Somewhat	Yes
There is a main idea/topic.	No	Somewhat	Yes

Content development

Adequate information or sufficient supporting detail about the main idea is presented.	No	Somewhat	Yes
Significant/relevant information is presented.	No	Somewhat	Yes
Accurate information is presented.	No	Somewhat	Yes

Organization

Type of writing	___ Descriptive	___ Narrative
	___ Expository	___ Persuasive

Logical progression/			
flow of information	No	Somewhat	Yes

Pattern of	___ Time order	___ Sequential order
organization	___ Spatial order	___ Definition
	___ Order of importance	___ Comparison
	___ Classification	

Organization of single paragraphs

Paragraph is indented	No	Somewhat	Yes
Clear, focused topic sentence	No	Somewhat	Yes
Conducting sentence	No	Somewhat	Yes

Organization of multiparagraphs			
Paragraphing is appropriate to content	No	Somewhat	Yes
Introductory paragraph that contains a clear, focused thesis	No	Somewhat	Yes
Introductory paragraphs outlines the organizational structure of the composition	No	Somewhat	Yes
Concluding paragraph	No	Somewhat	Yes
Cohesiveness			
Intraparagraph transition words/phrases	No	Somewhat	Yes
Interparagraph transition words/phrases	No	Somewhat	Yes
Repeated words, synonyms, parallelisms that co-occur	No	Somewhat	Yes
Unity			
Every sentence is related to the main idea	No		Yes

Source: B. J. Scott and Michael R. Winter (2000). Reprinted with permission of the Helen Dwight Reid Educational Foundation. Published by Heldref Publications, 1319 18th St., NW, Washington, DC 20036-1802. Copyright © 2000.

ganize examples of their efforts on a variety of assignments, classified according to type, over an entire unit, or more likely, an entire semester or year. With a summative portfolio, the emphasis is generally on having students save examples of their best work. Formative portfolios are less often used, but can provide very useful indications of students' progress. Instead of emphasizing students' best work, a formative portfolio includes examples of students' work that emphasize their development over a period of time. For instance, instead of simply saving only final drafts of written work, students could be asked to save early drafts as well. Any rubrics used to assess written work also should be included. The qualitative comments from the papers and rubrics would provide the chief indicators to students about their problem areas as well as ways they have improved. In this way, a formative portfolio provides useful reminders to the teacher and student about their improvement. They are also useful for helping students to reflect on how their skills have improved, and about the ways they might improve their performance or skills in other areas in the future.

Some of the student work samples that lend themselves particularly well to formative portfolio collections include:

- essays, research papers, written projects, and other written exercises;
- cooperative learning group outcomes;
- skill demonstrations (e.g., using reference materials);
- authentic creations (e.g., oral history projects, exhibits, videos, audiotapes, artifacts, photographs, bulletin boards, posters, Web sites);
- rating forms, checklists, and observation forms;
- diaries, journals, and logs;
- experiments; and
- teacher interviews.

These items lend themself to formative assessment particularly because each generally require multiple drafts or needs to be accomplished in stages. At the same time, as discussed in the next chapter, each can be useful in summative portfolios as well.[13]

Chapter 15

Formal Assessment and Evaluation Strategies

If the only tool you have is a hammer, you tend to see every problem as a nail.
—Abraham Maslow

Performance assessment has given paper and pencil tests a bad name. As discussed at length in the next chapter, performance assessment provides students with opportunities to demonstrate real world, authentic competencies. Many educators believe that performance assessment is a much more authentic, and therefore preferable, type of summative evaluation.[1] Yet objective and subjective formal assessments and evaluations still have an important place in history, social science, and social studies classrooms. Standardized tests certainly are an important part of the academic world. They typically are easier to design and implement than performance assessments. They are less subject to teacher grading bias when well constructed compared to essay or other authentic assessments. Secondary level students need to be prepared to take a variety of important paper and pencil type tests if they hope to do well on SAT, ACT, AP, LSAT, MCAT, GRE, and other types of precollegiate, collegiate, and graduate school examinations. Furthermore, objective and subjective (essay) tests, when developed carefully to reflect the important instructional objectives in teacher's units, can provide valuable summative evidence of students' learning. Indeed, essay tests, in particular, provide students with valuable writing practice, a skill that most certainly is authentic and valuable in the real world.

Nevertheless, it is important to consider both the strengths and weaknesses of paper and pencil objective type tests, especially, before weighing their results too heavily in your evaluation system. To be sure, critics of this type of formal assessment point out many valid concerns. There usually is only one right answer in objective test questions. This in turn promotes convergent thinking. The standard objective test formats, true-false, multiple choice, matching, and fill in the blank or sentence completion, focus primarily on the two lowest levels of Bloom's taxonomy—knowledge and comprehension. Knowledge-level testing also emphasizes memorization, a skill that tends to be overemphasized throughout elementary and secondary education. Studies of teacher-made tests suggest that the overwhelming majority of them are written at the knowledge level.[2] Memorization emphasis also lends itself to the problem of students cramming for tests and then forgetting the information soon after the test is over. The fact that objective test formats lend themselves to numerical grading also contributes to the widespread problem of students' concern for grades as opposed to real learning. Performance assessment is much more conducive to evaluation that is descriptive or narrative rather than scoring those results in a percentage and a letter grade.[3]

Given all the pitfalls of paper and pencil objective tests, what redeeming features do they have? As all social studies teachers know, the nature of history and the social sciences as disciplines requires extensive knowledge and comprehension of basic facts. History is especially dependent on knowledge of basic facts. It often is tempting to focus exclusively on knowledge and comprehension of facts in social studies classes, but it seems safe to say that at the very least students do need to have a grasp of facts if they are going to use relevant information for an issue-centered problem or if they are going to analyze and evaluate documents for a paper or other more authentic project. Objective tests can therefore provide an important and relatively painless evaluation format for assessing students' lower order, but still essential, thinking abilities. Objective type tests should therefore be used in combination with more authentic assessments, including essays, which are more suitable for evaluating students' higher-order thinking skills.

Objective Evaluation Formats

True-false statements are the most basic type of objective evaluation format. However, this simplicity is deceptive. Teachers need to use care when constructing their own true-false statements. They are best used for testing knowledge level information. As a result, they can sometimes lend themselves to testing trivial issues. History teachers, in particular, sometimes go overboard with constructing true-false statements focused on obscure dates, for instance, in their objective tests. Here, as with any form of assessment, teachers need to refer back to their instructional objectives. True-false statements should focus on the most essential as opposed to trivial facts.

Be sure to construct statements that are either definitely true or false. Sometimes teachers are tempted to include interpretive issues in their true-false test section. For instance, in a unit on World War II, some teachers might posit: American military leaders thought German soldiers were better trained than Japanese soldiers. While some historians might feel this is true, it is not definitely true without exception. It is a statement of opinion rather than a statement of fact. If a history teacher wants students to focus on such issues, they are better suited for explanation and elaboration in an essay or other open-ended format.

Because true-false statements also lend themselves to fairly successful guessing, since the odds are always 50–50, teachers should consider ways to encourage students to demonstrate their knowledge of the facts rather than their ability to guess successfully. One way to credit students' knowledge is to give extra credit to students who can successfully transform a false statement into a true statement. When the test items are designed, simply leave space below the statement for such transformations. If the correct answer is worth one point, then you might consider awarding students additional one or two points for a correct transformation of a false to a true statement.

Multiple choice questions are the most commonly used objective evaluation format in history, social science, and social studies classes. They are especially good for testing students' comprehension abilities. It is also possible to construct application-level test items. Although some might argue that higher-level multiple choice items can also be written, it is preferable to use essay format questions for allowing students to demonstrate their analysis, synthesis, and evaluation abilities.

As noted, multiple choice questions are especially useful for evaluating students' comprehension skills. For instance, the multiple choice format lends itself quite well to questions focused on important terms and concepts. Such questions normally start: Which statement about . . . is most accurate? The concept of . . . is best represented by . . . ? Multiple choice items also are very useful for testing cause and effect relationships. Examples of this include: Which was a significant cause of . . . ? Which incident led to . . . ? Which one of the following is a long-term result of . . . ? Key generalizations can also be successfully assessed through multiple choice items. In this case, questions might start: Which is the most accurate statement about . . . ? The idea that . . . is best illustrated by . . . ?

Application-level multiple choice questions can also be written. Here, since application ability requires students to use previously learned information or ideas in a new situation, it is best to remind students to review previous specific information that might be included on the evaluation. For instance, in a unit on World War I in a United States history class, a teacher might remind students to review military innovations that they had learned in the unit on the Civil War. A multiple choice question might then fairly ask: Which of the following military innovations developed during the Civil War was also used during World War I? Another application level multiple choice item requires students to arrange events in correct chronological order based on previously learned material. In this case an appropriate format might be: Which sequence of events best describes the historical development of . . . ? Each possible answer would then include a plausible sequence of such events.

Another somewhat more complicated type of multiple choice format is the database question. Unlike standard multiple choice questions, database multiple choice questions are based on data presented in maps, political cartoons, graphs, charts, tables, time lines, or readings. They lend themselves to testing higher-order thinking skills. There are four general categories of such questions: comprehension, explanatory, conclusion or generalization, and prediction. Comprehension questions simply require students to explain what the data means.

Explanatory questions ask students to choose the best answer that explains the data presented. Conclusion or generalization questions require students to synthesize from the data presented. For instance, what does the cartoon suggest . . . ? Which conclusion is best supported by the graph? Prediction questions ask students to predict based on the data presented. Database questions can test higher-order thinking skills, but require more time to develop and, more important, require students to use a good deal of time when taking the test to study the data and come up with their answers. This is time that might be better used in preparing an essay answer.[4]

One of the most important considerations when writing multiple choice questions is making sure that all choices are plausible. Avoid answers that are "throwaways" on topics unrelated to the subject at hand. Not only should the possible answers be closely related, they should also be approximately the same length. Students very often use their "meta–test-taking" skills to look for clues to the right answer when they do not know the material. One of these clues is an answer that is either much longer or shorter than the others. You should also use four or five possible answers and avoid "none of the above" or "all of the above" answers. Too often "none of the above" or "all of the above" are the correct answers when infrequently used. In addition, the stem part of the question should be stated positively and clearly. Avoid negatives and double negatives. It is important that students focus on the material stated in the question and not on uncovering the meaning of obscurely written or trick questions. Finally, be sure to vary the location of the correct response in your multiple choice section. Again, students often look for discernible patterns in multiple choice tests, especially when they are unsure of the material.

The *matching* format is also good for testing students' comprehension-level abilities. Use this format to test students' understanding of significant people, places, terms, and concepts. It is preferable to provide a list of related material in each column or section. For instance, list the key people, places, terms, or concepts in the left column and the possible definitions in the right column. You can also list the key people, places, terms, or concepts on top and the possible definitions on the bottom. In either case, the point to remember is that in the English language, people read from left to right and top to bottom. The items to be defined should be fairly concise while the definitions can be longer. To reduce the effect of guessing, provide more possible definitions than items to be defined. Also, be sure your directions indicate if definitions can be used for more than one item.

The *fill in the blank* or *sentence completion* format is similar to the true-false format, though more challenging, in that it emphasizes knowledge-level information recall. Consequently, be sure to emphasize specific factual items. The surrounding statement should contain enough information for the student to know what response to include. Nevertheless, teachers should expect alternative responses from students and be prepared to allow at least partial credit to these alternatives. Students are often quite creative about these alternatives. Also, since students usually are expected to know the correct name, place, or term that goes in the blank, you need to decide before the test (and inform the students) if they need to spell these names, places, or terms correctly. One variation that makes this format more similar to matching formats (but also less time consuming) is to provide a list of possible answers that students can refer to. As in the case of matching type questions, be sure to provide more possible responses than blank spaces. Worksheet 15.1 provides summary suggestions to consider when designing true-false, multiple choice, matching, and fill in the blank or sentence completion test questions.

Essay and Open-Ended Evaluation Formats

Essay questions provide the best way to formally assess students' higher-order thinking skills. They also encourage students to think creatively as well as critically. As is true of performance assessments, essay tests encourage divergent thinking. Writing is a "real life" skill that is unfortunately too often neglected in middle and high school history and social studies classes. Too many social studies teachers assume the language arts teacher will take care of writing issues. Given society's demands for professional skills and proficiencies, however, good writing ability will become even more crucial in the workplaces of the twenty-first century. The information economy, in fact, demands that people have good reading and writing skills to best use electronic information, communication, and other media.[5] Essay tests are one way to provide your students with help in developing their critical writing skills. This is just as true of middle level students as with high school students, though obviously teachers' expectation

Worksheet 15.1

Essential Considerations in Designing Objective Tests

True-False Questions

1. Focus on knowledge-level issues. Be sure your statements are definitely true or false.
2. Do not test trivial information. Focus on essential factual issues discussed in the unit.
3. Consider giving extra credit to students who can successfully transform false statements into true statements. This helps to reward students who actually know the facts instead of simply having guessed the answer successfully.

Multiple Choice Questions

1. Focus on comprehension and application-level issues.
2. Database multiple choice questions can test students' higher-order thinking skills.
3. Be sure all possible choices are plausible. Avoid throwaway answers.
4. Make each possible choice approximately equal in length. Use four or five possible choices.
5. Avoid "none of the above" or "all of the above" choices.
6. Avoid negatives or double negatives in the stem.
7. Vary the location of the correct answer so that students do not look for possible patterns.

Matching Questions

1. Focus on comprehension-level issues that test students' understanding of people, places, terms, or concepts.
2. Construct this section so that the names, places, terms, or concepts to be defined are either on the right or the top while the definitions are on the left or bottom. This increases readability and lessens confusion.
3. Be sure to provide more possible definitions than names, places, terms, or concepts to be defined to reduce the effect of guessing.

Fill in the Blank/Sentence Completion Questions

1. Focus on specific knowledge-level information. Be sure the surrounding material provides students with adequate context.
2. Give students partial credit for close answers.
3. Tell students whether or not they need to know exact spelling.

levels need to vary according to students' ages, developmental abilities, and skill level.

Essay writing is also an authentic skill used by practitioners of history and social studies. While preferable perhaps to incorporate writing assignments into performance assessments based on student-initiated projects, in-class formal exams that include essays or other kinds of open-ended writing are still valuable. Teachers need to be aware, though, that not all students will be equally proficient in demonstrating their writing skills under the conditions involved with in-class essay tests. For instance, students with learning disabilities may require more leeway in terms of extra time or privacy to work on their essays, in accordance with their Individual Education Plan (IEP). Students who are nonnative speakers of English may also need modifications in terms of essay writing expectations. Nevertheless, all students as much as possible should experience some in-class essay writing.

Essay tests certainly are not without their own problems, though. While relatively easy to design, essays are quite time consuming to read and grade. More problematic, perhaps, is the issue of validity and reliability in scoring essays. Be sure that the essay questions focus on key themes elaborated on in the unit. As in the case of objective test questions, it is important to test what was taught. In terms of grading essay responses, considerable care and thought needs to go into construction of your rubric for evaluating students' work.[6]

There are two main elements involved in developing effective essay questions. The first is the elements that should be considered when constructing good essay questions. It is good teaching practice to reinforce the major themes that you are focusing on in your units, and remind students that these themes are likely to be the subject of possible essay questions. Think carefully about your word choices and phrasings when constructing essay questions. Generally, good essay questions are concisely worded. Avoid long descriptions, multiple parts, or long antecedents or scenarios that precede the actual question. These types of questions tend to distract and confuse students. Avoid asking questions that simply ask for recall of factual information. Instead, focus on phrasings that encourage students to use analysis, synthesis, or evaluation skills. For example, an essay that wants students to analyze a process or a development could start: *Explain how* the industrial revolution developed between 1790 and 1820. Similarly, an essay that expects evaluation might say: *Explain why* the industrial revolution developed between 1790 and 1820. This phrasing is much preferable to essay questions that begin: *List* the events in the industrial revolution between 1790 and 1820, or *Describe* the events in the industrial revolution between 1790 and 1820. With the latter two questions, some students will simply provide a long laundry list of events with no attempt to explain their significance or the relationships among them.[7]

The second, and most important, element in designing essay questions is the scoring rubric. Generally, essays should be evaluated based on the *structure* of students' responses rather than simply on the amount of information conveyed in them. Structure refers to proper essay format, particularly the inclusion of a *thesis paragraph* that is followed by well-organized *explanatory evidence*.[8] The thesis paragraph in a history or social studies essay needs to be specific and direct in terms of stating what the students' position is. This paragraph might also convey information about the general background or context for the explanatory evidence to follow. It generally is not appropriate for a thesis paragraph to simply restate the question or say that this essay will address several points. In an essay responding to the question about why the industrial revolution developed between 1790 and 1820, an effective thesis might be: Master craftsmen who then became entrepreneurs revolutionized workplaces through development of division of labor and new marketing techniques. An ineffective thesis statement would be: This essay will discuss why the industrial revolution occurred between 1790 and 1820. The first thesis statement is effective precisely because it contains two specific references to issues that could be explained in subsequent paragraphs.

In addition to a strong thesis statement, a well-structured essay response includes organized explanatory evidence. If the thesis statement suggests two main ideas, then it is generally appropriate that the evidence include at least two explanatory paragraphs. Encourage students to think in terms of paragraph structure and development of topic sentences with transitions between each paragraph. The rubric that is used to evaluate the essays should reward students for these two main elements. It is important to explain to students that there is no one "right" essay answer, but that a well-developed essay with a strong thesis and explanatory evidence is better structured (and thus more "right") than an essay with a weak thesis and evidence that does not support or only vaguely supports the thesis.[9]

Especially for essays written during an in-class test, the rubric should not penalize students for misspellings or other mechanical problems unless those problems are so severe that they impede an understanding of the essay's underlying structure. Early in the year, when students are just starting to understand your essay expectations, it is good practice to provide models of good essays. Using students' actual essay responses, perhaps saved from another year and typed to protect students' identities, is a good way to model your expectations. Of course, it is important to tell students that you are not looking for one type of answer or that they should simply mimic what the student did in the model used in class.

Another consideration is allowing students to prepare outlines of the essays ahead of the test. In this case, it is necessary to give students two or three essay question possibilities before the test and indicate that you will choose only one question for the test. However, you should tell students to prepare for each possible essay question by outlining answers for each. Allowing students to use outlines eliminates some of the problems associated with test anxiety and actually encourages the teacher to weigh their scoring more on structure than memorized content. Students' outlines can include all the facts they think they may need. So instead, teachers should stress that their scoring will focus on how well students use and explain these facts rather than simply throwing them all into a laundry list response.

While use of a scoring rubric that reinforces emphasis on an essay's structure is vital to consistent scoring of students' work, two other scoring issues should also be considered. Be sure to give greater weight to the relative importance of the essay part of a test than to the individual objective test components. For instance, a typical in-class middle or high school level history or social studies test should include some objective questions and one essay question. The essay should constitute a larger proportion of the test's overall value than the true-false, multiple choice, matching, or fill in the blank portions of the objective part of the test. A good rule of thumb is to make the essay worth about half of the test's value unless the objective section is particularly long. In addition, as much as possible teachers should try to provide focused narrative explanatory remarks when providing comments on students' essays. This can be done on the rubric that is

---

Worksheet 15.2

Considerations in Constructing and Scoring Essay Tests

Constructing Essay Questions

1. Inform your students of the key issues they should think about as you teach the unit. Then ask them essay questions that pertain to those issues.
2. Think carefully about the words and phrases you use in constructing your questions. Avoid essay questions that have multiple parts or long antecedents.
3. Avoid essay questions that ask only for recall of factual information.
4. Explain to students that most essay questions have more than one "right" answer. Be sure your grading gives credit for divergent thinking.
5. Consider allowing students to use outlines and prepare for their essay responses ahead of the test.

Scoring Essay Responses

1. Develop a scoring rubric that focuses attention on the structure of students' answers. Tell students to develop their answers in proper essay format, including a thesis statement and an explanatory body of evidence.
2. Reward students for appropriate use of structure and content, but usually not on spelling or poor mechanics unless these elements detract significantly from the essay's meaning.
3. Consider modeling appropriate essay responses. Show students anonymous examples of previous students' work. Caution students about not mimicking such work and that you are not looking for one type of answer.

---

attached to the essay, for instance. Of course, writing fairly detailed comments adds to the time that it takes to evaluate essay tests, but such comments, particularly when they highlight the strengths of students' work, adds immensely to the value and authenticity of the experience for students. Worksheet 15.2 highlights the essential points about constructing and evaluating essay responses.

Considering the amount of time it takes to score essay tests, one variation on having students write a full answer to an essay question is having students write the thesis paragraph only. Since the thesis portion of an essay is usually the most direct evidence of students' higher-order thinking abilities, writing just the thesis paragraph is still a valuable writing experience. Similarly, many teachers effectively use open-ended short answer responses for the same purpose; they provide students with some writing practice and allow the teacher to gauge students' analytical, synthetic, or evaluative skills. For instance, directions for such short answer responses might state: Please highlight the most essential contribution or significance of each of the following names or terms. State the contribution or significance in no more than three sentences. Either of these two alternatives to a more formal essay test saves teachers valuable time in evaluating students' work but still gives students invaluable practice in critical writing.[10]

Chapter 16

Performance-Based Assessment

Education is not the filling of a pail, but the lighting of a fire.
—William Butler Yeats

Over the course of the past decade we have witnessed the dramatic swing of the educational assessment pendulum.[1] With the emergence of performance assessment, some educators have suggested the "3 Rs" are being eclipsed by the "3 Ps"—performance, portfolios, and products.[2] Although it is referred to by a variety of titles—authentic, alternative, nontraditional—there are certain common characteristics or elements germane to performance-based assessment.

Numerous classroom teachers have integrated performance assessment activities into their social studies curricula, the results of which have been examined and scrutinized by state and national professional organizations, government agencies, and researchers. The lessons learned from these observations, in particular the questions that should be answered prior to introducing performance assessment into the curriculum, as well as various examples of performance-based assessment activities are addressed in this chapter. Perhaps the pendulum swing that performance assessment represents is best summed up by educational researcher Grant Wiggins: "Assessment is something we do with and for the student, while traditional testing was something we did to the student."[3]

Definition of Performance Assessment

Just as there are numerous titles associated with performance assessment, so too are there countless definitions. While the search for a definition is, in itself, a fruitless semantic quest, it is important to understand what the term or concept means. Following are some of the more popular and widely accepted definitions of performance assessment:

> Performance assessment is a philosophy that asks students to use their knowledge and skills to produce a product that is as 'authentic' as the teacher can make it.[4]

> Performance assessment, also known as alternative or authentic assessment, is a form of testing that requires students to perform a task rather than select an answer from a ready-made list. For example, a student may be asked to explain historical events, generate scientific hypotheses, solve math problems, converse in a foreign language, or conduct research on an assigned topic.[5]

> [Performance assessments are] testing methods that require students to create an answer or product that demonstrates their knowledge and skills.[6]

> A performance assessment task is one that requires actual student performance in a context that reflects activities that are real and relevant to the student.[7]

History of Performance Assessment

Performance assessment is not a product of the late twentieth century. Its roots date back to the Han Dynasty in 210 B.C. It was during this period in Chinese history that two meritocratic examination systems were implemented for civil service and military selection.[8] From that period on, other manifestations of performance assessment could be found in every civilization throughout the globe. The European craft guilds of the fourteenth century serve as yet another example. To rise in this hierarchical structure from apprentice to journeyman and finally to master level, one had to demonstrate proficiency by undergoing "an examination (the so-called masterpiece) which was then both simple and practical."[9]

During the nineteenth and twentieth century, however, the emphasis on performance assessment was replaced with pencil and paper exams. In 1845, Horace Mann replaced oral exams with written essay devices for utilization in Boston public schools.[10] This trend continued throughout the remainder of the nineteenth century. By 1920, however, the written essay test that had dominated the previous century was being replaced with multiple-choice exams as the principal means of assessment.[11] Finally, in the last part of the twentieth century, critical reports such as 1983's *A Nation at Risk* provided the impetus for the swing in the educational assessment pendulum to where it is today.[12]

Purpose of Performance Assessment

One question all classroom teachers ask, when inundated with myriad forms of new educational strategies or programs, is "Why should I add this to my teaching repertoire?" Given the tremendous demands on teachers' time, this is a valid question that must be answered by advocates of any new curricular or instructional strategy or program if it is to be introduced into the classroom. Many teachers and researchers who have implemented and evaluated performance assessment have attempted to respond to this question. Their list of rationale for adopting the performance assessment model is:

- It allows for active student learning.
- Those student aptitudes and abilities not addressed by traditional tests are assessed.
- A wider range of data on student progress can be collected.
- Higher order and divergent thinking skills can be assessed.
- It provides for individual and group assessment.
- Both learning process and result/product are measured.
- It empowers students to make choices and thus is highly motivating.
- It can provide an impetus for improved instruction and enhanced student understanding.[13]

Role of Teachers

As with any curricular or instructional innovation, there are certain critical elements and/or questions that must be addressed if there is any chance of classroom success. Performance assessment certainly is no exception in this regard. Following are critical questions teachers may want to consider prior to implementing performance assessment activities in the classroom:

- Does this activity address course objectives?
- Is it curriculum centered?
- Does the activity integrate the other social studies and content areas?
- Is the activity feasible, with respect to time and resources?
- Is the activity engaging and thought provoking?
- Does the activity allow for both individual and collaborative work?
- Does the activity involve "real world" processes, resulting in authentic products?
- Does the task allow all students to succeed?
- Are evaluation criteria clearly understandable and presented prior to the task?
- Are models of excellent work provided to students?
- Are student learning styles and ability levels taken into consideration?
- Are students allowed the opportunity for self-assessment?
- Is there more than one right answer or approach?
- Is there a "feedback loop" that allows for students to continually revise their product?
- Does the task allow students to use higher order thinking skills?
- Are students allowed to participate in the development of assessment goals and criteria?[14]

Role of Students

One of the hallmarks of performance assessment is student empowerment. As in a democracy, there are responsibilities that go along with those rights provided to students under this form of assessment. Imogene Forte and Sandra Schurr provide teachers with the following list of responsibilities students should be accountable for while engaged in performance assessment activities:

- Be able to relate the performance to specific skills or concepts.
- Clearly explain the purpose and outcome.
- Critique exemplary and flawed examples of previous student perform-ances.
- Identify and explain assessment criteria.
- Be able to plan, monitor, and evaluate their progress.
- Conduct a self-evaluation of the final product or performance.
- Participate in the "feedback loop" between student and teacher.
- Use teacher critique and self-evaluation to set new goals for the next performance activity.[15]

Development of Performance Assessment Activities

For many teachers, it seems as though performance assessment activ-ities are specifically designed for social studies education, perhaps more so than any other discipline. While it is a viable form of as-sessment, worthy of being added to every classroom teacher's reper-toire, the transition can be daunting.[16] Although there is no one universally accepted approach to developing performance assessment activities, there are certain steps that most educators and researchers agree should be included in any model. Seven critical steps in the development process are outlined below.

- Determine what issue or concepts you want students to grapple with, learn and understand.
- Integrate previously learned essential skills and knowledge from the other content areas.
- Determine the appropriate activity or task that allows students to dem-onstrate understanding.
- Provide students with examples of both exemplary and flawed work.
- Develop and disseminate assessment criteria.
- Observe and collect data or evidence of student achievement throughout the process.
- Provide students with feedback and the opportunity for self-evaluation.[17]

Once teachers have established the protocol for using performance-based assessment activities in the classroom, they must next turn to the selection of those activities (See Appendix C for an outline of how the following performance assessment strategies correlate with various national standards). The more popular activities include the use of graphic organizers (Appendix B).

Graphic Organizers

The first few moments of a class are perhaps the most important in teaching; both setting the instructional stage and establishing the instructional momentum for the period. The integration of activities that incorporate graphic organizers not only sets the stage for history lessons but also serves as an ideal means for assessing prior student learning. Such activities may be integrated in the following manner:

- Teachers may choose to create handouts and distribute them to students, write them on the chalkboard/dry-erase board, or display them on a transparency or *PowerPoint* slide.
- Students then have the opportunity to immediately begin engaging in the activity. When completed, teachers may have students turn in their work, maintain it in their student portfolio, and/or use student responses as the focus of a classroom discussion.

The following is a brief overview of five of the most popular graphic organizers that history teachers may use for preinstructional or preassessment purposes (examples of each are included in the Appendices).

Timelines

Timeline activities are ideal for gauging student understanding of historical perspectives and causal relationships. They not only allow students to engage in chronological thinking, but they also provide an opportunity for them to refine their ability to identify temporal structure of historical narratives and establish temporal order in their own historical narratives. Students should be encouraged to use their textbooks, class notes, and other resources to assist in the design of historical timelines.

Decision-Making Scenarios

Decision-making scenarios allow students to demonstrate both convergent and divergent thinking skills. They also provide a way for students to participate in activities that introduce historical empathy as an instructional means for building student understanding. Teachers may elect to have student responses recorded in the form of an essay or require students to use a decision-making grid.

Concept Maps

Historical concepts, to include issues, movements, innovations, theories, and other events, are ideal foci for students' concept mapping or pattern noting activities, and are designed to help teachers determine the breadth and depth of student knowledge and understanding. Teachers should have students write the listed concept in the center circle on the map and then expand on that concept using one or two word phrases to describe related characteristics (e.g., individuals, events, consequences). Students can either design a semantic concept map, placing these related characteristics in the appropriate location (circle or box), or teachers can ask students to design a structured overview concept map that also includes the listing of the verb on the stem or line that connects these items.

Venn Diagrams

Venn diagrams are great vehicles for engaging students in analytical and convergent thinking. Teachers can instruct students in the number of differences and similarities that should be included in their response, and whether students should simply list or list and describe each of these items. Venn diagrams are primarily used as an organizational and conceptual tool for students to compare and contrast individuals, events, movements, and innovations in history; however, they also may be used for convergent and divergent thinking exercises.

Vee Heuristics

With a somewhat similar format to that of a Venn diagram, a Vee heuristic is designed for students to analyze dichotomous positions, policies, theories, decisions, movements, innovations, and events in American history. The Vee heuristic encourages students to delve further into the dichotomous positions addressed in the focus question, because there is no provision for a comparison as there would be in a Venn diagram activity. The focus question should be listed in the center of the Vee heuristic, with the two dichotomous positions labeled to the left and right of the question. Although graphic organizers provide useful intellectual scaffolding for students to engage in historical thinking, the absence of such constructs does not prevent such thinking from occurring in the classroom. One of the more traditional types of performance assessment that serves the same function as graphic organizers, absent the use of schemata replicating graphics, is journal writing.

Journal Writing

Journal writing is an ideal performance assessment strategy for engaging students in higher order cognitive-level thinking as well as for achieving many of the affective learning goals that are often requisite to deeper understanding. In addition, journal writing is a very effective means for integrating all of the elements of historical thinking into the curriculum. Historical thinking, as defined by in the *National Standards for History,* includes the following components:

- Chronological thinking
- Historical comprehension
- Historical analysis and interpretation
- Historical research capabilities
- Historical issues-analysis and decision making[18]

Although some instructional strategies demand that teachers sacrifice content for process, journal writing does not require that of those who choose to use it in the classroom. Another benefit of journal writing is the tremendous flexibility indigenous to its design. Journal writing activities can be assigned on a daily, weekly, and/or semester basis and can be worked out in various formats: notebooks, index cards, typed documents, floppy computer disks, protected/secure Web pages, and e-mail messages. Just as student journals may be maintained in a variety of formats, so too are there numerous types of journal writing classroom activities. The following forms of journal writing activities and implementation strategies serve as a reminder of the axiom put forth by the Bradley Commission on History in Schools that "variety is the spice of learning, just as it is of life."[19]

Integration Techniques

The following is an overview of five ways in which journal writing may be introduced in the middle and high school history classroom, within the curricular context of the *National Standards for History*.

Text Review Journal

The authors of the *National Standards for History* call chronological thinking the "heart of historical reasoning."[20] One way for students to identify the role and importance of temporal order, historical causation, and change and continuity is for history instructors to build this mental scaffolding. The type of journal assignment that appears best suited for this task is a text review. Text review journal writing encourages students to use the chronological timeline of the text as a baseline for other primary and secondary source materials they encounter in their readings, research, and class lectures. Students should place the items they come across in these other sources on the timeline provided by the textbook authors. This allows them to establish temporal order and to compare and contrast the varying historical accounts and interpretations they encounter during the course of their research and classroom discussion. For example, students can respond to journal prompts or assignments that ask them to

- identify the temporal order of the text's narrative;
- identify the interpretation of historical causation, events, and individuals in the text;
- compare historical interpretations in the text with those presented in class lectures/discussions;
- compare historical interpretations in the text with those presented in other course readings;
- compare historical interpretations in the text with those presented in research sources;
- place historical individuals, events, and movements encountered in other sources on the chronological timeline presented in the text's narrative; and

- discuss contradictions or inconsistencies between the text's chronological timeline and that of other sources.

Dialogue Journal Writing

The Bradley Commission's report on history teaching argues that one of history's "habits of the mind" is for students to develop an understanding of the "significance of the past to their own lives, both private and public, and to their society."[21] For this to occur, they must develop a degree of historical comprehension necessary to appreciate historical perspectives and avoid present-mindedness. To achieve this goal, students must be provided with opportunities to discuss historical issues and general learning concerns. Although many students take advantage of that period of time before and after school, as well as voice and electronic mail to address classroom issues and concerns, most do not. Dialogue journal writing provides a medium for discussing these issues in a manner integrated into the curriculum. Students might be asked to

- note general observations about course material;
- make suggestions or recommendations that might enhance student understanding;
- identify "lessons learned" thus far, including application to their own life and present society;
- list those lessons or topics they would like to learn more about;
- discuss individual learning progress, both positive and negative features;
- identify learning obstacles, including areas of concern, confusion or misunderstanding; and
- propose possible courses of action to overcome these barriers to learning and understanding.

Primary Document Analysis Journal Writing

According to the authors of the *National Standards for History,* the art of analysis "obliges the student to assess the evidence on which the historian has drawn and determine the soundness of interpretations created from that evidence."[22] Such an intellectual undertaking is possible only when students are allowed the opportunity to analyze, evaluate, compare, and contrast numerous primary source materials. As noted by some of the authors of the *National Standards for History*, "innumerable, and memorable, insights are to be gained from longer, closer looks at selected episodes, and all the more so by the deft use of primary sources."[23] Journal writing provides students with a means for recording their observations and conclusions in a comprehensive and systematic manner, thereby bringing a greater degree of consistency and authenticity to the learning process. For example, in their primary document analysis journals, students may be asked to

- identify the historical context in which the document was written;
- discuss the attitudes, beliefs, and values which are held by the author(s) of the document;
- determine the ideas, principles, beliefs, and values that are reflected in the document;
- identify the impact and legacy of the document, in particular causal relationships with other events or documents;
- compare and contrast historians' interpretations, similar documents, and other historical perspectives; and
- evaluate the role of the document in our nation's history.

Research Journal Writing

The authors of the *National Standards for History* best summarize the sentiments of most middle and high school history teachers by noting that, "perhaps no aspect of historical thinking is as exciting to students or as productive of their growth in historical thinking as 'doing history.'"[24] As with the other historical thinking skills, historical inquiry can also benefit from student journal writing, though in a much different manner. Students can benefit at every step of the inquiry process from maintaining a companion research journal to record their thought- and decision-making processes. A research journal provides students with a designated space to

- formulate historical questions and a thesis statement;
- list primary and secondary historical data sources;
- evaluate historical source materials; and
- record researcher's reflective thoughts and observations throughout the research process.

Classroom Discussion Journal Writing

One of the most engaging forms of journal writing is that which literally takes place in the classroom. When integrated into the history curriculum, classroom discussion journals have the potential to develop what certain architects of the *National Standards for History* have referred to as "perhaps the surest path to engagement and thereby to acquiring other habits of critical thought and perspective," historical empathy.[25] Well-structured journal writing prompts can spark the type of thought and reflection that allows students to develop both a deeper understanding and historical empathy. Journal writing activities may be introduced at various strategic points in the classroom discussion, including prior to instruction, as a transition technique, to check for student understanding, or as a summary activity. These journal prompts also may be designed to teach a number of historical facts, concepts, themes or issues, as well as to facilitate the development of a variety of historical thinking skills. For example, classroom journal writing can encourage students to

- identify salient issues relevant to understanding of historical events and movements;
- relate these historical issues to current societal concerns;
- discuss the problems and dilemmas that confronted individuals in history;
- discuss the role of historical context and antecedent circumstances;
- determine the alternative courses of action available to individuals during specific events in history;
- identify the beliefs, attitudes, and values that played a role in the decision-making process of individuals in history; and
- evaluate decisions made by individuals in history.[26]

Although journal writing has been modified as a result of the introduction of technology and the Internet in the classroom, other performance assessment activities trace their genesis to the dawn of the digital age. In particular, the following performance-based activities rely solely upon the Internet for their pedagogical existence.

Internet-Based Activities

There are many hurdles to be jumped before computers and the Internet become as commonplace as chalkboards and overhead projectors. Even if a teacher is fortunate enough to have a computer lab available for use, it still is necessary to clear the Internet access and use waiver hurdles before incorporating Internet-based performance assessment strategies into the history curriculum. For those teachers who have overcome these obstacles, however, there are still questions to be answered. Perhaps foremost is the question of how best to utilize the Internet to enhance the learning that already is taking place in the classroom.

The six Internet-based performance assessment strategies outlined here represent a linear pedagogical approach that allows students to build upon previous learning, while at the same time engage in more complex types of higher-order thinking. In addition, the varying levels of difficulty among these strategies allow teachers to select the one that is most congruent with their students' computer ability level. Many of these activities are adapted from the pedagogical model developed by Tom March of San Diego State University.[27] In addition, the conceptual basis for these performance assessment activities is traced back to the learning theory outlined by Joseph Novak and Bob Gowin.[28] Finally, the CARS Internet evaluation checklist, which calls for students to evaluate the *c*redibility, *a*ccuracy, *r*easonableness, and *s*upport of research sources, is taken from a framework developed by Robert Harris, Southern California College.[29] Overall, these activities are intentionally simplistic in design, with the intent being to seek simplicity while providing complexity for students. Unlike Alfred North Whitehead's cautionary note, "Seek simplicity, but distrust it," teachers should both seek it and trust it.[30]

Thematic Links Page

This activity allows students to explore the Internet in a relatively open environment. This is ideal for those students with little background in utilizing either computer technology and/or the Internet. First, provide students with an orientation in navigating the Internet and using a word processing program that provides for HTML conversion. Include in your orientation a discussion of how to download and insert images (e.g., backgrounds, bullets, pictures) and how to hyperlink text and images. Finally, outline the guidelines for the project, which include the following:

- List of potential themes from which to choose
- Minimum number of sites/links
- Textual data required on links page
  —URL
  —name of site
- Appearance of links page
  —background
  —main/heading Image
  —hyperlinked bullet images

Multimedia Scrapbook

The multimedia scrapbook activity allows students to conduct Internet research for images, text, audio, and video clips germane to a particular topic or theme. Once students have completed the thematic links page activity, they will have the skills necessary to prepare a multimedia scrapbook. Students will again conduct research on the Internet, although this time they will attempt to find a variety of multimedia items pertaining to the topic they identified in the thematic links page activity. They will construct a Web page that either links users to these varied multimedia items the students have indexed and hyperlinked, or they will display these items on their Web page. The students again should be provided with guidelines that address the following:

- Minimum number of multimedia items on multimedia scrapbook Web page
- Type of multimedia items required to be hyperlinked or displayed, for example:
  —photographs
  —paintings
  —political cartoons
  —maps
  —charts or graphs
  —documents

—video clips
—audio clips
—broadsides
—advertisements
—illustrations

- Appearance of multimedia scrapbook Web page
  —background
  —scroll or kiosk format

Internet Annotated Bibliography

Students familiar with the research and writing process will find this performance assessment activity to be a natural extension. Following completion of either of the above activities, students will have sufficient computer and Internet knowledge necessary for designing an Internet annotated bibliography. Teachers should reference Web sites for their students that address citing of Internet or electronic sources. Once students are familiar with the correct way to evaluate and cite Internet resources, the research phase of this activity should begin. Upon completion of the research phase, students should develop an annotated bibliography for their particular topic or theme. Included in their annotation should be a discussion of the information available at each particular site, the result of their CARS evaluation of the site and any additional information required. If the students are using a word processing program, such as *Microsoft Word*, the citations will be automatically hyperlinked. If not, have the students hyperlink the URL for each citation. Once students have completed the annotated bibliography have them convert the word document to HTML and insert a background and any images you might require. The guidelines for this activity are as follow:

- List of potential themes to choose from
- Minimum number of citations
- Web pages addressing citation of Internet resources
- Appearance of annotated bibliography Web page
  —background
- Main/heading image

Left Brain/Cognitive WebQuest

Three WebQuest activities are outlined in this section. Teachers may choose to have students work on any one or all of the activities. With the left brain or cognitive WebQuest activity, teachers provide students with a minimum of five Web sites to investigate. As students navigate through these Web sites they must respond to specific questions concerning data found at that site. Teachers should develop questions representative of the cognitive domain identified in Bloom's taxonomy. At the conclusion of the WebQuest, students should also respond to a "big question" that pulls together all of the information students encountered on their WebQuest, in a summative or evaluative manner. Unlike the previous activities, WebQuests are teacher created or designed, however they still involve a great deal of student involvement in navigating and responding to teacher queries. Teachers may display the hyperlinked WebQuest they want students to visit, along with the questions, on their home page, or they can simply create a handout for students to follow. The format for a left brain or cognitive WebQuest is as follows:

- Knowledge: Web site 1—listed or hyperlinked URL
  —Question 1.1
  —Question 1.2
- Comprehension: Web site 2—URL listed or hyperlinked URL
  —Question 2.1
  —Question 2.2
- Application: Web site 3—listed or hyperlinked URL
  —Question 3.1
  —Question 3.2
- Analysis: Web site 4—listed or hyperlinked URL
  —Question 4.1
  —Question 4.2
- Synthesis: Web site 5—listed or hyperlinked URL
  —Question 5.1
  —Question 5.2
- Evaluation: big question

Right Brain/Affective WebQuest

This WebQuest activity is very similar to the previous one with certain exceptions. First, the Web sites selected by the teacher should be ideal prompts for more reflective type questions that are not dichotomous in nature. Teachers should attempt to elicit reflection and personal interpretation from their students through queries representative of the affective domain. As with the previous activity, however, teachers should have their students navigate through the Web sites they have selected, responding to questions at each site. At the conclusion of the WebQuest, students should again respond to a "big question" that pulls together all of the information they encountered on their Web-Quest. Teachers may again choose to display the hyperlinked Web sites and questions on their home page or in a student handout. The format for a right brain or affective WebQuest is as follows:

- Receiving: Web site 1—listed or hyperlinked URL
  —Question 1.1
  —Question 1.2
- Responding: Web site 2—URL listed or hyperlinked URL
  —Question 2.1
  —Question 2.2
- Valuing: Web site 3—listed or hyperlinked URL
  —Question 3.1
  —Question 3.2
- Organization: Web site 4—listed or hyperlinked URL
  —Question 4.1
  —Question 4.2
- Characterization: Web site 5—listed or hyperlinked URL
  —Question 5.1
  —Question 5.2
- Summative: big question

Issue Investigation WebQuest

Unlike previous WebQuest activities, the issue investigation Web-Quest model requires students to work in teams. This inquiry-based activity calls for students to work in investigative teams attempting to research one aspect of a multifaceted problem or dilemma. Teachers should set the conceptual stage prior to this activity, using the WebQuest to enhance previous learning. This activity would be a great addition to any jurisprudential inquiry lesson, for example. Before embarking on their issue investigation WebQuest, students should identify the elements of the problem or dilemma they want to investigate further. Next, teams should be formed and assigned specific elements (e.g., issues, perspectives, characteristics) to investigate and report on. Upon completion of the research phase, students should prepare electronic or print reports addressing their findings. A culminating activity should follow, in which new teams are formed, consisting of one representative from each of the original teams, to discuss their findings and formulate a final position paper. Teachers may conclude with this activity or bring the class back together to discuss each group's final position paper. The teacher must provide students with guidelines for conducting the issue investigation WebQuest, to include the following:

- Student generated list of research elements
- Minimum number of sites/links to investigate
- Team report format—electronic or print
- Final position paper format

CARS Internet Evaluation Checklist

For each of these Internet-based performance assessment activities it is critical that students be equipped with the requisite knowledge necessary to evaluate the many Web sites they encounter along the way. One of the most widely used models for history students is the CARS method, developed by Robert Harris, Southern California College, which provides students with a systematic means for the evaluation of Web-based data/resources. The syntax of Harris's method is as follows:

- Credibility
  —Why should you believe this source over another?
  —Is the source trustworthy and respected?
- Accuracy
  —Is the information actually correct today?
  —Is the information accurate, detailed, and comprehensive?

- Reasonableness
  - —Is the information fair, balanced, objective, and reasoned?
  - —Does the source engage the subject in a thoughtful and reasonable man-
    ner?
- Support
  - —Do other sources agree with the information?
- Are sources listed?

Summary

No one claims performance assessment is an educational panacea. In
fact, both advocates and critics agree that research on this topic is
often inconclusive or contradictory. What remains true, however, is
that American education finds itself at a crossroads in which it must
decide which assessment road teachers and students will venture
down. Perhaps Elliot Eisner best summarized this current assessment
dilemma history teachers are faced with:

> One option, of course, is to employ two different kinds of assessment.
> One of these would be the continued use of large-scale, temperature-
> taking testing intended to provide comparative data on the performance
> of schools or school districts. Such a practice would not allow for the
> description of distinctive forms of individual student performance. A
> second assessment would need to be designed to reveal the distinctive
> talents of individual students and the effects of school practice on their
> development. One form of assessment would focus on the general; the
> other, on the particular.[31]

Chapter 17

Advanced Placement Assessment Strategies

Education would be much more effective if its purpose was
to ensure that by the time they leave school every boy and
girl should know how much they do not know, and be
imbued with a lifelong desire to know it.
—Sir William Haley

Arguably, the most challenging instruction in history and the social sciences in the secondary schools today occurs in Advanced Placement (AP) courses. Administered by the College Board and Educational Testing Service (ETS), the AP program began in 1955. Currently, more than 57 percent of United States secondary schools participate in the AP program. In 2001, over 820,000 students took thirty-five AP exams in nineteen subject areas. Most of this growth came in the past two decades as more schools added more AP courses to their curricula and opened up their AP courses to more students. Today, more students take the United States history exam than any of the other AP tests. In history and the social sciences, AP also offers tests in European history, world history, macroeconomics, microeconomics, human geography, United States government and politics, comparative government and politics, and psychology.[1]

Although AP courses typically provide thorough preparation for college-level work, their main purpose is to provide students with an avenue through the AP exams for receiving college credit. Just over 60 percent of the AP exams taken result in a grade that is recommended for college credit, normally at least a 3 on the 5-point AP scale. More than 90 percent of the colleges and universities in the United States recognize AP exam grades. Over 1,400 institutions, approximately 50 percent of colleges and universities in the United States, grant a full year's credit to students receiving satisfactory grades on a specific number of AP exams. Of course, this gives such students more opportunities to pursue advanced college courses, take a wider variety of courses, or pursue double majors or other academic opportunities.[2]

AP provides course descriptions to help guide the instruction of the highly qualified teachers who teach AP courses. AP teachers typically have more flexibility to use greater varieties of instructional materials to help them prepare their students for the examinations. The most successful AP teachers use intensive and highly creative instructional strategies and provide more informal and formal assessment than other teachers.[3] Many AP teachers also attend AP workshops and summer institutes for professional development and specific assistance in helping them prepare their AP courses. The College Board also suggests that AP teachers have advanced degrees in their fields before taking on AP course instruction. While schools are not charged for participating in the AP program, students pay $78 for each exam. The school keeps $7 of this fee as a rebate. More than forty states currently offer funding to subsidize low-income students' AP exam fees.[4]

The AP U.S. history examination is just over three hours in length and includes both a multiple choice and free-response (essay) section. The multiple-choice section includes questions at all levels of Bloom's taxonomy. The inclusion of database multiple-choice questions allows the higher-order end of Bloom's taxonomy to be addressed. This section is fifty-five minutes long and includes eighty questions, which account for one-half of the total score. The remaining time is allotted to the free-response section, which includes a required document-based question (DBQ) and two other essays in which students choose from one of two questions for each. The DBQ accounts for 22.5 percent of the total score and each essay counts for 13.75 percent. The overall U.S. history exam includes 35 percent political history, 35 percent social history, 15 percent diplomatic history, 10 percent economic history, and 5 percent cultural and intellectual history.[5]

U.S. History DBQ Preparation Strategies

While it is especially tempting for AP course instructors to teach strictly to the test, the best way to prepare students overall for the AP exam is to teach an intensive course on United States history that requires students to frequently practice database multiple choice questions, essay writing, and, particularly, preparation for the DBQ.[6] Introduced as part of the AP U.S. history exam in 1973, the DBQ requires students to think critically about eight to ten primary source documents centered on a question, often reflecting professionals' historiographical concerns, and analyze the meaning of these materials.[7] But students cannot simply succeed through perceptive analysis of the documents. Students are also required to weave outside information into their analytical narrative.

One suggestion for preparing students to write a good DBQ response is to have them read the question for the DBQ and then list all relevant facts that come to mind before examining the documents themselves. Students should then construct an outline for their response using these facts. After completing the first two steps, students can read the documents and decide how they fit into the outline they have already prepared. This outline can be adjusted according to the document analysis and an effective response constructed.[8]

The DBQ essay itself should start with a thesis paragraph with an explicit argument. Although graders of the DBQ essays are allowed to give credit to students who state a thesis in the essay's conclusion, more powerful DBQ responses, as is true of good essay construction in general, state a thesis in the introduction. The second paragraph should provide historical context. Subsequent paragraphs need to weave outside information into the document analysis. Importantly, students are not required to use all eight to ten documents to score at the top levels of the DBQs, but they do need to use most of the documents. Students should not quote excessively from the documents themselves and it is better to mention the author or subject of document rather than noting "Document A" or "Document D" in the narrative. Good DBQ conclusions, as is true of good essay conclusions, should not state new ideas or alter the thesis.[9]

The *Teacher's Guide to the Advanced Placement Course in United States History* provides several AP teachers' course syllabi that give insight into other methods good instructors use to help their students to prepare for the DBQ. In Robert W. DiLorenzo's AP class at DeWitt Clinton High School in New York City, students participate in an activity called "document shuffles" where each small group is given the same set of documents and then given the same analytical task to perform with them. Students also do take-home DBQs as well as in-class DBQs to help them prepare for this portion of the AP exam. DiLorenzo also notes that he spends considerable time in class discussing the grading of the exams. Bill Mendelsohn, an AP instructor at Clayton High School in suburban St. Louis, encourages students to develop projects for History Day and participate in student-teacher conferences about two history monographs read during the year on a single topic.[10]

Rosemary Ennis, a longtime AP history instructor and AP United States history consultant, suggests that the best way to help students prepare for the DBQ is by having them examine DBQs from earlier years. The College Board publishes a booklet titled *Doing the DBQ: Advanced Placement U.S. History Examination* that contains all the DBQs that have been given (see resource list at the end of the chapter). She uses a range of students' DBQ responses, obtained from past readings, from the very low to the top end of the scoring range, to show students the elements that constitute poor, average, better, and best responses. Ennis also suggests that instructors use the DBQ tutorials that AP makes available on their Web site (AP U.S. History is available at http://www.collegeboard.com/ap/students/ushistory/index.html and AP World History is available at http://www.collegeboard.com/ap/students/worldhistory/index.html). Additional DBQ resources are available from the College Board on CD-ROM.[11]

In another study based on close examination over an entire year of five students in an AP United States history course, Kathleen McCarthy Young and Gaea Leinhardt examined how the students became historically literate in the process of preparing for the AP examination. Young and Leinhardt contend that disciplinary literacy requires knowledge of the content area and as its "rhetorical processes." They examined the students' DBQ essay writing as "acts of discourse synthesis," where new texts are composed through selecting, organizing, and connecting previous knowledge to new information. They found that the instructor of the class was able to promote historical literacy by presenting "historical knowledge as interpreted rather than absolute." The course "challenged students with deep and broad reading of historical sources, frequent practice in interpreting documents, and varied forms of writing." Almost all of the instructor's writing assignments required students to evaluate multiple sources.[12]

Specifically in terms of preparation for the DBQ on the AP exam, Young and Leinhardt found that the course instructor assigned four timed DBQ essays over the course of the year. In preparing students for the DBQ essay, the instructor stressed four main points: answer the question that is posed; draw on knowledge of the period as historical context; interpret the documents instead of paraphrasing them; and provide and implement an organized argument for the essay. Young and Leinhardt also found that the instructor implicitly stressed a fifth point—authorship. Students need to see themselves as authors and make their cases as powerfully as possible. Young and Leinhardt also note that the instructor reinforced her instructions through "congruent and explicit" comments on their written work.[13]

Studies of the AP exam's evolution have found, like Young and Leinhardt's research, that successful AP instructors "teach to the test."[14] Although generally a bad practice in courses that focus more heavily on memorization, this is not a bad thing in helping students to prepare for the AP exam, since the AP test requires considerable higher-level thinking and good writing skills. In this respect it is also important to know how the AP graders, called readers, evaluate the DBQ essays. The approximately 600 readers of the U.S. history essays and DBQs gather at the same place, for the past several years at Trinity University in San Antonio, for one week in June to read and score the essays. There, so-called table leaders train the readers, about half of whom are high school AP instructors and the other half college professors, in applying consistent standards in their evaluations of the essays. Each essay and DBQ is scored on a 0 to 9 point scale. This 10-point scale avoids problems of too few points, which would allow only general distinctions, and too many points, which would require overly complicated gradations. The question and table leaders meet before the rest of the readers arrive for the grading session and determine the standards for each essay question. The scale is used as a ranking.[15]

Table leaders normally spend the better part of one day acquainting the six or so readers at their table with the standards for a particular essay or DBQ. About eight hours each day are devoted to reading and ranking essays. The objective is to blend readers' professional judgments with the standards developed for each essay or DBQ. Scoring on the AP exam is dependent on consistent assessment of the free responses. Importantly, a different reader scores each student's three free responses. Also, no reader knows the identity of any of the students' work that they score. To further enhance the reliability of the scoring process, table leaders randomly score essays to check their scores against the readers at their tables. Sometimes readers are asked to reread essays they previously scored.[16]

Although the DBQ differs from the other essays on the exam in terms of blending document analysis with outside information, readers score the DBQs and the essays based on similar attention to the incorporation of a thesis and supporting evidence. The readers look for both analysis and synthesis in the DBQ responses. To receive a score of 8 or 9 on the DBQ, students must successfully blend considerable outside information into their thorough analysis of the documents. To receive a score of 5, 6, or 7, students must state a thesis and present an organized response, but usually fail to thoroughly analyze the documents and/or use limited outside information. A 2-, 3-, or 4-point essay is superficial in both these respects, while a 0- or 1-point essay usually contains no thesis and an extremely superficial treatment of the issues.[17]

Because the AP exams are administered in early May, most AP instructors are faced with the dilemma of what to do with their students for the remaining month of the school year. This dilemma is made more vexing by the fact that about three-quarters of AP United States history instructors have already taught recent history to their students to help them prepare for the entire chronological range of the exam. One study, based on extensive surveys with AP instructors, found that most AP instructors reduced their class intensity level after the exam and "spent time discussing current events, engaging in group projects, and seeing movies." Other instructors spent more time on simulations and debates. In addition to these activities, some other posttest activities might include engaging students in authentic local history projects, such as oral history. Students might also apply their DBQ skills to development of a research project based on a topic of particular interest to them.[18] Worksheet 17.1 is a sample DBQ, similar in design to that included in an actual AP U.S. history exam.

For further information from the College Board on AP courses, examinations, and related materials, see their Web site (at apcentral. collegeboard.com). AP U.S. history instructors may access and/or purchase the following resources at this site:

- *Teacher's Guide to the AP Course in United States History*
- *Doing the DBQ*
- Free-Response Questions with Scoring Guides and sample student responses
- Student Guide to the AP United States History Course and Examination
- *AP Bulletin for Students and Parents*

Worksheet 17.1

Sample U.S. History Document-Based Question (DBQ)

UNITED STATES HISTORY
SECTION II
Part A
(Suggested writing time—45 minutes)
Percent of Section II score—45

Directions: The following question requires you to construct a coherent essay that integrates your interpretation of Documents A–K **and** your knowledge of the period referred to in the question. High scores will be earned only by essays that both cite key pieces of evidence from the documents and draw on outside knowledge of the period.

1. What problems did working-class Americans face in the 1930s? How effective were New Deal programs in addressing farmers and workers' problems?

Use the documents and your knowledge of the New Deal period to construct your response.

(continued)

Worksheet 17.1 *(continued)*

Document A

Source: Martha Gellhorn, "Report, Gaston County, North Carolina, November 11, 1934," FDR Library, Hopkins Papers, Box 66.

I have been seeing mill workers; and in every mill when possible, the local Union president. There has been widespread discrimination in the south; and many mills haven't reopened since the strike. Those open often run on such curtailment that workers are getting from 2 to 3 days work a week. The price of food has risen (especially the kind of food they eat: fat-back bacon, flour, meal, sorghum) as high as 100%. It is getting cold; and they have no clothes. The Union presidents are almost all out of work, since the strike. In many mill villages, evictions have been served; more threatened. These men are in a terrible fix.

Document B

Source: Wayne W. Parrish, "Report, Brooklyn, New York, November 24, 1934," FDR Library, Hopkins Papers, Box 66.

Relief rolls in Brooklyn are still going up. There are signs of jobs and clients invariably answer that "business is worse." In Bensonhurst I took a dozen new applicants for relief aside for interviews and found that most of them had been working until a few months ago. A widow with a 19-year-old daughter, lost her job because automatic machines had been installed in her uniform polishing plant where she had worked many years. A stone cutter out of work two years finally comes on relief. A single woman over fifty who used to work in a hospital is down to last cent and is obviously ashamed to apply. . . . several administrators thought business was better and coming back gradually, although one administrator said, "I don't see how private jobs are coming back. I don't feel that they will."

Document C

Source: Louisa Wilson, "Report, Flint, Michigan, November 30, 1934," FDR Library, Hopkins Papers, Box 66.

Since Flint lives and has its being through General Motors, the staggered production-plan, by which fewer families will get work but they have more steady employment, will it is generally agreed make less high peaks in relief but by the same token prevent the minimum drops of last Spring and Summer here.

The relief load up to the present has gone over the top with the net increase of cases accepted the largest in history between November 19 and 23, averaging 141 cases a day. The total current load is more than 8,500.

I could see little physical suffering, perhaps because the town is used to so little. But morally disintegrating, on the whole unrevolting humanity one did see.

Document D

Source: Works Progress Administration, "Soil Erosion in the Rosebud Country, South Dakota," 1935, National Archives and Records Administration.

Document E

Source: Dorothea Lange, Farm Security Administration, "Squatter Camp," California, November 1936, FDR Library.

(continued)

Worksheet 17.1 *(continued)*

Document F

Source: "More New Deal Co-operation," *New York Herald Tribune*, March 3, 1938, FDR Library, Cartoon Files.

Document G

Source: Henry A. Wallace, "The War at Our Feet," *Survey Graphic 29* (February 1, 1940), 109ff.

The Agricultural Adjustment Administration, first organized in 1933, was not set up to save soil, but to sustain our farm income. Yet it started almost immediately to sustain and improve soil. Even after that first smashing plow-up of cotton, a maneuver only to be countenanced in the light of the fact that another year of 5-cent cotton would have brought the South to absolute disaster—even after that first plow-up, you began to see in parts of the one-crop cotton country something rare and new: bright fields, bright with the living green of grass. Brooding upon what they had done, probably, and provided now with some money, both from an improved crop price and from Triple-A adjustment payments, thousands of farmers went out on their own volition and sowed those plowed-down strips to binding sod.

Document H

Source: Charles R. Walker, "Homesteaders—New Style," *Survey Graphic 28* (June 1939), 377ff.

Though Farm Security has helped 400,000 farm families—victims of drought, flood or other disaster—with grants in direct relief, the main body of its work has been directed toward permanent rehabilitation of farm families. This has involved far more than loans for seed, tools and livestock. When a family applies for aid, their resources and needs are carefully analyzed. Continued guidance and supervision in actual farm and home management insures both the government's loan and the farmer himself against a return to old inefficient methods and is regarded as even more important than the loans in restoring borrowers to self-sufficiency. To date nearly 693,000 families have received loans, averaging around $500 apiece.

Provision of medical services at low cost for families on the rehabilitation program . . . is considered by Farm Security part of the job of getting the farmer onto his feet and keeping him there. In cooperation with local medical societies, Farm Security has already some 60,000 low income farm families in eighteen states within a plan providing medical care at a cost the farmers can afford.

Document I

Source: George C. Stoney, "A Valley to Hold To," *Survey Graphic 29* (July 1, 1940), 391ff.

The first principle of TVA's grass roots philosophy of administration is to let the people make the first move.

TVA is a *regional* authority. Its policies have been made fit a section of the country that is fairly homogeneous. The local committees, as best they can, must make their local situation fit patterns prepared for the nation at large.

(continued)

Worksheet 17.1 *(continued)*

The job of TVA—control of land and waters in a region that forms a natural unit—it can handle as a whole, little hampered by political subdivisions or artificial segmentation.

Its method of adapting its programs to those of local and state agencies has reduced to a minimum the ugliest and most constant companion of public service—the fight for credit.

Document J

Source: Florence Kerr, "America's Unfinished Business," National Archives, May 6, 1939, WPA Papers, Record Group 69, Series 737, Box 7.

Those who wish to destroy the Federal work program used to assure the American people that WPA workers were only a lot of bums and loafers—they didn't really work, they just leaned on their shovels. Tales of WPA shovel-leaners have had an immense circulation. But the publication of the inventory of accomplishments on WPA projects has sort of taken the humor out of those jokes. Two hundred and eighty thousand miles of roads and streets built and improved by WPA—try to get a laugh out of that. Nearly three thousand new schoolhouses for our children, and over 21,000 repaired and modernized—what is there so funny about that?

It has been one of the principles of our work program to provide work as far as possible that makes use of every worker's skill and ability. We do not put a bricklayer to digging ditches when there are schools and firehouses to be built. Why should we not try to make use of the special abilities of unemployed teachers, nurses, artists, engineers and other professional workers? This, too, we have done.

Document K

Source: Eleanor Roosevelt, "Workers Should Join Trade Unions," *American Federationist* 48 (March 1941), 14–15.

I have always been interested in organizations for labor. I have always felt that it was important that everyone who was a worker join a labor organization, because the ideals of the organized labor movement are high ideals.

I wish those of us who are employers would learn that it is through cooperation that we achieve more—that through stating our problems and asking people to work with us to solve them that we really get somewhere.

I hope the day will come when all people of this country will understand that cooperation will bring us greater happiness, and will bring us in the end a better life for the whole country and enable us to exert a greater influence on the world as a whole.

Appendix A: Developing Instructional Objectives

Use the following list of objectives to answer the following set of questions.

I. Which of the following objectives are stated in behavorial language?
II. Which of the following objectives are cognitive? Which are process? And which are affective?

1. Students will learn to appreciate the benefits of American democracy.
2. Students will role play Booker T. Washington's and W.E.B. DuBois's positions regarding African American's participation in American society and compare/contrast their differences.
3. Students will discern the intellectual achievements of the ancient Greeks and Romans.
4. Students will interview soldiers who fought in the Vietnam War and document their key observations.
5. Students will heighten their grasp of the differences between Cubism and Expressionism.
6. Students will infer the causes of the South's failures at the Battle of Gettysburg by viewing the film *Gettysburg*.
7. Students will compare their religious beliefs to those of their parents.
8. Students will become good citizens by participating in a ten-week course on American democracy and citizenship.
9. Students will classify Indiana cities according to population and economic base.
10. Students will understand that all people express cultural behavior in different ways.

Appendix B: Performance Assessment Graphic Organizers

Figure A.1 **Graphic Organizer: Timeline**

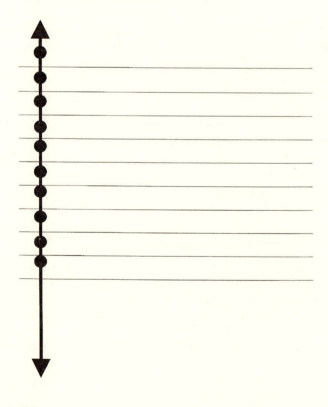

Figure A.2 **Graphic Organizer: Decision-Making Grid**

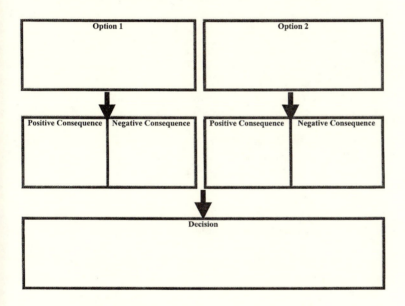

Figure A.3 **Graphic Organizer: Concept Map**

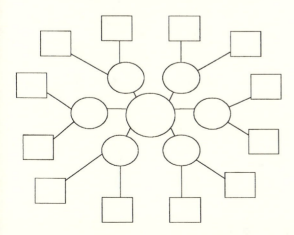

Figure A.4   **Graphic Organizer: Venn Diagram**

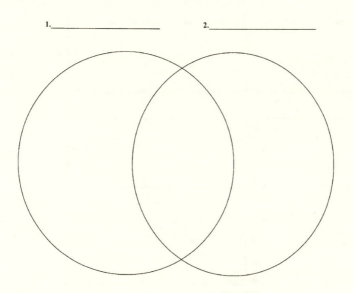

1._____   2._____

Figure A.5   **Graphic Organizer: Vee Heuristic**

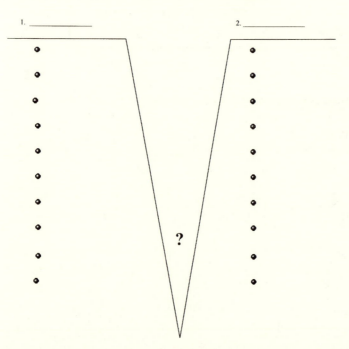

1. _____   2. _____

Appendix C: Performance Assessment—National Standards Correlation

National Standards for History[1]

Historical Thinking Skills	Journal Writing	Timeline	Decision Making	Concept Map	Venn Diagram	Vee Heuristic
Chronological Thinking	✖	✖		✖		
Historical Comprehension	✖		✖		✖	✖
Historical Analysis and Interpretation	✖	✖	✖	✖	✖	✖
Historical Research Capabilities		✖		✖		
Historical Issues Analysis and Decision Making	✖		✖	✖	✖	✖

National Council for History Education[2]

Habits of the Mind	Journal Writing	Timeline	Decision Making	Concept Map	Venn Diagram	Vee Heuristic
Understand the significance of the past	✖		✖		✖	✖
Develop discriminating memory	✖	✖	✖	✖		
Develop historical empathy	✖		✖			
Acquire a comprehension of diverse cultures	✖	✖	✖	✖	✖	✖
Understand how things happen and change	✖	✖	✖		✖	✖
Comprehend the interplay of change and continuity		✖		✖	✖	✖
Prepare to live with uncertainties	✖		✖			
Grasp the complexity of historical causation		✖			✖	✖
Appreciate tentative nature of judgments about past	✖		✖		✖	✖
Recognize the importance of individuals in history	✖	✖	✖	✖		
Appreciate the force of the nonrational in history	✖		✖	✖	✖	✖
Understand relationship between geography & history		✖		✖	✖	✖
Read widely and critically	✖	✖		✖		

National Council for the Social Studies Curriculum Standards[3]

Theme II—Time, Continuity, and Change	Journal Writing	Timeline	Decision Making	Concept Map	Venn Diagram	Vee Heuristic
Demonstrate historical knowledge is socially influenced	✖		✖		✖	✖
Apply key concepts such as time, chronology, causality	✖	✖	✖	✖	✖	✖
Identify significant historical periods and patterns of change	✖	✖	✖			
Systematically employ process of critical historical inquiry	✖		✖	✖	✖	✖
Investigate and interpret multiple historical viewpoints	✖	✖	✖	✖	✖	✖
Apply modes of historical inquiry to analyze developments	✖		✖		✖	✖

1. National Center for History in the Schools, *National Standards for History: Basic Edition* (Los Angeles: National Center for History in the Schools, 1996).

2. Bradley Commission on History in Schools, *Building a History Curriculum: Guidelines for Teaching History in Schools* (Westlake, OH: National Council for History Education, 1995); Paul Gagnon and the Bradley Commission on History in Schools, eds., *Historical Literacy: The Case for History in American Education* (Boston: Houghton Mifflin, 1991), 25.

3. National Council for the Social Studies, *Expectations of Excellence: Curriculum Standards for Social Studies* (Washington, DC: National Council for the Social Studies, 1994).

Notes

Preface

1. Carol Tell, "The I-Generation—From Toddlers to Teenagers: A Conversation with Jane M. Healy," *Educational Leadership* 58, no. 2 (2000): 8–9.
2. Quoted in Michael J. Berson et al., *Social Studies on the Internet* (Upper Saddle River, NJ: Prentice-Hall, 2001), v.
3. Ibid., 7.
4. D. Mark Meyers, "Teacher Education," in *Surfing the Social Studies: The Internet Book*, ed. Joseph A. Braun, Jr. and C. Frederick Risinger (Washington, DC: National Council for the Social Studies, 1999), 113.
5. Ibid.

Chapter 1. Origins and Rationale for Teaching History and the Social Studies in the Middle and High School Curriculum

1. H. Wells Singleton, "Problems of Democracy: The Revisionist Plan for Social Studies Education," *Theory and Research in Social Education* 8 (Fall 1980): 89–90; George L. Mehaffy, "Social Studies in World War One: A Period of Transition," *Theory and Research in Social Education* 15 (Winter 1987): 24; David Warren Saxe, *Social Studies in Schools: A History of the Early Years* (Albany: State University of New York Press, 1991); and Gary B. Nash, Charlotte Crabtree, and Ross E. Dunn, *History on Trial: Culture Wars and the Teaching of the Past* (New York: Alfred A. Knopf, 1998), 25–26.
2. Singleton, "Problems of Democracy," 92–94; Michael Lybarger, "The Political Context of the Social Studies: Creating a Constituency for Municipal Re-

form," *Theory and Research in Social Education* 8 (Fall 1980): 18–21; and Wilma S. Longstreet, "Social Science and the Social Studies: Origins of the Debate," *Social Education* 49 (May 1985): 357.

3. Oliver M. Keels, Jr., "The Collegiate Influence on the Early Social Studies Curriculum: A Reassessment of the Role of Historians," *Theory and Research in Social Education* 8 (Fall 1980): 106–111; and Saxe, *Social Studies in Schools.*

4. Saxe, *Social Studies in Schools*; Murry Nelson, "First Efforts Toward a National Curriculum: The Committee of Ten's Report on History, Civil Government, and Political Economy," *Theory and Research in Social Education* 20 (Spring 1992): 247, 249–257; and Michael Whelan, "Albert Bushnell Hart and the Origins of Social Studies Education," *Theory and Research in Social Education* 22 (Fall 1994): 423–432.

5. Keels, "The Collegiate Influence on the Early Social Studies Curriculum," 118–119; Saxe, *Social Studies in Schools;* Nelson, "First Efforts Toward a National Curriculum," 257–258.

6. David Nasaw, *Schooled to Order: A Social History of Public Schooling in the United States* (New York: Oxford University Press, 1979), 132–143; Singleton, "Problems of Democracy," 92–94; Longstreet, "Social Science and the Social Studies," 357–358; Saxe, *Social Studies in Schools;* Whelan, "Albert Bushnell Hart," 423–424.

7. James L. Barth and S. Samuel Shermis, "Nineteenth Century Origins of the Social Studies Movement: Understanding the Continuity Between Older and Contemporary Civic and U.S. History Textbooks," *Theory and Research in Social Education* 8 (Fall 1980): 39–41; Saxe, *Social Studies in Schools;* and idem, "An Introduction to the Seminal Social Welfare and Efficiency Prototype: The Founders of 1916 Social Studies," *Theory and Research in Social Education* 20 (Spring 1992): 158–164.

8. Lybarger, "The Political Context of the Social Studies," 18; Saxe, *Social Studies in Schools;* and Saxe, "An Introduction to the Seminal Social Welfare and Efficiency Prototype," 164–170.

9. John W. Kidd, "Social Science or Social Studies," *Social Education* 17 (May 1953): 207; Singleton, "Problems of Democracy," 92–94; Saxe, *Social Studies in Schools*; and Nash et al., *History on Trial,* 37–38.

10. Paul Robinson, "The Conventional Historians of the Social Studies," *Theory and Research in Social Education* 8 (Fall 1980): 75; Singleton, "Problems of Democracy," 92–94; Mehaffy, "Social Studies in World War One," 24–28; Nash et al., *History on Trial,* 37–38.

11. Stanley P. Wronski, "Edgar Bruce Wesley (1891–1980): His Contributions to the Past, Present and Future of the Social Studies," *Journal of Thought* 17 (Fall 1982): 58–64; and Shirley H. Engle, "Alan Griffin, 1907–1964," *Journal of Thought* 17 (Fall 1982): 50–51.

12. Murry R. Nelson, "The Rugg Brothers in Social Education," *Journal of Thought* 17 (Fall 1982): 71; and idem, "The Voice of Harold Rugg," *Social Education* 50 (November/December 1986): 489.

13. Nelson, "The Rugg Brothers in Social Education," 72; S. Samuel Shermis and James L. Barth, "Indoctrination and the Study of Social Problems: A Re-Examination of the 1930s Debate in The Social Frontier," *Social Education* 49 (March 1985): 192; and Nash et al., *History on Trial,* 40–45.

14. Murry R. Nelson, "Some Possible Effects of World War II on the Social Studies Curriculum," *Theory and Research in Social Education* 14 (Fall 1986): 267–275; and Nash et al., *History on Trial,* 68–69.

15. Maurice P. Hunt and Lawrence E. Metcalf, *Teaching High School Social Studies: Problems in Reflective Thinking and Social Understanding,* 2d ed. (New York: Harper and Row, 1968), 24, 33–35; John Dewey, *How We Think* (Boston: D.C. Heath, 1933).

16. Shirley H. Engle, "Decision Making: The Heart of Social Studies Instruction," *Social Education* 24 (November 1960): 301–304, 306.

17. Jerome Bruner, *The Process of Education* (Cambridge, MA: Harvard University Press, 1960), 12, 20–26; Edwin Fenton, "History in the New Social Studies," *Social Education* 30 (May 1966): 325–326; Mark M. Krug, "Bruner's New Social Studies: A Critique," *Social Education* 30 (October 1966): 400–406.

18. Edgar Bruce Wesley, "Let's Abolish History Courses," *Phi Delta Kappan* 49 (September 1967): 3–8; S. Samuel Shermis, "Six Myths Which Delude History Teachers," *Phi Delta Kappan* 49 (September 1967): 9–12; Shirley H. Engle, "Exploring the Meaning of the Social Studies," *Social Education* 35 (March 1971): 281–288; and Barth and Shermis, "Nineteenth Century Origins of the Social Studies Movement," 35.

19. Krug, "Bruner's New Social Studies," 401–406; and Derek Heater, "History and the Social Sciences," in *New Movements in the Study and Teaching of History,* ed. Martin Ballard (Bloomington: Indiana University Press, 1970), 135–136, 141–142.

20. Nash et al., *History on Trial,* 105–115.

21. Wilfred M. McClay, "History for a Democracy," *The Wilson Quarterly* 25 (Autumn 2001): 103.

22. James L. Barth, "Social Studies: There Is a History, There Is a Body, But Is It Worth Saving?" *Social Education* 57 (February 1993): 57.

23. The Committee of Seven, Report to the American Historical Association, *The Study of History in Schools* (New York: The Macmillan Committee, 1914), 16–26.

24. Charles A. McMurry, *Special Method in History: A Complete Outline of a Course of Study in History for the Grades Below the High School* (New York: Macmillan, 1909), 1–17.

25. The Bradley Commission on History in Schools, "Building a History Curriculum: Guidelines for Teaching History in Schools," in *Historical Literacy: The Case for History in American Education,* ed. Paul Gagnon (Boston: Houghton Mifflin, 1989), 21; and The Committee of Seven, *The Study of History in Schools,* 18.

26. Saxe, "An Introduction to the Seminal Social Welfare and Efficiency Prototype," 164–168.

27. Shirley H. Engle, "Foreword," in *Handbook on Teaching Social Issues,* ed. Ronald W. Evans and David Warren Saxe (Washington, DC: National Council for the Social Studies, 1996), viii.

28. Anna S. Ochoa-Becker, "Building a Rationale for Issues-Centered Education," in *Handbook on Teaching Social Issues,* 6–7.

29. Shirley H. Engle and Anna S. Ochoa, *Education for Democratic Citizenship: Decision Making in the Social Studies* (New York: Teachers College Press,

1988), 8–9; and Ochoa-Becker, "Building a Rationale for Issue-Centered Education," 12.

Chapter 2. Overview of the Structure and Standards for History, the Social Sciences, and Social Studies

1. R.G. Collingwood, *The Idea of History* (Oxford, UK: Oxford University Press, 1946), 7, 9; Mark Krug, *History and the Social Sciences: New Approaches to the Teaching of Social Studies* (Waltham, MA: Blaisdell, 1967), 4, 42.

2. Collingwood, *The Idea of History*, 9; Krug, *History and the Social Sciences*, 5; Norman F. Cantor and Richard I. Schneider, *How to Study History* (Arlington Heights, IL: AHM Publishing Corporation, 1967), 17–21; and William H. Dray, *Philosophy of History*, 2d ed. (Englewood Cliffs, NJ: Prentice-Hall, 1993), 8–19.

3. Cantor and Schneider, *How to Study History*, 20; and Oscar Handlin, *Truth in History* (Cambridge, MA: Belknap Press of Harvard University Press), 163–226.

4. Collingwood, *The Idea of History*, 282; Lester D. Stephens, *Probing the Past: A Guide to the Study and Teaching of History* (Boston: Allyn and Bacon, 1974), 62; and Dray, *Philosophy of History*, 56.

5. Krug, *History and the Social Sciences*, 47; Stephens, *Probing the Past*, 10; and Dray, *Philosophy of History*, 26–29.

6. Collingwood, *The Idea of History*, 247–254, 282, 302; Krug, *History and the Social Sciences*, 20–21, 26, 43; Stephens, *Probing the Past*, 41–56.

7. National Center for History in the Schools, *National Standards for History* (Los Angeles: University of California Press, Los Angeles, 1996).

8. National Council for the Social Studies, *National Standards for Social Studies Teachers*, 1997, www.ncss.org/standards/teachers/.

9. Jerome S. Bruner, *The Process of Education* (Cambridge, MA: Harvard University Press, 1960), 21–24.

10. National Council for the Social Studies, *National Standards for Social Studies Teachers*.

11. Ibid.

12. Ibid.

13. Ibid.

14. Mark M. Krug, "History and the Social Sciences: The Narrowing Gap," *Social Education* 29 (December 1965): 518–520; and idem, *History and the Social Sciences*, 69–72.

15. Maurice P. Hunt and Lawrence E. Metcalf, *Teaching High School Social Studies: Problems in Reflective Thinking and Social Understanding*, 2d ed. (New York: Harper and Row, 1968), 288–290. Also see chapters 13–19.

16. C. Benjamin Cox and Byron G. Massialas, ed., *Social Studies in the United States: A Critical Appraisal* (New York: Harcourt, Brace and World, 1967), 334–343.

17. Donald W. Oliver and James P. Shaver, *Teaching Public Issues in the High School* (Boston: Houghton Mifflin, 1966), 6, 9, 13–14.

18. Shirley H. Engle and Anna S. Ochoa, *Education for Democratic Citizen-*

ship: Decision Making in the Social Studies (New York: Teachers College Press, 1988), 92–93, 106; and James P. Shaver, "James Michener and the Historical Future of Social Studies," *Social Education* 59 (November/December 1995): 446–450.

19. Derek Heater, "History and the Social Sciences," in *New Movements in the Study and Teaching of History,* ed. Martin Ballard (Bloomington: Indiana University Press, 1970), 135–143; Matthew T. Downey, ed., *History in the Schools, NCSS Bulletin 74* (Washington, DC: National Council for the Social Studies, 1985), 11; Kieran Egan, "Social Studies and the Erosion of Education," *Curriculum Inquiry* 13 (Summer 1983): 202–204, 207; and Stephen J. Thornton, "Social Studies Misunderstood: A Reply to Kieran Egan," *Theory and Research in Social Education* 12 (Spring 1984): 43–47.

20. Interstate New Teacher Assessment and Support Consortium (INTASC), *Model Standards for Beginning Teacher Licensing and Development*, 1992, www.ccsso.org/intascst.html; National Council for the Social Studies (NCSS), *Expectation for Excellence; Curriculum Standards for Social Studies,* 1994.

21. Ibid.

22. Ibid.

23. Ibid.

24. Ibid.

25. Michael Whelan, "History and the Social Studies: A Response to the Critics," *Theory and Research in Social Education* 20 (Winter 1992): 12.

Chapter 3. Technology Integration in Preservice History Teacher Education

1. Margaret W. Smithey and Bradley W. Hough, "Creating Technology Advocates: Connecting Preservice Teachers with Technology," *T.H.E. Journal* 26, no. 8 (March 1999).

2. Ibid.; Martyn Wild, "Technology Refusal: Rationalizing the Failure of Student and Beginning Teachers to Use Computers," *British Journal of Educational Technology* 27 (May 1996); D.D. Kumar, "Science Teacher Education in an Era of Standards Based Reform: Policy Perspectives," *Contemporary Education* 70, no. 2 (Winter 1999).

3. Martyn Wild, "Technology Refusal."

4. D.D. Kumar, "Science Teacher Education."

5. Judith O'Donnell Dooling and Karen I. Case, "Integrating Technology Into Teacher Preparation Programs," *Teaching Education* 8 (Winter/Spring 1997).

6. Ibid.

7. President Bill Clinton, quoted in Denise Johnson, "We're Helping To Be Good Teachers: Using Electronic Dialoguing To Connect Theory and Practice in Preservice Teacher Education," *Journal of Computing in Childhood Education* 7, no. 2 (1996): 3.

8. Judy M. Parr, "Extending Educational Computing: A Case of Extensive Teacher Development and Support," *Journal of Research on Computing in Education* 31, no. 3 (Spring 1999): 281.

9. Ed Coughlin, "Professional Competencies Digital Age Classroom,"

Learning and Leading with Technology 27, no. 3 (November 1999); Smithey and Hough, "Creating Technology Advocates."

10. Coughlin, "Professional Competencies," 24.

11. Mark Warner and Maureen Akins, "Training Today's Teachers for Tomorrow's Classrooms," *T.H.E. Journal* 27, no. 3 (October 1999): online.

12. O'Donnell Dooling and Case, "Integrating Technology."

13. Cameron White, "It's Not Another New Thing: Technology as a Transformative Innovation for Social Studies Teacher Education," *Journal of Technology and Teacher Education* 7, no. 3 (1999).

14. President Clinton, quoted in Ranae Stetson and Troy Bagwell, "Technology and Teacher Preparation: An Oxymoron?" *Journal of Technology and Teacher Education* 7, no. 2 (1999).

15. Sean J. Smith, Kerri F. Martin, and John Wills Lloyd, "Preparing Preservice Teachers on the Web," *Teaching Exceptional Children* 30, no. 5 (May/June 1998); International Society for Teacher Education, "Will New Teachers Be Prepared to Teach in a Digital Age?" *The Education Digest* 65, no. 2 (October 1999).

16. Stetson and Bagwell, "Technology and Teacher Preparation."

17. Pamela Taylor Northrup and Wesley Little, "Establishing Instructional Technology Benchmarks for Teacher Preparation Programs," *Journal of Teacher Education* 47, no. 3 (May/June 1996): 214.

18. Jerry W. Wills and Howard D. Mehlinger, "Information Technology and Teacher Education," in John Sikula, Thomas J. Buttery, and Edith Guyton, eds., *Handbook of Research on Teacher Education,* 2d ed. (New York: Macmillan, 1996), 978.

19. Stetson and Bagwell, "Technology and Teacher Preparation," 146.

20. Wills and Mehlinger, "Information Technology," 979.

21. Thomas A. Brush, "Teaching Preservice Teachers to Use Technology in the Classroom," *Journal of Technology and Teacher Education* 6, no. 4 (1998): 258.

22. Stetson and Bagwell, "Technology and Teacher Preparation."

23. National Governors' Association, *The Governors' 1991 Report on Education: Results on Education 1990* (Washington, DC: National Governors' Association, 1991).

24. Roger W. Bybee and Susan Loucks-Horsley, "Standards as a Catalyst for Change in Technology Education," *The Technology Teacher* 59, no. 5 (February 2000), 15.

25. Ibid.

26. Interstate New Teacher Assessment and Support Consortium, *INTASC Core Standards.* Available at Council of Chief State School Officers Home Page http://www.ccsso.org/intascst.html (August 1, 2001).

27. National Board for Professional Teaching Standards, *Social Studies-History Standards for National Board Certification* [draft] (Washington, DC: National Board for Professional Teaching Standards, 1994), 31.

28. Ibid.

29. International Society for Technology in Education, *National Standards for Technology in Teacher Preparation* (Eugene, OR: International Society for

Technology in Education, 1996). Available at http://www.iste.org/Standards/ NCAE/found.html (August 2001).

30. International Society for Technology in Education, *NCATE Unit Accreditation Guidelines* (Eugene, OR: International Society for Technology in Education, 1996), http://www.iste.org/Standards/NCAE/found.html (August 1, 2001); Wills and Mehlinger, "Information Technology"; Regina Halpin, "A Model of Constructivist Learning in Practice: Computer Literacy Integrated into Elementary Mathematics and Science Teacher Education," *Journal of Research on Computing in Education* 32, no. 1 (Fall 1999).

31. International Society for Technology in Education, *National Standards for Technology in Teacher Preparation.*

32. Wills and Mehlinger, "Information Technology"; Halpin, "A Model of Constructivist Learning," 136.

33. Northrup and Little, "Establishing Instructional Technology."

34. Ibid., 218.

35. Christy J. Falba et al., "Choreographing Change One Step at a Time: Reflections on Integrating Technology into Teacher Education Courses," *Action in Teacher Education* 21, no. 1 (Spring 1999): 63.

36. Smith, Martin, and Lloyd, "Preparing Preservice Teacher," 62.

37. Ibid.; Stetson and Bagwell, "Technology and Teacher Preparation."

38. Halpin, "A Model of Constructivist Learning."

39. Wills and Mehlinger, "Information Technology," 999.

40. International Society for Teacher Education, "Will New Teachers Be Prepared to Teach in a Digital Age?"

41. Ibid.

42. Ibid.

43. Ibid.

44. Wills and Mehlinger, "Information Technology," 1000.

45. Dale S. Niederhauser, Donna J. Salem, and Matt Fields, "Exploring Teacher Learning and Instructional Reform in an Introductory Technology Course," *Journal of Technology and Teacher Education* 7, no. 2 (1999).

46. Wills and Mehlinger, "Information Technology."

47. Ibid.

48. Niederhauser, Salem, and Fields, "Exploring Teacher Learning."

49. Donna Read and Ralph Cafolla, "Multimedia Portfolios for Preservice Teachers: From Theory to Practice," *Journal of Technology and Teacher Education* 7, no. 2 (1999).

50. White, "It's Not Another New Thing," 3–4.

51. Niederhauser, Salem, and Fields, "Exploring Teacher Learning."

52. Ibid.

53. White, "It's Not Another New Thing."

54. International Society for Teacher Education, "Will New Teachers Be Prepared to Teach in a Digital Age?"

55. Read and Cafolla, "Multimedia Portfolios."

56. Ibid.

57. White, "It's Not Another New Thing," 10.

58. Steven J. Rakow, "Involving Classroom Teachers in the Assessment of

Preserve Intern Portfolios," *Action in Teacher Education* 21, no. 1 (Spring 1999).

59. Read and Cafolla, "Multimedia Portfolios."

60. James Takacs et al., "The Effect of Online Multimedia Project Development, Learning Style, and Prior Computer Experiences on Teachers' Attitudes Toward the Internet and Hypermedia," *Journal of Research on Computing in Education* 31, no. 4 (Summer 1999).

61. Matthew T. Downey and Linda S. Levstik, "Teaching and Learning History," in ed. James P. Shaver, *Handbook of Research on Social Studies Teaching and Learning* (New York: Macmillan, 1991).

62. Beverly J. Armento, "The Professional Development of Social Studies Educators," in *Handbook of Research on Teacher Education,* ed. John Sikula, Thomas J. Buttery, and Edith Guyton (New York: Macmillan, 1996).

63. Christopher Moersch, "Assessing Current Technology Use in the Classroom: A Key to Efficient Staff Development and Technology Planning," *Learning and Leading with Technology* 26, no. 8 (May 1999).

64. Beverly J. Armento, "The Professional Development of Social Studies Educators," 498.

65. Stetson and Bagwell, "Technology and Teacher Preparation."

66. Wills and Mehlinger, "Information Technology."

Chapter 4. History Teachers' Beliefs

1. CEO Forum on Education and Technology, *Second Annual Report, 1998*, [online]; http://www.ceoforum.org/REPORTS/REPORT99/HIGHLIGHTS.html; INTERNET.

2. R. Coley, J. Cradler and P.K. Engel, *Computers in the Classroom: The Status of Technology in U.S. Schools* (Princeton, NJ: Educational Testing Service Policy Information Report, 1997) RIE record no. ED 412 893.

3. C.M. Clark and M. Lampert, "The Study of Teacher Thinking: Implications for Teacher Education," *Journal of Teacher Education* 37, no. 5 (1986).

4. M.F. Pajares, "Teachers' Beliefs and Educational Research: Cleaning Up a Messy Construct," *Review of Educational Research* 62, no. 3 (1992).

5. J. Dewey, *How We Think* (Boston: D.C. Heath, 1933), 6.

6. Pajares, "Teachers' Beliefs," 307.

7. C.M. Clark and P.L. Peterson, "Teachers' Thought Processes," in *Handbook of Research on Teaching,* 3d ed., ed. M.C. Wittrock (New York: Macmillan, 1986).

8. P.W. Jackson, *Life in Classrooms* (New York: Holt, Rinehart and Winston, 1968).

9. As quoted in C.M. Clark and P.L. Peterson, "Teachers' Thought Processes," 256.

10. Ibid.

11. Ibid., 256.

12. P. Ernest, "The Knowledge, Beliefs and Attitudes of the Mathematics Teacher: A Model," *Journal of Education for Teaching* 15, no. 1 (1989).

13. J. Nespor, *The Teacher Beliefs Study: An Interim Report* (Austin, TX:

Research and Development Center for Teacher Education, 1984); J. Nespor, "The Role of Beliefs in the Practice of Teaching," *Journal of Curriculum Studies* 19, no. 4 (1987).

14. H. Munby, "The Place of Teachers' Beliefs in Research on Teacher Thinking and Decision Making, and an Alternative Methodology," *Instructional Science* 11 (1982).

15. Pajares, "Teachers' Beliefs."

16. Quoted in Nespor, "Teacher Beliefs Study," 9.

17. Pajares, "Teachers' Beliefs."

18. P.R. Pintrich, "Implications of Psychological Research on Student Learning and College Teaching for Teacher Education," in ed. W.R. Houston, *Handbook of Research on Teacher Education* (New York: Macmillan, 1990).

19. Pajares, "Teachers' Beliefs."

20. Ibid., 308.

21. Parker, "Teachers' Mediation in Social Studies," *Theory and Research in Social Education* 15, no. 1 (1987).

22. Ibid.

23. Nespor, "The Role of Beliefs."

24. D.P. Sanders and G. McCutcheon, "The Development of Practical Theories of Teaching," *Journal of Curriculum and Supervision* 2, no. 1 (1986).

25. A.G. Thompson, "Teachers' Beliefs and Conceptions: A Synthesis of the Research," in ed. D.A. Grouws, *Handbook of Research on Mathematics Teaching and Learning* (New York: Macmillan, 1992), 127.

26. S.N. Nicholas and M.J. Fleener, "Nine Preservice Teachers' Beliefs About Teaching and Teaming Mathematics: A Case Study–Part 1," *National Forum of Applied Educational Research Journal* 7, no. 2 (1994–1995).

27. Ernest, "Knowledge, Beliefs and Attitudes."

28. As quoted in D.M. Kagan, "Ways of Evaluating Teacher Cognition: Inferences Concerning the Goldilocks Principle," *Review of Educational Research* 60, no. 3 (1990).

29. Clark and Lampert, "The Study of Teacher Thinking," 27.

30. Jackson, *Life in Classrooms*; D.C. Lortie, *Schoolteacher: A Sociological Study* (Chicago: University of Chicago Press, 1975).

31. According to Clark and Peterson.

32. Ibid., 255–256.

33. Lortie, *Schoolteacher*.

34. Ibid., ix.

35. Ibid., vii-viii.

36. Clark and Peterson, "Teachers' Thought Processes."

37. H. Borko and R.J. Shavelson, "Speculations on Teacher Education: Recommendations from Research on Teachers' Cognitions," *Journal of Education for Teaching* 9, no. 3 (1983): 211.

38. R.J. Shavelson and P. Stern, "Research on Teachers' Pedagogical Thoughts, Judgments, Decisions, and Behavior," *Review of Educational Research* 51, no. 4 (1981).

39. Ibid.

40. Ibid.

41. P.L. Peterson, R.W. Marx, and C.M. Clark, "Teacher Planning, Teacher

Behavior, and Student Achievement," *American Educational Research Journal* 15 (1978).

42. Ibid.

43. C.M. Clark and R.J. Yinger, "Research on Teacher Thinking," *Curriculum Inquiry* 7, no. 4 (1977).

44. C.M. Clark and J.L. Elmore, *Teacher Planning in the First Weeks of School,* Research Series No. 56 (East Lansing: Michigan State University, Institute for Research on Teaching, 1979).

45. Ibid.

46. J.A. Zahorik, "Teachers' Planning Models," *Educational Leadership* 33 (1975).

47. J.A. Zahorik, "The Effects of Planning on Teaching," *Elementary School Journal* 71 (1970).

48. Clark and Peterson, 268.

49. Ibid.

50. P.L. Peterson and C.M. Clark, "Teachers' Reports of Their Cognitive Processes During Teaching," *American Educational Research Journal* 15 (1978).

51. Shavelson and Stern, "Research on Teachers' Pedagogical Thoughts."

52. Ibid.

53. Ibid., 482.

54. Ibid.

55. K. McNair, "Capturing Inflight Decisions," *Educational Research Quarterly* 3, no. 4 (1978–1979).

56. C.M. Clark, "Asking the Right Questions About Teacher Preparation: Contributions of Research on Teacher Thinking," *Educational Researcher* 17, no. 2 (1988), 6.

57. Kagan, "Ways of Evaluating Teacher Cognition."

58. Pajares, "Teachers' Beliefs," 307.

59. Clark and Yinger, "Research on Teacher Thinking," 301.

60. A. Thompson, "Teachers' Beliefs and Conceptions: A Synthesis of Research," in ed. D.A. Grouws, *Handbook of Research on Mathematics Teaching and Learning* (New York: Macmillan, 1992).

61. Ibid.

62. Ibid., 129.

63. Ibid., 307.

64. F. Elbaz, *Teacher Thinking: A Study of Practical Knowledge* (New York: Nichols Publishing, 1983).

65. Ibid., 3.

66. Ibid., 132.

67. Ibid., 133.

68. Ibid., 134.

69. M. Rokeach, *Beliefs, Attitudes, and Values: A Theory of Organization and Chance* (San Francisco: Jossey–Bass, 1968).

70. Ibid.

71. P.W. Marland, *A Study of Teachers' Interactive Thoughts*, unpublished Ph.D. diss., University of Alberta, 1977.

72. Pajares, "Teachers' Beliefs," 324–326.

73. Ibid.

74. C.A. Beard, *The Nature of the Social Sciences in Relation to Objectives of Instruction* (New York: Charles Scribner's Sons, 1934), 182.

75. J.P. Shaver and H. Berlak, "Curriculum Decisions in the Social Studies," in J.P. Shaver and H. Berlak, eds., *Democracy, Pluralism, and the Social Studies* (Boston: Houghton Mifflin, 1968).

76. J. Brophy and T. Good, *Teacher–Student Relationships: Causes and Consequences* (New York: Holt, Rinehart, and Winston, 1974).

77. H. W. Hertzberg, *Social Studies Reform: 1880–1980* (Boulder, CO: Social Science Education Consortium, 1981).

78. S. Adler, "A Field Study of Selected Student Teacher Perspectives Toward Social Studies," *Theory and Research in Social Education* 12, no. 1 (1984).

79. Ibid., 13.

80. E.W. Ross, "Teacher Perspective Development: A Study of Preservice Social Studies Teachers," *Theory and Research in Social Education* 15, no. 4 (1987).

81. Ibid., 228.

82. Ibid., 237.

83. R.W. Evans, "Teachers' Conceptions of History," *Theory and Research in Social Education* 17, no. 3 (1989).

84. Ibid.

85. C. Bennett and E. Spalding, "Teaching the Social Studies: Multiple Approaches for Multiple Perspectives," *Theory and Research in Social Education* 20, no. 3 (1992).

86. Ibid., 264.

87. Ibid.

88. Ibid., 267.

89. R.D. Barr, J.L. Barth, and S.S. Shermis, *Defining the Social Studies* (Washington, DC: National Council for the Social Studies, 1977); D.S.G. Carter, "Knowledge Transmitter, Social Scientist or Reflective Thinker: Three Images of the Practitioner in Western Australian High Schools," *Theory and Research in Social Education* 18, no. 3 (1990).

90. Carter, "Knowledge Transmitter," 305.

91. S.S. Stodolsky and P.L. Grossman, "The Impact of Subject Matter on Curricular Activity: An Analysis of Five Academic Subjects," *American Educational Research Journal* 32, no. 2 (1995).

92. Ibid.

93. S.S. Wineburg and S.M. Wilson, "Models of Wisdom in the Teaching of History," *Phi Delta Kappan* 70, no. 1 (1988).

94. Ibid., 50.

95. Ibid.

96. S.J. Thornton, "Teacher as Curricular-Instructional Gatekeeper in Social Studies," in ed. J.P. Shaver, *Handbook of Research on Social Studies Teaching and Learning* (New York: Macmillan, 1991).

97. Ibid.

98. Ibid., 241.

99. M.H. Romanowski, "Teacher's Lives and Beliefs: Influences That Shape the Teaching of U.S. History," *Mid-Western Educational Researcher* 11, no. 2 (1998): 2–3.

Chapter 5. Developing Objectives and Plans for History and Social Studies Instruction

1. Lorin W. Anderson, "Research on Teaching and Teacher Education," in *Bloom's Taxonomy: A Forty-year Retrospective, Ninety-Third Yearbook of the National Society for the Study of Education*, Part II, ed. Lorin W. Anderson and Lauren A. Sosniak (Chicago: University of Chicago Press, 1994), 138–139.

2. David Kobrin, *Beyond the Textbook: Teaching History Using Documents and Primary Sources* (Portsmouth, NH: Heinemann, 1996), 6–9.

3. Benjamin Bloom, ed., *Taxonomy of Educational Objectives: Handbook I—The Cognitive Domain* (New York: David O. McKay, 1956), 7. In distinguishing between the cognitive and process ends of the domain, this chapter follows the work of Arthur K. Ellis, Jeffrey T. Fouts, and Allen D. Glenn, as indicated in their text, *Teaching and Learning Secondary Social Studies* (New York: HarperCollins, 1991), 106–111.

4. Bloom, ed., *Taxonomy of Educational Objectives*, vol. 1.

5. Bloom, ed., *Taxonomy of Educational Objectives*, vol. 1. Two excellent Web sites elaborating on Bloom's cognitive domain are: "Major Categories in the Taxonomy of Educational Objectives," http://faculty.washington.edu/krumme/guides/bloom.html and "Bloom et al. Taxonomy of the Cognitive Domain," http://Chiron.Valdosta.edu/whuitt/col/cogsys/bloom.html.

6. David R. Krathwohl, Benjamin S. Bloom, and Bertram B. Masia, *Taxonomy of Educational Objectives: Handbook II—Affective Domain* (New York: David McKay, 1964), 7, 48–53.

7. Krathwohl, Bloom, Masia, *Taxonomy of Educational Objectives: Handbook II—Affective Domain*, Appendix A. Also see Krathwohl et al., "Taxonomy of the Affective Domain," http://chiron.valdosta.edu/whuitt/col/affsys/affoom.html.

8. Since 1956 when Bloom's *Taxonomy of Educational Objectives* was published, many educational and psychological theorists have questioned the perspectives embodied in it. Behaviorism, neobehaviorism and neoassociationism, information processing, cognitive development, and cognitive science theories of cognitive development have all questioned some elements of how Bloom's taxonomy is structured. However, many educational theorists note that it still stands up well to all such questions. See, for instance, William D. Rohwer, Jr. and Kathryn Sloan, "Psychological Perspectives," in *Bloom's Taxonomy: A Forty-Year Retrospective*, 41–63.

9. The format for social issue unit plans draws extensively on Joseph J. Onosko and Lee Swenson, "Designing Issue-Based Unit Plans," in *Handbook on Teaching Social Issues, NCSS Bulletin 93*, ed. Ronald W. Evans and David Warren Saxe (Washington, DC: National Council for the Social Studies, 1996), 89–98.

10. On unit lesson plan design, see R.M. Gagne and L. Briggs, *Principles of Instructional Design* (New York: Holt, Rinehart, and Winston, 1979); and Madeline Hunter, "Knowing, Teaching, and Supervising," in *Using What We Know about Teaching*, ed. P. Hosford (Alexandria, VA: Association for Supervision and Curriculum Development, 1984).

Chapter 6. Teaching Early American History: A Curricular Model for Integrating Online Resources

1. National Center for History in the Schools (NCHS), *National Standards for History: Basic Edition* (Los Angeles: NCHS, 1996), 62.
2. Charlotte Crabtree et al., eds., *Lessons from History: Essential Understandings and Historical Perspectives Students Should Acquire* (Los Angeles: NCHS, 1992), 51.
3. Ibid., 59.
4. Ibid., 69–70.
5. NCHS, *National Standards,* 85.
6. Ibid.; Paul Gagnon and the Bradley Commission on History in Schools, *Historical Literacy: The Case for History in American Education* (Boston: Houghton Mifflin, 1989); Bradley Commission on History in Schools, *Building a History Curriculum: Guidelines for Teaching History in Schools* (Westlake, OH: National Council for History Education, 1995), 9.
7. NCHS, *National Standards,* 76–84; National Council for the Social Studies, *Expectations of Excellence: Curriculum Standards for Social Studies* (Washington, DC: National Council for the Social Studies, 1994), 113–117; Bradley Commission, *Building a History.*
8. Gagnon and the Bradley Commission, *Historical Literacy,* 25–26; Bradley Commission, *Building a Curriculum,* 9.
9. Howard Mehlinger, quoted in C. Frederick Risinger, "Teaching History," in *Surfing Social Studies: The Internet Book,* ed. Joseph A. Braun, Jr., and C. Frederick Risinger (Washington, DC: National Council for the Social Studies, 1999), 27.
10. Charlotte Crabtree et al., *Lessons from History,* 52.
11. NCHS, *National Standards,* 77–78.
12. Passage quoted in Howard Zinn, *A People's History of the United States,* Teaching ed. (New York: The New Press, 1997), 3.
13. NCHS, *National Standards,* 79.
14. Quoted in John J. Newman and John M. Schmalbach, *United States History: Preparing for the Advanced Placement Examination* (New York: Amsco, 1998), 1.
15. NCHS, *National Standards,* 81–82.
16. Quoted in Newman and Schmalbach, *United States History,* 42.
17. NCHS, *National Standards,* 82–83.
18. Quoted in Alan L. Lockwood and David E. Harris, *Reasoning with Democratic Values: Ethical Problems in United States History,* vol. 1 (New York: Teachers College Press, 1985), 55.
19. NCHS, *National Standards,* 83–84.
20. Ibid., 86–87.
21. Charlotte Crabtree et al., eds. *Lessons from History,* 69.
22. NCHS, *National Standards,* 87–88.
23. Crabtree et al., *Lessons from History,* 77.
24. NCHS, *National Standards,* 89–90.

25. Gagnon and the Bradley Commission, *Historical Literacy*, 25–26; Quote from Bradley Commission, *Building a Curriculum*, 9.

Chapter 7. Active Learning, World History, and the Internet: Creating Knowledge in the Classroom

1. Joseph A. Braun, Jr. and C. Frederick Risinger, "The Internet," in *Surfing Social Studies: The Internet Book,* ed. Joseph A. Braun, Jr. and C. Frederick Risinger (Washington, DC: National Council for the Social Studies, 1999), 7.

2. Cameron White and Trenia Walker, "Technorealism: Addressing the Issues of Technology in Social Studies," *Computers in the Social Studies.* Available at http://www.cssjournal.com/journal/cwhite99.html (August 28, 1999).

3. Gary B. Nash, "The History Wars of the 1990s," paper delivered at the Lawrence F. Brewster Lecture in history at East Carolina University, November 1996. Available at http://personal.ecu.edu/wilburnk/b196.htm (10 January 2000). See National Center for History in the Schools (NCHS), "World History Standards for Grades 5–12," in *National Standards for History* (Los Angeles: National Center for History in the Schools, University of California, Los Angeles, 1996). The standards are also available at http://www.ssnet.ucla.edu/nchs (January 5, 2000) and are summarized in *The New World History: A Teacher's Companion,* ed. Ross E. Dunn (Boston: Bedford/St. Martin's, 2000), 394–405. Finally, see Gary B. Nash, Ross E. Dunn, and Charlotte Crabtree, *History on Trial* (New York: Knopf, 1997), 120.

4. NCHS, "World History Standards for Grades 5–12." All following quotes in this section are from this source unless otherwise indicated.

5. Ibid. The ecological issue is one this author has added to the five already present in the world history standards.

6. Dunn, *New World History,* 394–405.

7. NCHS, "World History Standards for Grades 5–12."

8. National Council for History Education, "Reinvigorating History in U.S. Schools: Reform Recommendations for the States." Available at http://63.70.163.70/nche/recommend.html (August 24, 1999).

9. Ibid.

10. Margaret L. Rice et al., "Social Studies Teachers and Technology: Activities for the Constructivist Classroom." Available at http://www.cssjournal.com/journal/rice.html (August 24, 1999).

11. Anthony Lorsbach and Fred Basolo, Jr., "Problem-Based Learning," in *Surfing Social Studies,* ed. Braun and Risinger, quote at page 122.

12. Ibid.

13. Ira Shor and Caroline Pari, eds., *Education Is Politics: Critical Teaching Across Differences, K-12* (New York: Heinemann, 1999).

14. Howard Gardner, *Frames of Mind: The Theory of Multiple Intelligences* (New York: Basic Books, 1983).

15. Waynne B. James and Michael W. Galbraith, "Perceptual Learning Styles: Implications and Techniques for the Practioner," *Lifelong Learning* 8, no. 4 (January 1985): 20–23; Katy Campbell, "Learner Characteristics and Instructional

Design." Available at http://www.atl.ualberta.ca/articles/idesign/learnchar.cfm. (July 9, 1999).

16. Campbell, "Learner Characteristics."

17. Barbara Brehm, "Effective Internet Searching," in *Surfing Social Studies,* ed. Braun and Risinger; Tim Dugan, "The Webmaster's Tale," in *Surfing Social Studies,* ed. Braun and Risinger; Jana Sackman Eaton, "The Social Studies Classroom on the Eve of the Cyber Century," *Computers in the Social Studies.* Available at http://www.cssjournal.com/journal/eaton99.html (August 28, 1999).

18. To get a sense of what it means to teach a class totally in cyberspace, see Alex Zukas, "Cyberworld: Teaching World History on the World Wide Web," *The History Teacher* 32 (1999), 495–516. The article deals with the problems and advantages of teaching a college-level world history course online.

19. Braun and Risinger, "The Internet," 7.

20. Gary Williams, "Computer Mediated Communication." Available at http://www.csu.edu.au/division/oli/celt/edtech/CMC/cmc.htm#online (September 7, 1999), has an excellent discussion of online teaching strategies, how to manage online discussions, the advantages and challenges of online teaching and learning, and the various kinds of computer-mediated communication teachers could employ in the classroom.

21. Eileen Giuffre Cotton, "The Virtual Tour," in *Surfing Social Studies,* ed. Braun and Risinger, 33–40. See also Rice et al., "Social Studies Teachers."

22. Eaton, "The Social Studies Classroom."

23. Brehm, "Effective Internet Searching," 15.

24. Timothy A. Keiper and Linda Bennett, "The Classroom Website," in *Surfing Social Studies*, ed. Braun and Risinger, 23–26.

25. See Michael Berson and Eileen Berson, "Safe Web Exploration," in *Surfing Social Studies*, ed. Braun and Risinger, 149–156.

26. Morten Flate Paulsen, "The Online Report on Pedagogical Techniques for Computer-Mediated Communication." Available at http://www.hs.nki.no/~morten/cmcped.htm (July 9, 1999).

27. Wren Bump et al., "Integrating Computer-Mediated Communication in the K-12 Curriculum." Available at http://www.cssjournal.com/journal/bump.html (August 24, 1999).

28. Bob Coulson and Alma Vallisneri, "Global Education," in *Surfing Social Studies,* ed. Braun and Risinger, 73–80.

29. Dennis A. Trinkle et al., *The History Highway: A Guide to Internet Resources* (Armonk, NY: M.E. Sharpe, 1997).

30. See C. Frederick Risinger, "Teaching History," in *Surfing Social Studies,* ed. Braun and Risinger, for a listing of these and other history and lesson plan Web sites.

31. Gregory A. Levitt, "Global Issues," in *Surfing Social Studies,* ed. Braun and Risinger, 81–92.

32. David B. Williams, "Art-Based Resources," in *Surfing Social Studies,* ed. Braun and Risinger, 93.

33. Joe Cain, "Have I Wasted My Summer on This Web Site?" *Perspectives* 37 (1999).

34. Ibid., 25.

35. Lorsbach and Basolo, "Problem-Based Learning," 123.

36. Ibid., 124.
37. Rice et al., "Social Studies Teachers."
38. Cain, "How I Wasted My Summer," 30.
39. Ibid., 28.
40. Campbell, "Learner Characteristics."
41. White and Walker, "Technorealism."

Chapter 8. Sequential Lesson Plan Frameworks

1. Walter Dick, "History of Instructional Design." Available at http://academic.udayton.edu/elearning/onlineTraining/InstructionalDesign/History/ (April 1, 2002).
2. Ibid.
3. Ibid.
4. Bruce Joyce, Marsha Weil, and Beverly Showers, *Models of Teaching*, 4th ed. (Boston: Allyn and Bacon, 1992), 1.
5. Lawrence Stenhouse, *An Introduction to Curriculum Research and Development* (London: Heineman, 1975), 4–5.
6. Decker F. Walker and Jonas F. Soltis, *Curriculum Aims*, 3d ed. (New York: Teachers College Press, 1997), 21.
7. Ibid.
8. Ralph W. Tyler, *Basic Principles of Curriculum and Instruction* (Chicago: University of Chicago Press, 1950).
9. Martin Briner, "Learning Theories Web Site." Available at http://curriculum.calstatela.edu/faculty/psparks/theorists/501learn.htm (March 15, 2002).
10. Walter Dick, "History of Instructional Design."
11. Robert Gagne, "Instruction in the Conditioning of Learning," in *Instruction: Some Contemporary Viewpoints,* ed. Laurence Siegel (New York: Harper & Row, 1967); Robert Gagne, *The Conditions of Learning* (New York: Holt, Rinehart, and Winston, 1965); Robert Gagne, *Psychological Principles in System Development* (New York: Holt, Rinehart, and Winston, 1962).
12. Ken Masters, "MCQs and Bloom's Taxonomy." Available at http://www.uct.ac.za/projects/cbe/mcqman/mcqappc.html (February 4, 2002).
13. Benjamin S. Bloom, ed., *Taxonomy of Educational Objectives: Cognitive Domain* (New York: David McKay, 1956).
14. Allison Drago, "Madeline Hunter." Available at http://www2.bc.edu/~ruedaju/MadelineHunter.html (January 17, 2002).
15. Madeline Hunter, *Mastery Teaching* (Thousand Oaks, CA: Corwin Press, 1982).
16. Arthur K. Ellis and Jeffrey T. Fouts, *Research on Educational Innovations*, 2d ed. (New York: Eye on Education, 1997).
17. Patricia Wolfe, "What the 'Seven-Step Lesson Plan' Isn't," *Educational Leadership* 44, no. 5 (February 1987).
18. SAGUARO Project, "Curriculum Design: The 5-E Learning Cycle." Available at http://saguaro.geo.arizona.edu/5–Epdf.pdf (April 16, 2002); Robert

Karplus and Herbert D. Thier, *A New Look at Elementary School Science* (Chicago: Rand McNally, 1967).

19. Ibid.

20. David T. Crowther, "Here We Grow Again: Applications of Research and Model Inquiry Lessons" *Electronic Journal of Science Education*. Available at http://unr.edu/homepage/crowther/ejse/crowedit4.html (February 4, 2002).

21. Robert Karplus and Herbert D. Their, *A New Look*; Robert Karplus, "The Learning Cycle," in *Workshop on Physics Teaching and the Development of Reasoning,* ed. Francis P. Collea, et al. (Stony Brook, NY: American Association of Physics, 1975); Rodger W. Bybee et al., *Science and Technology Education for the Elementary Years: Frameworks for Curriculum and Instruction* (Washington, DC: The National Center for Improving Instruction, 1989).

22. Donald W. Oliver and James P. Shaver, *Cases and Controversy: A Guide to Teaching the Public Issues Series* (Middletown, CT: American Education Publishers, 1971); Donald W. Oliver and James P. Shaver, *Teaching Public Issues in High School* (Boston: Houghton Mifflin, 1966).

23. Ibid.

24. John Dewey, *Democracy in Education* (New York: Macmillan, 1916), 37.

25. Lawrence Stenhouse, *An Introduction,* 142.

Chapter 9. Brain-Based Lesson Plan Frameworks

1. Howard Gardner, *Frames of the Mind: The Theory of Multiple Intelligences* (New York: Basic Books, 1983).

2. Thomas R. Hoerr, "Focusing on the Personal Intelligences as a Basis for Success," *NASSP Bulletin* 80, no. 583 (November 1996): 36.

3. Howard Gardner, *Multiple Intelligences: The Theory in Practice* (New York: Basic Books, 1993), 249; As quoted in Howard Gardner, "Multiple Intelligences as a Catalyst," *English Journal* 84, no. 8 (December 1995): 16.

4. Gardner, *Multiple Intelligences as a Catalyst*, 250–251; Kathy Checkley, "The First Seven . . . and the Eighth: A Conversation with Howard Gardner," *Educational Leadership* 55, no. 1 (September 1997): 8.

5. Howard Gardner, "Probing More Deeply Into the Theory of Multiple Intelligences," *NASSP Bulletin* 80, no. 583 (November 1996): quote at 1; Howard Gardner, "Reflections on Multiple Intelligences: Myths and Messages," *Phi Delta Kappan* 77, no. 3 (November 1995): quote at 201.

6. Jean Sausele Knodt, "A Think Tank Cultivates Kids," *Educational Leadership* 55, no. 1 (September 1997): 37; Andrew S. Latham, "Quantifying MI's Gains," *Educational Leadership* 55, no.1 (September 1997): 84.

7. Howard Gardner, "Educating for Understanding," *The American School Board Journal* 180, no. 7 (July1993): quote at 21.

8. Garet Nelson, "Internet/ Web-Based Instruction and Multiple Intelligences," *Educational Media International* 35, no. 2 (June 1998): 90.

9. Howard Gardner, "Multiple Intelligences as a Partner in School Improvements," *Educational Leadership* 55, no. 1 (September 1997): 21.

10. Thomas R. Hoerr, "Introducing the Theory of Multiple Intelligences," *NASSP Bulletin* 80, no. 583 (November 1996): 9.

11. Ibid., 9.
12. Gardner, "Multiple Intelligences as a Catalyst," 16.
13. David Lazear, *Seven Ways of Teaching: The Artistry of Teaching with Multiple Intelligences* (Palatine, IL: IRI/Skylight Publishing, 1991), v-vi.
14. Thomas R. Hoerr, *Implementing Multiple Intelligences: The New City School Experience* (Bloomington, IN: Phi Delta Kappa Educational Foundation, 1996); Lazear, *Seven Ways of Teaching*, vi-vii.
15. Hoerr, "Introducing the Theory of Multiple Intelligences," 8.
16. Maggie Meyer, "The GREENing of Learning: Using the Eighth Intelligence," *Educational Leadership* 55, no.1 (September 1997).
17. Gardner, "Multiple Intelligences as a Partner in School Improvement," 20.
18. Gardner, "Educating for Understanding," 21.
19. Howard Gardner, "Six Afterthoughts: Comments on 'Varieties of Intellectual Talent,'" *Journal of Creative Behavior* 31, no. 2 (1997): 120; Howard Gardner and Thomas Hatch, "Multiple Intelligences Go to School," *Educational Researcher* 18, no. 8 (November 1989): 5.
20. Gardner and Hatch, "Multiple Intelligences Go to School," 6; Sue Teele, "Redesigning the Educational System to Enable All Students to Succeed," *NASSP Bulletin* 80, no. 583 (November 1996): 65.
21. Teele, "Redesigning the Educational System," 75.
22. Peter Smagorinsky, "Multiple Intelligences in the English Class: An Overview," *English Journal* 84, no. 8 (December 1995): 25.
23. Gardner, *Multiple Intelligences: The Theory in Practice,* 251.
24. Kathleen M. Noonan, "Untangling the Web: The Use of the World Wide Web as a Pedagogical Tool in History Courses," *The History Teacher* 31, no. 2 (February 1998): 205.
25. Nelson, "Internet/Web-Based Instruction and Multiple Intelligences."
26. As quoted in Wendy Ecklund Lambert, "From Crockett to Tubman: Investigating Historical Perspectives," *Educational Leadership* 55, no. 1 (September 1997): 52.
27. Gardner, "Educating for Understanding," 24.
28. Gardner, "Reflections on Multiple Intelligences," 208.
29. Michelle D. Walker, "Multiple Intelligences and the World Wide Web: A New Approach to Teaching About the War," *OAH Magazine of History* 12, no.3 (Spring 1998); Nina Mjagkij and D. Antonio Cantu, "'The Public Be Damned!' A Thematic and Multiple Intelligences Approach to Teaching the Gilded Age," *OAH Magazine of History* 13, no. 4 (Summer 1999).
30. Ibid.
31. Teele, "Redesigning the Educational System," 68.
32. Latham, "Quantifying MI's Gains," 84–85.
33. Shirley E. Jordan, "Multiple Intelligences: Seven Keys to Opening Closed Minds," *NASSP Bulletin* 80, no. 583 (November 1996): 35.
34. Ellen Weber, "Creative Communities in High School: An Interactive Learning and Teaching Approach," *NASSP Bulletin* 80, no. 583 (November 1996). Quote at 77.
35. Joseph D. Novak and D. Bob Gowin, *Learning How To Learn* (Cambridge, UK: Cambridge University Press, 1984), xi.

36. Carol Tell, "The I-Generation—From Toddlers to Teenagers: A Conversation with Jane M. Healy," Educational *Leadership* 58, no. 2 (2000): 8–9.

37. Michael J. Berson et al., *Social Studies on the Internet* (Upper Saddle River, NJ: Prentice-Hall, 2001), v.

38. Bernice McCarthy and Susan Morris, *The 4MAT CourseBook,* Vol. 1 (Barrington, IL: Excel, 1994), 7.

39. Chris Dede, quoted in D. Mark Meyers, "Teacher Education," in *Surfing the Social Studies: The Internet Book,* ed. Joseph A. Braun, Jr. and C. Frederick Risinger (Washington, DC: National Council for the Social Studies, 1999), 113.

Chapter 10. Teaching Authentic History

1. Doug A. Archibald and Fred M. Newmann, *Beyond Standardized Testing: Assessing Authentic Academic Achievement in Secondary School* (Reston, VA: National Association of Secondary Principals, 1988); Geoffrey Scheurman and Fred M. Newmann, "Authentic Intellectual Work in Social Studies: Putting Performance before Pedagogy," *Social Education* 62 (January 1998): 23–25.

2. Bruce Fehn and Kim E. Koeppen, "Intensive Document-Based Instruction in a Social Studies Methods Curse and Student Teachers' Attitudes and Practice in Subsequent Field Experiences," *Theory and Research in Social Education* 26 (Fall 1998): 461–484.

3. James W. Loewen, *Lies My Teacher Told Me: Everything Your American History Textbook Got Wrong* (New York: The New Press, 1995), 1; and Howard Gardner, *The Disciplined Mind: Beyond Facts and Standardized Tests, The K-12 Education That Every Child Deserves* (New York: Penguin Books, 2000).

4. Andrew McMichael, "The Historian, the Internet, and the Web: A Reassessment." *Perspectives* (American Historical Association Newsmagazine) 36 (February 1998): 29–32; Phillip J. van Fossen and James M. Shively, "Using the Internet to Create Primary Source Teaching Packets," *The Social Studies* 91 (November/December 2000): 244–252; U.S. Department of Education, *The Condition of Education, 1998* (Washington, DC: National Center for Education Statistics, 1999).

5. David Kobrin, *Beyond the Textbook: Teaching History Using Documents and Primary Sources* (Portsmouth, NH: Heinemann, 1996), 95; O.L. Davis, Jr. and Elizabeth Yeager, "Classroom Teachers' Thinking about Historical Texts: An Exploratory Study," *Theory and Research in Social Education* 24 (Spring 1996): 146–166; Marcy Singer Gabella, "Beyond the Looking Glass: Bringing Students into the Conversation of Historical Inquiry," *Theory and Research in Social Education* 22 (Summer 1994): 340–363; Steven A. Stahl, Cynthia R. Hynd, Bruce K. Britton, Mary M. McNish, and Dennis Bosquet, "What Happens When Students Read Multiple Source Documents in History?" *Reading Research Quarterly* 31 (November/December 1996): 430–456; James A. Percoco, *A Passion for the Past: Creative Teaching of U.S. History* (Portsmouth, NH: Heinemann, 1998); and Bruce A. Van Sledright, "Arbitrating Competing Claims in the Classroom Culture Wars," *OAH Newsletter* 27 (February 1999): 7–8.

6. Lawrence Kohlberg, "Cognitive-Development Approach to Moral Edu-

cation," in *Social Studies Strategies: Theory into Practice*, ed. Peter H. Marto-rella, 127–142 (New York: Harper and Row, 1976).

7. Ronald W. Evans, "Teacher Conception of History Revisited: Ideology, Curriculum, and Student Belief," *Theory and Research in Social Education* 17 (Spring 1990): 101–138; James P. Shaver, ed., *Handbook of Research on Social Studies Teaching and Learning: A Project of the National Council for the Social Studies* (New York: Macmillan, 1991); Andrew S. Hughes, "Toward a More Thoughtful Professional Education for Social Studies Teachers: Can Problem-Based Learning Contribute?" *Theory and Research in Social Education* 25 (Fall 1997): 431–445; and Steven Zemelman, Harvey Daniels, and Arthur Hyde, *Best Practice: New Standards for Teaching and Learning in America's Schools* (Portsmouth, NH: Heinemann, 1998).

8. Kieran Egan, "Layers of Historical Understanding." *Theory and Research in Social Education* 17 (Fall 1989): 280–294; Peter J. Frederick, "Four Reflections on Teaching and Learning History," *Perspectives* (American Historical Association Newsmagazine) 39 (October 2001): 28; and Ronald W. Evans and David Warren Saxe, *Handbook on Teaching Social Issues, NCSS Bulletin 93* (Washington, DC: National Council for the Social Studies, 1996).

9. Laurel R. Singleton and James R. Giese, "American Memory: Using Library of Congress On-Line Resources to Enhance History Teaching," *Social Education* 62 (March 1998): 142–144; Lee Ann Porter, "National Archives Expands Digital Classroom," *Perspectives* (American Historical Association Newsmagazine) 37 (February 1999): 3–4; van Fossen and Shiveley, "Using the Internet to Create Primary Source Teaching Packets"; and Stephen Kneeshaw, "Bringing the Internet and World Wide Web into the History Classroom," in *History.edu: Essays on Teaching with Technology*, ed. Dennis A. Trinkle and Scott A. Merriman (Armonk, NY: M.E. Sharpe, 2001), 153–170.

10. Van Fossen and Shiveley, "Using the Internet to Create Primary Source Packets."

Chapter 11. The Montage Class: Teaching Historical Thinking with Audiovisual and Information Technology

1. These percentages are from Wagner Thielens, Jr., "The Disciplines and Undergraduate Lecturing," paper presented at the annual meeting of the American Educational Research Association (Washington, DC, April 20–24, 1987). The paraphrase is taken from Charles C. Bonwell and James A. Eison, *Active Learning: Creating Excitement in the Classroom,* ASHE-ERIC Higher Education Report No. 1 (Washington, DC: George Washington University, School of Education and Human Development, 1991), 3.

2. Bonwell and Eison, *Active Learning,* 9.

3. Steven W. Keele, *Attention and Human Performance* (Pacific Palisades, CA: Goodyear, 1973), 56–57.

4. Barry K. Beyer, *Practical Strategies for the Teaching of Thinking* (Boston: Allyn and Bacon, 1987), 44.

5. Barry K. Beyer, "Practical Strategies for the Direct Teaching of Thinking Skills," in *Developing Minds: A Resource Book for Teaching Thinking*, vol. 1,

rev. ed., ed. Arthur L. Costa (Alexandria, VA: Association for Supervision and Curriculum Development, 1991), 274. Hereinafter cited as "Direct Teaching."

6. Beyer, "Direct Teaching," 275.

7. Wilbur J. McKeachie, "Teaching Thinking," *NCRIPTAL UPDATE,* 2, no. 1 (September 1988): 1.

8. Joanne Gainen Kurfiss, "Critical Thinking by Design," *The Professional and Organizational Development Network in Higher Education's Teaching Excellence: Toward the Best in the Academy,* Fall 1989, http://www.ucet.ufl.edu/ProgramService/topic3-4.htm.

9. Beyer, "Direct Teaching," 275–276.

10. Beyer, "Direct Teaching," 278.

11. Hogue's article appears in the *Organization of American Historians Magazine of History for Teachers of History* 15, no. 1 (Fall 2000): 70–72. As outlined in the national standards, historical thinking includes these skills: chronological thinking, historical comprehension, historical analysis and interpretation, historical research capabilities, and historical issues-analysis and decision making. Available at http://www.sscnet.ucla.edu/nchs/standards/.

12. Hogue, "Using Computer Technology," 70.

13. Doug Stewart, "Teachers Aim at Turning Loose the Mind's Eyes," *Smithsonian,* August 1985, 54.

14. Ibid., 53.

15. Ibid., 47.

16. *Visual Thinking* (Berkeley: University of California Press, 1969), v.

17. Jacob Bronowski, *The Identity of Man,* rev. ed. (Garden City, NY: American Museum Science Books, 1971), 28.

18. J.A. Miller, "Paying Attention at Many Levels," *Science News* (November 9, 1985): 295.

19. Robert H. McKim, "The Imaginarium: An Environment and Program for Opening the Mind's Eye," in *Visual Learning, Thinking, and Communication,* ed. E. Bikkar, S. Randhawa, and W.E. Coffman (New York: Academic Press, 1978), 61–62.

20. Richard L. Hopkins, "Educating the Right Brain: Why We Need to Teach Patterning," *The Clearinghouse* 58, no. 3 (November 1984): 132.

21. J.R. Kidd, *How Adults Learn,* rev. ed. (New York: Association Press, 1973), 205.

22. Ibid., 263–264.

23. David Berliner and Ursula Cassanova Pinero, "How Memory Works: Implications for Teachers," *Instructor* 94, no. 5 (1985): 14–15: and Kidd, 219.

24. Stewart, "Teacher's Aim," 44–46.

25. Ibid., 46–52.

26. Hopkins, "Educating the Right Brain," 133–134.

27. Ibid., 133.

Chapter 12. Cooperative Learning

1. Harry Wong and Rosemary Wong, *The First Day of School* (Mountain View, CA: Harry K. Wong Publications, 1998), 246, 313.

2. James W. Loewen, *Lies My Teacher Told Me : Everything Your American History Textbook Got Wrong* (New York: The New Press, 1995).

3. R. Brandt, "On Cooperation in Schools: A Conversation with David and Roger Johnson," *Educational Leadership* 45 (1987): 16.

4. Loewen, *Lies My Teacher Told Me*.

5. Brandt, "On Cooperation in Schools," 16.

6. David Johnson, Roger Johnson, E. Holubec, and P. Roy, *Circles of Learning* (Alexandria, VA: Association for Supervision and Curriculum Development, 1984), 1.

7. Roger Johnson, David Johnson, and M. Stanne, "Effects of Cooperative, Competitive, and Individualistic Goal Structures on Computer-Assisted Instruction," *Journal of Educational Psychology* 77 (1985): 669.

8. Ibid., 668.

9. Johnson et al., *Circles of Learning*, 2.

10. R. Slaven, "Cooperative Learning and the Cooperative School," *Educational Leadership* 45 (1987): 7.

11. Ibid.

12. Y. Sharan and S. Sharan, "Training Teachers for Cooperative Learning" *Educational Leadership* 45 (1987): 13.

13. Brandt, "On Cooperation in Schools," 15–16.

14. Ibid., 16.

15. Wong and Wong, *First Day of School*, 254.

16. Ibid.

17. Brandt, "On Cooperation in Schools," 16.

18. David Johnson, Roger Johnson, and E. Holubec, *Advanced Cooperative Learning* (Edina, MN: Interaction Book, 1988), 12–13.

19. Ibid., 4.

20. Ibid.

21. David Johnson and Roger Johnson, *Learning Together and Alone* (Englewood Cliffs, NJ: Prentice-Hall, 1975).

22. Wong and Wong, *First Day of School*, 255.

23. Ibid.

24. Roger Johnson, David Johnson, and B. Bryant, "Cooperation in the Classroom: Perceptions and Preferences as Related to Students' Feelings of Personal Control," *Elementary School Journal* 73 (1973).

25. Johnson and Johnson, *Learning Together*.

26. Ibid.

27. Ibid.

28. Ibid.

29. Ruby K. Payne, *A Framework of Understanding Poverty* (Baytown, TX: RFT Publishing, 1998), 116.

30. Johnson et al., *Circles of Learning,* 391.

31. M. Sepon-Sheve and N. Schniedwind, "Selling Cooperative Learning Without Selling It Short," *Educational Leadership* 47 (1989–90): 64.

32. Ibid., 63.

33. Johnson et al., *Circles of Learning,* 13.

34. Ibid., 13–14.

35. J.M. Rich, *Innovations in Education,* 6th ed. (Needham Heights, MA: Allyn and Bacon, 1992), 4.

36. Ibid.

37. Johnson et al., *Circles of Learning,* 14.

38. H. Ozman and S.M. Craver, *Philosophical Foundations of Education,* 2d ed. (Columbus, OH: Charles E. Merrill, 1981).

39. Brandt, "On Cooperation in Schools," 16.

40. Johnson et al. *Circles of Learning,* 14.

41. Johnson and Johnson, *Learning Together,* 15.

42. Johnson et al. *Circles of Learning,* 7.

43. Ibid.

44. Ibid.

45. D. Antonio Cantu, *Take Five Minutes: American History Class Openers* (Westminister, CA: Teacher Created Materials, 2002), 6–11.

46. J.L. Schultz, "Cooperative Learning: Refining the Process," *Educational Leadership* 47 (1989–90): 44.

47. Ibid.

48. David W. Johnson and Roger J. Johnson, "Social Skills for Successful Group Work," *Education Leadership* 47 (1989–90): 30.

49. Johnson and Holubec, *Advanced Cooperative Learning,* 31.

50. Wong and Wong, *First Day of School,* 206.

51. Johnson et al., *Circles of Learning,* 55.

52. Peter M. Senge, *The Fifth Discipline: The Art & Practice of The Learning Organization* (New York: Currency Doubleday, 1990).

53. David W. Johnson and Roger T. Johnson, "Research Shows the Benefits of Adult Cooperation," *Educational Leadership* 45 (1987): 27.

54. S.S. Ellis and S.F. Whalen, "Keys to Cooperative Learning," *Instructor* (1992): 37.

55. Johnson, and Holubec, *Advanced Cooperative Learning,* 33.

56. Brandt, "On Cooperation in Schools," 16.

57. Ibid.

58. B.T. Vasquez, R.E. Slavin, M.D'Arcangelo, and L.J. Kiernan, *ASCD Cooperative Learning Series* (Alexandria, VA: Association for Supervision and Curriculum Development, 1990), 1.

59. Spencer Kagan, *Cooperative Learning SmartCard* (San Clemente, CA: Kagan Cooperative Learning, 1998).

Chapter 13. Teaching Strategies and Resources for History and Social Studies Education

1. Associated Press, "FCC Chief Sees Wireless U.S.," *Bloomington Pantagraph,* February 14, 2000, A4.

2. Jamie MacKenzie, *Beyond Technology: Questioning, Research, and the Information Literate School* (Bellingham, WA: FNO Press, 2000).

3. Joseph A. Braun, Jr., "Past Possibilities, and Potholes on the Information Superhighway," *Social Education* 60 (March 1996): 149–153.

4. Barry Beyer, "Critical Thinking: What Is It?" *Social Education* 49, no. 4 (1985): 278–276.

5. Mackenzie, *Beyond Technology,* 2.

6. Barbara Brehm, "Effective Internet Searching," in *Surfing Social Studies: The Internet Book,* ed. Joseph A. Braun, Jr. and C. Frederick Risinger (Washington, DC: National Council for the Social Studies, 1999), 9–16.

7. Danny Sullivan, ed., "Search Engine Watch." Available from http://searchenginewatch.com/ (August 16, 2000).

8. C. Frederick Risinger, "Separating the Wheat from the Chaff: Why Dirty Pictures Are Not the Real Dilemma in Using the Internet in Social Studies," *Social Education* 62 (March 1998): 148–150; M. Berson and Eileen Berson, "Safe Web Exploration," in *Surfing Social Studies,* ed. Braunn and Risinger (Washington, DC: National Council for the Social Studies, 1999), 149–156.

9. Brehm, "Effective Internet Searching," 15.

10. Risinger, "Separating the Wheat from the Chaff," 149.

11. Fred Newmann, *Authentic Achievement: Restructing Schools for Intellectual Quality* (San Francisco: Jossey-Bass, 1996).

12. Joseph A. Braun, Jr. "Social Studies Rubrics." Available from http://searchenginewatch.com/ (August 16, 2000); http://www.Coe.ilstu.edu/jabraun/braun/professional/rubric.html.

13. Mackenzie, *Beyond Technology,* 130.

14. Ibid., 14.

15. Ibid., 134.

16. Ibid., 135.

17. Susan Davis Lenski, Mary Ann Wham, and Jerry L. Johns, *Reading and Learning Strategies for Middle & High School Students* (Dubuque, IA: Kendall Hunt, 1999).

18. B. Hunter and E.K. Lodish, *Online Searching in the Curriculum* (Santa Barbara, CA: ABC/Clio, 1989).

19. Jan McCoy, "Databases in the Social Studies: Not Why But How," *Social Studies and the Young Learner* (Fall 1990): 13–15.

20. Hunter and Lodish, *Online Searching,* 33.

21. Joseph A. Braun, Jr., Phyllis Maxey Fernlund, and Charles S. White, *Technology Tools in the Social Studies Curriculum* (Wilsonville, OR: Franklin Beedle & Associates, 1998).

22. James R. Paul and Colette Kaiser, "Do Women Live Longer than Men? Investigating Graveyard Data with Computers," *Learning and Leading with Technology* 23, no. 8 (May1996): 13–15.

23. Hollylyne Stohl Dreyer and Lee K. John, "Learning About Climate: An Exploration of Geography and Mathematics," *Social Studies and the Younger Learner* (September/October 1999): 6–10.

24. L. Anderson-Inman, L. Ditson and M.T. Ditson, "Computer-Based Concept Mapping: Enhancing Literacy with Tools for Visual Thinking," *Journal of Adolescent and Adult Literacy* 40, no. 4 (1985): 302–306.

25. Inspiration Software, http://www.inspiration.com/.

26. Nicholas Negroponte, *Being Digital* (New York: Alfred Knopf, 1995).

27. "MultiMedia Mania 2000." Available from http://www.ncsu.edu/midlink/rub.multi.htm (August 16, 2000); Joseph A. Braun, Jr., "A Rubric for Evaluation

Social Studies World Wide Web Pages." Available from http://www.coe.ilstu.edu/jabraun/braun/professional/wwwrubric.html (August 16, 2000).

28. "Web66 International School Web Site Registry." Available from http://web66.coled.umn.edu/schools.html (August 16, 2000).

29. Madeleine Decker, "The Webquest Page." Available from http://www.pekin.net/pekin108/wash/wq/wqpage.html (August 16, 2000).

30. Jamie McKenzie, "Grazing the Net: Raising a Generation of Free-Range Students," *Phi Delta Kappan* (September 1998): 26–31.

31. Jamie McKenzie, "Module Makers." Available from http://questioning.org/module/module.html (August 16, 2000).

32. Braun, Fernlund, and White, *Technology Tools,* 5.

33. Bill Bigelow, "On the Road to Cultural Bias: A Critique of 'The Oregon Trail CD-ROM,'" *Social Studies and the Young Learner* (January/February 1996): 26–29.

34. Marianne Teague and Gerald Teague, "Planning with Computers: A Social Studies Simulation," *Learning and Leading with Technologies* 23, no. 1 (September 1995): 20–22.

35. John Chiodo and Mary Flaim, "The Link Between Computer Simulations and Social Studies Learning: Debriefing," *The Social Studies* (May/June 1993): 119–121.

36. Corsandra Stallworth and Joseph A. Braun, Jr., "GIS Programs: Geography Tools for Teachers and Students," *Social Education* 64 (April 2000): 161–164.

37. Timothy Keiper, "Connecting Authenticity, Technology, and Geography," *Social Studies and the Young Learner* 12 (January/February 1999): 22–28.

38. Alvin Toffler, *Future Shock* (New York: Bantam Books, 1971).

39. Peshe Kuriloff, "If John Dewey Were Alive Today, He'd be a Webhead," *Chronicle of Higher Education*, April 28, 2000, A72.

40. International Society for Technology Education, "Standards Projects." Available from http://www.iste.org/Standards/index.html (August 16, 2000).

41. Marsha Albrandi, Candy Beal, Ann Thompson, and Anna Wilson, "Reconstructing a School's Past Using Oral Histories and GIS Mapping," *Social Education* 64 (April 2000): 134–140; John Zola and Andri Ionnidou, "Learning and Teaching with Interactive Simulations," *Social Education* (April 2000): 142–145.

42. Howard Mehlinger, "Amy Wallace: Information Age Teacher," *Social Education* (April 2000): 146–148.

43. As quoted in John O'Niel, "Fads and Fireflies: The Difficulties of Sustaining Change," *Educational Leadership* (April 2000): 8.

44. John Goodlad, *A Place Called School: Prospects for the Future* (New York: McGraw-Hill, 1984).

Chapter 14. Informal Assessment and Evaluation Strategies

1. George F. Madaus and Laura M. O'Dwyer, "A Short History of Performance Assessment: Lessons Learned," *Phi Delta Kappan* 80 (May 1999): 689.

2. Ibid., 690–693.

3. Thomas A. Angelo and K. Patricia Cross, *Classroom Assessment Techniques: A Handbook for College Teachers*, 2d ed. (San Francisco: Jossey-Bass, 1993), 5.

4. Ibid., 132–137.

5. Margaret E. McIntosh, "Formative Assessment in Mathematics," *Clearing House* 71 (November/December 1997): 92–97; D.W. Ogle, "K-W-L: A Teaching Model that Develops Active Reading of Expository Text," *The Reading Teacher* 39 (1986): 564–570; and E. Carr and D.W. Ogle, "K-W-L-Plus: A Strategy for Comprehension and Summarizing," *Journal of Reading* 30 (1987): 626–631.

6. David Kobrin, *Beyond the Textbook: Teaching History Using Documents and Primary Sources* (Portsmouth, NH: Heinemann, 1996), 76–78.

7. Angelo and Cross, *Classroom Assessment Techniques*, 168–171.

8. McIntosh, "Formative Assessment in Mathematics."

9. Angelo and Cross, *Classroom Assessment Techniques*, 258–262.

10. Ibid., 263–270.

11. B.J. Scott and Michael R. Vitale, "Informal Assessment of Idea Development in Written Expression: A Tool for Classroom Use," *Preventing School Failure* 44 (Winter 2000): 67–72.

12. Angelo and Cross, *Classroom Assessment Techniques*, 322–329.

13. Peter H. Martorella, *Teaching Social Studies in Middle and Secondary Schools,* 2d ed. (Englewood Cliffs, NJ: Prentice-Hall, 1996), 403.

Chapter 15. Formal Assessment and Evaluation Strategies

1. Steven Zemelman, Harvey Daniels, and Arthur Hyde, *Best Practice: New Standards for Teaching and Learning in America's Schools,* 2d ed. (Portsmouth, NH: Heinemann, 1998), 245–249.

2. Lorin W. Anderson, "Research on Teaching and Teacher Education," in *Bloom's Taxonomy: A Forty-year Retrospective, Ninety-Third Yearbook of the National Society for the Study of Education*, Part II, ed. Lorin W. Anderson and Lauren A. Sosniak (Chicago: University of Chicago Press, 1994), 134–135.

3. Zemelman, Daniels, and Hyde, *Best Practice,* 247–249; James A. Banks and Cherry A. McGee-Banks, *Teaching Strategies for the Social Studies: Decision-Making and Citizen Action*, 5th ed. (New York: Longman, 1999), 474–475; Peter H. Martorella, *Teaching Social Studies in Middle and Secondary Schools*, 2d ed. (Engelwood Cliffs, NJ: Prentice-Hall, Inc., 1996), 408; and Arthur K. Ellis, Jeffrey T. Fouts, and Allen D. Glenn, *Teaching and Learning Secondary Social Studies* (New York: HarperCollins, 1991), 134–137.

4. James Killoran, "In Defense of the Multiple-Choice Question," *Social Education* 56 (February 1992): 107–108. For perceptive defenses of the legitimacy of multiple choice tests in history classes, see Ann McCormick Scott, "Life is a Multiple-Choice Question," in *History Anew: Innovations in the Teaching of History Today,* ed. Robert Blackey (Long Beach: The University Press, California State University, 1993), 59–72; and Ray W. Karras, "A Multidimensional Multiple-Choice Testing System," in *History Anew*, Blackey, ed., 73–81.

5. See, for instance, Beatriz Pont and Patrick Werquin, "How Old Are the New Skills?" *The OECD Observer*, no. 225, March 2001, 15–17.

6. For a brief but balanced assessment of the pros and cons of essay testing in history classes, see Myron A. Marty, "Wrestling with Testing in American History," *Social Education* 40 (November-December 1976): 524–527. The entire November–December 1976 issue of *Social Education* is devoted to practical testing ideas for social studies teachers. Also see Douglas D. Adler, "Teacher-Made Tests in History," *Teaching History: A Journal of Methods* 4 (Spring 1979): 24–30.

7. On essay test construction, see Robert Blackey, "A Guide to the Skill of Essay Construction in History," in *History Anew,* Blackey, ed., 49–58.

8. For particularly good insights on the importance of essays that make an argument, see Ray W. Karras, "Writing Essays That Make Historical Arguments," *OAH Magazine of History* 8 (Summer 1994): 54–57.

9. For further suggestions about helping students write effective essay responses, see Jules R. Benjamin, *A Student's Guide to History,* 7th ed. (Boston: Bedford Books, 1998), 46–52; Joel S. Poetker, "Preparing for Essay Tests," *The Social Studies* 67 (May/June 1976): 113–115; John C. Bartul, "Teaching the Value of Inquiry through the Essay Question," in *History Anew,* 85–89; Virginia S. Wilson, James A. Litle, and Gerald L. Wilson, "No Solo Venture: Essay Writing in History," in *History Anew,* 91–94; and Robert Blackey, "Bull's-Eye: A Teacher's Guide for Developing Student Skill in Responding to Essay Questions," in *History Anew*, 95–101.

10. On other types of formal writing exercises that can be used in social studies classes, see Beverly Rinehart Banks, "Writing: A Tool for Learning in Social Science," *Social Studies Review* 23 (Winter 1984): 11–15.

Chapter 16. Performance-Based Assessment

1. Heidi Hayes Jacobs, *Social Studies Handbook on Alternative Assessment* (Upper Saddle River, NJ: Prentice-Hall, 1997), 2.

2. George F. Madaus and Laura M. O'Dwyer, "A Short History of Performance Assessment," *Phi Delta Kappan* 80, no. 9 (May 1999): 688.

3. As quoted in William W. Joyce, "Performance Assessment: The Wave of the Future?" *Michigan Social Studies Journal* 11, no. 1 (Spring 1999): Wiggins quoted at 27.

4. K. Michael Hibbard, *Glencoe World Geography: Performance Assessment Strategies and Activities* (New York: Glencoe, 1995), 1.

5. Office of Research, "Performance Assessment," *Education Consumer Guide* 2 (September 1993). Available at http://www.ed.gov/pubs/OR/Consumer Guides/perfasse.html (April 20, 1999).

6. Stephen N. Elliott, "Creating Meaningful Performance Assessments," in *ERIC Digest* E531 [database online] (Reston, VA: ERIC Clearinghouse on Disabilities and Gifted Education, 1995). ERIC document no. ED381985. Available at http://www.ed.gov/databases/ERIC_Digests/ed381985.html (April 20, 1999).

7. Steven L. McCollum, *Performance Assessment in the Social Studies*

Classroom: A How-To Book for Teachers (Joplin, MO: Chalk Dust Press, 1994), 7.

8. Madaus and O'Dwyer, "A Short History," 690.

9. Ibid.

10. Ibid., 692.

11. Ibid., 693.

12. Edward H. Haertel, "Performance Assessment and Education Reform," *Phi Delta Kappan* 80, no. 9 (May 1999): 662.

13. Janet Alleman and Jere Brophy, "Assessment at the Classroom Level" *Michigan Social Studies Journal* 11, no. 1 (Spring 1999): 21; Elliot W. Eisner, "The Uses and Limits of Performance Assessment," *Phi Delta Kappan* 80, no. 9 (May 1999): 658; Imogene Forte and Sandra Schurr, *Making Portfolios, Products, and Performances Meaningful and Manageable for Students and Teachers* (Nashville, TN: Incentive Publications, 1995), 88; McCollum, *Performance Assessment,* 9.

14. Hibbard, *Glencoe World Geography,* 4–5; Forte and Schurr, *Making Portfolios,* vii, 93; McCollum, *Performance Assessment,* 7–8.

15. Forte and Schurr, *Making Portfolios,* 94.

16. Joyce, "The Wave of theFuture," 28.

17. McCollum, *Performance Assessment,* 12–15; Hibbard, *Glencoe World Geography,* 1, 11; Forte and Schurr, *Making Portfolios,* 89.

18. National Center for History in the Schools (NCHS), *National Standards for History: Basic Edition* (Los Angeles: National Center for History in the Schools, 1996).

19. Bradley Commission on History in Schools, *Building a History Curriculum: Guidelines for Teaching History in Schools* (Westlake, OH: National Council for History Education, 1995), 24.

20. NCHS, *National Standards,* 62.

21. Paul Gagnon and the Bradley Commission on History in Schools, eds., *Historical Literacy: The Case for History in American Education* (Boston: Houghton Mifflin, 1991), 25.

22. NCHS, *National Standards,* 65.

23. Charlotte Crabtree et al., eds., *Lessons from History: Essential Understandings and Historical Perspectives Students Should Acquire* (Los Angeles: National Center for History in the Schools, 1992), 18.

24. NCHS, *National Standards,* 67.

25. Crabtree et al., *Lessons from History,* 153.

26. Bradley Commission, *Historical Literacy,* 24.

27. Tom March, "What's on the Web?" *Computer-Using Educators' Newsletter* (July/August 1995).

28. Joseph D. Novak and D. Bob Gowin, *Learning How to Learn* (New York: Cambridge University Press, 1998).

29. Robert Harris, "Evaluating Historical Research on the World Wide Web" *NCHE History Matters* 11, no. 2 (1998).

30. As quoted in Novak and Gowin, *Learning How to Learn,* 1.

31. Eisner, "Uses and Limits," 660.

Chapter 17. Advanced Placement Assessment Strategies

1. The College Board, *A Guide to the Advanced Placement Program, May 2000* (Princeton, NJ: Educational Testing Service, 1999), 7, 15–20; and "AP Central: The College Board's Online Home for AP Professionals." Available at apcentral.collegeboard.com.teachers. On the history of the AP program, also see Eric Rothschild, "Four Decades of the Advanced Placement Program," *History Teacher* 32 (February 1999): 175–206. Rothschild's article (p. 200) suggests that as many as 45 percent of students in AP courses end up not taking the AP examination. (Note that the entire February 1999 issue of *History Teacher* is devoted to AP history related issues.) For a defense of the AP program's reinforcement of authentic historical instruction, see Harriet Lillich, "Teaching Skills and Habits of Mind in World History," *History Teacher* 32 (February 1999): 293–296. On the connection between the addition of the AP human geography exam and the resurgence of geography as a high school subject, see Alexander B. Murphy, "Advanced Placement Geography: Opportunities and Challenges for Geographers," *Journal of Geography* 97 (May–June 1998): 132–136.

2. "AP Central" Web site. On instructors and students' views about the purpose of AP courses, see Michael Henry, "Advanced Placement U.S. History: What Happens after the Examination?" *The Social Studies* 82 (May/June 1991): 94–97. On the issue of AP scores and compatibility with college and university course requirements, see Raymond M. Hyser, "Is a 3 a C?: The Reliability of the Advanced Placement United States History Test for College Credit," *History Teacher* 32 (February 1999): 223–235. For perspectives that stress limitations of AP programs, see Eric Neutuch, "Advanced Placement United States History: A Student's Perspective," *History Teacher* 32 (February 1999), 245–248; and Pete Blagaich, "Advanced Placement Courses Are Not for Everyone," *History Teacher* 32 (February 1999): 259–262.

3. On the characteristics of successful AP United States history instructors, see James Henderson, "Effective Teaching in Advanced Placement Classrooms," *Journal of Classroom Instruction* 31 (Winter 1996): 29–35.

4. "AP Central" Web site.

5. Eric Rothschild, *Teacher's Guide to the Advanced Placement Course in United States History* (Princeton, NJ: Educational Testing Service, 1996), 21–22. The inclusion of greater social and cultural history in the AP exams is discussed in George Fain, "Teaching History," *Clearing House* 72 (November/December 1998): 68–69; and Michael S. Henry, "The AP United States History Exam: Have Free Response Essays Changed in the Last Thirty Years?" *Social Education* 58 (March 1994): 145–148.

6. For suggestions on how to teach the entire span of U.S. history within a one-year course, see Thomas E. Morrissey, "Teaching Advanced Placement American History," *Social Studies Journal* 18 (Spring 1989): 12–15. For ideas on preparing students in an urban, minority high school, see Robert DiLorenzo, "Teaching Advanced Placement United States History in the Urban, Minority High School: Successful Strategies," *History Teacher* 32 (February 1999): 207–221.

7. On the value of the DBQ for testing students' critical thinking, see John E. Stovel, "Document-Based Questions (DBQ) and Testing for Critical Thinking," *Social Science Record* 24 (Spring 1987): 11–12.

8. Rothschild, *Teacher's Guide,* 22–23.

9. Ibid., 23–24.

10. Ibid., 50, 90.

11. Rosemary Ennis, "Resources for AP United States History," *History Teacher* 32 (February 1999): 239–240.

12. Kathleen McCarthy Young and Gaea Leinhardt, "Writing from Primary Documents," *Written Communication* 15 (January 1998): 44–69.

13. Ibid.

14. See Henry, "The AP United States History Exam."

15. The College Board, *The Advanced Placement Examination in United States History, Free-Response Scoring Guide with Multiple-Choice Section, 1996* (Princeton, NJ: Educational Testing Service, 1997), 2. For further information on how the composite 0–5 AP exam scores are computed based on the scores from both the multiple choice and free response sections, see pages 92–93 of this booklet.

16. Ibid.

17. Ibid., 41.

18. Henry, "Advanced Placement U.S. History."

Bibliography

Adler, A. "A Field Study of Selected Student Teacher Perspectives Toward Social Studies." *Theory and Research in Social Education* 12, no. 1 (1984): 13–30.

Adler, Douglas D. "Teacher-Made Tests in History." *Teaching History: A Journal of Methods 4* (Spring 1979): 24–30.

Albrandi, Marsha, Candy Beal, Ann Thompson, and Anna Wilson. "Reconstructing a School's Past Using Oral Histories and GIS Mapping." *Social Education* 64 (April 2000): 134–140.

Alleman, Janet, and Jere Brophy. "Assessment at the Classroom Level." *Michigan Social Studies Journal* 11, no. 1 (Spring 1999): 21–26.

Anderson-Inman, L., L. Ditson, and M.T. Ditson. "Computer-Based Concept Mapping: Enhancing Literacy with Tools for Visual Thinking." *Journal of Adolescent and Adult Literacy* 40, no. 4 (1985): 302–306.

Anderson, Lorin W., and Lauren A. Sosniak, eds. *Bloom's Taxonomy, A Forty-year Retrospective. Ninety-Third Yearbook of the National Society for the Study of Education.* Chicago: University of Chicago Press, 1994.

Angelo, Thomas A., and K. Patricia Cross. *Classroom Assessment Techniques: A Handbook for College Teachers.* 2d ed. San Francisco: Jossey-Bass, 1993.

Archibald, Doug A., and Fred M. Newmann. *Beyond Standardized Testing: Assessing Authentic Academic Achievement in Secondary School.* Reston, VA: National Association of Secondary Principals, 1988.

Associated Press. "FCC Chief Sees Wireless U.S." *Bloomington Pantagraph,* February 14, 2000, A4.

Attig, John C. "Writing Essays on the U.S. History Examination." *Social Studies Review* 26 (Winter 1987): 49–51.

Azzara, Judy. "Training Teachers for Technology." *Principal* 79, no. 3 (January 2000): 22–25.

Ballard, Martin, ed. *New Movements in the Study and Teaching of History.* Bloomington: Indiana University Press, 1970.

Banks, Beverly Rinehart. "Writing: A Tool for Learning in Social Science." *Social Studies Review* 23 (Winter 1984): 11–15.

Banks, James A., and Cherry A. McGee-Banks. *Teaching Strategies for the Social Studies: Decision-Making and Citizen Action.* 5th ed. New York: Longman, 1999.

Barr, R.D., J.L. Barth, and S.S. Shermis. *Defining the Social Studies.* Washington, DC: National Council for the Social Studies, 1977.

Barth, James L. "Social Studies: There Is a History, There Is a Body, But Is It Worth Saving?" *Social Education* 57 (February 1993): 56–57.

Barth, James L., and S. Samuel Shermis. "Nineteenth Century Origins of the Social Studies Movement: Understanding the Continuity Between Older and Contemporary Civic and U.S. History Textbooks." *Theory and Research in Social Education* 8 (Fall 1980): 29–50.

Beard, C.A. *The Nature of the Social Sciences in Relation to Objectives of Instruction.* New York: Charles Scribner's Sons, 1934.

Benjamin, Jules R. *A Student's Guide to History.* 7th ed. Boston: Bedford Books, 1998.

Bennett, C., and E. Spalding. "Teaching the Social Studies: Multiple Approaches for Multiple Perspectives." *Theory and Research in Social Education* 20, no. 3 (1992): 263–292.

Berg, Roger. "Resisting Change: What the Literature Says About Computers in the Social Studies Classroom." *Social Education* 47, no. 5 (May 1983): 314–316.

Bergman, Sally. *A Multiple Intelligences Road to a Quality Classroom.* Palatine, IL: IRI/Skylight Training and Publishing, 1995.

Berson, Michael J., Barbara C. Cruz, James A. Duplas, and J. Howard Johnson. *Social Studies on the Internet.* Upper Saddle River, NJ: Prentice-Hall, 2001.

Beyer, Barry K. "Critical Thinking: What Is It?" *Social Education* 49, no. 4 (1985): 278– 276.

———. *Practical Strategies for the Teaching of Thinking.* Boston: Allyn and Bacon, 1987.

Bigelow, Bill. "On the Road to Cultural Bias: A Critique of 'The Oregon Trail CD-ROM.'" *Social Studies and the Young Learner* (January/February 1996): 26–29.

Bikkar, E., S. Randhawa, and W.E. Coffman, eds. *Visual Learning, Thinking, and Communication.* New York: Academic Press, 1978.

Blackey, Robert, ed. *History Anew: Innovations in the Teaching of History Today.* Long Beach: The University Press, California State University, 1993.

Blagaich, Pete. "Advanced Placement Courses Are Not for Everyone." *History Teacher* 32 (February 1999): 259–262.

Bloom, Benjamin S., Mas D. Englehart, Edward J. Furst, Walker H. Hill, and David R. Krathwohl, eds. *Taxonomy of Educational Objectives: The Classification of Educational Goals. Handbook I: Cognitive Domain.* New York: Longmans, Green, 1956.

Bonwell, Charles C., and James A. Eison. *Active Learning: Creating Excitement in the Classroom,* ASHE-ERIC Higher Education Report No. 1. Washington, DC: The George Washington University, School of Education and Human Development, 1991.

Borko, H., and R.J. Shavelson. "Speculations on Teacher Education: Recommendations from Research on Teachers' Cognitions." *Journal of Education for Teaching* 9, no. 3 (1983): 210–224.

Bradley Commission on History in Schools. *Building a History Curriculum: Guidelines for Teaching History in Schools.* Westlake, OH: National Council for History Education, 1995.

Brady, H. Robert. "An Overview of Computer Integration into Social Studies Instruction." *Social Education* 58, no. 5 (September 1994): 312–314.

Brady, H. Robert, and James L. Barth. "Social Studies Standards that Effectively Integrate Technology." *Social Education* 56, no. 1 (January 2000): 14–16.

———. "Reclaiming the Spirit of the Social Studies." *Social Education* 59 (April/May 1995): 208–210.

Brandt, Ron. "On Cooperation in Schools: A Conversation with David and Roger Johnson." *Educational Leadership* 45 (1987).

Braun Jr., Joseph A. "Past Possibilities, and Potholes on the Information Superhighway." *Social Education* 60 (March 1996): 149–153.

Braun Jr., Joseph A., and C. Frederick Risinger. *Surfing Social Studies: The Internet Book.* Washington, DC: National Council for the Social Studies, 1999.

Braun Jr., Joseph A., Phyllis Maxey Fernlund, and Charles S. White. *Technology Tools in the Social Studies Curriculum.* Wilsonville, OR: Franklin Beedle & Associates, 1998.

Briner, Martin. "Learning Theories Web Site." Available at http://curriculum.calstatela.edu/faculty/psparks/theorists/501learn.htm.

Bronowski, Jacob. *The Identity of Man.* rev. ed. Garden City, NY: American Museum Science Books, 1971.

Brooks, Diane L. "Technology as Basic to History-Social Science: It's Long Overdue." *Educational Technology* 34, no. 7 (September 1994): 19–20.

Brophy, J., and T. Good. *Teacher–Student Relationships: Causes and Consequences.* New York: Holt Rinehart and Winston, 1974.

Bruner, Jerome S. *The Process of Education.* Cambridge, MA: Harvard University Press, 1960.

Brush, Thomas A. "Teaching Preservice Teachers to Use Technology in the Classroom." *Journal of Technology and Teacher Education* 6, no. 4 (1998): 243–258.

Bump, Wren, A. Durand, J. Durall, K. Holliday, and L. Wang. "Integrating Computer-Mediated Communication in the K-12 Curriculum." *CSS Journal* 7, no. 3 (1999): online. Available at www.cssjournal.com/journal/bump.html.

Bybee, Roger W., and Susan Loucks-Horsley, "Standards as a Catalyst for Change in Technology Education." *The Technology Teacher* 59, no. 5 (February 2000): 14–16.

Bybee, Roger W. et al. *Science and Technology Education for the Elementary Years: Frameworks for Curriculum and Instruction.* Washington, DC: The National Center for Improving Instruction, 1989.

Cain, Joe. "Have I Wasted My Summer on This Web Site?" *Perspectives* 37 (1999): 25–30.

Campbell, Katy. "Learner Characteristics and Instructional Design." Available at www.atl.ualberta.ca/articles/idesign/learnchar.cfm.

Campbell, Linda, Bruce Campbell, and Dee Dickenson. *Teaching & Learning Through Multiple Intelligences.* Needham, MA: Allyn & Bacon, 1996.

Cantor, Norman F., and Richard I. Schneider. *How to Study History.* Arlington Heights, IL: AHM Publishing Corporation, 1967.

Cantu, D. Antonio. *Take Five Minutes: American History Class Openers.* Westminister, CA: Teacher Created Materials, 2002.

Carr, E., and D.W. Ogle. "K-W-L-Plus: A Strategy for Comprehension and Summarizing." *Journal of Reading* 30 (1987): 626–631.

Carter, D.S.G. "Knowledge Transmitter, Social Scientist or Reflective Thinker: Three Images of the Practitioner in Western Australian High Schools." *Theory and Research in Social Education* 18, no. 3 (1990): 274–309.

CEO Forum on Education and Technology. *Second Annual Report, 1998.* Available from http://www.ceoforum.org/REPORTS/REPORT99/HIGHLIGHTS.html.

Chapman, Carolyn. *If the Shoe Fits . . . How to Develop Multiple Intelligences in the Classroom.* Palatine, IL: IRI/Skylight Publishing, 1993.

Checkley, Kathy. "The First Seven . . . and the Eighth: A Conversation with Howard Gardner." *Educational Leadership* 55, no. 1 (September 1997): 8–13.

Chiodo, John, and Mary Flaim. "The Link Between Computer Simulations and Social Studies Learning: Debriefing." *The Social Studies* (May/June 1993): 119–121.

Clark, C.M. "Asking the Right Questions About Teacher Preparation: Contributions of Research on Teacher Thinking." *Educational Researcher* 17, no. 2 (1988): 5–12.

Clark, C.M., and J.L. Elmore. *Teacher Planning in the First Weeks of School* [Research Series No. 56]. East Lansing: Michigan State University, Institute for Research on Teaching, 1979.

Clark, C.M., and M. Lampert. "The Study of Teacher Thinking: Implications for Teacher Education." *Journal of Teacher Education* 37, no. 5 (1986): 27–31.

Clark, C.M., and R.J. Yinger. "Research on Teacher Thinking." *Curriculum Inquiry* 7, no. 4 (1977): 279–304.

Coley, R., J. Cradler, and P.K. Engel. *Computers in the Classroom: The Status of Technology in U.S. Schools,* Princeton, NJ: Educational Testing Service, 1997 (Policy Information Report, RIE record no. ED 412 893).

Collea, Francis P., ed. *Workshop on Physics Teaching and the Development of Reasoning.* Stony Brook, NY: American Association of Physics, 1975.

Collingwood, R.G. *The Idea of History.* Oxford, UK: Oxford University Press, 1946.

Coughlin, Ed. "Professional Competencies Digital Age Classroom." *Learning and Leading with Technology* 27, no. 3 (November 1999), 22–27.

Cox, C. Benjamin, and Byron G. Massialas, eds. *Social Studies in the United States: A Critical Appraisal.* New York: Harcourt, Brace and World, 1967.

Crabtree, Charlotte, Gary B. Nash, Paul Gragnon, and Scott Waugh, eds. *Lessons from History: Essential Understandings and Historical Perspectives Students Should Acquire.* Los Angeles: National Center for History in the Schools, 1992.

Crowther, David T. "Here We Grow Again: Applications of Research and Model

Inquiry Lessons." *Electronic Journal of Science Education*. Available at http://unr.edu/homepage/crowther/ejse/crowedit4.html.

Davis Jr., O.L., and Elizabeth Yeager. "Classroom Teachers' Thinking about Historical Texts: An Exploratory Study." *Theory and Research in Social Education* 24 (Spring 1996): 146–166.

Decker, Madeleine. "The Webquest Page." Available from www.pekin.net/pekin108/wash/wq/wqpage.html.

Deluca, Nicholas M. "Social Studies Teachers and Computer Technology: An Administrator's Perspective." *Social Education* 47, no. 5 (May 1983): 333–334.

Dewey, John. *Democracy in Education*. New York: Macmillan, 1916.

———. *How We Think*. Boston: D. C. Heath, 1933.

Dick, Walter. "History of Instructional Design." Available from http://academic.udayton.edu/elearning/onlineTraining/InstructionalDesign/History/ (April 1, 2002).

Diem, Richard A. "Technology and the Social Studies: Issues and Responsibilities." *Social Education* 47, no. 5 (May 1983).

DiLorenzo, Robert. "Teaching Advanced Placement United States History in the Urban, Minority High School: Successful Strategies." *History Teacher* 32 (February 1999): 207–221.

Dooling, Judith O'Donnell, and Karen I. Case. "Integrating Technology Into Teacher Preparation Programs." *Teaching Education* 8 (Winter/Spring 1997): 279–300.

Downey, Matthew T., ed. *History in the Schools*. Washington, DC: National Council for the Social Studies, 1985.

Drago, Allison. "Madeline Hunter." Available at www2.bc.edu/~ruedaju/MadelineHunter.html.

Dray, William H. *Philosophy of History*. 2d ed. Englewood Cliffs: Prentice Hall, 1993.

Dunn, Ross E., ed. *The New World History: A Teacher's Companion*. Boston: Bedford/St. Martin's, 2000.

Eaton, Jana Sackman. "The Social Studies Classroom on the Eve of the Cyber Century." *Computers in the Social Studies*. Available at http://www.cssjournal.com/journal/eaton99.html.

Egan, Kieran. "Layers of Historical Understanding." *Theory and Research in Social Education* 17 (Fall 1989): 280–294.

———. "Social Studies and the Erosion of Education." *Curriculum Inquiry* 13 (Summer 1983): 195–214.

Eisner, Elliot W. "The Uses and Limits of Performance Assessment." *Phi Delta Kappan* 80 no. 9 (May 1999): 658–660.

Elbaz, F. *Teacher Thinking: A Study of Practical Knowledge*. New York: Nichols Publishing, 1983.

Elliott, Stephen N. "Creating Meaningful Performance Assessments," In ERIC Digest E531 [database online] Reston, VA: ERIC Clearinghouse on Disabilities and Gifted Education, 1995. ERIC document no. ED381985. Available at www.ed.gov/databases/ERIC_Digests/ed381985.html.

Ellis, Arthur K., and Jeffrey T. Fouts. *Research on Educational Innovations*. 2d ed. New York: Eye on Education, 1997.

Ellis, Arthur K., Jeffrey T. Fouts, and Allen D. Glenn. *Teaching and Learning Secondary Social Studies*. New York: HarperCollins, 1991.

Ellis, S.S., and S.F. Whalen. "Keys to Cooperative Learning." *Instructor* 101, no. 6 (1992): 34–37.

Engle, Shirley H. "Alan Griffith, 1907–1964." *Journal of Thought* 17 (Fall 1982): 45–54.

———. "Decision Making: The Heart of Social Studies Instruction." *Social Education* 24 (November 1960): 301–304, 306.

———. "Exploring the Meaning of the Social Studies." *Social Education* 35 (March 1971): 280–288, 344.

Engle, Shirley H., and Anna S. Ochoa. *Education for Democratic Citizenship: Decision Making in the Social Studies*. New York: Teacher College Press, Columbia University, 1988.

Ennis, Rosemary. "Resources for AP United States History." *History Teacher* 32 (February 1999): 237–243.

Ernest, P. "The Knowledge, Beliefs and Attitudes of the Mathematics Teacher: A Model." *Journal of Education for Teaching* 15, no. 1 (1989): 13–33.

Evans, Ronald W. "Teacher Conception of History Revisited: Ideology, Curriculum, and Student Belief." *Theory and Research in Social Education* 17 (Spring 1990): 101–138.

———. "Teachers' Conceptions of History." *Theory and Research in Social Education* 17, no. 3 (1989): 210–240.

Evans, Ronald W., and David Warren Saxe. *Handbook on Teaching Social Issues*. Washington, DC: National Council for the Social Studies, 1996.

Fain, George. "Teaching History." *Clearing House* 72 (November/December 1998): 68–69.

Falba, Christy J., Neal Strodler, Thomas W. Bean, Juli K. Dixon, Patricia A. Markos, Marilyn McKinney, and Stanley J. Zehm. "Choreographing Change One Step at a Time: Reflections on Integrating Technology into Teacher Education Courses." *Action in Teacher Education* 21, no. 1 (Spring 1999): 61–76.

Fehn, Bruce, and Kim E. Koeppen. "Intensive Document-Based Instruction in a Social Studies Methods Curse and Student Teachers' Attitudes and Practice in Subsequent Field Experiences." *Theory and Research in Social Education* 26 (Fall 1998): 461–484.

Flood, James, Julie M. Jensen, Diane Lapp, and James R. Squire, eds. *Handbook of Research on Teaching the English Language Arts*. New York: Macmillan, 1991.

Forte, Imogene, and Sandra Schurr. *Making Portfolios, Products, and Performances Meaningful and Manageable for Students and Teachers*. Nashville, TN: Incentive Publications, 1995.

Frederick, Peter J. "Four Reflections on Teaching and Learning History." *AHA Perspectives* 39 (October 2001): 28–30.

Gabella, Marcy Singer. "Beyond the Looking Glass: Bringing Students into the Conversation of Historical Inquiry." *Theory and Research in Social Education* 22 (Summer 1994): 340–363.

Gagne, Robert. "Instruction in the Conditioning of Learning." In *Instruction: Some Contemporary Viewpoints*, ed. Laurence Siegel. New York: Harper & Row, 1967.

————. *The Conditions of Learning.* New York: Holt, Rinehart, and Winston, 1965.

————. *Psychological Principles in System Development.* New York: Holt, Rinehart, and Winston, 1962.

Gagnon, Paul, ed. *Historical Literacy: The Case for History in American Education.* Boston: Houghton Mifflin, 1989.

Gardner, Howard. *Frames of Mind: The Theory of Multiple Intelligences.* New York: Basic Books, 1983.

————. *The Disciplined Mind: Beyond Facts and Standardized Tests, The K-12 Education That Every Child Deserves.* New York: Penguin Books, 2000.

————. *Multiple Intelligences: The Theory in Practice.* New York: Basic Books, 1993.

————. "Educating for Understanding." *The American School Board Journal* 180, no. 7 (July 1993): 20–24.

————. "Multiple Intelligences as a Catalyst." *English Journal* 84, no. 8 (December 1995): 16–18.

————. "Reflections on Multiple Intelligences: Myths and Messages." *Phi Delta Kappan* 77, no. 3 (November 1995): 200–203.

————. "Probing More Deeply Into the Theory of Multiple Intelligences." *NASSP Bulletin* 80, no. 583 (November 1996): 1–7.

————. "Multiple Intelligences as a Partner in School Improvement." *Educational Leadership* 55, no. 1 (September 1997): 20–21.

————. "Six Afterthoughts: Comments on 'Varieties of Intellectual Talent.' " *Journal of Creative Behavior* 31, no. 2 (1997): 120–24.

Gardner, Howard, and Thomas Hatch. "Multiple Intelligences Go to School." *Educational Researcher* 18, no. 8 (November 1989): 4–9.

Geography Education Standards Project. *Geography for Life: National Geography Standards.* Washington, DC: National Geographic Research and Exploration, 1994.

Gilderhus, Mark T. *History and Historians: A Historiographical Introduction.* 3d ed. Englewood Cliffs, NJ: Prentice-Hall, 1996.

Goodlad, John. *A Place Called School: Prospects for the Future.* New York: McGraw-Hill, 1984.

Gutloff, Karen, ed. *Multiple Intelligences.* West Haven, CT: NEA Professional Library, 1996.

Haertel, Edward H. "Performance Assessment and Education Reform." *Phi Delta Kappan* 80, no. 9 (May 1999): 662–666.

Hall, Marc Elliot. "Training Key to Understanding Technology's Value." *Educational Leadership* 29, no. 2 (November/December 1999): online. Available at http://www.acsa.org/publications/Leadership.

Halpin, Regina. "A Model of Constructivist Learning in Practice: Computer Literacy Integrated into Elementary Mathematics and Science Teacher Education." *Journal of Research on Computing in Education* 32, no. 1 (Fall 1999): 128–138.

Handlin, Oscar. *Truth in History.* Cambridge: Belknap Press, 1979.

Harris, Robert. "Evaluating Historical Research on the World Wide Web." *NCHE History Matters* 11, no. 2 (1998): 3.

Hatfield, Mary M. "Using Multimedia in Preservice Education." *Journal of Teacher Education* 47, no. 3 (May/June 1996): 223–228.

Henderson, James, Catherine Eggleston Hackney, and Kathleen R. Kesson. "Effective Teaching in Advanced Placement Classrooms." *Journal of Classroom Interaction* 31 (Winter 1996): 29–35.

Henry, Michael. "Advanced Placement U.S. History." *The Social Studies* 82 (May/June 1991): 94–97.

———. "The AP United States History Exam: Have Free Response Essays Changed in the Last Thirty Years?" *Social Education* 58 (March 1994): 145–148.

Hertzberg, H.W. *Social Studies Reform: 1880–1980.* Boulder, CO: Social Science Education Consortium, 1981.

Hibbard, K. Michael. *Glencoe World Geography: Performance Assessment Strategies and Activities.* New York: Glencoe, 1995.

Hill, Janette R. "Teaching Technology: Implementing a Problem-Centered, Activity-Based Approach." *Journal of Research on Computing in Education* 31, no. 3 (Spring 1999): 261–279.

Hoerr, Thomas R. "Introducing the Theory of Multiple Intelligences." *NASSP Bulletin* 80, no. 583 (November 1996): 8–10.

———. "Focusing on the Personal Intelligences as a Basis for Success." *NASSP Bulletin* 80, no. 583 (November 1996): 36–42.

———. *Implementing Multiple Intelligences: The New City School Experience.* Bloomington, IN: Phi Delta Kappa Educational Foundation, 1996.

Hopkins, Richard L. "Educating the Right Brain: Why We Need to Teach Patterning." *The Clearinghouse* 58, no. 3 (November 1984): 132–134.

Hughes, Andrew S. "Toward a More Thoughtful Professional Education for Social Studies Teachers: Can Problem-Based Learning Contribute?" *Theory and Research in Social Education* 25 (Fall 1997): 431–445.

Hunt, Maurice P., and Lawrence E. Metcalf. *Teaching High School Social Studies: Problems in Reflective Thinking and Social Understanding.* 2d ed. New York: Harper and Row, 1968.

Hunter, B., and E. K. Lodish. *Online Searching in the Curriculum.* Santa Barbara, CA: ABC/Clio, 1989.

Hunter, Beverly. "Social Studies Education in the Information Society." *Social Education* 47, no. 5 (May 1983): 321–324.

Hunter, Madeline. *Mastery Teaching.* Thousand Oaks, CA: Corwin Press, 1982.

Hyser, Raymond M. "Is a 3 a C?: The Reliability of the Advanced Placement United States History Test for College Credit." *History Teacher* 32 (February 1999): 223–235.

International Society for Technology Education, "Standards Projects." Available from www.iste.org/standards/index.html.

Interstate New Teacher Assessment and Support Consortium. *Model Standards for Beginning Teacher Licensing and Development: A Resource for State Dialogue.* Washington, DC: INTASC, 2000.

Jackson, P.W. *Life in Classrooms.* New York: Holt, Rinehart & Winston, 1968.

Jacobs, Heidi Hayes. *Social Studies Handbook on Alternative Assessment*. Upper Saddle River, NJ: Prentice Hall, 1997.

James, Waynne B., and Michael W. Galbraith, "Perceptual Learning Styles: Implications and Techniques for the Practitioner," *Lifelong Learning* 8, no. 4 (January 1985): 20–23.

Johnson, Denise. "We're Helping to Be Good Teachers: Using Electronic Dialoguing to Connect Theory and Practice in Preservice Teacher Education." *Journal of Computing in Childhood Education* 7, no. 2 (1996): 3–11.

Johnson, David W., and Roger T. Johnson. "Research Shows the Benefits of Adult Cooperation." *Educational Leadership* 45 (1987): 27–30.

Johnson, David, and Roger Johnson. *Learning Together and Alone*. Englewood Cliffs, NJ: Prentice-Hall, 1975.

Johnson, Roger, David Johnson, and B. Bryant. "Cooperation in the Classroom: Perceptions and Preferences as Related to Students' Feelings of Personal Control." *Elementary School Journal* 73 (1973): 306–313.

Johnson, David, Roger Johnson, and E. Holubec. *Advanced Cooperative Learning*. Edina, MN: Interaction Book, 1988.

Johnson, Roger, David Johnson, and M. Stanne. "Effects of Cooperative, Competitive, and Individualistic Goal Structures on Computer-Assisted Instruction." *Journal of Educational Psychology* 77 (1985): 668–677.

Johnson, David, Roger Johnson, E. Holubec, and P. Roy. *Circles of Learning*. Alexandria, VA: Association for Supervision and Curriculum Development, 1984.

Jordan, Shirley E. "Multiple Intelligences: Seven Keys to Opening Closed Minds." *NASSP Bulletin* 80, no. 583 (November 1996): 29–35.

Joyce, Bruce, Marsha Weil, and Beverly Showers. *Models of Teaching*. 4th ed. Boston: Allyn and Bacon, 1992.

Joyce, William W. "Performance Assessment: The Wave of the Future?" *Michigan Social Studies Journal* 11, no. 1 (Spring 1999): 27–33.

Kagan, D.M. "Ways of Evaluating Teacher Cognition: Inferences Concerning the Goldilocks Principle." *Review of Educational Research* 60, no. 3 (1990): 419–469.

Kagan, Spencer. *Cooperative Learning SmartCard*. San Clemente, CA: Kagan Cooperative Learning, 1998.

Karplus, Robert, and Herbert D. Thier. *A New Look at Elementary School Science*. Chicago: Rand McNally, 1969.

Karras, Ray W. "Writing Essays that Make Historical Arguments." *OAH Magazine of History* 8 (Summer 1994): 54–57.

Keele, Steven W. *Attention and Human Performance*. Pacific Palisades, CA: Goodyear, 1973.

Keels, Oliver M., Jr. "The Collegiate Influence on the Early Social Social Studies Curriculum: A Reassessment of the Role of Historians." *Theory and Research in Social Education* 8 (Fall 1980): 105–128.

Keiper, Timothy. "Connecting Authenticity, Technology, and Geography." *Social Studies and the Young Learner* 12 (January-February 1999): 22–28.

Kidd, J.R. *How Adults Learn*. rev. ed. New York: Association Press, 1973.

Killoran, James. "In Defense of the Multiple-Choice Question," *Social Education* 56 (February 1992): 107–108.

Kneeshaw, Stephen. "Bringing the Internet and World Wide Web into the History Classroom." In *History.edu: Essays on Teaching with Technology,* ed., Dennis A. Trinkle and Scott A. Merriman. Armonk, NY: M.E. Sharpe, 2001.

Knodt, Jean Sausele. "A Think Tank Cultivates Kids." *Educational Leadership* 55, no. 1 (September 1997): 35–37.

Kobrin, David. *Beyond the Textbook: Teaching History Using Documents and Primary Sources.* Portsmouth, NH: Heinemann, 1996.

Kornbluh, Mark Lawrence. "H-Net Humanities and Social Sciences OnLine." *AHA Perspectives* 37, no. 2 (February 1999): 6–49 passim.

Krathwohl, David R., Benjamin S. Bloom, and Bertram B. Masia, eds. *Taxonomy of Educational Objectives: The Classification of Educational Goals. Handbook II: Affective Domain.* New York: David McKay, 1964.

Krug, Mark M. "Bruner's New Social Studies: A Critique." *Social Education* 30 (October 1966): 400–406.

———. *History and the Social Sciences: New Approaches to the Teaching of Social Studies.* Waltham, MA: Blaisdell Publishing, 1967.

———. "History and the Social Sciences: The Narrowing Gap." *Social Education* 29 (December 1965): 515–520.

Kumar, David D. "Science Teacher Education in an Era of Standards Based Reform: Policy Perspectives." *Contemporary Education* 70, no. 2 (Winter 1999): 222–234.

Kuriloff, Peshe. "If John Dewey Were Alive Today, He'd Be a Webhead." *Chronicle of Higher Education* (April 28, 2000): A72.

Lambert, Wendy Ecklund. "From Crockett to Tubman: Investigating Historical Perspectives." *Educational Leadership* 55, no. 1 (September 1997): 51–54.

Latham, Andrew S. "Quantifying MI's Gains." *Educational Leadership* 55, no. 1 (September 1997): 84–85.

Lazear, David. *Seven Ways of Teaching: The Artistry of Teaching with Multiple Intelligences.* Palantine, IL: IRI/Skylight Publishing, 1991.

———. *Teaching for Multiple Intelligences.* Bloomington, IN: Phi Delta Kappa Educational Foundation, 1992.

Lenski, Susan, Mary Ann Davis, and Jerry L. Johns. *Reading and Learning Strategies for Middle & High School Students.* Dubuque, IA: Kendall Hunt, 1999.

Levitt, Gregory A. "Global Issues." In *Surfing Social Studies: The Internet Book,* ed. Joseph A. Braun, Jr. and C. Frederick Risinger. Washington, DC: National Council for the Social Studies, 1999.

Lillich, Harriet. "Teaching Skills and Habits of Mind in World History." *History Teacher* 32 (February 1999): 293–296.

Lockwood, Alan L., and David E. Harris. *Reasoning with Democratic Values: Ethical Problems in United States History,* vol. 1. New York: Teachers College Press, 1985.

Loewen, James W. *Lies My Teacher Told Me: Everything Your American History Textbook Got Wrong.* New York: New Press, 1995.

Longstreet, Wilma S. "Social Science and the Social Studies: Origins of the Debate." *Social Education* 49 (May 1985): 356–359.

Lorsbach, Anthony, and Fred Basolo Jr., "Problem-Based Learning." In *Surfing Social Studies: The Internet Book,* ed. Joseph A. Braun Jr. and C. Frederick Risinger. Washington, DC: National Council for the Social Studies, 1999.

Lortie, D.C. *School Teacher: A Sociological Study.* Chicago: University of Chicago Press, 1975.

Lybarger, Michael. "The Political Context of the Social Studies: Creating a Constituency for Municipal Reform." *Theory and Research in Social Education* 8 (Fall 1980): 1–28.

Madaus, George F., and Laura M. O'Dwyer. "A Short History of Performance Assessment: Lessons Learned." *Phi Delta Kappan* 80 (May 1999): 688–695.

Manoucherhri, Azita. "Computers and School Mathematics Reform: Implications for Mathematics Teacher Education." *Journal of Computers in Mathematics and Science Teaching* 18, no. 1 (1999): 31–48.

March, Tom. "What's on the Web?" *Computer-Using Educators' Newsletter* (July/August 1995).

Marker, Gerald, and Howard Mehlinger. "Social Studies." In *Handbook of Research on Curriculum,* ed. Philip W. Jackson. New York: Macmillan, 1992.

Marland, P. W. *A Study of Teachers' Interactive Thoughts.* Unpublished Ph.D. diss., University of Alberta, 1977.

Martorella, Peter H. *Teaching Social Studies in Middle and Secondary Schools.* 2d ed. Englewood Cliffs, NJ: Prentice-Hall, 1996.

———. *Social Strategies: Theory into Practice.* New York: Harper and Row, 1976.

Marty, Myron A. "Wrestling with Testing in American History." *Social Education* 40 (November–December 1976): 524–527.

Masters, Ken. "MCQs and Bloom's Taxonomy." Available at http://www.uct.ac.za/projects/cbe/mcqman/mcqappc.html.

McCarthy, Bernice, and Susan Morris. *The 4MAT CourseBook,* vol. 1. Barrington, IL: Excel, 1994.

McClay, Wilfred M. "History for a Democracy." *The Wilson Quarterly* 25 (Autumn 2001): 99–106.

McCollum, Steven L. *Performance Assessment in the Social Studies Classroom: A How-To Book for Teachers.* Joplin, MO: Chalk Dust Press, 1994.

McCoy, Jan. "Databases in the Social Studies: Not Why But How." *Social Studies and the Young Learner* (Fall 1990): 13–15.

McKenzie, Jamie. *Beyond Technology: Questioning, Research, and the Information Literate School.* Bellingham, WA: FNO Press, 2000.

———. "Grazing the Net: Raising a Generation of Free-Range Students." *Phi Delta Kappan* (September 1998): 26–31.

———. "Module Makers." Available from http://questioning.org/module/module.html.

McMichael, Andrew. "The Historian, the Internet, and the Web: A Reassessment." *AHA Perspectives* 36 (February 1998): 29–32.

McNair, K. "Capturing Inflight Decisions." *Educational Research Quarterly* 3, no. 4 (1978–1979): 26–42.

Mehaffy, George L. "Social Studies in World War One: A Period of Transition." *Theory and Research in Social Education* 15 (Winter 1987): 23–32.

Mehlinger, Howard. "Amy Wallace: Information Age Teacher." *Social Education* (April 2000): 146–148.

Melton, Louisa, and Winston Pickett. *Using Multiple Intelligences in Middle*

School Reading. Bloomington, IN: Phi Delta Kappa Educational Foundation, 1997.

Meyer, Maggie. "The GREENing of Learning: Using the Eighth Intelligence." *Educational Leadership* 55, no. 1 (September 1997): 32–34.

Meyers, D. Mark. "Teacher Education." In *Surfing the Social Studies: The Internet Book*, ed. Joseph A. Braun Jr. and C. Frederick Risinger. Washington, DC: National Council for the Social Studies, 1999.

Miller, J.A. "Paying Attention at Many Levels." *Science News* (November 9, 1985).

Mjagkij, Nina, and D. Antonio Cantu. "'The Public Be Damned!' A Thematic and Multiple Intelligences Approach to Teaching the Gilded Age." *OAH Magazine of History* 13, no. 4 (Summer 1999): 56–60.

Moersch, Christopher. "Assessing Current Technology Use in the Classroom: A Key to Efficient Staff Development and Technology Planning." *Learning and Leading with Technology* 26, no. 8 (May 1999).

Morrissey, Thomas E. "Teaching Advanced Placement American History." *Social Studies Journal* 18 (Spring 1989): 12–15.

Murphy, Alexander B. "Advanced Placement Geography: Opportunities and Challenges for Geographers." *Journal of Geography* 97 (May–June 1998): 132–136.

Munby, H. "The Place of Teachers' Beliefs in Research on Teacher Thinking and Decision Making, and an Alternative Methodology." *Instructional Science* 11 (1982): 201–225.

Nasaw, David. *Schooled to Order: A Social History of Public Schooling in the United States*. New York: Oxford University Press, 1979.

Nash, Gary B. "The History Wars of the 1990s." Paper delivered at the Lawrence F. Brewster Lecture in History at East Carolina University, November 1996. Available at http://personal.ecu.edu/wilburnk/b196.htm.

Nash, Gary B., Charlotte Crabtree, and Ross E. Dunn. *History on Trial: Culture Wars and the Teaching of the Past*. New York: Alfred A. Knopf, 1998.

Nash, Gary B., Ross E. Dunn, and Charlotte Crabtree. *History on Trial*. New York: Knopf, 1997.

National Center for History in the Schools. *National Standards for History: Basic Edition*. Los Angeles: National Center for History in the Schools, 1996.

National Council for History Education. "Reinvigorating History in U.S. Schools: Reform Recommendations for the States." Available at http://63.70.163.70/nche/recommend.html.

National Council for the Social Studies. *Expectations of Excellence: Curriculum Standards for Social Studies*. Washington, DC: National Council for the Social Studies, 1994.

———. *National Standards for Social Studies Teachers*. Available from www.ncss.org/standards/teachers/home.html.

Negroponte, Nicholas. *Being Digital*. New York: Alfred Knopf, 1995.

Nelson, Garet. "Internet/Web-Based Instruction and Multiple Intelligences." *Educational Media International* 35, no. 2 (June 1998): 90–94.

Nelson, Murry R. "First Efforts Toward a National Curriculum: The Committee of Ten's Report on History, Civil Government, and Political Economy." *Theory and Research in Social Education* 20 (Spring 1992): 242–262.

————. "The Rugg Brothers in Social Education." *Journal of Thought* 17 (Fall 1982): 68–82.

————. "Social Studies: Something Old, Something New, and All Borrowed." *Theory and Research in Social Education* 8 (Fall 1980): 51–64.

————. "Some Possible Effects of World War II on the Social Studies Curriculum." *Theory and Research in Social Education* 14 (Fall 1986): 267–275.

————. "The Voice of Harold Rugg." *Social Education* 50 (November/December 1986): 488–490.

Nespor, J. *The Teacher Beliefs Study: An Interim Report.* Austin, TX: Research and Development Center for Teacher Education, 1984.

————. "The Role of Beliefs in the Practice of Teaching." *Journal of Curriculum Studies* 19, no. 4 (1987): 317–328.

Neutuch, Eric. "Advanced Placement United States History: A Student's Perspective." *History Teacher* 32 (February 1999): 245–248.

Newman, John J., and John M. Schmalbach. *United States History: Preparing for the Advanced Placement Examination.* New York: Amsco, 1998.

Newmann, Fred. *Authentic Achievement: Restructing Schools for Intellectual Quality.* San Francisco: Jossey-Bass, 1996.

Nicaise, Molly, and David Barnes. "The Union of Technology, Constructivism, and Teacher Education." *Journal of Teacher Education* 47, no. 3 (May/June 1996): 205–212.

Nicholas, S.N., and M.J. Fleener. "Nine Preservice Teachers' Beliefs about Teaching and Teaming Mathematics: A Case Study–Part 1." *National Forum of Applied Educational Research Journal* 7, no. 2 (1994–1995): 3–12.

Niederhauser, Dale S., Donna J. Salem, and Matt Fields. "Exploring Teacher Learning and Instructional Reform in an Introductory Technology Course." *Journal of Technology and Teacher Education* 7, no. 2 (1999): 153–172.

Noonan, Kathleen M. "Untangling the Web: The Use of the World Wide Web as a Pedagogical Tool in History Courses." *The History Teacher* 31, no. 2 (February 1998): 205–219.

Northrup, Pamela Taylor, and Wesley Little. "Establishing Instructional Technology Benchmarks for Teacher Preparation Programs." *Journal of Teacher Education* 47, no. 3 (May/June 1996): 213–222.

Novak, Joseph D., and D. Bob Gowin. *Learning How To Learn.* Cambridge, UK: Cambridge University Press, 1984.

Ogle, D.W. "K-W-L: A Teaching Model that Develops Active Reading of Expository Text." *The Reading Teacher* 39 (1986): 564–570.

Oliver, Donald W., and James P. Shaver. *Cases and Controversy: A Guide to Teaching the Public Issues Series.* Middletown, CT: American Education Publishers, 1971.

————. *Teaching Public Issues in the High School.* Boston: Houghton Mifflin, 1966.

O'Niel, John. "Fads and Fireflies: The Difficulties of Sustaining Change." *Educational Leadership* (April 2000): 6–9.

Ozman, H., and S.M. Craver. *Philosophical Foundations of Education.* 2d ed. Columbus, OH: Charles E. Merrill, 1981.

Pajares, M.F. "Teachers' Beliefs and Educational Research: Cleaning Up a Messy Construct." *Review of Educational Research* 62, no. 3 (1992): 307–332.

Parker, Walter C. "Teachers' Mediation in Social Studies." *Theory and Research in Social Education* 15, no. 1 (1987): 1–22.

Parr, Judy M. "Extending Educational Computing: A Case of Extensive Teacher Development and Support." *Journal of Research on Computing in Education* 31, no. 3 (Spring 1999): 280–291.

Paul, James R., and Colette Kaiser. "Do Women Live Longer than Men? Investigating Graveyard Data with Computers." *Learning and Leading with Technology* 23, no. 8 (May 1996): 13–15.

Paulsen, Morten Flate. "The Online Report on Pedagogical Techniques for Computer-Mediated Communication." Available at http://www.hs.nki.no/~morten/cmcped.htm.

Payne, Ruby K. *A Framework of Understanding Poverty.* Baytown, TX: RFT Publishing, 1998.

Percoco, James A. *A Passion for the Past: Creative Teaching of U.S. History.* Portsmouth, NH: Heinemann, 1998.

Peterson, P.L., and C.M. Clark. "Teachers' Reports of Their Cognitive Processes During Teaching." *American Educational Research Journal* 15 (1978): 555–565.

Peterson, P.L., R.W. Marx, and C.M. Clark. "Teacher Planning, Teacher Behavior, and Student Achievement." *American Educational Research Journal* 15 (1978): 417–432.

Pintrich, P.R. "Implications of Psychological Research on Student Learning and College Teaching for Teacher Education." In *Handbook of Research on Teacher Education,* ed. W.R. Houston. New York: Macmillan, 1990.

Poetker, Joel S. "Preparing for Essays Tests." *The Social Studies* 67 (May/June 1976): 113–115.

Porter, Lee Ann. "National Archives Expands Digital Classroom." *AHA Perspectives* 37 (February 1999): 3–4.

Rakow, Steven J. "Involving Classroom Teachers in the Assessment of Preservice Intern Portfolios." *Action in Teacher Education* 21, no. 1 (Spring 1999).

Read, Donna, and Ralph Cafolla. "Multimedia Portfolios for Preservice Teachers: From Theory to Practice." *Journal of Technology and Teacher Education* 7, no. 2 (1999).

Rice, Margaret L. et al. "Social Studies Teachers and Technology: Activities for the Constructivist Classroom." Available at www.cssjournal.com/journal/rice.html.

Rich, J.M. *Innovations in Education.* 6th ed. Needham Heights, MA: Allyn and Bacon, 1992.

Risinger, C. Frederick. "Teaching History." In *Surfing Social Studies: The Internet Book,* ed. Joseph A. Braun Jr., and C. Frederick Risinger. Washington, DC: National Council for the Social Studies, 1999.

Risinger, C. Frederick. "Separating the Wheat from the Chaff: Why Dirty Pictures Are Not the Real Dilemma in Using the Internet in Social Studies." *Social Education* 62 (March 1998): 148–150.

Robin, Bernard R., Kip T. Tellez, and Robert W. Mudge Miller. "A Comparison of Text-Based and Graphical Internet Tools in Preservice Teacher Training." *Journal of Technology and Teacher Education* 6, no. 4 (1998): 259–272.

Robinson, Paul. "The Conventional Historians of the Social Studies." *Theory and Research in Social Education* 8 (Fall 1980): 65–88.

Rokeach, M. *Beliefs, Attitudes, and Values: A Theory of Organization and Chance*. San Francisco: Jossey–Bass, 1968.

Romanowski, M.H. "Teacher's Lives and Beliefs: Influences That Shape the Teaching of U.S. History." *Mid-Western Educational Researcher* 11, no. 2 (1998): 2–8.

Ropp, Margaret Merlyn. "Exploring Individual Characteristics Associated with Learning to Use Computers in Preservice Teacher Preparation." *Journal of Research on Computing in Education* 31, no. 4 (Summer 1999): 402–424.

Ross, E. Wayne. "Teacher Perspective Development: A Study of Preservice Social Studies Teachers." *Theory and Research in Social Education* 15, no. 4 (1987): 225–243.

Rothschild, Eric. "Four Decades of the Advanced Placement Program." *History Teacher* 32 (February 1999): 175–206.

———. *Teacher's Guide to the Advanced Placement Course in United States History*. Princeton, NJ: Educational Testing Service, 1996.

SAGUARO Project. "Curriculum Design: The 5-E Learning Cycle." Available at http://saguaro.geo.arizona.edu/5–Epdf.pdf.

Sanders, D.P., and G. McCutcheon. "The Development of Practical Theories of Teaching." *Journal of Curriculum and Supervision* 2, no. 1 (1986): 50–67.

Saxe, David Warren. "An Introduction to the Seminal Social Welfare and Efficiency Prototype: The Founders of 1916 Social Studies." *Theory and Research in Social Education* 20 (Spring 1992): 156–178.

———. *Social Studies in Schools: A History of the Early Years*. Albany: State University of New York Press, 1991.

Scheurman, Geoffrey, and Fred M. Newmann. "Authentic Intellectual Work in Social Studies: Putting Performance before Pedagogy." *Social Education* 62 (January 1998): 23–25.

Schneider, Donald O. "History, Social Sciences, and the Social Studies." *Social Education* 53 (March 1989): 148–154.

Schultz, James L. "Cooperative Learning: Refining the Process." *Educational Leadership* 47 (1989–90): 43–45.

Scott, B.J., and Michael R. Vitale. "Informal Assessment of Idea Development in Written Expression: A Tool for Classroom Use." *Preventing School Failure* 44 (Winter 2000): 67–72.

Searles, John E. "Information Technology and the Social Studies." *Social Education* 47, no. 5 (May 1983): 335–337.

Senge, Peter M. *The Fifth Discipline: The Art & Practice of The Learning Organization*. New York: Currency Doubleday, 1990.

Senn, Peter R. "Six Checklists to Prepare Your Classroom for Technology." *Social Education* 47, no. 5 (May 1983).

Sepon-Sheve, M., and N. Schniedwind. "Selling Cooperative Learning Without Selling it Short." *Educational Leadership* 47 (1989–1990): 63–65.

Sharan, Yael, and Shlomo Sharan. "Training Teachers for Cooperative Learning." *Educational Leadership* 45 (1987): 20–25.

Shaver, James P., ed. *Handbook of Research on Social Studies Teaching and Learning*. New York: Macmillan, 1991.

Shaver, James P. "James Michener and the Historical Future of Social Studies." *Social Education* 59 (November/December 1995): 446–450.

Shaver, James P., and H. Berlak. "Curriculum Decisions in the Social Studies." In *Democracy, Pluralism, and the Social Studies,* ed. J.P. Shaver and H. Berlak. Boston: Houghton Mifflin, 1968.

Shavelson, R.J., and P. Stern. "Research on Teachers' Pedagogical Thoughts, Judgments, Decisions, and Behavior." *Review of Educational Research* 51 no. 4 (1981): 455–498.

Shermis, S. Samuel. "Six Myths Which Delude History Teachers." *Phi Delta Kappan* 49 (September 1967): 9–12.

Shermis, S. Samuel, and James L. Barth. "Indoctrination and the Study of Social Problems: A Re-Examination of the 1930s Debate in *The Social Frontier.*" *Social Education* 49 (March 1985): 190–193.

Shor, Ira, and Caroline Pari, eds. *Education Is Politics: Critical Teaching Across Differences, K-12.* New York: Heinemann, 1999.

Sikula, John, Thomas J. Buttery, and Edith Guyton, eds. *Handbook of Research on Teacher Education.* New York: Macmillan, 1996.

Singleton, H. Wells. "Problems of Democracy: The Revisionist Plan for Social Studies Education." *Theory and Research in Social Education* 8 (Fall 1980): 89–104.

Singleton, Laurel R., and James R. Giese. "American Memory: Using Library of Congress On-Line Resources to Enhance History Teaching." *Social Education* 62 (March 1998): 142–144.

Slaven, R. "Cooperative Learning and the Cooperative School," *Educational Leadership* 45 (1987): 7–13.

Smagorinsky, Peter. "Multiple Intelligences in the English Class: An Overview." *English Journal* 84, no. 8 (December 1995): 19–26.

Smith, Sean J., Kerri F. Martin, and John Wills Lloyd. "Preparing Preservice Teachers on the Web." *Teaching Exceptional Children* 30, no. 5 (May/June 1998): 60–64.

Smithey, Margaret W., and Bradley W. Hough. "Creating Technology Advocates: Connecting Preservice Teachers with Technology." *T.H.E. Journal* 26, no. 8 (March 1999): 78–79.

Soares, Louise M. "Structure, Content, and Process in Teacher Training: The Relevance of Copernicus, Gardner, and Dewey." *The Clearing House* 71, no. 4 (March/April 1998): 217–220.

Stahl, Steven A., Cynthia R. Hynd, Bruce K. Britton, Mary M. McNish, and Dennis Bosquet. "What Happens When Students Read Multiple Source Documents in History?" *Reading Research Quarterly* 31 (November/December 1996): 430–456.

Stallworth, Corsandra, and Joseph A. Braun Jr. "GIS Programs: Geography Tools for Teachers and Students." *Social Education* 64 (April 2000): 161–164.

Stenhouse, Lawrence. *An Introduction to Curriculum Research and Development.* London: Heineman, 1975.

Stephens, Lester D. *Probing the Past: A Guide to the Study and Teaching of History.* Boston: Allyn and Bacon, 1974.

Stetson, Ranae, and Troy Bagwell. "Technology and Teacher Preparation: An

Oxymoron?" *Journal of Technology and Teacher Education* 7, no. 2 (1999): 145–152.

Stewart, Doug. "Teachers Aim at Turning Loose the Mind's Eyes." *Smithsonian* 16, no. 5 (August 1985): 38–40.

Stodolsky, S.S., and P.L. Grossman. "The Impact of Subject Matter on Curricular Activity: An Analysis of Five Academic Subjects." *American Educational Research Journal* 32, no. 2 (1995): 227–249.

Stovel, John E. "Document-Based Questions (DBQ) and Testing for Critical Thinking." *Social Science Record* 24 (Spring 1987): 11–12.

Sweeney, Jacqueline. *Incredible Quotations.* New York: Scholastic, 1997.

Takacs, James, W. Michael Reed, John G. Wells, and Lynn A. Dombrowski. "The Effect of Online Multimedia Project Development, Learning Style, and Prior Computer Experiences on Teachers' Attitudes Toward the Internet and Hypermedia." *Journal of Research on Computing in Education* 31, no. 4 (Summer 1999): 341–355.

Teague, Marianne, and Gerald Teague. "Planning with Computers: A Social Studies Simulation." *Learning and Leading with Technologies* 23, no. 1 (September 1995): 20–22.

Teele, Sue. "Redesigning the Educational System to Enable All Students to Succeed." *NASSP Bulletin* 80, no. 583 (November 1996): 65–75.

Tell, Carol. "The I-Generation—From Toddlers to Teenagers: A Conversation with Jane M. Healy," *Educational Leadership* 58, no. 2 (2000): 8–9.

Thielens, Jr., Wagner. "The Disciplines and Undergraduate Lecturing," Paper presented at the Annual Meeting of the American Educational Research Association. Washington, DC, April 20–24, 1987.

Thomas, Laurie, Renee T. Clift, and Taku Sugimoto. "Telecommunication, Student Teaching, and Methods Instruction: An Exploratory Investigation." *Journal of Teacher Education* 47, no. 3 (May/June 1996): 165–174.

Thompson, A. "Teachers' Beliefs and Conceptions: A Synthesis of Research." In *Handbook of Research on Mathematics Teaching and Learning,* ed. D.A. Grouws. New York: Macmillan, 1992.

Thornton, Stephen J. "Social Studies Misunderstood: A Reply to Kieran Egan." *Theory and Research in Social Education* 12 (Spring 1984): 43–47.

Thornton, S.J. "Teacher as Curricular-Instructional Gatekeeper in Social Studies." In *Handbook of Research on Social Studies Teaching and Learning,* ed. J.P. Shaver. New York: Macmillan, 1991.

Toffler, Alvin. *Future Shock.* New York: Bantam Books, 1971.

Trinkle, Dennis A. et al. *The History Highway: A Guide to Internet Resources.* Armonk, NY: M.E. Sharpe, 1997.

Tyler, Ralph W. *Basic Principles of Curriculum and Instruction.* Chicago: University of Chicago Press, 1950.

United States Department of Education. *The Condition of Education 1998.* Washington, DC: National Center for Education Statistics, 1999.

VanFossen, Phillip J., and James M. Shiveley. "Using the Internet to Create Primary Source Teaching Packets." *The Social Studies* 91 (November/December 2000): 244–252.

VanSledright, Bruce A. "Arbitrating Competing Claims in the Classroom Culture Wars." *OAH Newsletter* 27 (February 1999): 7–8.

Vasquez, B.T., R.E. Slavin, M.D'Arcangelo, and L.J. Kiernan. *ASCD Cooperative Learning Series*. Alexandria, VA: Association for Supervision and Curriculum Development, 1990.

Walker, Decker F., and Jonas F. Soltis. *Curriculum Aims*. 3d ed. New York: Teachers College Press, 1997.

Walker, Michelle D. "Multiple Intelligences and the World Wide Web: A New Approach to Teaching About the War." *OAH Magazine of History* 12, no. 3 (Spring 1998): 44–47.

Warner, Mark, and Maureen Akins. "Training Today's Teachers for Tomorrow's Classrooms." *T.H.E. Journal* 27, no. 3 (October 1999): online. Available at http://www.thejournal.com/magazine/vault/A2293.cfm.

"Web66 International School Web Site Registry." Available from http://web66.coled.umn.edu/schools.html.

Weber, Ellen. "Creative Communities in High School: An Interactive Learning and Teaching Approach." *NASSP Bulletin* 80, no. 583 (November 1996): 76–86.

Wesley, Edgar Bruce. "Let's Abolish History Courses." *Phi Delta Kappan* 49 (September 1967): 3–8.

Whelan, Michael. "Albert Bushnell Hart and the Origins of Social Studies Education." *Theory and Research in Social Education* 22 (Fali 1994): 423–440.

———. "History and the Social Studies: A Response to the Critics." *Theory and Research in Social Education* 20 (Winter 1992): 2–16.

White, Cameron. "It's Not Another New Thing: Technology as a Transformative Innovation for Social Studies Teacher Education." *Journal of Technology and Teacher Education* 7, no. 3 (1999): 3–12.

White, Cameron, and Trenia Walker. "Technorealism: Addressing the Issues of Technology in Social Studies." *Computers in the Social Studies*. Available from www.cssjournal.com/journal/cwhite99.html.

Wild, Martyn. "Technology Refusal: Rationalizing the Failure of Student and Beginning Teachers to Use Computers." *British Journal of Educational Technology* 27 (May 1996): 134–143.

Williams, David B. "Art-Based Resources." In *Surfing Social Studies: The Internet Book*, ed. Joseph A. Braun Jr. and C. Frederick Risinger. Washington, DC: National Council for the Social Studies, 1999.

Williams, Gary. "Computer Mediated Communication." Available at www.csu.edu.au/division/oli/celt/edtech/CMC/cmc.htm#online.

Wineburg, S.S., and S.M. Wilson. "Models of Wisdom in the Teaching of History." *Phi Delta Kappan* 70, no. 1 (1988): 50–58.

Wittrock, Merlin, ed. *Handbook of Research on Teaching*. 3d ed. New York: Macmillan, 1986.

Wolfe, Patricia. "What the 'Seven-Step Lesson Plan' Isn't." *Educational Leadership* 44, no. 5 (February 1987): 70–71.

Wong, Harry, and Rosemary Wong. *The First Day of School*. Mountain View, CA: Harry K. Wong Publications, 1998.

Wright, Thomas. "Are You Caught in a Time Warp?" *Tech Directions* 57 (February 1998): 34–38.

Wronski, Stanley P. "Edgar Bruce Wesley (1891–1980): His Contributions to the

Past, Present and Future of the Social Studies." *Journal of Thought* 17 (Fall 1982): 55–67.

Young, Kathleen McCarthy, and Gaea Leinhardt. "Writing from Primary Documents." *Written Communication* 15 (January 1998): 44–69.

Zahorik, J.A. "The Effects of Planning on Teaching." *Elementary School Journal* 71 (1970): 143–151.

———. "Teachers' Planning Models." *Educational Leadership* 33 (1975): 134–139.

Zemelman, Steven, Harvey Daniels, and Arthur Hyde, ed. *Best Practice: New Standards For Teaching and Learning in America's Schools.* 2d ed. Portsmouth, NH: Heinemann, 1998.

Zinn, Howard. *A People's History of the United States.* New York: The New Press, 1997.

Zola, John, and Andri Ionnidou. "Learning and Teaching with Interactive Simulations." *Social Education* (April 2000): 142–145.

Zukas, Alex. "Cyberworld: Teaching World History on the World Wide Web." *The History Teacher* 32 (1999): 495–516.

About the Authors and Contributors

D. Antonio Cantu is an associate professor of history at Ball State University. He received his M.A. in history from Arkansas State University and Ph.D. in curriculum and instruction from Southern Illinois University at Carbondale, and has nine years experience as a high school American history teacher and department chair, as well as four years experience teaching U.S. history and social studies methods at the university level. He is the author of *Presidential Elections: 1789–1996*, *The Vietnam War: A National Dilemma*, *Early Education in the Arkansas Delta*, *An Investigation of the Relationship Between Social Studies Teachers' Beliefs and Practices*, and *Take Five Minutes: Reflective and Critical Thinking American History Class Openers*. He also is the editor of the *International Journal of Social Education*.

Wilson J. Warren is an associate professor of history at Western Michigan University. He received his M.A. in history from the University of Iowa and Ph.D. in history from the University of Pittsburgh. He taught middle and high school history and English in the United States and Japan for three years as well as social studies methods and history at the undergraduate and graduate levels for the past nine years. He is author of *Struggling with "Iowa's Pride": Labor Relations, Unionism, and Politics in the Rural Midwest since 1877* (University of Iowa Press, 2000) and several articles in labor history and social studies instruction and pedagogy.

John R. Barber earned an M.A.T. and a Ph.D. in modern European history at Vanderbilt University. He has taught for thirty-nine years and earned six teaching excellence awards, including the American Historical Association's Eugene Asher Distinguished Teaching Award. His publications include *Modern European History* and numerous articles and papers pertaining to his research fields and history teaching methods. His work on methods has focused especially on visual techniques and teaching for improved thinking.

Joseph A. Braun, Jr. is professor of elementary social studies education in the Department of Curriculum and Instruction at Illinois State University. He is the coeditor of the National Council for the Social Studies' Annual Bulletin, *Surfing the Social Studies: The Internet Book*. He also is the author of numerous other books and articles on technology and social studies education.

Sandy Cantu is a high school teacher at Muncie Central High School in Muncie, Indiana. She has taught United States history and psychology for three years and has an additional ten years teaching experience at the elementary, middle school, and high school level. Sandy has been a facilitator and presenter at numerous education conferences focusing on cooperative learning and teaching strategies. She is also the coauthor of *The Vietnam War: A National Dilemma*.

Alex Zukas is associate professor of history at National University in San Diego, California, where he also serves as director of the Institute for Community and Oral History of the Center for Cultural and Ethnic Studies. He has published articles in *Contemporary European History, The History Teacher, Radical History Review,* and *Perspectives*.

Index

Toffler, Alvin, 234
Transparency projection, 190
Trinkle, Dennis, 174
True-false test items, 253, 257
Tyler, Ralph: educational theory,
131, 132; Tyler's "teaching
by objectives," 132–34;
Tyler's teaching by
objectives method syntax,
133; lesson title, 133;
educational goals, 133;
instructional objectives, 133–
34; curricular resources, 133–
34; instruction, 133–34;
evaluation, 133–34; post-
reflection, 133–34

U.S. Department of Education, x
U.S. Office of Technology
Assessment, 35–37, 43

Vee heuristics, 269
Venn diagrams, 269

Visual: primacy, 191; teaching, 194;
thinking, 192

Walker, Decker F., 133
Walker, Trenia, 124
WebQuest, 49, 103, 115, 118–20,
125, 222, 232, 280
Weil, Marsha, 132
Wesley, Edgar Bruce, 7, 11
Whelan, Michael, 34
White, Cameron, 44, 124
Wiggins, Grant, 263
Williams, David, 118
Willis, Jerry, 38
Wilson, Suzanne, 64–65
Wineburg, Samuel, 64–65
Winter, Michael R., 249
Wong, Hurry, 201, 215
Word Processing, 226–28
Wraga, William G., 79

Young, Kathleen McCarthy, 286–
87